The Asian American Experience

Series Editor
Roger Daniels, University of Cincinnati

Books in the Series

The Hood River Issei: An Oral History of Japanese Settlers
in Oregon's Hood River Valley
Linda Tamura

Americanization, Acculturation, and Ethnic Identity:
The Nisei Generation in Hawaii
Eileen H. Tamura

Sui Sin Far/Edith Maude Eaton: A Literary Biography
Annette White-Parks

Mrs. Spring Fragrance and Other Writings
Sui Sin Far
Edited by Amy Ling and Annette White-Parks

Sui Sin Far/Edith Maude Eaton

Sui Sin Far/Edith Maude Eaton:
A Literary Biography

Annette White-Parks
Foreword by Roger Daniels

University of Illinois Press
Urbana and Chicago

Library of Congress Cataloging-in-Publication Data

Sui Sin Far/Edith Maude Eaton : a literary biography / Annette
White-Parks ; foreword by Roger Daniels.
    p.   cm.
Includes bibliographical references and index.
ISBN 0–252–02113–4 (cloth)
1. Sui Sin Far, 1865–1914. 2. Canadian literature—Chinese
authors—History and criticism. 3. Women authors, Canadian—19th
century—Biography. 4. Women authors, Canadian—20th century—
Biography. 5. Chinese—Canada—Biography. 6. Chinese in
literature.   I. Title.
PR199.2.S93Z97   1995
813′.4—dc20
[B]   94–6448
CIP

Title page photo: Sui Sin Far (Edith Maude Eaton), December 1903.
Courtesy of the Southwest Museum, Los Angeles, California (photo
no. N.35626).

To the Women Writers
of Mendocino County, California,
who have inspired and nourished this book
in all of its stages

Contents

Foreword

One of the concomitant phenomena of the growing awareness of America's multicultural past, a past this series is dedicated to exploring, analyzing, and sometimes celebrating, is the rereading of lost literatures, the rehearing of long-silenced voices, the rediscovery of forgotten writers and sometimes their previously unpublished writings. Annette White-Parks has been engaged for some years not in deconstruction but in the reconstruction of a long-forgotten pioneer of Asian North American literature, the English-born Chinese Canadian woman who signed much of her work Sui Sin Far.

Sui Sin Far/Edith Maude Eaton, although well known in her own time, had until recently slipped from public consciousness. A few specialists knew that she existed, that she was what is usually called Eurasian, and that she had some claim to be the first serious Asian North American writer of fiction. Now, thanks to White-Parks, we know much more. White-Parks has, by dint of research that was truly detective work on both sides of the 49th parallel, pieced together what will almost certainly be the definitive life story. She has for the first time compiled what is probably the complete corpus of Sui Sin Far's published work, including unsigned material in newspapers.

Sui Sin Far's work appeared in what was, for Asians, the era of exclusion, when Chinese and other Asians in North America were at the very bottom of the ethnocultural pyramid, with a legal status lower than that of African Americans or African Canadians. Sui Sin Far's voice is not a militant one, but it does depict Chinese North Americans not as exotics but as ordinary human beings trying to live normal lives.

Some critics, usually on the right, have questioned the value or utility of examining long-forgotten writers and have insisted that resurrecting ethnic and/or female writers is merely a perverse, retroactive affirmative action. Many of them are appalled at the suggestion that more of these writers should be added to the canon of American literature. Such views, it seems to me, are misguided. It is always important to know about beginnings. A canon that has a place for, say, Michael Wigglesworth (1631–1705), author of a lugubrious poem in jog-trot ballad measure, can surely find room for Yung Wing (1828–1912), author of the first book-length Chinese American autobiography, or for Sui Sin Far (1865–1914), the first Asian North American author of fiction. Ethnic writers are particularly important when their subject matter delineates an aspect of race and ethnicity in North American life, a topic certainly germane to current concerns.

In this particular instance, there is another reason. We are currently experiencing a veritable explosion of Chinese American women writers, the most gifted of whom, Maxine Hong Kingston, recently testified how much it meant to her to discover *Fifth Chinese Daughter* (1950) by Jade Snow Wong (she calls her "the Mother of Chinese American Literature") in a public library, to discover a book by "a person who looked like me." But Sui Sin Far, of whom the young Maxine Hong was not aware, began publishing more than half a century before Wong. Because her works were all but lost for a time, much of Chinese North American literature developed unaware of Sui Sin Far's pioneering role. But she was there, and all students of the subject are indebted to Annette White-Parks for this exploration of her life and career.

Roger Daniels

Preface

We are always talking about power relationships in society; facts are never objective. Meaning that—as writers—we must be always aware of where everyone is located and at what point in time.

—Dionne Brand, American Studies Conference, Toronto, 1989

I began researching the life and writings of Sui Sin Far/Edith Maude Eaton, an author of Chinese and English parentage, in 1986. In the early years of my work, a question frequently raised was "Why are you, a white woman, doing scholarship on a woman of color?" The question presumes a world of divisions that I must respond to by moving back to 1969, when, after completing my M.A. in English, I realized that even the most visible of women writers (Willa Cather and Katherine Anne Porter, for instance)[1] had been left out of my education. The years of reading, teaching, and research that I have spent trying to correct this deficit led in 1979 to a Women Writers Project in northern California, on which I worked with female students of many backgrounds, recovering women who had written historically in our region and then joining their work with our own in the pages of an annual journal. This project led to my recognition that the writing voices of women from cultures other than European simply were not turning up. "Oh, they didn't write, they mainly stayed in the kitchen," I was told of Asian American women, a stereotype in direct contradiction to the major roles that I knew women of all races and cultures had played in Pacific Coast history. In 1985 I began a doctoral program with the goal of locating women who had written from the perspectives of racial, ethnic, or class minorities that had been historically prominent in North America since the European invasion yet who have been kept literarily invisible. At this time, I was not yet aware that my work connected with a burgeoning national movement to redefine the canon of American literature or that the writer I would research needed to be part of that canon.

I first became acquainted with Sui Sin Far at a slide show entitled "Chinese Women in America," given by Judy Yung and Ruthanne Lum McCunn. During this presentation, Sui Sin Far was identified as a Eurasian who had written and published from Seattle at the turn of the century. A grant from the Canadian Embassy led me to the home of her more permanent roots in eastern Canada—Montreal, where her family had settled in 1873, where she was raised and lived as an adult until age thirty-two, where she returned intermittently between working and publishing in the United States, and where she died and is buried. A fellowship from the American Association of University Women allowed me to trace the outline of Sui Sin Far's path in the United States, as she traversed the continent from San Francisco to Los Angeles, from Seattle to Boston, seeking work, publishers, and her Chinese ancestry. Anyone who has sought to retrieve a writer from the silences imposed by gender, race, class, or whatever other marginalizing factors society creates can probably understand why I say "outline." I found that Sui Sin Far wrote continuously but in the mere cracks of time she could eke out in her continuous struggle for survival—economic, social, and spiritual. Her work often found print in such outlets as railway brochures or local newspapers, and even during her lifetime it was printed anonymously. She wrote for journals and magazines that quickly went out of print and remained accessible, if at all, only in archives. Her personal papers have never been found and likely were not considered, by her descendants, worth saving. Interpretations in the critical biography I offer here are limited to the writings that have been located. Leaping the spaces between knowns in Sui Sin Far's life has long reminded me of leaping stones between waters as a child crossing a creek. The gaps between footholds loom vast.

That Sui Sin Far was of Chinese English descent and I of Scotch-Irish I did not initially consider. That is, the part of my mind that believes women of all cultures, places, and times share a perspective we all depend on to survive never considered it—the part that believes with Sui Sin Far in a "one-family vision,"[2] that follows Audrey Kobayashi and Peter Jackson in the belief that "race" is a social construction,[3] artificial, contrived, and divisive. Another part of me, however, understands that the results of this construction, in which superficial physical differences between people are exploited to create social divisions—a process Robert Miles termed *racialization*[4]—were very real and that they had been manifested in abuse against Sui Sin Far, a child of parents who represented two warring cultures (in her terms, the "East" and the "West") during the decades at the turn of the century, when she was doing most of her writing. Notwithstanding their artificiality, it was these constructions, I knew, against which Sui Sin Far had fought all her life; they were major reasons why she had neither married nor had children and were factors in her early death at age forty-nine. Her experience was my own in so many ways: as a woman, a writer, an eldest daughter in a family whose economic fortunes had plummeted in a society that expects just the opposite—we even both had Irish grandmothers. But it all stopped at the construct of race, and—walking through the streets she had walked in Montreal and Boston, viewing the neighborhoods where she had lived on the borders of Seattle's turn-of-the-century Chinatown—I deliberated the question: How could I present Sui Sin Far's story from her own, as she termed it, "Eurasian" perspective?

Important to defining my stance here was a session at the American Studies Association International Conference in Toronto in November 1989, during which various women writers and scholars from many cultures helped me brainstorm guidelines for doing interracial scholarship. The suggestions I found most useful were: (1) never remove a text from its original matrix; always take into account the sociocultural background of any specific text; (2) point out the uniqueness of each writer's viewpoint; do not assume that literature by writers from any two cultures shares the same vantage point, much less that literature by writers of color offers the same perspective as literature by writers who are white; and (3) challenge your own assumptions and try out alternate perspectives, especially those of the cultures whose works you are using. As Dionne Brand, an African Canadian poet who was at this conference, suggested, being aware of where everyone is located and at what point in time affects everything, from the job one has (or has not) to the neighborhood where one lives.

The complex distinctions of doing scholarship across races were examined in essay form in "Have We Got a Theory for You! Feminist Theory, Cultural Imperialism and the Demand for 'the Woman's Voice,' " in which a dialogue between the Anglo writer Elizabeth V. Spelman and the Hispana writer María C. Lugones examined "the use of two voices" but "without presupposing unity of expression or of experience." Suggesting that "if white/Anglo women are to understand our voices, they must understand our communities and us in them," Lugones cautioned that "this learning calls for circumspection, for questioning of yourselves and your roles in your own culture." The dialogue generated leads women of diverse cultures to become, in the words of these writers, "both outsider and insider in respect to each other."[5]

These writers and many others have been of enormous help in my effort to arrive at my own decisions. Through them, I am learning to recognize the diverse backgrounds through which we all travel to arrive at the boundaries where we intermittently touch and form bridges based on respect for one another. As Sui Sin Far reaches forward from the past and I reach back from the present, I believe that we speak across racial divisions and, in Michelle Cliff's words, the "resonance of interruptions" that impede women's literary tradition.[6] It is a dialogue of growing importance to all women moving toward the turn of a new century. To quote Lugones and Spelman,

"When we speak in unison, it means just that—there are two voices and not just one."[7]

Because I am working in overlapping discourse communities, during a period when scholars are struggling to find language that acknowledges current ideological debates about the nature and boundaries of culture, some discussion of terms is necessary. Sui Sin Far might have coined the most central of these, *Chinese American,* and might have been the first to use it in literature when she announced that her concern was with "those Chinese who came to live in this land, to make their homes in America.... Chinese-Americans I call them."[8] Amy Ling brings the question into contemporary scholarship: "How does one define a Chinese American? At what point does an immigrant become an American?"[9] Sau-ling C. Wong suggests we use the term *Chinese American* for "all persons of Chinese ancestry residing permanently in the United States."[10] I generally use the term *Chinese American* for persons of Chinese ancestry who live in the United States, *Chinese Canadian* for persons of Chinese ancestry who live in Canada, and *Chinese North American* for persons of Chinese ancestry who live in either nation.

To avoid distorting Sui Sin Far's own voice to coincide with language usage in the 1990s, when quoting from her I use terms as she did. These include *Chinaman,* a generic slang term for Chinese in North America at the turn of the century; *American,* residents of the United States of European descent, often synonymous with the word *white; Chinese,* residents of China, Chinese immigrants to North America, and people born in North America of Chinese ancestry; *Eurasians,* people of Chinese and white parentage, the progeny of interracial marriages; and *Americanization,* the adaptation of Western manners and culture by Chinese or Chinese Americans, which, if it involves denying Chinese culture, becomes assimilation at its most negative, implying betrayal and loss of roots.

Another premise concerns Sui Sin Far's name. Although cited on her birth certificate as Edith Maude Eaton, the name Sui Sin Far seems to be not a pseudonym but a term of address her family used from early childhood. In the autobiographical "Leaves from the Mental Portfolio of an Eurasian," she mentions being called "Sui" as a toddler. That she saw both names as part of who she was is illustrated in her response in 1900 to a letter from a student at Dartmouth: "Of course I shall be glad to let you have my autograph ... perhaps I should say *they* as I have both an English and a Chinese name." She closed with both signatures.[11] In this text I purposefully use "Sui Sin Far" to underline the personal choice she made to distinguish herself from the English Canadian identity that most of her family maintained and to help make visible the Chinese heritage for which she fought throughout her life.[12] The family name comes first in Chinese, but in Sui Sin Far's case, the syllables cannot be separated: "Far, Sui Sin" or simply "Far," as is the convention in English.

Meaning depends on the sequence, "Sui Sin Far," and does not work if the sequence is broken. In the writer's evolving life and career, "Sui Sin Far" came to express her Chinese identity, as "Edith Eaton" expressed her English one.

The reader will notice Sui Sin Far's repeated use of the same name for different characters throughout her fiction. The most prominent is "Ku Yum," a name given to various fictional women and children. According to Jinqi Ling of the University of California, Los Angeles, in Chinese "Ku Yum" is not a name at all but a description, approximating a miserable person or someone in need of help—in traditional China virtually synonymous with a daughter.[13] That Sui Sin Far uses this descriptive phrase as a proper noun—it is the most common name for Chinese female characters in her fiction—may indicate her feeling about the way Chinese females often were treated. Her characters who bear that name share difficult predicaments, with which they all struggle and many find means to overcome.

The work that emerges here is obviously a result of much scholarly cooperation, which befits both its themes and its content. Previous Sui Sin Far scholars have been generous, sharing materials and ideas that provided a vital and timesaving base from which to work. Paramount here is S. E. Solberg, a Seattle-based scholar who offered me his pioneering research on Sui Sin Far and has served as a continuing resource. James Doyle, professor of English at Wilfred Laurier University in Ontario, shared his work on the Eaton family, on Walter Blackburn Harte, and on the locations of Sui Sin Far's first Chinese Canadian stories. Other scholars and critics have given invaluable hours of consultation and reading time. My deepest gratitude is to Alexander Hammond, who aided in the text's initial design and editing and has been ever generous in helping to sharpen ideas and offer moral support. I am grateful to Sue Armitage, in whose Women of the West class I discovered my subject and who has read my rough drafts, offering continuing advice and encouragement. I thank Stephen Sumida for introducing me to Asian American literary scholarship and for our work together over the years; Margaret Andrews for comment on the Canadian component; Janet Lecompte, a writing friend who has consulted with me every step of the way, from conception of the idea to final drafts; and Amy Ling, Elizabeth Ammons, and Roger Daniels for reading and commenting on the manuscript in its final stages.

For invaluable assistance with my research in eastern Canada, I am grateful to L. Charles Laferrière, Sui Sin Far's grandnephew, for information on the Eaton family, for reading my biographical chapter, and for serving as a research buddy in Montreal throughout this project; Marie Baboyant, an archivist at the Bibliothèque Centrale, Ville de Montréal, for supplying research assistance both on site and by long distance; Audrey Kobayashi, a geography professor at McGill University, for providing bibliographical resources and helping me understand the history of Asian-European race relations in Canada; Rejean Charbonneau, a conservateur d'histoire, Hochelaga-Maissonneuve, for familiarizing me with Sui Sin Far's childhood environment through numerous hours of consultation, walking tours, and video presentations; Nancy Williatte-Batlet and Jim Shields, archivists at the Canadian Pacific Railway, for their generous sharing of materials and office space; James Wing, for a firsthand account of immigration from China to Montreal, a tour of the Chinese Canadian section of Mont Royal Cemetery, and a translation of the Chinese characters on Sui Sin Far's monument; Howard Roiter, a professor of English at the University of Montréal, for orienting me to the research environment and serving as a local academic resource; and the Lesemann family, which offered me hospitality, friendship, and a home base. Other Eaton family members I wish to thank are Eileen Lewis, Hubert Lewis, Elizabeth Rooney, and Paul Rooney.

This critical biography would not have been possible without the resources and support of many libraries and their staffs. Most important are the Boston, Los Angeles, New York, and San Francisco public libraries; the National Library and National Archives at Ottawa, Canada; the Special Collections Division, University of Calgary; the Presbyterian Church Library in Montreal; the McLennan Library at McGill University; and the Nottman Collection, McCord Museum, Montreal. I offer special thanks to the Bibliothèque Centrale, Ville de Montréal, and its staff for the many bound volumes of the *Montreal Daily Witness* they carted up for me from the basement. Particular thanks are extended to the reference librarians at Holland Library at Washington State University, to the staff at Holland's Interlibrary Loan, and to Jean Bonde at Murphy Library's Interlibrary Loan at the University of Wisconsin–La Crosse. Copies of Sui Sin Far's letters were made available to me through the courtesy of the Dartmouth College Library, the Huntington Library, the New York Public Library, and the Southwest Museum. I thank the Newberry Library for sending me information from their A. C. McClurg and Co. collection.

A large dose of gratitude goes to the agencies that supported this project with funding: the Canadian Embassy, for a fellowship in 1989; the American Association of University Women, for a fellowship in 1990–91; the Office of Grants and Reseach Development at Washington State University, for a research assistantship in 1990; and the College of Arts, Letters and Sciences at the University of Wisconsin–La Crosse, for a research grant in 1992 and released time in 1993. For technical assistance in early drafts, I thank the Humanities Resource Center at Washington State University, with special gratitude to Rhonda Blair, Jian Wang, and Jeannie Anderson. I am grateful to Diane Cannon and Phyllis Bedessom in the English Department at the University of Wisconsin–La Crosse and to Dave Faulkner at the Computer Center at the University of Wisconsin–La Crosse. I thank Melanie Austin and

and Karen Weathermann at Washington State University for assistance with final corrections and indexing. Many thanks to Jane Mohraz for her diligent editing.

Finally, I must thank three special people: Nancy Corbin, Kathy Chambery, and my husband, Wilbur Parks, for their ongoing support.

Notes

1. Willa Cather and Katherine Anne Porter are two of the few women writers to appear in some literary anthologies prior to the movement of the last two decades to redefine the American literary canon. For more on this subject, see Paul Lauter, "Race and Gender in the Shaping of the American Literary Canon: A Case Study from the 20s," *Feminist Studies* 9 (Fall 1983); reprinted in Paul Lauter, *Canons and Contexts* (New York: Oxford University Press, 1991), 22–47.

2. The one-family vision is referred to in Sui Sin Far's autobiographical "Leaves from the Mental Portfolio of an Eurasian," *Independent* 66 (21 January 1909): 132, and in many other of her writings. Basically, it means a vision of community that respects cultural differences but dissolves social barriers based on race.

3. Audrey Kobayashi and Peter Jackson, "Japanese Canadians and the Racialization of Labour in the British Columbia Sawmill Industry, 1900–1930" (Paper presented at the Sixth British Columbia Studies Conference, University of British Columbia, Vancouver, 2–3 November 1990). See also P. Jackson, *Race and Racism* (London: Unwin Hyman, 1987), 3–21.

4. For more on this theory, see Robert Miles, *Racism and Labour Migration* (London: Routledge and Kegan, 1982) and *Racism* (London: Routledge, 1990).

5. Elizabeth V. Spelman and María C. Lugones, "Have We Got a Theory for You! Feminist Theory, Cultural Imperialism and the Demand for 'the Woman's Voice,'" *Women's Studies International Forum* 6 (1983): 581, 577.

6. Michelle Cliff, "Resonance of Interruptions," *Chrysalis* 8 (August 1979): 29–37.

7. Spelman and Lugones, "Have We Got a Theory for You!" 573. See Gloria Anzaldúa, *Making Face, Making Soul—Haciendo Caras: Creative and Critical Perspectives by Women of Color* (San Francisco: Aunt Lute Books, 1990), for various essays that speak to women's interracial relationships.

8. Sui Sin Far (Edith Eaton), "The Chinese in America," *Westerner* 10 (May 1909): 24.

9. Amy Ling, *Between Worlds: Women Writers of Chinese Ancestry* (New York: Pergamon, 1990), 104.

10. Sau-ling C. Wong, "What's in a Name? Defining Chinese American Literature of the Immigrant Generation," in *Frontiers of Asian American Studies,* ed. Gail M. Nomura et al. (Pullman: Washington State University Press, 1989), 159. Wong describes this definition as of recent coinage and limited currency, however.

11. Letter from Edith Eaton to Harold Rugg, 18 January 1900, MS 900118.1, Special Collections, Dartmouth College Library, Dartmouth College, Hanover, N.H.

12. Compare Elizabeth Ammons, *Conflicting Stories: American Women Writers at the Turn into the Twentieth Century* (New York: Oxford University Press, 1992), 118: "I consistently use Sui Sin Far because that is the name she published under and that is how she referred to herself in her autobiographical essay."

13. Jinqi Ling, Interview, Pullman, Wash., 15 October 1990.

Introduction

Then you might begin to comprehend the lives of our "crazy," "Sainted" mothers and grandmothers. The agony of the lives of women who might have been Poets, Novelists, Essayists, and Short-Story Writers (over a period of centuries), who died with their real gifts stifled within them.
— Alice Walker, "In Search of Our Mothers' Gardens"

This is the first book-length study of the life and writings of Sui Sin Far/Edith Maude Eaton, who published between 1888 and 1913 and founded a tradition of Chinese North American literature in Canada and the United States. Sui Sin Far's significance lies in several realms. First, she presents portraits of turn-of-the-century North American Chinatowns, not in the mode of the "yellow peril" literature popular in her era but with an empathy that has caused critics from her time to the present to recognize her as the first to write from an insider viewpoint on Chinese in North America. Second, her stories give voice and protagonist roles to Chinese and Chinese North American women and children, thus breaking the stereotypes of silence, invisibility, and the "bachelor society" in which pioneer Chinese Americans are said to have lived. Third, she used the very divisions society handed her to ground an identity and to find strategies for her art that would communicate to a dual audience, experimenting with trickster characters and tools of irony that share a paradigm with other writers marginalized by race, class, or gender who found ways to get published at the turn of the century. Finally, Sui Sin Far was the first writer in North America to depict the ambiguous position of the Eurasian. Appropriately, her writings are unique in initiating a dialogue between North Americans of Chinese and European descents.

Sui Sin Far's career included publication of numerous short stories, count-less pieces of journalism, and one book. Her death in 1914 produced several appreciative obituaries, followed by sixty-one years of silence, a silence broken only by brief discussion in two dissertations on Asian American literature[1] and citations in two Canadian dictionaries.[2] In 1975 *Aiiieeeee! An Anthology of Asian American Writers* recognized Sui Sin Far's pioneer role in the development of an Asian American literature. Crediting her as "one of the first to speak for an Asian-American sensibility that was neither Asian nor white American," the editors of *Aiiieeeee!* asserted that the tradition Sui Sin Far founded was "authentic," in contrast to "a white tradition of Chinese novelty literature, would-be Chinese writing about America for the entertainment of Americans" that prevailed in her era.[3]

The further critical attention that Sui Sin Far received in the 1970s and 1980s was basically by two scholars, S. E. Solberg and Amy Ling. Both reinforced her position as a pioneer Chinese North American writer and as the first to deal with the Chinese North American experience as an insider. In 1981 Solberg suggested that Sui Sin Far's fiction, unlike that of many turn-of-the-century writers, sought "not to exploit, but rather to record, explain, and somehow give meaning to the experience of the Chinese in America."[4] In 1983 Ling agreed: "No one before [Sui Sin Far] has written so sympathetically and extensively about the Chinese in America, and never before from this far inside."[5] In his 1982 book *The Yellow Peril: Chinese Americans in American Fiction, 1850–1940,* William Wu referred to Sui Sin Far as "maybe the earliest writer of American fiction to have Chinese ancestry" and saw her fiction as "clearly that of an insider."[6]

It is in the 1990s, though, centennial of the decade when her work began to appear internationally, that Sui Sin Far's reputation as a writer and champion of Chinese North Americans is coming into its own. Her name shows up increasingly at national conferences and in scholarly articles;[7] two critical studies, Amy Ling's *Between Worlds: Women Writers of Chinese Ancestry* and Elizabeth Ammons's *Conflicting Stories: American Women Writers at the Turn into the Twentieth Century,* devote full chapters to her life and work.[8] Selections from Sui Sin Far's book-length collection *Mrs. Spring Fragrance* are being recovered individually in literary anthologies.[9]

Such recognition brings with it certain critical questions, some which have followed Sui Sin Far over the years. Was she, for example, breaking or perpetuating popular stereotypes in her portrayals of Chinese North American immigrants and resident populations? This issue was first raised in 1932 by William Purviance Fenn, who saw Sui Sin Far as essentially "stamped from the same die" as most writers of Chinatown literature, who were only interested in depicting "the sinister and evil character of the quarter and most of its inhabitants."[10] In 1987 Lorraine Dong and Marlon K. Hom expressed similar doubts. Although they maintained that Sui Sin Far's stories "reveal a sympathetic, if not empathetic, perception of Chinese Americans," they argued that "she has nevertheless perpetuated certain negative images of the Chinese in her characterizations."[11] In an unpublished 1976 study, Solberg suggested that the reason some modern readers perceive such contradictory images in Sui Sin Far's work may lie in the gap between her intent and her ability to achieve a form for her themes. Viewing the writings in the context of Fenn's description of "Chinatown literature," Solberg observed, "Edith Eaton as Sui Sin Far did manage to dip into those deeper currents [of Chinatown] beneath the surface color, but no matter what she saw and understood, there was no acceptable form to shape it to. Had she been physically stronger and had a more sophisticated literary apprenticeship she might have been able to create that new form. As it was she was defeated. . . ."[12]

Addressing this same issue fifteen years later, Elizabeth Ammons raises the question, "If we approach [Sui Sin Far] as a writer who succeeded rather than failed at what she did . . . what do we see?"[13] I argue that what we see is Sui Sin Far conceiving "that new form" in process, molding and shaping it word by word out of the tensions generated by her border position, in joint response to her determination to plant "a few Eurasian thoughts in Western literature"[14] and to meet the demands on her as a writer marginalized by race, gender, and class in the imperialistic marketplace of her era. The ambivalent stance of this writer's art reflects both the ambiguity of her identity, wrought from the division between the colonizer and the colonized in the North America in which she was working, and the vision of irony that she evolved. In the process, she left a literary legacy of the identity ambivalence so familiar to such contemporary writers as Cherrié Moraga, Michelle Cliff, and Hans Suyin, and she demonstrated what it means to be the child of a biracial union in a racist society. In the words of Ammons, "Sui Sin Far did not flounder in a formless field. Instead, like Jewett before her and Anderson after her, she manipulated to her advantage the tradition of regional and sketch fiction that she inherited primarily from women to offer not a long narrative about one individual but a multifaceted, collective narrative about a group of people and a network of issues."[15] As anyone whose parents are of different races knows, Sui Sin Far's identity was not either-or but existed on a continuum. Rather than accommodate the ruggedly individualistic code of a West steeped in Social Darwinism during the era she wrote, her aesthetics focus on a world vision that is largely communal in its insistence that humans and other living beings must exist in harmony to survive. In this sense, Sui Sin Far's aesthetic is far ahead of her time and is startlingly contemporary. Appropriately, then, the underlying theme we see from her first work to her last is that people are not single-faceted; human experience and interrelationships turn on ambiguity.

In a world that emphasizes nationalism, however, which of her countries of residence Sui Sin Far really "belongs to" has been seen as important. Perhaps because many of her stories were published in the United States, modern critics of Sui Sin Far's work generally have referred to her as an Asian American writer. Research discloses, however, that in her travels on the southerly side of the Canadian-U.S. border, we are seeing only temporary detours in this writer's life and that the main road—that of "home"—invariably started from and led back to eastern Canada. Montreal was the site of her early materials and the testing ground for later stories. It was the place where she learned stenography, the vocation that supported her writing; the place where she became acquainted with her first Chinese North American community and entered the career of journalism; and the place where she enjoyed her first publications. Montreal was where she lived from age eight to thirty-two, traveled back to whenever she could save enough money, returned to die, and is buried. Like many Canadian writers at the turn of the century, Sui Sin Far came to the United States to earn a living and find publishing outlets. The irrelevance of nationalism to Sui Sin Far herself, as a child of two races and four countries, she clearly asserted: "I have no nationality and am not anxious to claim any."[16]

A related critical question involves Sui Sin Far's status as an "invisible minority," an issue that is sometimes raised with the discovery that Sui Sin Far looked like a white European and thus could enjoy the dubious luxury of "passing," a choice that "more visible minorities" do not have. For crossing borders in an age of exclusion acts in the United States and head taxes in Canada, this was an undisputed advantage. Yet all of her writings demonstrate that Sui Sin Far's ambiguous racial status made her the butt of racist attitudes from both sides of her heritage and held her in thrall to the unending decision of how and to whom to assert the Chinese heritage to which her sense of self and art was committed. Audrey Kobayashi believes that the issue of passing is a red herring: "The very fact that she had to pretend indicates the depths of the racism. It wouldn't be an issue if the racist thinking wasn't there, and we must approach it in context."[17] As Ling argues in *Between Worlds,* Sui Sin Far's choice not to deny her Chinese heritage is a key difference between this writer and her sister Winifred, who fabricated a Japanese background and wrote under the name Onoto Watanna.[18] Recognition that such choices were available *and* that Sui Sin Far chose as she did must be central to any effort to understand Sui Sin Far's writing.

While I address such issues, my central concern is how was Sui Sin Far—a woman of Chinese-English parentage writing about socially taboo and politically controversial subjects during a period of severe anti-Chinese sentiment and nativism throughout the regions where she worked—getting published at all? My general hypothesis is that the particular strategies Sui Sin Far devised to write against the dominant racial and cultural ideologies of her time cannot be understood in isolation from either her life experiences or the marketplaces and audiences for which she wrote. Her writings share techniques with those of other women who were writing and publishing from similarly marginalized situations during this period. These include the writer's creation of dual fictional voices, the first level providing "entertainment" by satisfying the popular formulas that a turn-of-the-century marketplace and reading audience of European descent demanded for public acceptance, and the second disturbing the stereotypes embedded in those formulas as the writer pursues her own personal and ideological themes. Drawing on a device writers from colonized populations in North America have used since the continent was invaded by Europeans, Sui Sin Far also employs trickster figures to slip past the censors and to upset her readers' monologic view of reality by opening multiple perspectives. In this sense, her aesthetic calls to mind Mikhail Bakhtin's "carnival," especially as Dale M. Bauer applies Bakhtin's concepts to writings by women. In Bauer's words, carnival "serves to make every voice in the communal performance heard and unrestricted by official or authoritative speech."[19]

Because my attempt is to understand Sui Sin Far's total located oeuvre— letters, journalism, essays, and short fiction—in the biographical and cultural contexts in which it was written and as it reflects the writer's voice as a whole, my organization follows the geographical path of Sui Sin Far's travels and the evolution of her development as an author. The first chapter, "A Bird on the Wing," constructs a biographical overview of Sui Sin Far's life and the life of her family in historical and cultural perspective from the mid-nineteenth century, when her parents were married, until the author's own death in 1914. It is concerned with establishing the framework in which Sui Sin Far's themes, style, and writing stance would develop. The second chapter, "Montreal: The Early Writings," explores the writer's beginning career in Montreal from the mid-1880s to 1898. The analysis includes her British Canadian stories, her journalism and rising voice as a defender of Chinese immigrants in eastern Canada, and her first Chinese stories in the environment of a growing Chinese Montreal community. The third chapter, "Pacific Coast Chinatown Stories," examines Sui Sin Far's writings on the U.S. West Coast in the context of Chinese American history, of the Chinatowns that she encountered, and of a literary marketplace caught up in the trend of "Chinatown literature," and it surveys her brief stint in Jamaica as a pivotal interlude in the development of her identity as a writer of Chinese heritage. The fourth chapter, "Boston: The Mature Voice and Its Art," covers Sui Sin Far's mature fiction, from approximately 1909 to 1913, when she was living mainly in Boston and selling her stories to eastern markets. The chapter focuses on the strategies that most illuminate the ironic voice she had been practicing since adolescence, including her development of trickster characters and an authorial stance that permits her to write for a dual audience. The final chapter, "Mrs. Spring Fragrance," concerns Sui Sin Far's only book and, in the absence of the novel she was apparently working on at the time of her death, the culmination of her life's work. The chapter examines *Mrs. Spring Fragrance*'s physical design and contents, the publisher's marketing strategies, and the book's reception.

My research convinces me beyond doubt that the tradition of writers in North America of Asian descent began with Sui Sin Far; more specifically, that she is the founder of the Chinese North American woman writer's tradition, foremother to the women writers of Chinese ancestry Ling traces in *Between Worlds,* to whom such contemporary writers as Maxine Hong Kingston and Amy Tan look for roots. This is not necessarily a conscious connection. We are not always aware of our writing traditions, especially if we represent cultures that fall off the margins of the conventional canon, whose works go out of print and remain inaccessible to the descendants who could most profit by them. If it seems ironic that Sui Sin Far looked back to William Shakespeare and Alfred Lord Tennyson for writing models, I can well understand it, because for years I believed Nathaniel Hawthorne and Henry James were my reference points. In her introduction to the 1990 edition of *Fifth Chinese Daughter,* Jade Snow Wong indicates that she is not aware of the tradition Sui Sin Far founded when she writes, "At a time when nothing had been published from a female Chinese American perspective, I wrote with the purpose of creating better understanding of the Chinese culture on the part of Americans."[20] Nevertheless, Sui Sin Far was writing from the Chinese American woman's perspective as early as the 1890s, and recognized or not by those who came after, she planted seeds for major themes that have recurred in Chinese North American literature over the century: a sense of exile and identity conflict, the oppression of Chinese by white society and of women by men, and a commitment to rendering visible and vocal the Chinese North American woman's face and voice.

Beyond race, Sui Sin Far's life and work joins the flow of women writers in a multicultural sense and on a global scale, women whose voices since the beginning of speech have "talked story" in oral cultures or guided our pens when we felt, existentially, we were working alone. Increasingly, we find that together we form a writing continuum as old as history and create a collage of pain and courage, ostracism and perseverance, struggle and triumph that Michelle Cliff has explored in her classic essay "Resonance of Interruptions."[21] Sui Sin Far is part of this tradition, both in the stories she gave us and in the fact that those stories were excluded from literature's ongoing current. In this sense she provides another example of the numerous writers Tillie Olsen refers to in *Silences,* for whom "the claims of creation cannot be primary, [resulting in] . . . atrophy; unfinished work; minor effort and accompanying silences." Moreover, Sui Sin Far shares the even more excruciating level of abandonment that Olsen recognizes when she suggests "class and/or color" as "the age-old silencers of humanity."[22] Perhaps the final challenge that such writers face, and that I have encountered since beginning my work, was framed by

Jane Tompkins in 1987 with the question, "But is she any good?"[23] It is otherwise phrased, "But was she really writing *literature?*" The irony is that the very strategies these writers were forced to use to get published in the late nineteenth century can keep them from getting reprinted in the late twentieth. A determination to break through such double-silencing is much of the impetus behind my work.

Notes

1. William Purviance Fenn, "Ah Sin and His Brethren in American Literature" (Ph.D. diss., State University of Iowa, 1932); John Burt Foster, "China and the Chinese in American Literature, 1850–1950" (Ph.D. diss., University of Illinois, 1952).

2. *The MacMillan Dictionary of Canadian Biography,* 3d ed. (London and Toronto: Macmillan, 1963); Reginald Eyre Watters, *A Checklist of Canadian Literature and Background Materials, 1628–1960,* 2d ed. (Toronto: University of Toronto Press, 1972), 282.

3. Frank Chin et al., eds., *Aiiieeeee! An Anthology of Asian American Literature* (Garden City, N.Y.: Anchor, 1991 [1974]), xii–xiii.

4. S. E. Solberg, "Sui Sin Far/Edith Eaton: First Chinese-American Fictionist," *MELUS* 8 (Spring 1981): 33.

5. Amy Ling, "Edith Eaton: Pioneer Chinamerican Writer and Feminist," *American Literary Realism* 16 (Autumn 1983): 292.

6. William F. Wu, *The Yellow Peril: Chinese Americans in American Fiction, 1850–1940* (Hamden, Conn.: Archon Books, 1982), 53–54.

7. See, for example, Annette White-Parks, "Introduction to 'Wisdom of the New' by Sui Sin Far," *Legacy: A Journal of Nineteenth-Century Women's Literature* 6 (Spring 1989): 34–49; and Xiao-Huang Yin, "Between the East and West: Sui Sin Far—The First Chinese American Woman Writer," *Arizona Quarterly* 7 (Winter 1991): 49–84.

8. Amy Ling, *Between Worlds: Women Writers of Chinese Ancestry* (New York: Pergamon, 1990); Elizabeth Ammons, *Conflicting Stories: American Women Writers at the Turn into the Twentieth Century* (New York: Oxford University Press, 1992).

9. Paul Lauter et al., eds., *The Heath Anthology of American Literature,* vol. 2 (New York: D.C. Heath, 1990); Susan Koppelman, *Women's Friendships* (Norman: University of Oklahoma Press, 1991); Judith Fetterley and Marjorie Pryse, eds., *American Women Regionalists, 1850–1910* (New York: W. W. Norton, 1992); Eileen Barrett and Mary Cullinan, *American Women Writers: Diverse Voices in Prose since 1845* (New York: St. Martin's Press, 1992); Wesley Brown and Amy Ling, *Imagining America: Stories from the Promised Land* (New York: Persea Books, 1991).

10. Fenn, "Ah Sen and His Brethren in American Literature," 116.

11. Lorraine Dong and Marlon K. Hom, "Defiance or Perpetuation: An

Analysis of Characters in *Mrs. Spring Fragrance*," in *Chinese America: History and Perspectives,* ed. Him Mark Lai, Ruthanne Lum McCunn, and Judy Yung (San Francisco: Chinese Historical Society of America, 1987), 140.

12. S. E. Solberg, "The Eaton Sisters: Sui Sin Far and Onoto Watanna" (Paper presented at the Pacific Northwest Asian American Writer's Conference, Seattle, Wash., 16 April 1976).

13. Ammons, *Conflicting Stories,* 117.

14. Sui Sin Far, "Sui Sin Far, the Half Chinese Writer, Tells of Her Career," *Boston Globe,* 5 May 1912.

15. Ammons, *Conflicting Stories,* 116.

16. Sui Sin Far, "Leaves from the Mental Portfolio of an Eurasian," *Independent* 66 (21 January 1909): 132.

17. Audrey Kobayashi, Interview, Vancouver, British Columbia, 2 November 1990.

18. Ling, *Between Worlds,* 32–39.

19. Dale M. Bauer, *Feminist Dialogics: A Theory of Failed Community* (New York: State University of New York Press, 1988), 13.

20. Jade Snow Wong, *Fifth Chinese Daughter,* 2d ed. (Seattle: University of Washington Press, 1990), viii.

21. Michelle Cliff, "Resonance of Interruptions," *Chrysalis* 8 (August 1979): 29–37.

22. Tillie Olsen, *Silences* (New York: Dell, 1965), 13, 46.

23. Jane Tompkins, *Sensational Designs: The Cultural Work of American Fiction, 1790–1860* (New York: Oxford University Press, 1985). For a thorough examination of the validity of traditional definitions of literary merit, see chapter 7, "But Is It Any Good?: The Institutionalization of Literary Value," 186–201.

1

A Bird on the Wing

When biographers came to write the life of a woman, they have had
to struggle with the inevitable conflict between the destiny of being
unambiguously a woman and the woman subject's palpable desire, or
fate, to be something else.

—Carolyn G. Heilbrun, *Writing a Woman's Life*

"At the age of seven, as it is today, a bird on the wing is my emblem of
happiness," Sui Sin Far wrote in 1909 for a New York *Independent* audience.[1]
The bird image with which this writer recurrently identifies in essays and
fiction capsules the major problem scholars encounter when setting out to
probe her life. After her birth to a Chinese mother and British father in
England in 1865 and her immigration to eastern Canada as a child in 1873, Sui
Sin Far lived and worked in Montreal until she was nearly thirty-two years
old, when she began a life of travel that interwove with her work and her
writing. In 1897 she spent a brief interval in Jamaica and in 1898 began her
travels in the United States, living in San Francisco, Los Angeles, Seattle, and
Boston over the next fifteen years. Her journeys were laced with intermittent
crossings of the continent and the border back into Canada, until her final
illness and death in Montreal in 1914. As a child in an impoverished family of
sixteen that frequently changed residences, and as an adult in continual search
of work, Sui Sin Far stayed almost continuously "on the wing," which led
Marie Baboyant, an archivist at the Bibliothèque Centrale, Ville de Montréal,
to remark, "No wonder we can't find out more—she is like a bird—flying
from place to place too fast for anyone to get to know her." As a prelude to
understanding her art, this chapter recovers, within the limits of the meager
evidence her flights left behind, Sui Sin Far's biography.

The ambiguous vision that Sui Sin Far would create in her art reflected the
tug between colonizer and colonized in the world of global politics in which
she was born and grew up. If ever two people represented this tug, it was Sui

Sin Far's parents. As a Chinese woman converted by the Christian mission movement invading nineteenth-century China, her mother, Lotus Blossom Trefusis, was among the colonized. As a British silk merchant, one of many exploiting China's silk coast, her father, Edward Eaton, was of the colonizer. Their two countries were at perpetual war, and their populations were segregated. Yet Lotus Blossom and Edward met, married, and had fourteen children. Sui Sin Far was the second child and the eldest daughter.

According to burial records at the Mont Royal Cemetery in Montreal, Quebec, Sui Sin Far's mother was born in China in 1846, four years after the Treaty of Nanking granted merchants, Christian missionaries, and military forces from Europe and North America a right for which they had been fighting for centuries—to move into China at key ports, most important, Shanghai. Family legend holds that her home province was Kuangtong and that she was Cantonese.[2] Though all public documents are recorded and signed with the English name Grace A., she is referred to familiarly as Lotus Blossom,[3] with the maiden name Trefusis providing a core of identity across cultural shifts. Her death certificate lists her father as A. Trefusis and her mother as Ah Cheun,[4] but her own given name at birth is unknown. The fact that the name Trefusis is not Chinese could suggest that Lotus Blossom herself was of mixed races, but no other family record supports this. According to one family legend, she was found in a circus somewhere in China after her parents, circus performers, had died.[5] In the autobiographical narrative *Me,* written by Sui Sin Far's younger sister Winifred Eaton Babcock, the narrator's claim that "my mother had been a tightrope dancer in her early youth" agrees with this version.[6] How Lotus Blossom left China and her age when she departed are equally hazy. According to Edward's obituary,[7] "his wife" was taken from China to England as the protégée of a Sir Hugh Matheson, who presumably brought her up and gave her an English education.[8] Sui Sin Far's recollection in the autobiographical "Leaves" suggests that her mother was old enough to recall the experience: "Though a child when she left her native land, she remembers it well, and I am never tired of listening to the story of how she was stolen from her home" (127).

What transpired between the time Lotus Blossom arrived in England and she returned to Shanghai where she met Edward is almost a total mystery. Edward's obituary claims that she was educated in England at the Home and Colonial School, "a training college for schoolmistresses";[9] but Sui Sin Far writes, and the obituary corroborates, that she "was in training for a missionary."[10] Upon returning to China, she might have lived in a mission station, a pivotal element of the British cultural communities that by the 1860s had infiltrated China's landscape, described by the historian Kenneth Scott Latourette as "bits of the West set down in China."[11] The mission school's function was primarily assimilative—to convert Chinese populations to the Christian religion, to

Lotus Blossom, Sui Sin Far's mother, date unknown.
Courtesy of L. Charles Laferrière.

teach Chinese the English language and culture, and to use Chinese, once converted, to carry the gospel to their own people in China's interior. Lotus Blossom's experience is representative of the mission practice of training Chinese abroad—in Europe or North America—and then sending them back to China as Christian missionaries.

The arrival of Sui Sin Far's father in Shanghai is grounded more concretely. Born in Macclesfield, England, in 1839[12]—the same year England's first war with China, commonly known as the Opium War, was launched in Hong Kong harbor—Edward Eaton came from a family whose roots on the side of his mother, Ellen, can be traced to Ireland but on the side of his father, Edward, extended deep in England. His father's family held mercantile interests that continued steadfastly in the silk center of Macclesfield.[13] "My father's an Oxford man and a descendant of the family of Sir Isaac Newton," Winifred's narrator claims in *Me* (26). *White's Cheshire Directory* in 1860 shows Edward's

Sui Sin Far's parents, Edward and Grace A. (Lotus Blossom) Eaton, circa 1910. Courtesy of L. Charles Laferrière.

grandfather, Isaac Eaton, to have been "actuary to Savings Bank, and registrar of births, deaths and marriages" during the era of Lotus Blossom's and Edward's meeting.[14] As an eldest son and a junior, Edward was expected to "follow a mercantile career"; Edward, though, had inclinations toward art. He studied in France and took a first prize at the Paris Salon. His "master" advised his father to encourage Edward's growth as an artist, but instead his father sent Edward to the Port of Shanghai, where he set him up in business. A second son, Isaac, was sent to Japan to buy silk.[15]

Sometime in the early 1860s, Lotus Blossom and Edward Eaton met and married, a date substantiated by Sui Sin Far's allusion to her father's age at the meeting: "My father, who was educated in England and studied art in France, was established in business by his father at the age of 22, at the Port of Shanghai, China. There he met my mother, a Chinese young girl, who had been educated in England, and who was in training for a missionary. They were married by the British Consul, and the year following their marriage returned to England" (*Globe*). The date is confirmed by records of "Merchant Vessels" in the *North China Herald* ("Her Majesty's Official Organ," published in Shanghai) that indicated "Edward Eaton & Co." ships appeared regularly in the Shanghai harbor during the spring and summer of 1863.[16]

It was near the end of the T'ai P'ing Rebellion, when crucial events in

Chinese-Anglo relations were playing themselves out, especially concerning who would attain hegemony over the resources of China's interior. A few years earlier, in 1858, the Treaties of Tientsin had been signed, opening China to both merchants and missionaries. One result was that both were now firmly ensconced, well protected by the military, inside Shanghai's city walls. The rapidity with which English residents moved to segregate Chinese residents in their own city after the Tientsin Treaties offers a microcosm of British colonization as it was being practiced in the mid-nineteenth century over the globe. It also indicates the attitudes of the British toward the Chinese. In 1861 the *North China Herald* reported that a municipal council had been founded and a voting electorate established to assist British residents in Shanghai to "rally as a pillar of strength" against Chinese residents, because "what discomforts, what nuisances we should suffer if Chinese buildings should encroach on our already narrow streets . . . filth would be everywhere . . . the city would become common."[17] The same issue that cited the arrival of an "Edward Eaton & Co." ship in Shanghai harbor in 1863 ran an article reminiscent to *Of Plymouth Plantation* in its comparison of the British stronghold in Shanghai with "one of the early colonies of America, located on the borders of an unexplored region tenanted by hostile savages who thirsted for our blood."[18] Ideologically, the point of common meeting is the attitude with which English viewed, internationally, people with skins darker than theirs and with languages and religions that differed from theirs.

Where would Edward and Lotus Blossom—he a British merchant and she a Chinese missionary, he of the colonizer and she of the colonized—have met in this city? That Edward might have been less imperialistic than some of his countrymen is indicated by his obituary description as "the one honest white man" in Shanghai and "the trusted friend of many Chinese," who introduced him to "the woman who would become his wife."[19] With the British presence in Shanghai in the early 1860s—soldiers in the military, merchants bargaining for chinoiserie to take back to Europe, and missionaries from all Christian denominations vying for souls—interracial relationships obviously developed in spite of hostilities. One potential meeting place for British and Chinese individuals would have been the Shanghai Mission Station, where merchants and missionaries gathered and Chinese converts could mix socially. It would have been another matter to marry across racial lines.

Sui Sin Far's father overturned family expectations and traditions, first by pursuing a career in art and then by marrying a Chinese woman. Sui Sin Far's mother, a Chinese woman who conventionally would have remained home-bound while awaiting an arranged marriage, was independent enough to travel and choose her own husband. The decision these two people made at this historical juncture profoundly affected their futures and those of their children to come. In this sense, they were mavericks, whose children had to decipher their own racial identities in the context of the European-dominated societies where they would find themselves.

The first of these children was Edward Charles, born in 1864 in China.[20] Sui Sin Far would be next, the first child Lotus Blossom would give birth to in England. Sui Sin Far would live in three countries for significant periods— England, Canada, and the United States. While diverse in geography, manners, and mores, the political, legal, and social systems of all three were rooted in England and operated from common racist assumptions about the Chinese. Moreover, all three countries were firmly allied in the missionary movement, synonymous in its time with assimilation. Sui Sin Far and her siblings were Christians and looked European, but their experience points to the reality beneath the illusion: mere knowledge of their Chinese mother was sufficient to incite racist attacks wherever they lived. Stigmatism against the children was magnified because they symbolized their parents' violation of cultural mores; furthermore, the Eatons' very existence as a family offered a vision of cultural pluralism that none of the countries in which they lived was willing to accept.

It was late 1864 or early 1865 when the English husband and Chinese wife arrived back in England with their infant son. We can only speculate about how the Eaton family and the village of Macclesfield responded to their marriage. Family legend relates that Edward senior met them at the port and drove them in his carriage through the village streets, shouting, "Behold my new daughter-in-law!"[21] Lotus Blossom and Edward probably moved in with his family, as the youngest of several generations who shared the same roof. A birth certificate records that Edith Maude Eaton was born on 15 March 1865 in Upton Cottage, Parish of Prestbury, County of Chester, Macclesfield, England,[22] a site she later described as "the birthplace of my father, grandfather, great-grandfather and . . . and . . ." (*Globe,* her ellipses). She described ancestors on her paternal grandmother's side as "unknown to local history" and her grandmother as "a pretty Irish lass from Dublin when she first won my grandfather's affections" (*Globe*).

In 1865 there were statistically speaking no Chinese populations living in England, although in reality Chinese individuals must have been arriving on English shores since the first British ships recruited the first Chinese sailors in the late eighteenth century, a process that accelerated as merchants attempted to sate the increasing English desire for chinoiserie and as missionaries returned from Asia with converts. As residents of a center for England's silk industry that had had continual interchange with China for over two hundred years, Macclesfield populations would have had more experience with Chinese culture than usual. The first silk mill was built in Macclesfield in 1756, during the same era that European ships were invading China's silk coast, and it had since sustained the town economically. During Sui Sin Far's early childhood—in the late 1860s and early 1870s—silk from China still supplied a livelihood for many families: "the rattle of the loom . . . in the cottages" over the village likely sounded in the writer's ears as a toddler.[23] Macclesfield census records of 1851 list Eaton family members in all facets of the silk industry—spinning, weaving, piecing, and mercantile. Flurries of publications—many sent back from missionaries or travelers in China and printed in London—stimulated interest, roused fascination, and created popular stereotypes about Chinese flora, fauna, and populations. A Chinese woman in person in rural England would, however, have been a rarity, much less a woman whom one of their village sons had married and with whom he was begetting children—how did this violate the traditionally maintained divisions on the map between East and West, regions that clearly not only had met but had mingled, producing children who were an admixture of both? To add to the ambiguity, these children looked European and bore an English name—Eaton.

Beyond glimpses offered in the historical relations between England and China and in Sui Sin Far's writings, our knowledge about the attitude of the average Macclesfield resident toward Lotus Blossom, or what part this attitude played in the couple's decision to migrate to North America for the first time when Sui Sin Far was an infant of about two, remains largely speculative. The migration is dated by birth records, which show a second daughter—Sui Sin Far's sister Grace—to have been born in Jersey City in 1867. *Trow's New York City Directory* lists Edward Eaton as a merchant, with a home address in Jersey City in 1868; *Trow's* cites Edward as owning a wholesale drug business in New York City, the failure of which, James Doyle conjectures, caused the Eatons to go back to England.[24]

By 1868 or 1869 the family had apparently returned to Macclesfield. All of Sui Sin Far's adult recollections of these primary years indicate that her initial self-image was as a British child. She was put in a private school in Macclesfield at age four, where she recalled being "very much interested in English history" ("Leaves," 126). Her remembered world of her English childhood centered on her eldest brother, Edward Charles, described as "a noble little fellow, whose heart and intelligence during the brief years of early childhood led and directed mine." Sui Sin Far describes her mother as "English bred, with British ways and manners of dress" (*Globe*), and a photo from this period portrays Lotus Blossom in a Victorian gown with a bustle. Because Sui Sin Far's mother had ostensibly been raised in England from an early age, the "costume" was not false but reflected who she was—part of who she was—an Anglicized Chinese woman married to a British citizen. Under social constructions of race, the Victorian bonnet could not cover the Chinese face, illustrating a major fallacy in presuming that full assimilation between races occurs in Anglo-American cultures. Since society has constructed race from such physical features as skin color, hair texture, and eyes and has used such constructions to divide people, race remains identifiable across cultural and national changes, and, barring intermarriage, cannot be disguised.[25]

In the privacy of her own family, Lotus Blossom may not have attempted to dismiss her native heritage as fully as the scant records of her public life indicate. It was undoubtedly she who instilled into their young lives what knowledge her children possessed of their Chinese ancestry. In Sui Sin Far's memory, much was passed down through stories. The home atmosphere created by her mother—"She sings us songs she learned at her English school. She tells us tales of China"—was culturally integrated and pluralistic. Her father's contribution to this atmosphere was suggested in his "French version of little Bo-peep" (Globe). In Sui Sin Far's recollections, the serpent entered this multicultural garden, as it would in numerous of her short stories to come, from outside the family circle.[26]

"The day on which I first learned I was something different and apart from other children" ("Leaves," 126) is clearly articulated by the adult author through a particular incident when she was "scarcely four years of age, walking in front of my nurse, in a green English lane, and listening to her tell another of her kind that my mother is Chinese." " 'Oh, Lord!' " the second nurse answered, turning the small Sui Sin Far around and examining her "curiously from head to foot" (125). In another episode the child was playing with a girlfriend when a third girl, passing by, called: " 'I wouldn't speak to Sui if I were you. Her mamma is Chinese.' " Again, at a children's party, she was "called from my play by the hostess for purposes of inspection" by "a white haired old man" who "adjusts his eyeglasses" and exclaimed—" 'Ah, indeed! . . . now I see the difference between her and other children . . . very interesting little creature' " (126). Sui Sin Far's growing awareness of racial conflict was reinforced at the English private school she attended, where she was taught "that China is a heathen country being civilized by England." Her response to such surprising behavior and attitudes was a mixture of curiosity, embarrassment, and defiance. What was Chinese? she inquired, passing the incident with the nurse along to her mother. The nurse protested, " 'Little Miss Sui is a storyteller,' " and her mother slapped Sui Sin Far. From the old man at the party, "I hide myself behind a hall door, and refuse to show myself until it is time to go home" (126). To the girlfriend—who insisted she liked Sui Sin Far better than the other girl, " 'even if your mamma is Chinese' "—she retorted, " 'But I don't like you.' "

By implication, these were the writer's fledgling steps toward a meeting with the border identity that society had laid out for children born of two races, an identity that Sui Sin Far was forced to face more explicitly in the three or four years that ensued before the Eatons' second migration to North America, during which time three more siblings were born. The 1881 census shows Sarah, distinguished by the narrator in her sister's novel Marion as "the prettiest baby in England" and her mother's "show child";[27] Ernest George, a second brother; and Christiana Mary, known to her family as "Agnes." The villagers' reactions, as Sui Sin Far recalled them, proved that, in spite of her "English ways," Macclesfield had not forgotten Lotus Blossom's native origins: "What a peculiar coloring! Her mother's eyes and hair and her father's features, I presume," the white-haired man inspecting Sui Sin Far had remarked ("Leaves," 126). Similar "inspections" of Eaton siblings would occur in Canada and the United States, suggesting that all three societies in which Sui Sin Far lived found the "border" phenomenon, which their invasions into Asia had provoked, as intriguing as they found it disturbing.

The Eaton children's perceptions of themselves would consequently be marked at a depth that transfigured their identities—culturally, socially, and psychically. Because their dual racial inheritance was not clearly evident, they were placed in the position of having to make excruciating decisions, not just once but over and over again as they grew up. "The greatest temptation was in the thought of getting away, to where no mocking cries of 'Chinese! Chinese!' could reach," Sui Sin Far admitted years later ("Leaves," 128). Their choices hovered between hiding their Chinese ancestry and passing as English—with the continual fear of exposure—or acknowledging their Chinese ancestry and confronting the racist attitudes and actions of white society. Sui Sin Far's English years, approximately her first seven, taught her to assume an English identity, for any deviance from this was perceived as strange and unacceptably different. Because the writer's innate sense of self denied this premise, apparently from an early age, a struggle to find her own script and define her own story was set into motion. " 'Why? Why?' " she would ask over a lifetime of inquiry, scrutinizing her mother and father: " 'Is she not every bit as good and dear as he?' " ("Leaves," 128).

Lotus Blossom and Edward would migrate from England the second time in 1871 or 1872, an era in which British citizens—because of "poverty, want of employment, higher rates of wages . . . love of change"—were heading for the North American continent at the rate of 200,000 or 300,000 a year.[28] The majority went to the United States; those who pushed on to eastern Canada customarily settled in small and culturally exclusive enclaves, which functioned to preserve, reinforce, and replenish memories and traditions of home in the new land.[29] Lotus Blossom's and Edward's decision to leave again and to settle permanently in Canada probably came about for several reasons. Perhaps North America's size and heterogeneous populations made it seem easier for a family that had violated social taboos to hide there than in a small English village. Perhaps the depression in the silk trade between England and China in the 1870s caused a slump in family business, adding a financial incentive. Or perhaps Edward's family asked them to leave.[30] "We know that it was his marriage to mamma that had cut him off from his kindred," Winifred writes of the father in *Me* (26). It also has been suggested that Edward was on a family remittance.[31]

Though Montreal was where the Eatons would eventually settle, Sui Sin Far remembers their being in the United States first: "My parents have come to America. We are in Hudson City, New York, and we are very poor." Here Sui Sin Far recalls encountering the first Chinese she had seen outside her own family, when she and her brother Edward Charles passed "a Chinese store," described as "a long, low room" with the door open. The children peeked in and saw two men: "uncouth specimens of their race, drest in working blouses and pantaloons with queues hanging down their backs." The little girl recoiled in shock. " 'Oh, Charlie . . . Are we like that?' " she asked. " 'Well, we're Chinese, and they're Chinese, too, so we must be!' " Charlie retorted with eight-year-old logic ("Leaves," 126). Of course, these men differed from the Eaton children in many ways, including the ocean they had sailed to arrive in North America, but all that was clear to Sui Sin Far, the child, was the key word, *Chinese.* It was this word, finally made comprehensible by an external referent, that formed a bridge in the child's mind between her and the two men before her. In her memory of the event, she looked at the men as into a reflexive mirror, as external manifestations of a term others had used to describe, often punitively, an unseen and unidentified part of herself.

What Sui Sin Far would quickly discover was that she and these men shared a common status as objects of the racist attitudes and actions of a European-dominated society. In North America, treatment went beyond the "curiosity" she had suffered in England to include physical violence. Attacks on Eaton children by boys and girls in New York streets reflected the temper of adults in the country. " 'Chinky, Chinky, Chinaman, yellow-face, pig-tail, rat-eater,' " a boy taunted. " 'Better than you,' " shouted Sui Sin Far's brother. " 'I'd rather be Chinese than anything else in the world,' " Sui Sin Far screamed. And the battle ensued. "They pull my hair, they tear my clothes, they scratch my face and all but lame my brother; but the white blood in our veins fights valiantly for the Chinese half of us," Sui Sin Far recollected. If it was on the streets of New York that Sui Sin Far first learned she must fight for her "Chinese-ness," experiences here also reinforced the lessons of England, that survival sometimes required one to hide. Her remembrance that one of the boys who attacked them "lives near us and has seen my mother" suggests that keeping Lotus Blossom undercover was one way the family protected itself from attacks ("Leaves," 126).

The Eatons' arrival in Canada in 1872 or 1873 necessitated an international border crossing that was probably managed by rail; Sui Sin Far recalled coming in at "the station." Since all citizens of Canada were identified as "British" until 1947, when the Canadian Citizenship Act created Canadian citizenship, the family presumably traveled on British passports.[32] The fact that Mrs. Eaton was Chinese would not be noted on immigration records, for all documentation was under "head of household" only. This household included Sui Sin Far and her brother Edward Charles, three sisters and another brother, and Lotus Blossom and Edward, both of whom—according to their oldest daughter—were "still in their twenties" ("Leaves," 127). Sui Sin Far's own age would have been seven or eight.[33] Because Montreal's British and French communities had been divided by language, religion, and education since the Peace of Paris in 1763, Sui Sin Far would find in her new home what a segregated community looked like. Here she discovered a model for the cultural tension between Chinese and white immigrants in North America that would furnish her subject matter as a writer.

The Eatons' first known Montreal address, appearing in *Lovell's Montreal Directory*, 1873–74, was 16 St. Sacrament, near the St. Lawrence River in the heart of the city. Edward's occupation was listed as "commission merchant."[34] By *Lovell's* next entry, 1874–75, the family had moved to rue du Iberville on the western border of Hochelaga, a home described by Sui Sin Far as "the little Indian village where I grew up,"[35] a play on the name Jacques Cartier gave to the Iroquois settlement when he arrived in 1535. Established on the east side of St. Laurent Boulevard, Montreal's recognized line of demarcation between the English and the French, Hochelaga had been a French working-class village since the 1850s, when land farmed under the French seignorial system for the past two hundred years suddenly blossomed with industry, encouraging French Canadians throughout rural Quebec to migrate to this now-burgeoning suburb of Montreal to find work. Because they were reputed to take any employment for survival, the French Canadians were referred to as "the Chinese of Canada"[36]—though persons of Chinese descent were almost as infrequent a sight in eastern Canada in the 1870s as they were in England. The gold fields and railroad construction in the United States and Canada first brought Chinese immigrants to the western regions of these nations in the mid-nineteenth century. In 1885 completion of the transcontinental railroad in Canada would lead to the building of a serious Chinese community in eastern Canada.[37] Montrealers, however, were well aware of China and the increasing Chinese migrations to North America. Canada, along with Britain and the United States, was also an active participant in the Christian mission movement, as we have observed in Shanghai. Further, since discovery of gold in 1858 on the Fraser River in British Columbia and subsequent construction of a transcontinental railroad, the question of whether to import Chinese labor, and to what extent, had been a continuing issue of national debate.[38]

That their new Canadian neighbors, both French and English, were alert to the family's Chinese racial connections is apparent in Sui Sin Far's portrayal of their arrival and her early childhood years in Montreal. A sleigh carried the family from "the station" to a little "French Canadian hotel," where her father helped her mother out, and then one-by-one the "little black heads" of the children emerged from "the buffalo robe." The sleigh was surrounded by "villagers," whose curiosity, Sui Sin Far writes, "is tempered with kindness" as they murmur, "Les pauvres. enfants . . . Chinoise, Chinoise." The abuse the Eaton children suffered in Montreal more or less duplicated their experience in New York. Other children refused to sit next to them at school, and when they went out, Sui Sin Far recalled, "our footsteps are dogged by a number of young French and English Canadians, who amuse themselves with specula-tions as to whether, we being Chinese, are susceptible to pinches and hairpulling, while older persons pause and gaze upon us, very much in the same way that I have seen people gaze upon strange animals in a menagerie." "Pitched battles" again ensued, and the children would "seldom leave the house without being armed for conflict." Sui Sin Far writes that her mother "takes a great interest in our battles, and usually cheers us on." As for her father, "peace is his motto, and he deems it wisest to be blind and deaf to many things." Yet, from Sui Sin Far's adult perspective, even her mother did not understand "the depths of the troubled waters through which her little children wade," for Lotus Blossom was "Chinese," as Edward was "English"—that is, "they know who they are." In her painful grappling for self-definition, Sui Sin Far would strive for a place in both worlds but from both would feel severed. "I do not confide in my father and mother," the adult woman wrote. "I am different to both of them—a stranger, though their own child" ("Leaves," 126–27).

Added to the traumas Sui Sin Far and her siblings experienced because of their race was an encroaching family impoverishment, which apparently began when the Eatons left England and grew gradually more intense during their first years in Montreal. The reason the Eatons, an English family in terms of loyalties, public records, and national identity, chose to settle in the industrial French suburb of a city that had sharply divided English and French for two hundred years might have been the same reason French Canadian farmers migrated from rural Quebec: housing was cheap, and there was promise of work in the new factories. The largest of those factories was Victor Hudon's cotton mill, constructed in 1874, the same year the Eatons' address first appears in Hochelaga. Owned by the English, Hudon's was the region's largest employer, offering separate doors for "hommes," "femmes," and "enfants," who were paid respectively $5.00–6.00, $4.50–5.00, and $1.50–1.80, for a sixty- to sixty-two-hour week. Since Hudon's employed many clerks, this might have been where Edward worked.[39]

Hudon's also offered long rows of "company houses" along Hochelaga's newly designed streets, close to the enormous mills by the waterfront.[40] In 1877 the Eatons' address was 62 Moreau; in 1878, it was 13 Marlborough; and during 1880–82, it became 42 Seaver and then 32 Seaver. All recorded addresses were located in "an English pocket" of a housing area that Hudon's provided for their workers. The dwelling places on these streets where Sui Sin Far and her siblings would grow up for approximately the next decade can be envisioned as a composite. They were row houses constructed of brick, mortar, or stone, materials required by ordinance after a fire in the 1850s almost consumed Montreal and led to the banning of wood construction. Designed in three stories, with a row of corniced windows along the top under the eaves, these dwellings looked ample enough, but only the relatively well-to-do had the full three stories to themselves; for working people the structure was shared, a floor to a family. This meant that privacy, a writer's most precious resource, was rare if not nonexistent. Set back a prescribed ten feet from the curb, front doors opened flush with the walkway, back doors onto a small garden space, usually supporting a few chickens, a pig, or a cow. The narrator of Winifred's *Marion* compares their garden to her family: "unkempt and wild and heathenish" (8).

Also in the back space was the toilet, or "backhouse"—indoor plumbing was unheard of for working-class housing. Carriers brought drinking water from the St. Lawrence and sold it door-to-door from barrels slung over their backs. Pollution from both factory and human waste caused this water to spread such diseases as typhoid and tuberculosis. Public baths made of wood and placed on strategic corners to be shared by the community likely spread as many germs as they eliminated. Poor sanitation, mixed with overcrowding, was largely responsible for one of the highest infant mortality rates in the world in St. Mary's of Hochelaga, the ward where the Eatons lived. In 1874 Sui Sin Far's brother, Ernest George, would succumb, becoming the first Eaton to be buried in Mont Royal Cemetery, on the Protestant slope of "The Mountain" around which Montreal grew.[41] It is in this family cycle of deaths and new births that Sui Sin Far, the eldest daughter in a family plummeting financially from "merchant" to "working" class, would live from age eight into adulthood. "In dat familee dere are eleven children, and more—they come!" a Canadian storekeeper in *Me* would exclaim (1). The birth of a new baby took place almost every year and, nearly as frequently, the move to a new address. Did the family move because it was forced to seek larger quarters as the old were outgrown? Because of increasing inability to pay the rent? Or perhaps because of racism directed against them, if someone "lives near us and has seen my mother" ("Leaves," 126)?[42]

Sui Sin Far's return to school in Hochelaga brought with it more pain because of continued attacks by other children and her sense of inferiority among her own siblings. All schools in the Montreal district were divided between French and English children. The Eaton children officially would have attended an English school, but since their names do not appear on public school records, they must have attended private schools. "I am in the same class with my brother, my sister next to me is in the class below," Sui Sin Far recollected. She recalled that her parents compared her with "the sister next to me" (that is, Grace), who "has a wonderful head for figures, and . . . helps my father with his night work accounts." Her father thought Grace was "more like my mother, who is very bright . . . ." Her brother was also regarded as "remarkably bright" ("Leaves," 127). Sui Sin Far's sense of inadequacy might have been somewhat offset when, at age eight, inspired by a particular teacher who professed that "the true fathers and mothers of the world were those who battled through great trials and hardships to leave to future generations noble and inspiring truths," she "conceived the ambition to write a book about the half-Chinese" (*Globe*). The girl's curiosity about her "Chinese-ness" was developing into a fierce determination to know, an impulse that apparently distinguished her from the rest of her family. " 'What are we?' " she asked Charlie. " 'It doesn't matter, sissy,' " he responded. " 'But,' " Sui Sin Far continued, " 'it does.' " She "dreams dreams of being great and noble; my sisters and brothers also," and "glor[ies] in the idea of dying at the stake and a great genie arising from the flames and declaring to those who have scorned us: 'Behold, how great and glorious and noble are the Chinese people!' " ("Leaves," 128).

A further difficulty for Sui Sin Far was her physical frailty. Here, too, she recalled that her parents compared her with Grace, who "is of sturdier build," as she compared herself with all her sisters. Such comparisons, perceived as moral judgments, affected her growing self-image. Years later she would remember her father's admonition that she "will never make half the woman that my mother is or that my sister will be." She was "prostrated at times with attacks of nervous sickness," diagnosed as having a heart "unusually large" ("Leaves," 127), and at age fourteen she suffered an attack of rheumatic fever, "a sickness which affected both head and heart and retarded development both mentally and physically" (*Globe*). Fearing "that the others will despise me for not being as strong as they," she tried to hide her illness, thus bringing increased isolation. Further, she felt "somewhat ashamed," especially because "I am the eldest little girl and more is expected of me" ("Leaves," 127).

The role of eldest daughter—in Victorian England, Canada, and the United States—was socially prescribed, which partially explains why Sui Sin Far was not free to pursue a life of her own until she was past thirty. As the eldest daughter, Sui Sin Far was in the role of second mother and thus responsible for her siblings' upbringing and care. Countless newspapers urged women to "make the home a blessing."[43] What society mandated, the family unit took for granted, and the church reinforced. For example, an item in the *Presbyterian Record,* a publication of the church where Sui Sin Far's "mother believes in sending us to Sunday School" ("Leaves," 126), held as exemplary a girl who "asked God to show her . . . what was her special work" and was told that she should "take her baby brother, only a few months old, and nurse him for the Lord." "So she took charge of the child, and relieved her mother in the work and care of the little ones. This was Godly and Christlike. Home duties and fireside responsibilities have the first claim upon every child of God."[44] Sui Sin Far recalled accepting similar responsibilities at age ten: "If there is any trouble in the house . . . between my mother and father, or if any child is punished, how I suffer! And when harmony is restored, harmony seems to be all around me." Most significant for the adolescent girl's developing gender identity was the empathy she felt with her mother's relentless childbearing—an experience excruciatingly intimate under conditions where births take place at home: "My mother's screams of agony when a baby is born almost drive me wild, and long after her pangs have subsided I feel them in my own body" ("Leaves," 127). Such identification obviously moved beyond physical pain to the awareness that every bout with birth resulted in a new infant for the eldest daughter to help feed, love, and protect.

In 1875, when Sui Sin Far was ten, May Darling, Lillie Winifred, and Christiana Mary ("Agnes") were baptized at Montreal's American Presbyterian Church.[45] The Eaton family fortunes must have suffered further decline that year because Sui Sin Far recalls that the children were taken from school and that she "shortly thereafter attracts the attention of a lovely old lady, Mrs. William Darling of Hochelaga, who induced my mother to send me to her for a few hours each day" (*Globe*).[46] Besides tutoring in music and French, Mrs. Darling offset Sui Sin Far's remorse about having "no head for figures" by telling her that she had "a marvelous memory," by inspiring her "with the belief that the spirit is more than the body," and by generally nourishing in the girl a positive self-perception. When Sui Sin Far finally achieved book publication at age forty-seven, she wrote, "It was Mrs. Darling who first, aside from my mother, interested me in my mother's people, and impressed upon me that I should be proud that I had sprung from such a race." The following year "family circumstances made it necessary to withdraw me from Mrs. Darling," and though Mrs. Darling "tried to persuade [Sui Sin Far's parents] to permit her to send me to a boarding school," her father would not agree—for he "was an Englishman, and the idea of having any of his children brought up on charity hurt his pride" (*Globe*).

It was a major turning point in the author's life, one that is integrally connected with issues of class. Since Montreal guaranteed a free public education from primary school through college to any "Protestant boy or girl of promise, no matter how humble in life or how straitened in circumstance their parents may be,"[47] it is hard to understand why the Eaton children should be taken from school because of lack of money. James Doyle suggests that "colonial schools" (i.e., Canadian public schools) were not good enough for "a Britisher's children," or so an Englishman of the merchant class would have seen it—no economic fall into poverty could dismiss this entrenched class distinction. In public schools children could not help but be exposed, for example, to the Irish who had immigrated to Canada in the decades following the potato famine in Ireland and who, by the 1870s, had formed large Montreal communities. As "English from England," Edward Eaton would have assumed that his family's status was above the French, and probably even above the Canadian-born British, a mind-set substantiated by *Marion*'s narrator when she speaks of someone's taking papa's paintings "back to England with him, as representative of Canadian art" and adds parenthetically, "(which it was not—papa had studied in France, and was an Englishman, not a Canadian)" (145). The Eatons were not merely English, Doyle points out, but *British*, an enclave unto themselves attempting to preserve home values in exile. If they could not afford to educate their children at a good private school, they were better off educating them at home.

That Lotus Blossom was able to do so is clear from her training as "a schoolmistress" and from the cultural atmosphere of learning that both Sui Sin Far and Winifred remembered as prevailing in their home. According to scenes in *Marion*, family composition of poetry was a daily activity, and family members regularly composed plays based on British models and acted them out for each other (99). Libraries were free, available, and probably well used. As Sui Sin Far remembered, "Whenever I have the opportunity, I steal away to the library and read everything I can find on China and the Chinese" ("Leaves," 128). A skillful command of the "King's English" is obvious in the writings of both Sui Sin Far and Winifred, as is their acquaintance with Eastern and Western classics and the Bible. The closely monitored home education of all of the daughters is evident in their achievements, most impressively illustrated when Grace becomes a lawyer.

Whatever the reasons, in 1876 when Sui Sin Far was eleven, all formal education for her and her siblings appears to have come to a halt. When Edward withdrew his children from formal education, one must assume that more than his pride was at stake, for according to both sisters' recollections, he used them in the creation of a family work force. "My sisters are apprenticed to a dressmaker; my brother is entered in an office. I tramp around and sell my father's pictures, also some lace which I make myself," Sui Sin Far recounted ("Leaves," 128). For a child who was intellectually inclined and found school one of her few pleasures in life, one can barely imagine the depths of this trauma.

Her strategy for rising out of it expresses the optimism of her nature and the gift that would serve her so well in her art—seeing life through dual lenses. Against the drudgery, humiliation, and dangers of having to take to the streets as a child of eleven to "earn [her] living" was set, first, the "opportunity to study human nature" and "to gratify [her] love for landscape beauty" and, second, the elation experienced in "starting out one morning with two pictures in one hand and coming home in the evening with twenty dollars," making everyone "happy." Tramping around Montreal streets to sell the Irish lace she designed and crocheted was probably Sui Sin Far's first experience at learning that creativity and earning an income can be mutually compatible. Most important, in the struggle to survive, she divided her mind into "two lives" or perspectives, creating a pattern in her psyche that seems to have laid the dual vision that would underlie her approach to both life and writing: "I, now in my 11th year, entered into two lives, one devoted entirely to family concerns; the other, a withdrawn life of thought and musing. This withdrawn life of thought probably took the place of ordinary education with me. I had six keys to it; one, a great capacity for feeling; another, the key of imagination; third, the key of physical pain; fourth the key of sympathy; fifth, the sense of being differentiated from the ordinary by the fact that I was an Eurasian; sixth, the impulse to create" (*Globe*).

It is especially interesting that, at eleven years of age, Sui Sin Far combined "the key of imagination" with "the impulse to create," both informed by "the sense of being differentiated from the ordinary by the fact that I was an Eurasian." While the practical life "devoted to family concerns" would encompass the duties of daily living and gain in dominance as Sui Sin Far and her younger siblings grew to be teenagers, in that "withdrawn life of thought and musing" the world of imagination would continue to flourish. That Sui Sin Far continued to nourish pride in her "Chinese-ness," though this feeling remained largely unspoken, is suggested in the attitude she recalled at age eighteen when she was working at the *Montreal Daily Star:* "What troubles me is not that I am what I am, but that others are ignorant of my superiority" ("Leaves," 128).

In this way, the girl struggling with family poverty grew to be "Miss Edith Eaton," the dutiful, hard-working eldest daughter of a large, rather Bohemian, English Canadian family. The decade of the 1880s was difficult and turbulent for the Eatons. More children were born—George in 1879, Rose in 1880, Lawrence in 1882, Florence in 1885, and Beryl, the fourteenth and last, in 1887. In 1884 Lawrence died and was buried beside Ernest George in the Mont Royal Cemetery. In 1880–81 Edward shifted his occupation from clerk to bookkeeper, in 1882–83 back to clerk, and in 1883–84 to artist, which he remained with for the rest of his life. A smallpox epidemic in 1885, accompanied by English attempts to take over a French hospital for a clinic and force the French to accept vaccinations, increased racial tensions in Montreal, as did the 1885 execution of Louis Riel, the Métis leader of an Indian rebellion in the West. The 1880s also saw the continuance of a distinct downward trend in eastern Canada's economy. This period is described by *Marion*'s narrator as "the grueling days of dire poverty that follow the plague" (14), with the fictional children's father "sitting at his easel, his blue eyes fixed absently on the canvas before him," painting "potboilers to feed [his] hungry children," the mother crying all night, and the children going to bed hungry (5). In the novel the father returns briefly to England—"to try to induce grandpa—that grandfather we have never seen—to help us" (14). Such evidence suggests the year of the smallpox epidemic probably would have been the year of Edward's last appeal to his Macclesfield family.

By 1883 Sui Sin Far's activities as eldest daughter had moved from "carrying our babies" at home and selling paintings and lace on the streets to joining those women who, since the late 1860s, had been entering the traditionally male world of office work.[48] "My 18th birthday saw me in the composing room of the Montreal Daily Star," Sui Sin Far recalled, "picking and setting type" (Globe). A passage in Marion describes Ada, probably modeled after Sui Sin Far, as "the most unselfish of girls" who "used to bring everything she earned to mama" when she worked on "The Star" (66). Presumably all the older Eaton children (Edward Charles, Grace, Sarah, Agnes) also handed over their earnings "to mama," while May and Winifred, aged ten and eight, assumed the care of oncoming babies. At the Montreal Daily Star, Sui Sin Far taught herself shorthand in preparation for entering the occupation of stenography, which the introduction of typewriters, among other factors, was opening to thousands of women. Stenography would sustain most of the Eaton sisters until each got married and would furnish Sui Sin Far a marginal income throughout most of her life. "Like my sister [Grace], I teach myself," Sui Sin Far recalled, "but, unlike my sister, I have neither the perseverance nor the ability to perfect myself.... Therefore, although I can always earn a moderately good salary, I do not distinguish myself in the business world as does she" ("Leaves," 128). Still, the eldest daughter's skills were sufficient that she obtained a position as stenographer for "Archibald and McCormick, advocates and commissioners for Ontario, 1724 Notre Dame," a law firm in Montreal's original riverfront business district.[49]

Though Sui Sin Far found stenographic work to be stultifying and "demeaning to one whose mind must create its own images," she sustained herself with a favorite myth women were fed in this era: "it brought me into contact with men of judgment and mental ability" (Globe). Somewhere between demands of family and employment, she nevertheless was finding time and space to write, for in the mid-1880s her first publications appeared—"humorous articles" in the radical U.S. newspapers Peck's Sun, Texas Liftings, and Detroit Free Press.[50] In "the senior member of the firm" for which she worked, the future Judge John Sprott Archibald of Montreal,[51] she likely met her first mentor. Archibald "read my little stories and verses as they appeared, and usually commented on them with amused interest," she recounted in the Globe. His condescending tone, coupled with his opinion "that it would be necessary . . . to acquire some experience of life and some knowledge of character" when Sui Sin Far confessed she "was ambitious to write a book," introduced her to the attitude of "great men" she would continue to encounter in the world of publishing. Her reply struck a note of independence and hinted at her position on future fictional characterizations: "I intended to form all my characters upon the model of myself" (*Globe*).

In the late 1880s that model would have been not only of a woman from a middle-class but rather down-at-the-heels English Canadian family whose daughter had to work for a living but also of a woman in her mid-twenties who was still single. Sui Sin Far's work implies that her family and friends were actively pressuring her to look for a husband. In 1888–89 six short stories and two essays came out in a new periodical devoted to the promotion of Canada, the *Dominion Illustrated,* most emphasizing the love adventures of European Canadian women. Each was signed "Edith Eaton," indicating that Sui Sin Far's "withdrawn life of thought and musing," inasmuch as her Chinese identity was concerned, was still in seclusion. These pieces also show that the keys to unlock that life—particularly those of imagination and the impulse to create—remained safely in the writer's hands. Each carries the dual vision of the trickster in her fledgling stages, the humorous and satirical barbs flung at romantic love and marriage that would become Sui Sin Far's hallmark.

Sui Sin Far's views about marriage are further illuminated in Winifred's depiction of Marion's oldest sister, Ada, who, as the fictional younger sisters move into their teens, is assigned the position of chaperone customarily assumed by a mother when younger sisters date or receive gentlemen callers. Ada is described as "the one who always sat up for anyone in the house who went out at night" and who put them through "cross-questioning" if they were late (50). When Marion (the fictional counterpart of Sui Sin Far's sister Sarah)[52] is being courted by the foppish young Britisher Bertie, Ada is said to have "settled down with her crochet work by the lamp," where she "sat there all evening with her eye on Mr. Bertie and occasionally saying something brief and sarcastic" (60). It is Ada (not "papa") who insists on knowing the "intentions" of her sisters' suitors. Ada's language—"If he doesn't propose soon, you ought to stop going out with him. It's bad form" (19)—reflects the courting mores of a Victorian age. Nevertheless, the prescribed role of marriage for a woman of this era was one that both Ada and Sui Sin Far knew very well and would avoid for themselves.

The men who call on the Eaton sisters in *Marion* are all either British or French Canadian. *Marion*'s narrator speaks of the "younger sons of aristocrats, who, not much good in England were often sent to Canada" and "liked to hang around papa, whose family most of them knew" (28–29). One of these is identified as "the son of the Earl of Albemarle," who "liked Ada," but for whom "Ada pretended she had only an indifferent interest" (29).[53] Prominent is Bertie, who professes to love Marion but can never tell his family in England of her existence because her family was so poor. That Bertie's reluctance could be influenced by Marion's Chinese ancestry is never suggested. The closest Winifred comes to mentioning the mother's race is in *Me* when the narrator says, "She was a native of a far-distant land, and I do not think she ever got over being a stranger in Canada" (3).[54]

In effect, *Marion* gives us the portrait of a family anomalous because of poverty and the father's choice to be an artist, not because that family is Chinese Canadian. Yet, to the reader with external knowledge, the narrator's very silence on the matter causes the mother's Chinese identity to glare from the text's margins. In *Marion* the mother of the family is a continuous presence, walking into or out of rooms, downstairs or up, usually with her eldest daughter. "I saw Ada glance at mamma, and I knew what was in their minds," the younger daughter Marion observes. But the character of the mother is granted neither name, physical description, nor power of speech, perhaps reflecting the invisibility of the actual Lotus Blossom. Again, however, the details of truth are darted through like threads of gilt in a curtain, as Ada and "mamma" move together between rooms, standing beside the piano to hear "In the Gloaming" sung to them by "a friend of papa's" (28). It illuminates the root of Ada's "passionate devotion and loyalty to the family" (51) and the closeness of the relationship between "mamma" and her eldest daughter—the only Eaton offspring to acknowledge and seek the Chinese roots they all shared.

Sometime in the early 1890s, when a "clergyman" visited Lotus Blossom with the request "that she call upon a young Chinese woman who has recently arrived from China as the bride of one of the local merchants," the first door inviting Sui Sin Far to step over the threshold from "outsider" to "insider" among the small but growing Chinese populations in eastern Canada suddenly opened. The fact that the clergyman approached Lotus Blossom suggests her presence in Montreal was not as completely hidden as the public records imply. "With the exception of my mother, there was but one other Chinese woman in the city besides the bride," Sui Sin Far wrote in the *Globe*.[55] When Lotus Blossom made the call, Sui Sin Far accompanied her. That a clergyman should have been the catalyst for such a meeting is consistent with Eaton family history and the history of the missionary movement, which—embryonic when Lotus Blossom met Edward in Shanghai—was reaching a fever pitch by this last decade of the century. Multiple Christian denominations in both Canada and the United States vied for the souls of incoming immigrants, constructing "home" mission societies that served the same function in North America as the mission stations did in China. The completion of the Canadian Pacific Railway in 1885, U.S. passage of the Chinese Exclusion Act in 1882, and Montreal's assumption of the "entrepôt"

Sui Sin Far in the 1890s. Courtesy of L. Charles
Laferrière.

position in the distribution of Chinese labor to Europe and the Americas all
contributed to the rapid growth of a Montreal Chinese community in these
last fifteen years of the century.[56] The Eaton family would have been well
aware of this because of their own Chinese identity and their involvement
with the Protestant church. For Sui Sin Far, the "clergyman's" call marked a
juncture: "From that time I began to go among my mother's people, and it did
me a world of good to discover how akin I was to them" (*Globe*).

Once over that threshold, the woman's life hints at no turning back. Her
opening "an office of my own" ("Leaves," 128) in the center of Montreal's
financial district is dated by this entry in *Lovell's,* 1894–95: "Eaton, Miss Edith,
stenographer and typewriter, 157 St. James, h 828 St. Lawrence."[57] Her
evolving career independence worked hand in hand with a deepening
involvement with Chinese Montrealers. As a free-lance journalist, Sui Sin Far

received "most of the local Chinese reporting" from local papers, implying that her withdrawn life of "Eurasian-ness" was beginning to stir ("Leaves," 128). Publicly, she was moving beyond sympathetic outsider to champion the Chinese Canadians against a new onslaught of racist laws and practices. On 21 September 1896 a letter captioned "A Plea for the Chinaman," addressed "To the Editor of the Star" and signed "E.E.," spoke out against a national petition to raise the head tax the Dominion had placed on Chinese immigrants.[58] Sui Sin Far's pride in her role of defender is evident: "I meet many Chinese persons, and when they get into trouble am often called upon to fight their battles in the papers. This I enjoy" ("Leaves," 128).[59] Of further interest is that both the Chinese and the newspapers recognized her in this role.

By the mid-1890s, when she was approximately thirty, Sui Sin Far had thus made a major choice, one inversely related to the dual existence she had created for survival at age eleven. When she was a child, her Chinese heritage could be relegated to the imaginative world and tucked out of sight; when she was a woman, it must be confronted in action. Since the 21 September 1896 letter was written about Chinese North Americans in New York as well as Montreal, her commitment to take a stand for Chinese North Americans clearly ignored national borders; this is also indicated when she speaks of a Chinese man from New York who visited her Montreal office. This shift in the workplace was joined by a new trend in her fiction. In 1896 her first "Chinese stories" appeared, the first in the New York journal *Fly Leaf,* published by her new brother-in-law, Walter Blackburne Harte; the next two in the *Lotus,* a Kansas City journal that Harte edited; and the other two in the Los Angeles *Land of Sunshine,* edited by Charles Fletcher Lummis.[60] All were signed from Montreal by "Sui Seen Far."

This passage from "Leaves" offers a clue to how Sui Sin Far's Eaton family reacted to her new visibility:

> "You were walking with a Chinaman yesterday," accuses an acquaintance.
> "Yes, what of it?"
> "You ought not to. It isn't right."
> "Not right to walk with one of my own mother's people? Oh, indeed!" (129)

This may be read as a conversation between Sui Sin Far and a brother or sister;[61] more likely, it is a composite expressing Sui Sin Far's choice to "walk" ideologically apart from her family. It was a choice at direct odds with those her siblings were making as, one by one during the 1890s, they married and became absorbed into the white community. Edward Charles started the trend in 1888 by marrying Isabella Maria Carter, according to *Marion's* narrator, "a girl we didn't like," because she "took precious care that the contribution [of income] should be of the smallest, and kept Charles from coming to see his family" (4).[62] In 1891 Grace married Walter Blackburn Harte, a writer from England, and the couple moved to New York, where Harte had been offered an editorial position on the *New England Magazine*.[63] Christiana Mary ("Agnes") married a French Canadian, E. E. Perrault, in 1893, gave birth to the first Eaton grandchild, and would be the only Eaton daughter to stay in Montreal.[64] May Darling entered a nunnery, where she would stay for several months[65] before migrating to San Francisco in response to an ad for work in a photographer's studio, and eventually married a San Franciscan named Winkelman. Sarah, who followed her father's path as a painter, moved to Boston and eventually married Karl Bosse, an artist.[66] In 1896 Winifred went as a stenographer to Jamaica. By 1897 only the three youngest sisters—Rose, Florence, and Beryl—and a sixteen-year-old brother, Hubert, remained at home. The need would have diminished, at least on a physical basis, for Sui Sin Far to serve as the household's "advisory head."

In 1897 *Lovell's* last entry for "Miss Edith Eaton, stenographer and typewriter" appeared, and on 30 January 1897 Sui Sin Far wrote Lummis a letter from Kingston, Jamaica, to thank him for a four-dollar check. The reason Sui Sin Far gave for her leave-taking was economic: "I gave up my office in Montreal and accepted a position as reporter on one of the Jamaican papers because of hard times, dullness in business, and c."[67]—a circumstance probably brought about by a tightening economic depression in eastern Canada throughout the 1890s, to which the narrator of *Me* may be alluding when she comments on the "departing of the older children to try their fortunes in more promising cities than Quebec" (6). All the Eaton offspring were expected to continue to contribute to the family income from wherever they moved. When Marion (Sarah) goes to Boston, Ada reminds her to "be sure and send something home each week just as Nora [Winifred] is doing" (*Marion,* 130); when Ellen (Grace) marries Wallace (Walter), she sends money regularly until Wallace becomes ill.

From the perspective of Sui Sin Far's developing artistic vision, a more critical factor was that until the sister-daughter-aunt, closely bonded by love and duty to her family, took the plunge—Lotus Blossom notwithstanding—of weaning herself geographically from the Montreal enclave, she could not establish herself independently. Carolyn Heilbrun's suggestion that "the unconscious decision to place one's life outside the bounds of society's restraints and ready-made narratives" is central to the development of some women artists is relevant to Sui Sin Far's life at this crossroad.[68] Her decision not to marry, her stand as a defender of Chinese North American populations, and her leave-taking from Montreal were all steps in the labyrinth through which she would probe the ambiguities of her identity apart from the rest and define her writing purpose.

In a preamble to Jamaica, Sui Sin Far took a trip, presumably for temporary work, to "a little town away off on the north shore of a big lake," situated generally in the "Middle West." The trip was crucial to her stand on her identity. Through "a transcontinental railway" that ran through the town, and a "population . . . in the main made up of working folks with strong prejudices against my mother's countrymen," the setting becomes a microcosm within which divisions between white and Chinese North America play themselves out. There Sui Sin Far worked as a stenographer, and while she was dining one day at a table with her employer and other business acquaintances, the conversation turned to the "cars full of Chinamen that past [*sic*] that morning by train." Listening to her dinner companions remark, "I wouldn't have one in my house," and "I cannot reconcile myself to the thought that the Chinese are human like ourselves," Sui Sin Far recalled that a "miserable, cowardly feeling" kept her "silent," for she realized that if she spoke, "every person in the place will hear about it the next day." Then she lifted her eyes and addressed her employer: " 'The Chinese may have no souls, no expression on their faces, be altogether beyond the pale of civilization, but whatever they are, I want you to understand that I am—I am a Chinese.' " Her employer apologized to her: " 'I know nothing whatever about the Chinese. It was pure prejudice.' " Sui Sin Far "admired" his "moral courage," yet she did "not remain much longer in the little town" ("Leaves," 129–30). Living for what was probably the first time in a community that did not know her family, she marks this as a turning point in her lifelong struggle to integrate "Sui Sin Far" and "Miss Edith Eaton." At this dinner table, she announced—and thus learned for herself—that in each was the other.

What began in the "little town" reached the proportions of a "rebirth" experience for Sui Sin Far in Jamaica. Our major sources for the Jamaican experiences of both Sui Sin Far and Winifred are their respective autobiographical accounts in "Leaves" and *Me.* Winifred's narrator in *Me* refers to herself as the fifth child to leave home, yet as "the first to leave for a land as distant as the West Indies" (4). Reading this, we might wonder how a young Canadian woman would find the opportunity to go to Kingston, Jamaica, a six-day trip by railroad and steamship. Implicit in *Me* is the existence of an imperial network that connected the West Indies and Canada, as well as many other nations in the nineteenth-century world. The Canadian agent for the Jamaican paper for whom the narrator works is described as a "family friend." After the agent sees a story she wrote for the *Montreal Daily Star,* he suggests that she "take the place of a girl out in Jamaica who is anxious to return to Canada" (5). When the narrator leaves Jamaica she is "replaced" by her sister, presumably Sui Sin Far, clearly suggesting that Canada, a British dominion, was supplying an ongoing force of women office workers to Jamaica, a British colony. Though fictionalized in *Me* as the *Lantern,* the paper for which both Winifred and Sui Sin Far went to work was probably the *News Letter,* which

Sui Sin Far gives as her return address in a letter to Lummis. Winifred Eaton Babcock's entry in *Who Was Who* confirms this supposition: "went to West Indies 1895, and worked as general writer and reporter on Jamaican News Letter."[69] For *Me*'s narrator, transportation costs were fifty-five dollars and paid by the paper (25); the salary was ten dollars a week plus free board and lodging at the "Myrtle Bank Hotel" (29). The narrators of both *Me* and the *Globe* article describe reporting for legislative council meetings and doing stenography, a skill that Sui Sin Far had probably taught Winifred (implied when *Me*'s narrator claims that a sister showed her the "rudiments of shorthand" [24]).

In such British colonies as Jamaica, the racist attitudes of the dominant white populations toward people with skins darker than Anglos' were similar to those Sui Sin Far knew as a child in Montreal. Indeed, Anglo ethnocentrism was approaching new heights in this period verging on the Boer War. According to the 1897 *Whitaker's Almanac,* Jamaica's racial composite was made up as follows: "Whites: 14,692; Blacks 488,624; Coloured, 121,955," plus "a number of coolies or Chinese."[70] Used in Jamaica to segregate mulattoes and people of varying shades of "black-ness" from the privileged whites, the "coloured" distinction could apply equally to Eurasians, as Winifred and Sui Sin Far knew. Both also recognized that if they were identified as the daughters of Lotus Blossom, they might not be traveling at all, unless as Chinese traveled, in bond.[71]

Hence, as the sisters began their treks across national borders, "passing" became an issue of more than social acceptance or even racist abuse but of survival at a primary level. It was an issue Sui Sin Far had already faced in the past, perhaps when she went to the "Middle West town," most certainly when she made a trip to New York in 1896.[72] Pressure to pass as white and the fear of being discovered must have plagued both sisters on all of their journeys; the conflict for Sui Sin Far would have been especially severe because of her loyalty to her Chinese descent. Both had been raised in the same marginalized conditions of racism, poverty, thwarted education, and untimely financial responsibility; both had ambitions to become writers and the courage to strike out for ways to fulfill their goals in environments in which they knew the odds were against them. Yet the lack of evidence of sisterly bonding is notable. No correspondence between them has surfaced, and mutual references in their essays and fiction are rare. Winifred chose to mask her Chinese identity by writing under the pseudonym "Onoto Watanna" and feigning a Japanese heritage, while Sui Sin Far used her writing to come to terms with her Chinese identity, which suggests that the sisters had contrary notions about how to deal with their interracial heritage and the purposes of their writing.[73]

The sisters' contrasting attitudes are nowhere better illustrated than in their accounts of Jamaica. *Me*'s narrator consistently elevates her father's status and relates to her English heritage: "My father's an Oxford man, and a descendant of the family of Sir Isaac Newton;" "the greatness of my father's people had been a sort of fairy story with us all . . ." (26, 94). The narrator of "Leaves" relates to her mother's culture: "Though a child when she left her native land she remembers it well, and I am never tired of listening to the story of how she was stolen from her home" (128). Both sisters dream of the day they can be free of caring for young children and out on their own, but the language with which each conveys her desire is markedly different. *Me*'s narrator dismisses her family and focuses only on personal escape: "with what fierce joy did I not now look forward to getting away at last from that same, noisy, tormenting brood, for whom it had been my particular and detested task to care" (6). The narrator of "Leaves" focuses on her siblings' well-being, which, once attained, can open the doors to her own independence: "I peeped into the future and saw all the family grown and settled down and myself, far away from all noise and confusion, with nothing to do but write a book" (*Globe*). Winifred expresses bitter dissatisfaction toward many aspects of herself—"My clothes were thick and woolen. . . . My coat was rough and hopelessly Canadian" (6)—including her non-English features: "In all my most fanciful imaginings and dreams I had always been golden-haired and blue-eyed" (41). Such rejection of her appearance reinforces the narrator's covert denial of her maternal ancestry and is accompanied by a denial of racism; at the same time she expresses racist feelings against other people of color. In Canada, "one color . . . is as good as another," *Me*'s narrator claims, and she rhetorically asks: "What should I, a girl who has never before been outside Quebec . . . know of race prejudice?"

This question is at odds with all of Sui Sin Far's memories of prejudice against her and her family and belies more objective evidence. As the historian Robin W. Winks has noted, "The patterns of discrimination practiced by whites against blacks in Canada differed but slightly from patterns of discrimination observed in the northern United States."[74] Furthermore, Winifred's denial of the issue of race through an autobiographical narrator directly contrasts with her sister's acute awareness of racism wherever she traveled. The difference between the two sisters' perceptions is not explained simply by their ten-year difference in age; rather, it reflects antithetical views of "self/other" identities, which set the pattern for the diverse contents and themes in each of their writings. *Me*'s narrator refers to Jamaica as "a hot, beastly old country where nearly everybody is black" (28), refuses to take the extended hand of one black man, runs in terror from another, and laments: "I myself was dark and foreign-looking, but the blonde type I adored" (41).

Sui Sin Far, whose sense of heterogeneous identity is also heightened in Jamaica, expresses herself antithetically. While she also must place herself in the category of "white" to travel and work, the opposition between socioeco-

Sui Sin Far's sister Winifred in the 1920s. Courtesy of L. Charles Laferrière.

nomic necessity and her inner sense of racial identity is ironically maintained throughout. When taken "to task" by her employer's wife for thanking a black maid, the narrator of "Leaves" inwardly comments that she is "mixing with people of fashion, and yet not one of them." She opposes a "warning" given her by "Englishmen" about the " 'brown boys' of the island" by completing the sentence with candid self-reflection: "little dreaming that I too am of the 'brown people' of the earth." She openly acknowledges her perilous status as an "invisible minority": "it begins to be whispered about the place that I am not all white." When these whispers cause " 'sporty' " types to seek her acquaintance, an irony of expectation moves into play, for the specified type is not "brown" but "a big, blonde, handsome fellow," a "naval officer," who invites her "out for a sail," tells her she "look[s] such a nice little body," and entertains her with stories of "the sweet little Chinese girls [he] met . . . at Hong Kong." Sui Sin Far's generic response to such men reverses their roles, allowing *her* to look at *them* condescendingly: "When . . . they discover that I am a very serious and sober-minded spinster indeed, they retire quite gracefully, leaving me a few amusing reflections." Implicit throughout this scene is an ironic assault on the imperialistic assumption that "little Chinese girls," like the land that they hail from, are the playthings of "big, handsome, blonde fellows" (130).

Sui Sin Far must have been in Jamaica less than a year when she contracted "malarial fever, the only cure for which, in my case," she wrote, "was a trip up North" (Globe). In "Leaves," she noted the pivotal position the Jamaican experience, brief as it was, occupied in her personal and professional growth: "The surroundings, people, manner of living, are so entirely different from what I have been accustomed to up North that I feel as if I were 'born again' " (130). Given her Christian background, the metaphor, cited in quotes, would not have been used accidentally. The entire West Indies junket was for Sui Sin Far a "rebirth," but not one of religious salvation. Rather, her experience with Jamaica's "brown people" helped the author break through her loneliness and isolation to perceive an affinity with them. In contrast to the path charted for the male identity search in the American literary tradition, in which "finding oneself" requires running away from community,[75] it is by running toward community that Sui Sin Far came to accept her relationship with her mother's people and her own commitment as artist.

By 1898, the same year her sister-in-law Isabella Maria Eaton gave birth to a son, Sui Sin Far was back in Montreal recuperating from malaria and living at 1257 Dorchester, her father's address. She worked as a stenographer for Hugh Graham ("now Sir Hugh") of the Montreal Daily Star[76] and for G. T. Bell of the Grand Trunk, Canadian Pacific Railway's independent competitor, but within the year she was "compelled to resign because of attacks of inflammatory rheumatism." Physicians told her that she would never regain strength in Montreal (Globe) and "ordered [her] beyond the Rockies" ("Leaves," 130). Hence, she wrote, "one afternoon in June [1898] what was left of me—84 pounds—set its face westward" (Globe). Her notation that "I travel on an advertising contract" with a "railway company that [assumed] in some way or other I will give them full value for their transportation across the continent" implied she was receiving train fare in return for writing railway ads, a common outlet for writers at the turn of the century ("Leaves," 130). Her first destination was San Francisco, where she would join her sister May (Globe).[77]

Although she had been working in offices for approximately fifteen years, at age thirty-three Sui Sin Far first experienced seeking work as "a stranger in a strange town," all her previous jobs having been obtained through "home influence." She was "surprised to find that there is no demand for my services in San Francisco and that no one is particularly interested in me." Accepting an offer to type correspondence at the San Francisco office of the Canadian Pacific for five dollars a month,[78] she remained "hopeful that the sale of a story or newspaper article may add to my income." Ill health contributed to a flagging self-image, however; she believed that because "I still limp and bear traces of sickness, I am fortunate to secure any work at all" ("Leaves," 130). The continuing network that Sui Sin Far maintained with Montreal is implied in the "letter of introduction" with which she approached the editor of the *San Francisco Bulletin.* This editor assigned her no writing but indirectly abetted her contacts with a local Chinese community when he sent her to canvas Chinatown for subscribers.[79]

Though the "battles" fought by Chinese Americans in San Francisco paralleled those fought by Chinese Canadians in Montreal, Sui Sin Far would find an older, larger, and more unified Chinatown community in San Francisco. It had begun its process of growth forty years earlier, was a rendezvous point for immigrants across the Pacific and throughout the United States, and had a population of up to thirty thousand, depending on the season. Here, she confronted a prejudice against the Anglo side of her heritage, the ironic mirror image of the "invisible minority" status granted by her appearance. "Chinese merchants and people generally are inclined to regard me with suspicion," she recollected, and "the Americanized Chinamen actually laugh in my face when I tell them that I am of their race" ("Leaves," 130–31).[80] From her own experience, Sui Sin Far was sensitive to the reasons: "They have been imposed upon so many times by unscrupulous white people." She also saw herself through Chinese American eyes as a pretender to *their* culture: "How . . . can I expect these people to accept me as their own countrywoman" when "save for a few phrases, I am unacquainted with my mother tongue?" But just as a Chinese immigrant woman had initiated her entrance into the Chinese Montreal community, so Chinese American women served as Sui Sin Far's guides to Chinatown San Francisco: "Some little women discover that I have Chinese hair, color of eyes and complexion, also that I love rice and tea. This settles the matter for them—and for their husbands" ("Leaves," 131).

By the end of 1898, Sui Sin Far—at age thirty-three and on the opposite side of the continent from her Montreal family—appears to have been acknowledging her Chinese ancestry openly and was ceasing to see Chinese North Americans as "other" in relation to whites. Her retrospective measure of this progress in "Leaves" implies a newfound affinity for Chinese North Americans as individuals, including the "Chinaman" inside herself: "My Chinese instincts develop. I am no longer the little girl who shrunk against my brother at the first sight of a Chinaman. Many and many a time, when alone in a strange place, has the appearance of even an humble laundryman given me a sense of protection and made me feel quite at home" (131). She contrasts herself with "Chinese Eurasians" who masquerade as Mexicans or Japanese (her sister Winifred), singling out the "poor child" in San Francisco (probably her sister May), who "lives in nervous dread of being 'discovered,'" and

Sui Sin Far's sister May, circa 1900. Courtesy of L. Charles Laferrière.

empathizes: "The unfortunate Chinese Eurasians! Are not those who compel them to thus cringe more to be blamed than they?" ("Leaves," 131).

The question of race assumed additional importance in the lives of Sui Sin Far and her sisters by influencing their marriage choices; her dual parentage is no doubt one root of Sui Sin Far's choice not to wed and have children. In 1880 the California state legislature had expanded its previous antimiscegenation law, which prohibited marriage between whites and "Negroes or mulattoes," to include "Mongolians."[81] The racist environment marked by such laws provided the context for a story in "Leaves" about a Eurasian who "allowed herself to become engaged to a white man after refusing him nine times. She had discouraged him in every way possible, had warned him that she was half Chinese; that her people were poor, that . . . she sent home a certain amount of her earnings, and that the man she married would have to do as much . . . that she did not love him and never would." Because the young man swore none of this mattered ("He loved her") and "because the young woman had a married mother and married sisters, who were always picking at her and gossiping over her independent manner of living, she finally consented to marry him, recording . . . in her diary thus: 'I have promised to become the wife . . . because the world is so cruel and sneering to a single woman—and for no other reason' " (131).[82] Provoking her fiancé about her Chineseness, the woman tells him that when they are married, she will give constant parties, filling their house with Chinese "laundrymen and vegetable farmers"; in response, the young man suggests that when they are married, it would be nice if "we allowed it to be presumed that you were—er—Japanese?" The young woman breaks the engagement and that evening writes in her diary words that catch the pulse of Sui Sin Far's own strike for liberation: "Joy, oh, joy! I'm free once more. Never again shall I be untrue to my own heart. Never again will I allow anyone to 'hound' or 'sneer' me into matrimony" (132).[83]

Family pressure on the sisters to marry and censure for those who did not conform are regularly hinted at in Winifred's *Marion*, in "Leaves," and in Sui Sin Far's other fiction in which women characters defy marriage plans laid out by their families and risk consequences, whatever the cost. Passages in her prose illustrate that she considered marriage with men from either side of her heritage and suggest why she would describe herself as a "serious and sober-minded spinster" ("Leaves," 130). Having met Chinese Canadian and American men in her Montreal office, the narrator of "Leaves" compared them "favorably with the white men of my acquaintance" and found them "quite handsome." When asked by "some little Chinese women whom I interview" if she would marry one of their race, Sui Sin Far recalled, "I do not answer No"; the women were, however, "a little doubtful as to whether one could be persuaded to care for me, full-blooded Chinese people having a prejudice against the half white" ("Leaves," 128–29). The short story "Sweet Sin" develops around a Eurasian protagonist who cries out against the double-bind in which Sui Sin Far was similarly caught: " 'But, Father, though I cannot marry a Chinaman, who would despise me for being an American, I will not marry an American, for the Americans have made me feel so [sic] I will save the children of the man I love from being called 'Chinese! Chinese!' "[84] When she meets the children of a Chinese man and his "American wife," her "heart throbs in sympathetic tune with the tales they relate of their experiences as Eurasians" ("Leaves," 128). Sui Sin Far, having spent over thirty years of her life helping to raise thirteen brothers and sisters, also must have been well aware of the relation that Tillie Olsen observes between marriage and diminishing literary possibilities for a woman: "In the last century, of the women whose achievements endure for us in one way or another, nearly all never married (Jane Austen, Emily Bronte, Cristina Rosetti, Emily Dickinson, Louisa Mae Alcott, Sarah Orne Jewett) . . . or, if married, have been childless."[85]

As the century reached its conclusion, Sui Sin Far's description of herself as "a serious and sober-minded spinster" was probably meant literally, as issues of marriage and childbearing gave way, for the woman in her mid-thirties, to finding means to survive economically and continue to write. The summer of 1899 marked her first trip to southern California. "The Canadian Pacific are giving me a trip down South on the P.C.S.S. Co's steamers about the middle of July," she wrote to Charles Lummis on 30 June. "I am going as far as San Diego, but shall stop for a day at Los Angeles."[86] This marks the date of Sui Sin Far's first visit to the Charles Lummis ranch, which she would write of a decade later: "I secure transportation to many California points. I meet some literary people, chief among whom is the editor of the magazine who took my first Chinese stories. He and his wife give me a warm welcome to their ranch" ("Leaves," 132).

These years were not as productive as Sui Sin Far had hoped, however, largely because of strapped finances, homesickness, and physical convalescence. In 1898 she published two more stories in *Land of Sunshine,* and in 1899 she published two more there, plus one in the *Overland Monthly.*[87] A sense of meager output is conveyed by the writer's reference to the Chinese San Franciscan she had "known in Montreal" who "inquired if I were still writing Chinese stories" and her note that "Mr. Charles Lummis made the same inquiry." In response to the queries, she recalls that "latent ambition aroused itself. I recommended writing Chinese stories. Youth's Companion accepted one" (*Globe*). On 2 December 1898 she wrote Lummis that she had "6 stories touring around at the present time" and expected "all but the one sent to Montreal to be rejected." She was also disappointed that she had "quarrelled with the Editor of the [San Francisco] Sunday 'Call,' the Editor of the 'Chronicle' . . . does not take fiction, the 'Examiner' has my 'Child of the 6 Companies,' and there is no other paper here worth trying."[88] Lummis's *Land of Sunshine* apparently remained the main outlet for her pen. In 1899 her discouragement was surely intensified by the news that in Chicago, Winifred, ten years her junior, had written her first novel, *Miss Nume of Japan,* and got it published by Rand McNally under the pseudonym Onoto Watanna.

The bonds with her family nevertheless remained intensely close and always with Sui Sin Far. Her attempts to deal with them reveal an ambivalence familiar to women who are caught between the desire to work and the urge to be with their families. "Whenever I had a little money put by, some inward impulse would compel me to use it for a passage home. The same impulse would drive me to work my way across the Continent, writing advertisements for different lines," she recounted in the *Globe.* In September 1899 she wrote the president of the Canadian Pacific Railway a letter requesting a pass to travel to Montreal from Vancouver.[89] By late summer of 1900 her letters to Lummis were again signed from the Eatons' Montreal address (1257 Dorchester). Admitting that the Montreal climate did not agree with her, she confessed, "I have to come home and see them all because I get so lonesome. I am always coming home and going away."[90] From the end of July until mid-October of 1900 Sui Sin Far stayed in Montreal. During this stay, her writing energy spiraled upward, and she made concerted efforts to forge links among published stories and build a marketing network. A new contact emerged at the *Chicago Evening Post,* which had reviewed a *Land of Sunshine* story, when she wrote Samuel T. Clover, the editor, asking for a copy of the review. Clover responded by asking her to write stories for him "on similar lines as the one in *Land of Sunshine*"; he accepted one of these and requested another. When Sui Sin Far mentioned she was writing a play and then revising it into a story of ten thousand words ("too long for an ordinary magazine short story—and yet not long enough for a serial"), Clover advised submitting it to *McClure's* and offered to send the editor of *McClure's* a letter.[91]

By the fall of the year, Sui Sin Far had left Montreal for Seattle, enclosing in a letter she sent to Lummis her "last little story which appeared in Saturday's paper" to read to his "little girl." She gave "Seattle Post Office, General Delivery" as her next address.[92] Motivated by "an urgent need for money," she moved there in response to a tip from a man for whom she had typed deeds in San Francisco and who, observing that she understood legal work, had recommended the "'old Siwash town.'" Arriving with a "sole fortune" of eight dollars, she noted that "before 5 o'clock of the first day here I had arranged for desk room in a lawyer's office and secured promise of patronage from several attorneys, a loan and mortgage company and a lumber and shingle merchant." The exhilaration was sufficient to prompt her to write her mother "that I had struck gold, silver, oil, copper . . . in proof of which I grandiloquently shoved into her envelope a part of my remaining wealth" (*Globe*).

Back on the West Coast, the writing energy generated in Montreal held its own for a while and then plummeted. In a letter thanking Lummis for his last "cheque" and "two notes," she relayed Samuel Clover's "nice little notice about me," enclosed her "last little story," and assured Lummis she was "going to try hard to do more writing," adding, "In fact, I want to earn my living that way."[93] The frustration of her determination to write set against an unremitting struggle to survive—physically, economically, and emotionally— weaves her personal essays and letters with a tone tautly held between doubt and elation. The pleasure she expressed to Lummis for putting her "into good company in your November number" was qualified by her hope that "I shan't feel out of my element." Her pride in "the fine paragraph you gave me" was followed by the promise "to try to write a more pretentious story than any I have hitherto sent you." She admitted that she had not been writing and "had about made up my mind to drop 'Literature' altogether when [Lummis's] letter arrived" but promised that "in a couple of weeks [I] will don my thinking cap again."[94]

Sui Sin Far's fragile self-image and appeals to the approval of a male editor-mentor manifest a frustration that more than one woman writer faced when she sought marketing outlets,[95] a situation that intensified if she was marginalized by race or class. The "skillful editing" of her *Post* story for which Sui Sin Far thanks Lummis, adding "without which it would have been rough reading indeed," illustrates her lack of confidence, as does the repeated use of the diminutive "little" mentioned earlier.[96] Such phrasing also illustrates a strategy women have always been taught, aptly portrayed in Virginia Woolf's angel: "Be sympathetic; be tender; flatter; deceive; use all the arts and wiles of our sex. Never let anybody guess that you have a mind of your own."[97] Sending Lummis a short story entitled "Sun Lin," begun in Montreal and reworked in Seattle, she asserted that it contained more "work and thought" than any story to date, adding, "I am not at all sure you will like it."[98] This story never appeared in *Land of Sunshine* or elsewhere. By February 1901 three stories had come back with rejections from various publishers, and Sui Sin Far wrote Lummis that she was "so disappointed in my literary ventures that I've given up story writing entirely." That the world of duty was again gaining an edge comes through in her remark, "I have taken a position which pays me very well and shall stay by it."[99]

Among Sui Sin Far's various landing points in her search to find work, Seattle was the closest to permanent, a city where she would live on and off for the first decade of the twentieth century. The Chinese American community in Seattle was close in size to Montreal's, numbering 438 in 1900, the year after Sui Sin Far arrived, and growing to 924 by 1910.[100] Her first lodgings were on Yessler Way, the border street from which Chinatown extended northward. Linda Popp DiBiase envisions the scene as "a little known group of people clustered in the Tenderloin district near Washington Street."[101] That Sui Sin Far was one of those people is evident in her reminiscences: "I taught in a Chinese mission school . . . and learned more from my scholars than ever I could impart to them"; "I managed to hold up my head and worked intermittently and happily at my Chinese stories" (*Globe*). In a series for the *Westerner,* published in Earlington, Washington, in the summer of 1909, she portrayed the experiences of West Coast Chinese Americans with an intimacy of voice that implied she mingled freely among them.[102]

During this decade, Sui Sin Far's addresses changed seven times,[103] and her letters express a lack of constancy, reflecting the numerous dwellings she had known since age eight. "I may change my room at any time," she wrote to Lummis in October 1900.[104] She continued to make her living as a legal stenographer, although there is no indication that she liked stenography any better than ever she had or felt that her skills were improved by routine work: "As always, on account of my inaccuracy as a stenographer and my inability to typewrite continuously, my earning capacity was small" (*Globe*). The tension between the financial needs of her family and her own need for creativity was perpetual. She put aside eighty-five dollars to buy time to "write the book of my dreams," but "news from home caused me to banish ambition for awhile longer; and I sent my little savings to pay a passage out West for one of my younger sisters." Keeping this sister for seven months, Sui Sin Far taught her shorthand and typing "so that upon her return to Montreal she would be enabled to earn her living" (*Globe*).[105]

Recognizing the dilemma between what family could give and also take away ("Thus did the ties of relation bind me, but at the same time strengthen"), she gained empowerment by bonding with women whose identities did not depend on socially prescribed family roles or "nationality."[106] Her description of these women embodies the "one world vision" that would become an ideal in her fiction: "I also formed friendships with women who braced and enlightened me, women to whom the things of the mind and the heart appealed; women who were individuals, not merely the daughters of their parents, the wives of their husbands; women who taught me that nationality was no bar to friendship with those whose friendship was worthwhile" (*Globe*).

The turn from the nineteenth to twentieth century, which saw the United States annex Hawaii, enter a war with the Philippines, and pass the 1882 Chinese Exclusion Act and witnessed a five-hundred-dollar head tax imposed by a Dominion Parliament on Chinese immigrants in 1904, also saw Sui Sin Far move toward her most intense commitment to writing and her most severe writing crisis. Ironically, the period began with her long-anticipated decision to give up stenography (listening to the "voices of others") and launch into exploring full-time her long pent-up desire to support herself by her pen.

Her sister Winifred's marriage in 1901 to Bertram Whitcomb Babcock, a newsman from New York, must have exacerbated the outsider position Sui Sin Far felt she had sealed for herself by remaining single, and it probably aroused bittersweet feelings. More tragically, the drowning of her twenty-one-year-old brother Hubert, in August 1902,[107] might have precipitated the "shock of sudden grief," which led her to quit her Seattle job and work her way south to Los Angeles, with the vow to "emancipate myself from the torture of writing other people's thoughts and words with a heart full of my own." "I struggled for many months," she would tell a *Globe* audience. "If there was nothing but bread to eat and water to drink, absorbed in my work I was immune to material things—for a while." But as she "gave way to my ruling passion—the passion to write all the emotions of my heart away," the writer encountered the dilemma that Olsen has noticed in many writers who, after too many years of listening to the voices of others, encounter predominantly nothingness when they reach for their own. "The habits of a lifetime when everything else had to come before writing are not easily broken," Olsen notes.[108] Sui Sin Far reflected on the effects of her personal paralysis: "I had been so long accustomed to dictation that when I sat down to compose, although my mind teemed with ideas tumultuously clamoring for release, I hesitated as if I were waiting for a voice behind me to express them." If this era reveals Sui Sin Far's writing efforts at their most grueling, it also proves her persistence and ongoing will: "I had to free myself from that spell. My writings might be imperfect, but they had got to bear the impress of thoughts begotten in my own mind and clothed in my own words" (*Globe*).

In the winter of 1903, she began a correspondence with Robert Underwood Johnson, the associate editor of *Century*. The letters illuminate in a painful immediacy the diligence with which Sui Sin Far was writing and seeking markets.[109] The first (4 December 1903) thanked Johnson for his "acceptance of my little story"[110] and the "generous check" he had sent, included news that another story had been published in *Out West,*[111] and proposed sending a story currently in process. The second (24 December 1903) enclosed a manuscript described as "not a Chinese story" and requested Johnson's advice about writing on "non-Chinese subjects." The third (undated) included "The Last Picture," "a little Canadian story which I have been working at ever since I came home" about "Hochelaga . . . the old fashioned little village in which I spent my childhood days." A fourth (19 March 1904) informed Johnson that "Taiko Takehishi," the story of "a little Japanese in the Puget Sound country," had been accepted by *Youth's Companion* and included samples from "a series of articles" Sui Sin Far was writing for the *Los Angeles Express.* A fifth (28 March 1904) enclosed a short story, "The Success of a Mistake." A final letter to Johnson (1 April 1904) offered the story "Lum Lin," which she said she had started "many years ago, but have only had time to finish during these last few weeks." The December letters were on *Los Angeles Express* letterheads; the remainder were addressed from Montreal.[112]

Repeated use of the word *little* to describe her stories and such comments as "I know I am not a fluent or artistic writer" (4 December 1903), "my phrases are not elegant," and "It is very slight" express a continuing deference and perhaps lack of confidence, but they also note her awareness of style. However ambitious Sui Sin Far's efforts to give publishers what they wanted, her personal agenda was of at least equal concern. Selling was important, but it was not enough, a distinction she would later make in the *Globe* article: "The Century Magazine took a story from me; but I remained discontented with my work." She clearly expressed the purpose of her "Chinese" fiction in a letter to Johnson on 4 December 1904: "to depict as well as I can what I know and see about the Chinese people in America." It was an approach she boldly distinguished from that of contemporaries: "I have read many clever and interesting Chinese stories written by American writers, but they all seem to me to stand afar off from the Chinaman—in most cases treating him as a 'joke.'" To characterize Chinese honestly meant reversing "yellow peril" stereotypes, as much in vogue in North American bookstalls as chinoiserie was in the shops. It meant plotting a defense less direct than in journalism, a strategy that would feed editors what they wanted while preserving the expectations of her own moral themes. In short, it meant being a trickster, finding a way to get past the censors. In an undated letter, Sui Sin Far requested advice from Johnson about restricting her subject matter by race: "Though I myself prefer to branch out, so many friends prefer to think that the Chinese should be my only theme." The comment hinted at her more far-reaching vision—to be accepted by editors without racialization.

From the spaces between Sui Sin Far's repeated appeals, one can feel her wince of rejection upon receiving Johnson's form letters. The fact that the *Century* never published any of Sui Sin Far's stories, except for "A Chinese Boy-Girl," leads one to wonder about the criteria behind this single acceptance. Was Johnson's decision based on considerations of "literary quality"—something for which the *Century,* running serialized novels by Edith Wharton and Jack London in the same issue in which "A Chinese Boy-Girl" was published, had a national reputation?[113] Or was the one story chosen, as Sui Sin Far's letters imply she suspected, because of its Chinese subject matter, that is, as a token, like the exhibit in Barnham's Museum that spotlighted a Chinese woman's "fairy feet," useful for display only once?[114]

It is notable that Winifred published a story in the *Century* in March 1903[115] and that throughout these same years Winifred's career was enjoying a heady advancement. Under the Japanese name "Onoto Watanna," she published five novels with such houses as Doubleday, Macmillan, and Harper, all of which won critical acclaim.[116] How much this had to do with standards of literature and how much with the mythology that the author was of Japanese ancestry has never been settled. There were several reasons why it might have been advantageous for a writer of Chinese ancestry in North America to disguise herself as Japanese at the turn of the century. To quote S. E. Solberg, "The Chinese were commonly perceived as mysterious, evil, nearby, and threatening, while the Japanese were exotic, quaint, delicate . . . and distant . . . the general fascination with the exotic (Japanese) was able to transcend racist ideas so long as distance was a part of the formula."[117] It was an issue under debate even at the time the two sisters were publishing. In a 13 December 1903 letter to Johnson commending Sui Sin Far's writing, Samuel T. Clover, former editor of the *Chicago Evening Post* who had promoted Sui Sin Far's stories in 1899 and was now her editor at the *Los Angeles Express,* offered a rare comparison between her writing and Winifred's: "Since [Sui Sin Far] came to Los Angeles she has been doing work for The Express and her Chinese sketches appeal to me particularly from their sympathetic point of view and lucidity of expression. I think she really has more talent than her sister who writes over the name of Onoto Watanna . . . [and] has claimed to be half Japanese and half English, but of course she is not. . . ."[118]

During October and November of 1903 the *Los Angeles Express* printed a series of articles with Sui Sin Far's byline, to which Clover was referring. Bearing such titles as "Chinatown Needs a School" and "Chinese Laundry Checking," the articles focused on Los Angeles's Chinatown community of more than five thousand people. The writings' frank and detailed efforts "to depict . . . what I know and see" were successful and were among the few pieces by Sui Sin Far to be found in the markets.[119] In 1900 she had four stories published, then three more between 1903 and 1905, in addition to her newspaper work.[120] After 1905 pages where her words might have appeared emit only an ominously blank publishing silence, the spaces themselves carrying the tension of the conflicts she faced—between writing and family, between writing and eating, and most important between speaking in her own voice and that plague of marginalization Clover, in his 13 December 1903 letter to Johnson, termed an "almost painful diffidence," the feeling she was never quite good enough. Sui Sin Far's letter to Johnson on 1 April 1904 noted the fight against time that she waged, foreshadowing what appears to be her five-year silence to come: "I am very anxious to push my stories as I am tired of earning my living as a stenographer, but if I find within a year that I am not fitted for literary work I will retire from the field and take up again with the honest old typewriter. I simply want to give myself a trial."

The frustration Sui Sin Far must have felt at rejection, along with her relentless pursuit of survival, helps explain why she spent much of that decade roaming, in her words, "back and forth across the continent" ("Leaves," 132)—working under advertising contracts for the Canadian Pacific Railway, writing for newspapers in various Chinese communities, and visiting her family in Montreal whenever she could afford the trip. In the four months of her correspondence with Johnson alone, she went from Seattle to Los Angeles to Montreal, frequently changing her address: "I am leaving here [L. A.] in early January and will be in Seattle sometime in February," she wrote on 24 December 1903. In the same letter she also mentioned her intentions to "reach my home in Montreal" and her dreams of going to China: "I expect to make arrangements with some railway to give me a trip to China or Japan. I will work my way, if I have the opportunity, by writing letters for some paper." In a 19 March 1904 letter to Johnson, she announced plans to go to New York, where she would "call upon the Century people," spend "a couple of weeks," then return "West by way of Chicago—making my way as a Chinaman." Three years later, in a 20 April 1907 letter to the "Editor, Century Magazine" (not necessarily Johnson), she wrote of a devastating event: "Through a wreck on the Great Northern Railway in North Dakota last Sunday night I have lost everything save life, my trunk containing all my manuscripts, scrap books etc., having been destroyed in the fire caused by the accident." The extent of her loss can be gauged by her request in the same letter to "kindly send me a copy of the letter in which you accepted my story 'A Chinese Boy Girl,' also a couple of copies of the Century Magazine in which that story appears." On 23 March 1912, she wrote asking Charles Lummis to return photographs she had given him years earlier, "because all of mine were burned in a railway fire."[121] We thus learn what happened to at least some of the manuscripts Sui Sin Far was writing during this period and—assuming that the wrecked trunks also held personal papers—one reason why documenting her life is so difficult.

Sui Sin Far's emancipation from the concern for "material things" was shortlived. As she admitted in the *Globe* article, "You have to come back to them in the end." The early years of the century that saw her forsake the voices of others to reach for her own also saw her return to material concerns, because "one cannot live on air and water alone, even if one is half-Chinese." Yet this time duty's return did not mean that imagination must recede to the background. The absence of Sui Sin Far's words during this period was like the silence of the moth inside the cocoon: something was happening. On 21 January 1909, with the appearance of "Leaves from the Mental Portfolio of an Eurasian" in the *Independent,* her voice came bursting forth—publicly, nationally —signaling unprecedented recognition and a cycle of writing and publishing energy for Sui Sin Far that would continue. Though the autobiographical essay was published in New York, Sui Sin Far was probably still in Seattle, for on 10 February of that year she sent a letter to Lummis enclosing an announcement describing "a series of articles on 'The Chinese in America' which I am writing for a northwest paper called the Westerner."[122] Running from May through August 1909, the *Westerner* articles dealt with the ambiguities of "Americanization" faced by Chinese Americans and with the problems of Chinese immigrants in their confrontations with whites. Such themes would dominate the last stage of her fiction.

Shortly after the last piece in this series appeared, Sui Sin Far moved from the West to Boston, where she resided at a single address, 146 Concord Street West.[123] During 1910 she published nine pieces of short fiction in publications ranging from the *Independent* to *Good Housekeeping.* Written under the name "Sui Sin Far" and using Chinese American content and themes, these stories reveal ironic control and artistic maturity. In this year also the scattered links of Sui Sin Far's existence—residences, jobs, personal relationships, and burdensome travels—showed evidence of coalescing around a common personal center. As she explained in the *Globe:* "While I was in Montreal my father obtained for me a letter of introduction from a Chinese merchant of that city to his brother in Boston, Mr. Lew Han Son. Through Mr. Lew Han Son I became acquainted with some Americans of the name of Austin who live in

Dorchester and who have been my good friends ever since. I am also acquainted with a lady in Charlestown, Mrs. Henderson, who is a sister of one of my Western friends." This passage suggests that the "one family" vision that Sui Sin Far's fiction and essays projected had become part of her life-style.

A composure and confidence emerged in the writer's voice now that had never before been present. In the *Globe* article, Sui Sin Far stated that she moved to Boston "with the intention of publishing a book and planting a few Eurasian thoughts in Western literature." Explaining that "during the past year [1911] I have been engaged in writing my first book, and completed it a couple of months ago," she credited the managing editor of the *Independent* (William Hayes Ward) for encouraging her in this undertaking because, she said with characteristic deference, "I am one of those people who has very little staying power." That new writing time had suddenly opened she attributed to Montreal patrons: "To accomplish this work, or to enable me to have the leisure in which to accomplish it . . . two of my lawyer friends in Montreal kindly contributed" (*Globe*). One could easily have been her first mentor, Montreal's Superior Court Judge John Sprott Archibald. On 13 July 1911 she wrote Lummis that "A. C. McClurg of Chicago are to bring out a book of my Chinese stories this spring. . . ."[124]

In June 1912 McClurg published twenty-five hundred copies of *Mrs. Spring Fragrance*—a collection of short stories, some of which had been previously published in magazines. Sui Sin Far probably wrote some of the previously unpublished stories during her "emancipation," when she took time off from her duties to write. Anticipating a warm reception from family and friends, she singled out Lotus Blossom in the *Globe* article: "My people in Montreal, my mother in particular, my Chinese friends in Boston and also American friends are looking forward to the advent of 'Mrs. Spring Fragrance' with, I believe, some enthusiasm." She went on to add, "I am myself quite excited over the prospect. Would not any one be who had worked as hard as I have—and waited as long as I have—for a book?" *Mrs. Spring Fragrance* was recognized in reviews on both sides of the Canadian-U.S. border. The first appeared in the *Montreal Daily Witness* and continued the trend of positioning Sui Sin Far on an ambiguous borderland between race and country: "One of the charming gift books of the season comes from the pen of a Canadian Chinese, or half Chinese, woman, whose sympathies range her on the side of the Chinese mother rather than of the British father."[125]

During 1911 and 1912 three more stories appeared under Sui Sin Far's name in the *New England Magazine*.[126] In 1913 the *Independent* published "Chinese Workmen in America," an interesting counterpoint to "The Chinese Woman in America," published in 1897.[127] After this, Sui Sin Far appears to have vanished from the public scene altogether. No more letters or names in public directories have been located. When she returned to Montreal is uncertain. In 1911 her eldest brother, Edward Charles—at that time the managing director of Canada's largest distributor of railway equipment, Montreal's Frothingham and Workman, where he had worked for thirty years—died at home in his bed at age forty-eight of a "bullet wound near his heart" from the revolver he "always slept with . . . under his pillow."[128] Between mourning the death of her brother (the "noble little fellow" of her childhood) and celebrating her first book, Sui Sin Far might have made the decision to return to her family. In 1913 she was reported seen by a young Eaton niece walking in the Victorian Square near 110 Agnes, Edward's last address listed in *Lovell's*. [129] "When I am East, my heart is West. When I am West, my heart is East," Sui Sin Far wrote in 1909. "Before long I hope to be in China. As my life began in my father's family it may end in my mother's" ("Leaves," 132).[130] Just as the deepest vein of her psychic identity ran back to her mother's homeland of China, so the region defined by her as "home" continued to be Montreal, where her mother resided.

The next time Sui Sin Far's name appeared in print was in a death notice in the *Montreal Daily Star* on 7 April 1914, followed by an obituary the next day. Acknowledging that Edith Eaton was "at one time . . . a member of the Montreal Star staff," the *Star* summed up her life in two columns and a photo. Written anonymously, presumably with information from family and acquaintances, this obituary offers the main clues we have to the final period of Sui Sin Far's life. "Years ago she had suffered from inflammatory rheumatism," the reporter stated, leading to "permanent heart trouble, which made itself again known just when she was getting in the public eye" and "retarded her work greatly." She had been living in Boston but had decided to reside in Montreal again, where she had gone to the Royal Victoria Hospital "for treatment" and had suddenly "died at dawn." The reporter noted that she was "working on a long novel . . . and planning and writing shorter stories to meet the demand, but her health broke down."[131] This novel is undoubtedly the same work that Sui Sin Far referred to on 5 May 1912 in the *Globe* piece ("I have also written another book which will appear next year if Providence is kind") and on 9 August 1911 in a letter to Lummis ("I think you will be more interested in my book, when it is written, than in my short stories").[132] No further trace of this second book has been found.

The *Star*'s obituary poses another question to haunt the researcher who turns through the newspaper's pages over Easter week of 1914, finding Sui Sin Far's death and then funeral notices between ads for flowered hats and news of the current election—including an offer by suffragists to provide transportation for local women so they could go cast their ballots. Why, the reporter inquired, did this woman die "just when the road which would have led to rewards commensurate with her hard work and continuous effort, had been thrown wide open to her."[133] The scanty records offer no obvious clues. Was

Sui Sin Far's "heart trouble" exacerbated by the excitement of publishing a
book after the long years of waiting? Was stress added when she tried "to meet
the demand" from publishers who were finally coming to her instead of she to
them? What part was played by the death of her brother and a return to a
climate where, fifteen years earlier, physicians had warned she "would never
regain . . . strength?" Words from "Leaves" connecting her ill health with her
lifelong fight against racism read like a foreshadowing: "I had no organic
disease, but the strength of my feelings seems to take from me the strength of
my body. . . . The doctor says that my heart is unusually large; but in the light
of the present [1909] I know that the cross of the Eurasian bore too heavily
upon my childish shoulders" (127).

The ambiguity that pervaded her life would follow Sui Sin Far into death
and, indeed, through posterity. Scarcely one month after her forty-ninth
birthday, 11 April 1914, the Reverend Dean Evans conducted her funeral in
the Trinity Anglican Church on Good Friday, after which she was buried
beside her younger brothers in the Eaton family plot at the Montreal cemetery.[134]
Her name in the Mont Royal records was cited as "Edith Maude Eaton" and
her religion as "Anglican." An obituary in the New York Times claimed that
"Edith Eaton, author known in the East as Sui Sin Far, the 'Chinese Lily,'"
was the daughter of "a Japanese noblewoman who had been adopted by Sir
Hugh Matheson as a child and educated in England." The piece added that
"one of Miss Eaton's sisters, Mrs. Bertram W. Babcock of New York, is an
author writing under the pen name of 'Onoto Watanna.'"[135] Though there
was no byline for this obituary, scholars have generally held Winifred to be the
author. Amy Ling refers to Winifred's "continuation of her deception even
into the obituary of her older sister."[136] S. E. Solberg argues more indirectly:
"The irony is that the obituary manages to skirt any meaningful summary of
Edith's life in favor of legitimizing family history for Winifred. . . . Perhaps the
obituary should be taken as one more proof of the hostility toward Chinese-
Americans against which Edith Eaton had fought during her lifetime."[137] This
apparent last breach of justice, capping the many that had touched this
woman's life, must be considered in light of the fact that the final word on Sui
Sin Far's identity—or on her relationship with Winifred—had not yet been
written. The following year, Winifred anonymously published her autobiography Me. In the text no writing sister named either "Edith" or "Sui Sin Far" is
mentioned, but one passage rings with the sense of its author's intimate truth:
"I thought of other sisters . . . the eldest, a girl with more real talent than I
who had been a pitiful invalid all her days. She is dead now, that dear big sister
of mine, and a monument marks her grave in commemoration of the work she
did for my mother's country" (194).[138]

Though Me's narrator does not name her "mother's country," when we
move outside the text and examine the monument that stands over Sui Sin
Far's grave in the Mont Royal Cemetery, the basic four words, "From Her

Sui Sin Far's monument in Mont Royal Cemetery,
Montreal.

Chinese Friends," tease the line between fact and fiction. No absolute answer
concerning when and by whom the monument was erected has emerged.[139]
Its most remarkable aspect is that the words on this headstone of simple gray
granite, maybe four feet in height and eighteen inches across, make a statement
through which the ambiguous components of Sui Sin Far's identity, counter-
poised and at odds through so much of her life, are resolved. Standing in the
"English" section of the Mont Royal Cemetery, conspicuous above shorter
stones all around it, the monument is engraved in a white so bright it looks as
if it were painted just yesterday.[140] English letters spell out both names, "Sui
Sin Far/Edith Eaton," and are juxtaposed against four Chinese characters that
roughly translate "It is right and good that we should remember China."[141]

    In 1915 Edward died of cancer and was buried beside his eldest daughter, and
seven years later Lotus Blossom—who had moved after Edward's death to
New York to live with her youngest daughter, Beryl, and Beryl's husband,

Walter Shaw—was brought back and buried beside her husband. A common stone identifies "Edward and Grace A. Eaton," a couple whose determination to be together shaped the course of their children's lives, which in turn altered the course, albeit awaiting recognition, of North American literary history. All the other adult children of Lotus Blossom and Edward would be buried with the families of their wives or husbands. Among the Eaton sisters only the bones of Sui Sin Far, the "bird on the wing," would mingle with those of her parents.

Sui Sin Far did not necessarily choose her pattern of flight. In her ideal "one-family vision," it would not have been necessary, but she was caught between warring cultures in an arena of racism, poverty, and sexual inequality. She was a woman determined to write, who did not, in Carolyn Heilbrun's words, "make a man the center of [her life] . . . [and] there were no models . . . no exemplars, no stories."[142] Sui Sin Far freed herself to create her own life, hence to bequeath models for future women. The most fascinating question to guide us, approaching the crisscrossing path between East and West that leads into her stories, is how she was able to use the very ambiguities handed to her by birth and society to interweave a "home" on the artistic borderland that she claimed for herself.

Notes

1. Sui Sin Far, "Leaves from the Mental Portfolio of an Eurasian," *Independent* 66 (21 January 1909): 127. Hereafter referred to as "Leaves."

2. Eileen Lewis, Telephone interview, Pullman, Wash., 20 September 1990. Eileen Lewis is Sui Sin Far's grandniece.

3. Jinqi Ling, Department of English, UCLA, Interview, Pullman, Wash., 15 October 1990, describes "Lotus Blossom" as the kind of "pet" flower name that Chinese families, especially rural families, have traditionally given their daughters. The name "Lotus Blossom" is not familiar to her two grandsons, Tim Rooney and L. Charles Laferrière. "Grace" or "Grace A. Trefusis" or "Grace A. Eaton" is the name listed on all Canadian and U.S. legal documents, the signature this woman uses (for example, on baptismal records) as an adult, and the name inscribed on her tombstone. "Lotus Blossom" is the name Eileen Lewis knew her great-grandmother by and the name she remembers using when constructing a family tree as a child. I cannot argue for the official authenticity of "Lotus Blossom" one way or the other. Because of my commitment to breaking through the invisibility brought to this woman's history largely through British nomenclature and to portraying her not only as Sui Sin Far's mother but as a Chinese immigrant woman to England and then Canada, I use the name "Lotus Blossom" throughout.

4. Standard Certificate of Death, Grace Eaton, Reg. No. 13638, 9 May 1922, Department of Health of the City of New York, Bureau of Records, State of New York.

5. Elizabeth Rooney, great-great-granddaughter of Lotus Blossom Trefusis, Interview, Toronto, Ontario, November 1989.

6. [Winifred Eaton Babcock,] *Me: A Book of Remembrance* (New York: Century, 1915), 3; published anonymously. Hereafter cited in the text as simply *Me.* I recognize that contemporary scholars generally spell Winifred with two *n*s. My basis for using one *n* is the baptismal certificate, which gives her name as "Lillie Winifred." Baptismal Records, 21 August 1875, Archives Nationales du Québec, Montreal.

7. Edward Eaton Obituary, *Montreal Gazette,* n.d.; courtesy of L. Charles Laferrière who, with his two children, is the last descendant of the Eaton family to still reside in Montreal. Although undated, the obituary can be set during 1915, the year, according to Mont Royal Cemetery records, of Edward Eaton's death. Like most obituaries, it is written anonymously and without documentation, so it must be viewed with caution.

8. The name Sir Hugh Matheson does not turn up in encyclopedias of British peerage.

9. John William Adamson, *English Education, 1789–1902* (Cambridge: Cambridge University Press, 1964), 116–17.

10. Sui Sin Far, "Sui Sin Far, the Half Chinese Writer, Tells of Her Career," *Boston Globe,* 5 May 1912. Hereafter referred to as *Globe.*

11. Kenneth Scott Latourette, *The Chinese: Their History and Culture* (New York: Macmillan, 1959), 345.

12. Burial Records, Mont Royal Cemetery, Montreal, Quebec.

13. Ellen and Edward Eaton are listed as husband and wife in Census Report, 1871, Prestbury Parish, Folio 79, Upton Township, England. Unmarried children living in the household included Sarah, Ellen Charles, Michael, Kate, and Maria. The grandfather, Isaac; his unmarried sister Ellen; and a servant, Ann Dooley, also lived in the houshold.

14. *White's Cheshire Directory,* 1860, 742.

15. Paul Rooney, grandson of Winifred Eaton Babcock Reeve, Interview, Toronto, Ontario, November 1989.

16. *North China Herald,* 27 March, 28 March, 4 April, 2 May, and 25 July 1863.

17. Ibid., 13 April 1861.

18. Ibid., 7 February 1863.

19. Edward Eaton Obituary, *Montreal Gazette,* [1915].

20. Census Report, 1881, District no. 91, S. District E., No. 1, 29, Village of Hochelaga, Quebec.

21. Paul Rooney interview.

22. Birth certificate, 8 April 1865, District of Macclesfield, Subdistrict of Prestbury, County of Chester, England.

23. T. A. Coward, *Cheshire* (Cambridge: Cambridge University Press, 1910), 6.

24. *Trow's New York City Directory,* vol. 81, comp. H. Wilson (1 May 1868).

25. For further discussion of concepts of "racialization," see Audrey Kobayashi and Peter Jackson, "Japanese Canadians and the Racialization of Labour in the British Columbia Sawmill Industry, 1900–1930" (Paper presented at the Sixth British Columbia Studies Conference, University of British Columbia,

Vancouver, 2–3 November 1990); and Alan Wold, "Theorizing Cultural Differences: A Critique of the 'Ethnicity School,'" *MELUS* 14 (Summer 1987): 21–33.

26. Attitudes about intermarriage were antagonistic and uncompromising in the views of both cultures.

27. [Winifred Eaton Babcock,] *Marion: The Story of an Artist's Model* (New York: W. J. Watt, 1916), 26. Hereafter referred to in the text as *Marion*.

28. Joseph Whitaker, *Whitaker's Almanac* (London: J. Whitaker, 1874), 143.

29. I am indebted to James Doyle for giving me the "feel" of a British enclave in nineteenth-century Canada.

30. See Amy Ling, *Between Worlds: Women Writers of Chinese Ancestry* (New York: Pergamon, 1990), 26: "Because Edward's parents disapproved of his marriage, the burgeoning family emigrated to America. . . ." The cause-and-effect relationship in this case has to be speculative, however.

31. L. Charles Laferrière, Interview, Montreal, Quebec, April 1989, noted the reference in the novel *Marion* to wealthy Britons sending their "Black Sheep" sons off to America and added, "This was the case of my greatgrandfather."

32. No records were kept of immigration by land between the United States and Canada in 1873. Passage of the Chinese Exclusion Act by the U.S. government in 1882, barring most Chinese from legally entering the United States, would be instrumental in tightening border crossings, as would the series of head taxes that Canada subsequently passed.

33. Sui Sin Far writes that Edward Charles was seven at this time, but this is at odds with his birthdate of 1864. She has already placed him as "ten months older than myself" ("Leaves," 126), which is consistent with census record evidence.

34. *Lovell's Montreal Directory*, 1873–74, Bibliothèque de Ville de Montréal.

35. Edith Eaton to Robert Underwood Johnson, n.d., Century Company Records, Rare Books and Manuscripts Division, New York Public Library (hereafter cited as NYPL).

36. Réjean Charbonneau, curator of Histoire de Hochelaga, Interview, Montreal, Quebec, Spring 1989. Roger Daniels equates this phrasing with "the Chinese of the East," in Daniels words "used in New England to denigrate French Canadian immigrants in the 1870's" (Letter to the author, 22 July 1992).

37. David Cheunyan Lai, *Chinatowns: Towns within Cities in Canada* (Vancouver: University of British Columbia Press, 1988), 9, postulates that as Chinatowns in the West "withered," those in the East were being born.

38. For two recent studies of racial issues involving immigrant labor in Canada during Sui Sin Far's era, see Kobayashi and Jackson, "Japanese Canadians and the Racialization of Labour"; and Timothy Stanley, "Defining the Chinese Other: White Supremacy and Leading Opinion in British Columbia, 1885–1925" (Paper presented at the Sixth British Columbia Studies Conference, University of British Columbia, Vancouver, 2–3 November 1990).

39. Two publications examine Hochelaga's history in depth: *L'Histoire du logement ouvrier à Hochelaga-Maisonneuve* (Montreal: l'Atelier d'Histoire

Hochelaga-Maisonneuve, 1980); and *De fil en aiguille: Chronique ouvrière d'une filature de coton à Hochelaga en 1880* (Montreal: l'Atelier d'Histoire Hochelaga-Maisonneuve, 1985).

40. I am grateful to Réjean Charbonneau, Interview, Montreal, Quebec, Spring 1989, for factual information and a sense of the atmosphere of Hochelaga in the late nineteenth century, on which this reconstruction of the Eatons' residency in Hochelaga is based.

41. Sepulchre Register, Archives du Québec, Montreal. In the Mont Royal Cemetery Company records, the Eaton family plot is described as "Section L, Lot No. 718, Registered in the name of Edward Eaton."

42. Gabrielle Roy's *Tin Flute* (Toronto: McClelland and Stewart, 1947) depicts conditions of poverty for a French Canadian family in Montreal in the 1940s, which parallels in many details, but without the component of racism, what I perceive the Eatons to have experienced seven decades earlier. The most grueling of all in Roy's novel, especially for the mother and eldest daughter, are the recurring births and forced removals to new living quarters.

43. See, for example, "Women's Realm," *Montreal Daily Star,* 12 June 1895.

44. "Home Duties First," *Presbyterian Record* (1885): 305.

45. Baptismal Records, Archives Nationales du Québec, Montreal. As previously noted, Christiana Mary was born three years earlier in England. Several children would often be born before a baptism took place.

46. This "Mrs. Darling" may be the wife of William Darling of "Wm. Darling & Co's Bloomfield House, 430 St. Mary, Hochelaga," as cited in *Lovell's Montreal Directory,* 1877–78, 699. The name "Darling" reappears in the Eaton family. One of Sui Sin Far's sisters is named "May Darling." *Me*'s narrator also speaks of "Mrs. Darling," a Hochelaga neighbor.

47. Protestant Board of School Commissioner of the City of Montreal, *Report, 1847–1889* (Montreal: Protestant Board of School Commissioner of the City of Montreal, 1889), 7.

48. Edith Eaton to Charles Lummis, 16 September 1900, Charles Fletcher Lummis Collection, Southwest Museum, Los Angeles, Calif. (hereafter cited as SWM). For two studies of women replacing men in offices of this era, see Graham S. Lowe, "Women, Work and the Office: The Feminization of Clerical Occupations in Canada, 1901–1931," in *Rethinking Canada: The Promise of Women's History,* ed. Veronica Strong-Boag and Anita Clair Fellman (Toronto: Copp Clark Pitman, 1986), 107–22; and Margery W. Davis, *Women's Place Is at the Typewriter: Office Work and Office Workers, 1870–1930* (Philadelphia: Temple University Press, 1985).

49. *Lovell's Montreal Directory,* 1885–86.

50. These articles have not yet been located.

51. I thank both L. Charles Laferrière and Geoff Ott, Manuscript Division, National Archives of Canada, for sending me information on John Sprott Archibald, which supplements and substantiates Sui Sin Far's memory.

52. I thank L. Charles Laferrière for supplying me with a list of Eaton family equivalencies for *Marion*'s fictional counterparts.

53. Sui Sin Far satirizes a suitor named Albemarle in the "Albemarle's Secret," *Dominion Illustrated* 3 (19 October 1889): 254.

54. Though the young British immigrants who called on the Eaton sisters obviously knew that their mother, "Grace," was Chinese and had probably grown up hearing about her, her manners might have been sufficiently British that—combined with the scarcity of acceptable mates and the sisters' attractiveness—the young men could pretend to overlook the matter of race. Telling parents in England that they wanted to marry daughters of the interracial union would have been another matter, however.

55. There is no way to know how many Chinese women were in Montreal in the mid-1890s. Denise Helly, *Les Chinois à Montréal, 1877–1951* (Montreal: Québecois de recherche sur la culture, 1987), 128, cites two Chinese women in Montreal in 1891 and two in 1901, though figures for Chinese males had risen to 1,030 during this decade. News articles, missionary reports, and photos show increasing numbers of Chinese women and children in Montreal during the 1890s. If demographics were settled by public records, Lotus Blossom and her nine daughters would go down in history as British.

56. Harry Con et al., *From China to Canada: A History of the Chinese Community in Canada,* ed. Edgar Wickberg (Toronto: McClelland and Stewart, 1988).

57. *Lovell's Montreal Directory,* 1894–95. The *h* stands for home; 828 St. Lawrence is the address listed for Edward.

58. E.E., "A Plea for the Chinaman: A Correspondent's Argument in His Favor," letter to the editor, *Montreal Daily Star,* 21 September 1896.

59. The three major English language newspapers in Montreal in the 1890s were the *Daily Star, Gazette,* and *Daily Witness.* Nothing indicates that Sui Sin Far was fluent in any language except English.

60. Sui Seen Far, "The Gamblers," *Fly Leaf* 1 (February 1896): 14–18; "The Story of Iso," *Lotus* 2 (August 1896): 117–19; "A Love Story of the Orient," *Lotus* 2 (October 1896): 203–7; "Ku Yum," *Land of Sunshine* 5 (June 1896): 29–31; "A Chinese Feud," *Land of Sunshine* 5 (November 1896): 236–37.

61. According to L. Charles Laferrière, characterizations in "Leaves" are all modeled on members of Sui Sin Far's family.

62. This episode from *Marion* is implicitly authenticated in Marriage Records, Archives du Québec, Montreal. The witnesses were the bride's father and two people of unknown relation; no Eatons were present.

63. I am indebted to James Doyle, who is currently writing a book on the literary life and times of Walter Blackburn Harte in Canada, for information about Harte. Doyle has uncovered the information that Harte wrote for Montreal newspapers, the *Star* and the *Gazette,* during the same years that Sui Sin Far did. Doyle conjectures that it was probably through Sui Sin Far that Harte met his future wife. Because Harte was a new English immigrant to Canada, Doyle explains, it would have been an assumed courtesy for Edith to invite him home for dinner.

64. According to L. Charles Laferrière, her grandson, Mary Agnes married on her birthday, 14 October 1893, in Montreal's Notre Dame Cathedral. In 1905 she was widowed and left with six children. She supported them and herself by taking in boarders and eventually by working as a stenographer for the Canadian Pacific Railway. She spent her last years in Detroit, where five of her children had moved in the early 1920s.

65. On 29 September 1906, Florence, the eighth Eaton sister, would also briefly enter a nunnery, the novitiate of the Nuns of Charity of the Province of Montreal, which she would leave on 12 March 1907. Registers of the Persons of the Community of the Nuns of Charity of the Province, Archives Province, 12055 rue Grenet, Montreal; researched and translated by Soeur Jeannine Blais and sent to me by L. Charles Laferrière. The fact that these two daughters from a traditional Protestant family both made choices to enter a Catholic nunnery and stayed there so briefly implies that Sui Sin Far might not have been the only Eaton sister seeking alternative options to marriage. See Marta Danylewycz, *Taking the Veil: An Alternative to Marriage, Motherhood, and Spinsterhood in Quebec, 1840–1920,* ed. Paul-André Linteau, Alison Prentice, and William Westfall (Toronto: McClelland and Stewart, 1987), 9, for, in the editor's words, "an innovative exploration of the lives and work of Quebec women who chose the veil and their fascinating relationship with turn-of-the-century feminism."

66. L. Charles Laferrière's description of Karl Bosse makes it hard to resist comparing Sarah's husband's life with her father's. Bosse was "a French German who, to please his parents, obtained a degree in medicine but never practiced after graduation and went back to his chosen life, that of an artist. Unlike his father-in-law, though," Laferrière adds, "Bosse held a reasonably successful career as a medical illustrator." Interview, April 1989.

67. *Lovell's Montreal Directory,* 1897; Edith Eaton to Charles Lummis, 30 January 1897, SWM.

68. Carolyn G. Heilbrun, *Writing a Woman's Life* (New York: Ballantine Books, 1988), 50.

69. Both sisters depart from the recorded facts about their ages. *Me's* narrator says she went to Jamaica when she was seventeen (3). In the *Globe* article, Sui Sin Far claims to have been twenty-seven when she made the same trip. Other evidence and dates appear to be more factually reliable. "Winnifred Eaton Babcock," in *Women's Who's Who of America: A Biographical Dictionary of Contemporary Women of the United States and Canada, 1914–1915* (New York: 1914), cites Winifred as being in Jamaica in 1895, when she would have been twenty. Sui Sin Far's letter to Lummis, 30 January 1897, SWM, places her age at thirty-one.

70. Whitaker, *Whitaker's Almanac,* 142.

71. Eileen Lewis, Telephone interview, Pullman, Wash., 20 September 1990, recalls her grandmother Florence's telling her that Lotus Blossom warned her children not to tell anyone they were Chinese because she feared they might be sold into "coolee labor."

72. See E.E., "A Plea for the Chinaman."

73. See S. E. Solberg, "The Eaton Sisters: Sui Sin Far and Onoto Watanna" (Paper presented at the Pacific Northwest Asian American Writer's Conference, Seattle, Wash., 16 April 1976), 16, who maintains, "They were both skillful writers, able to plot and tell a story. The essential difference was in the quality of their perceptions. Edith cut straight through to her point, she saw clearly and well. Winnifred, in most cases, was more concerned with detail, with, if you will, what would sell"; and Ling, *Between Worlds,* 39, who points out that "Edith's response to racism was a frontal assault, direct and confrontational. Winnifred's response, in contrast, was indirect, covert, and subversive. . . ."

74. Robin W. Winks, *Canadian-West Indies Union: A Forty-Year Minuet* (London: Athlone Press, 1968), 11.

75. Nina Baym, "Melodramas of Beset Manhood," *American Quarterly* 33 (Summer 1981): 123–39, reprinted in *The New Feminist Criticism,* ed. Elaine Showalter (New York: Pantheon Books, 1985), 63–80, examines the difference between female and male identity searches.

76. Information on Hugh Graham comes from Canada's *Who Was Who, 1929–40,* courtesy of L. Charles Laferrière. In 1869 Hugh Graham founded the *Evening Star,* which later became the *Montreal Daily Star,* and the *Family Herald and Weekly Star.* His wealth and philanthropic tendencies make Graham a candidate as one of the unnamed patrons who provided Sui Sin Far with financial backing to write *Mrs. Spring Fragrance* in 1912.

77. May Eaton's residency in San Francisco is documented in *Crocker-Langley San Francisco Directory,* 1898: "Eaton, May Miss, finisher, Thors Photographic Co., residence 1226 Mission." The address of Thors Photographic Co., Louis Thors, President, is listed as 14 Grant Avenue, San Francisco.

78. Sui Sin Far mentions that she was doing typing at five dollars a month in "Leaves" (130). The company she was working for is documented in letters to Charles Lummis, 2 December 1898 and 30 June 1899, SWM; and in *Crocker-Langley San Francisco Directory,* 1899: "Edith Eaton, stenographer, C.P.R., 921 A Fulton."

79. Sui Sin Far, "Leaves," 130.

80. Audrey Kobayashi, Interview, Vancouver, British Columbia, 2 November 1990, stated that individuals who can "pass" are often the butt of reverse racism, explaining, "It's the way I experience racism." Ling, *Between Worlds,* 39, writes, "The special reality for Chinese Eurasians was rejection from both sides."

81. Nobuya Tsuchida, "Asians and California's Anti-miscegenation Law," in *Asian and Pacific American Experiences* (Asian/Pacific American Learning Resource Center, University of Minnesota, 1982), 16–31.

82. This passage refers to a class issue, namely that the bottom line in a Victorian woman's choice not to marry was economic independence, the line Virginia Woolf recognizes in *A Room of One's Own.* The assumption behind it is that if a woman could provide her own livelihood, she would not have to depend on a man. In much of the fiction by women writers of Sui Sin Far's

period—Sarah Orne Jewett and Mary Wilkins Freeman, for instance—the heroines who make the decision to remain single usually enjoy a private income. As Michele Clark writes of Freeman's women in Mary E. Wilkins Freeman, *The Revolt of Mother and Other Stories,* with an afterword by Michele Clark (New York: Feminist Press, 1974), 194, "Economic independence is their most valued position: your own backyard's dandelion greens are preferable to all the fancy puddings and delicate sauces of another." The generally proffered options for poor women—or so society liked to believe—were between marriage and a life on the streets. In this context Sui Sin Far represents women who broke the mold. She was a poor woman who chose not to marry, yet she was able to survive on the marginal income of her own earnings and to achieve important work beyond the domestic sphere.

83. See Amy Ling, "Edith Eaton: Pioneer Chinamerican Writer and Feminist," *American Literary Realism* 16 (Autumn 1983): 289, who maintains, "The authentic ring of this story, the intimate details of the diary entries, and the fact that Edith Eaton never married point strongly to the conclusion that this was her own story." This is an example of a woman's declaration of independence that is fully cross-cultural. It may be compared with the narrator in Kate Chopin, "The Story of an Hour," in *Kate O'Flaherty Chopin: The Complete Works,* ed. Peter Seyersted, (Baton Rouge: Louisiana State University Press, 1969), 353, who declares, "Free! Body and soul free!" and the narrator in Estela Portillo Trambley, "If It Weren't for the Honeysuckle," in *Rain of Scorpions and Other Writings* (Berkeley, Calif.: Tonatiuh-Quinto Sol International, 1975), 108, who says, "It was a joyous idea. . . . Free . . . free." All relate to stands for sexual independence.

84. Sui Seen Far, "Sweet Sin," *Land of Sunshine* 8 (April 1898): 226.

85. Tillie Olsen, *Silences* (New York: Dell, 1965), 16.

86. Edith Eaton to Charles Lummis, 30 June 1899, SWM.

87. Sui Seen Far, "Sweet Sin"; Sui Seen Far, "The Sing-Song Woman," *Land of Sunshine* 9 (October 1898): 225–28; Sui Sin Fah, "Lin John," *Land of Sunshine* 10 (January 1899): 76–77; Sui Sin Fah, "The Story of Tin-A," *Land of Sunshine* 12 (December 1899): 101–3; Sui Sin Fah, "A Chinese Ishmael," *Overland Monthly* 34 (July 1899): 43–49.

88. Edith Eaton to Charles Lummis, 2 December 1898, SWM. Neither of the stories to which she refers has been located.

89. Register of President's Correspondence, Canadian Pacific Rail Corporate Archives Collection, Windsor Station, Montreal.

90. Edith Eaton to Charles Lummis, 16 September 1900, SWM.

91. Ibid. Clover accepted Sui Sin Far, "Ku Yum's Little Sister," *Chicago Evening Post,* 13 October 1900.

92. Edith Eaton to Charles Lummis, 8 October 1900, SWM. All Seattle addresses and employers for Sui Sin Far in the *Seattle Directory* were located by S. E. Solberg and compiled in an unpublished "Bibliographic Note," 7 April 1976.

93. Edith Eaton to Charles Lummis, 25 October 1900, SWM.

94. Edith Eaton to Charles Lummis, 2 November 1900, SWM.

95. The most obvious example is the relationship between Emily Dickinson and Thomas Wentworth Higginson.

96. Edith Eaton to Charles Lummis, 16 September 1900, SWM.

97. Virginia Woolf, "Professions for Women," in *Women and Writing* (New York: Harcourt Brace Jovanovich, 1979 [1904]), 59.

98. Edith Eaton to Charles Lummis, 8 January 1901, SWM.

99. Edith Eaton to Charles Lummis, 13 February 1901, SWM.

100. Karen Wong, *Chinese History in the Pacific Northwest* (Seattle: n.p., 1972), n.p.

101. Linda Popp DiBiase, "A Chinese Lily in Seattle," *Seattle Weekly,* 10 September 1986.

102. Sui Sin Far (Edith Eaton), "The Chinese in America: Intimate Study of Chinese Life in America, Told in a Series of Short Sketches—An Interpretation of Chinese Life and Character," *Westerner* 10, 11 (May–August 1909).

103. According to Solberg, "Bibliographic Note," these are 519 Yessler Way in 1900; 1026 Marion in 1901; 1003 Yessler Way in 1902; 318 James in 1903; 807 Madison in 1905; 319 Boren in 1906; and 412 Terry Avenue in 1908. Some entries in the *Seattle Directory* cite no occupation; one (1908) lists her as "an occasional journalist."

104. Edith Eaton to Charles Lummis, 25 October 1900, SWM.

105. This was probably Sui Sin Far's next-to-youngest sister, Florence.

106. *Nationality* may be Sui Sin Far's euphemism for *race.*

107. Sepulchre Register, Archives du Québec, Montreal.

108. Olsen, *Silences,* 38.

109. Edith Eaton to Robert Underwood Johnson, NYPL.

110. Sui Sin Far, "A Chinese Boy-Girl," *Century* 67 (April 1904): 828–31.

111. Sui Sin Far, "The Horoscope," *Out West* 19 (November 1903): 521–24.

112. None of these manuscripts has been located.

113. These serializations were of Wharton's "Roman Villas" and London's "Sea-Wolf."

114. The example is from Judy Yung, *Chinese Women in America: A Pictorial History* (Seattle: University of Washington Press, 1986), 35.

115. Onoto Watanna, "The Loves of Sakura Jiro and the Three-Headed Maid," *Century* 65 (March 1903): 755–60.

116. Onoto Watanna, *Miss Nume of Japan: A Japanese-American Romance* (Chicago: Rand McNally, 1899); *A Japanese Nightingale* (New York: Harper and Bros., 1901); *The Wooing of Wisteria* (New York: Harper and Bros., 1902); *The Heart of Hyacinth* (New York: Harper and Bros., 1903); *The Daughters of Nijo: A Romance of Japan* (New York: Macmillan, 1904).

117. S. E. Solberg, "Sui Sin Far/Edith Eaton: First Chinese-American Fictionist," *MELUS* 8 (Spring 1981): 29.

118. Samuel T. Clover to R. U. Johnson, Esq., 13 December 1903, NYPL.

119. Edith Eaton to R. U. Johnson, Esq., 4 December 1903, NYPL.

120. Sui Sin Fah, "The Smuggling of Tie Co," *Land of Sunshine* 13 (July

1900): 100–104; Edith Eaton (Sui Sin Far), "A Chinese Tom-Boy," *Montreal Daily Witness,* 16 October 1900; Sui Sin Far, "Ku Yum's Little Sister"; Sui Sin Fah, "O Yam—A Sketch," *Land of Sunshine* 13 (November 1900): 341–43; Edith Eaton (Sui Sin Far), "The Coat of Many Colors," *Youth's Companion* 76 (April 1902): n.p.; Sui Sin Far, "The Horoscope"; Sui Sin Far, "A Chinese Boy-Girl"; Sui Sin Far (Edith Eaton), "Aluteh," *Chautauquan* 42 (December 1905): 338–42.

The changing names by which Sui Sin Far signed her stories tells us a lot about her identity conflict.

121. Edith Eaton to Charles Lummis, 23 March 1912, Charles Fletcher Lummis Collection, Huntington Library, San Marino, Calif. (hereafter cited as HL).

122. Edith Eaton to Charles Lummis, 10 February 1909, SWM.

123. The 146 Concord Street West address is documented in letters to Charles Lummis, 13 July 1911, 9 August 1911, 23 March 1912, 19 April 1912, and 22 June 1912, HL. I walked past the residence in August 1990 and found that the neighborhood still appears much as described in the Thirteenth Census of the United States, Boston City, Mass., Ward 12, Sheet 23 (1910). Census entries document West Concord as having been a neighborhood of lodging houses, filled with mainly working-class residents (seamstresses, machinists, clerks, nurses), who listed their race as singularly "white" and their birthplaces as mainly New England, although a number defined themselves as "Canadian English."

124. Edith Eaton to Charles Lummis, 13 July 1911, HL.

125. "Mrs. Spring Fragrance and Her Friends, Chinese and American," *Montreal Daily Witness,* 18 June 1912.

126. Sui Sin Far, "A Love Story from the Rice Fields of China," *New England Magazine* 45 (December 1911): 343–45; "Who's Game?" *New England Magazine* 45 (February 1912): 573–79; "Chan Hen Yen, Chinese Student," *New England Magazine* 45 (June 1912): 462–66.

127. Sui Sin Far, "Chinese Workmen in America," *Independent* 75 (3 July 1913): 56–58; Sui Seen Far, "The Chinese Woman in America," *Land of Sunshine* 6 (January 1897): 60–65.

128. Information on Edward Charles's death is from his undated obituary in the *Montreal Gazette.* L. Charles Laferrière, Interview, Montreal, Quebec, Spring 1989, noted that Edward Charles belonged to the "Pistol Section" of the Montreal Amateur Athletic Association, a very exclusive WASP club that would not have accepted him if his Chinese ancestry had been known. According to Laferrière's grandmother, Sui Sin Far's sister Agnes, Edward Charles had not returned to see his family since his marriage.

129. L. Charles Laferrière, Interview, Montreal, Quebec, Spring 1989.

130. Recognizing her talent for exploiting the multiple ambiguities of her identity on the printed page, I assume that Sui Sin Far intends "East" in this context to refer to both Montreal (the eastern North American continent) and China, and "West" to refer to both North America and the Pacific United States.

131. Death notice, *Montreal Daily Star,* 7 April 1914; "Well-Known Author of Chinese Stories Who Died Yesterday," *Montreal Daily Star,* 8 April 1941 (quotes).

132. Edith Eaton to Charles Lummis, 9 August 1911, HL.

133. "Well-Known Author of Chinese Stories Who Died Yesterday."

134. Funeral notice, *Montreal Daily Star,* 11 April 1914.

135. "Edith Eaton Dead: Author of Chinese Stories under the Name of Sui Sin Far," *New York Times,* 9 April 1914.

136. Ling, *Between Worlds,* 36–37.

137. Solberg, "Sui Sin Far/Edith Eaton," 29.

138. See Amy Ling, "Revelation and Mask: Autobiographies of the Eaton Sisters," *a/b Auto/Biography Studies* 3 (Summer 1987): 49, who comments, "Perhaps the obituary she [Winifred] wrote for Edith was weighing heavily on her conscience."

139. According to Mont Royal Cemetery records, permission to pour the foundation for this monument was not requested until 15 October 1927, which raises the question of when and by whom Sui Sin Far's monument was erected. Ling, *Between Worlds,* 32, writes, "To memorialize their gratitude after her death, the 'Chinese community of Montreal and Boston' placed on her tomb in the Protestant cemetery in Montreal, a special headstone. . . ." L. Charles Laferrière suggests the possibility that Winifred, in her own trickster manner and in an attempt to atone, might have had the monument put up some years later. An undocumented newspaper article in the Winifred Babcock Eaton Collection, McKimmie Library, University of Calgary, entitled "Chinese Tribute to Montreal Writer: Monument to Edith Eaton (Sui Sin Far) Unveiled Yesterday" comes the closest to actual verification. It records the unveiling of a monument "to the memory of Miss Edith Eaton (Sui Sin Far) who died about a year ago," a ceremony that was attended only by her "parents and near relatives and a few of the prominent Chinese of Montreal." I believe that the monument probably was erected by the Montreal Chinese community in 1915 but that it was 1927 before a permanent foundation was commissioned.

140. This is explained by L. Charles Laferrière's caretaking.

141. I am grateful to James Wing, a Chinese Canadian who has lived in Montreal since 1923, for going to the Mont Royal Cemetery with me and offering this translation. Compare Ling's translation in *Between Worlds,* 32: " 'Yi bu wong hua' ('The righteous or loyal one does not forget China')."

142. Heilbrun, *Writing a Woman's Life,* 30.

2

Montreal:
The Early Writings

Women understand—only women altogether—what a dreary will-o-the-
wisp is this old, common, I had almost said commonplace experience.
"When the fall sewing is done," "When the baby can walk," "When house-
cleaning is over" . . . "When I am a little stronger," then I will write the
poem, or learn the language . . . or master the symphony; then I will act,
dare, dream, become.

—Tillie Olsen, *Silences*

Sui Sin Far's first audience was undoubtedly her family. The "doggerel verse"
she speaks of writing at age eleven is corroborated by the narrator in Winifred's
Marion: "Ada made up poems about every little incident in our lives," with
examples ranging from "a lovely poem about God hearing us" when the
family prayed for Edward to come back from England to "a lovely poem
about our Panama hen who died."[1] None of these poems has been located,
however. The first of Sui Sin Far's recovered writings date from 1888 and
were published in Montreal's new monthly dedicated to the promotion of
Canada, the *Dominion Illustrated.*[2] These pieces, eight in all, were written
during her employment with Archibald and McCormick as a stenographer.
Less than a thousand words each, they recall Virginia Woolf's observation that
women have frequently written in short forms—an analogy to quilt blocks is
pertinent, what can be completed in a single, small section of time, perhaps
after dinner dishes are done or before the babies awake in the morning.[3] We
know that Sui Sin Far lived with her family while she was writing them and
that her two sisters Beryl and Florence would still have been toddlers. Twenty-
two years later Sui Sin Far would refer to these writings as "juvenile pieces,"[4]
though she was between twenty-three and twenty-five years old when they
were published.

Sui Sin Far never testifies in a first-person voice about her own decision not to marry, but the wry attitude toward marriage revealed in her early writings suggests biographical origins. These writings also suggest the struggle that Sui Sin Far, as a Victorian woman, must have gone through in the decision to deviate from the norms ascribed to her by society and by both sides of her ancestry—that is to say, women should marry. If marriage was a major issue in her life during the years her first stories were published, she was facing a problem with which many women writers struggled, especially those who were poor, were members of a large family household, and occupied roles as eldest daughters.

Events in Sui Sin Far's literary environment of eastern Canada are relevant to these first writings also. When the movement to become a nation independent of England, which had been felt as a ground swell in Canada all through the century, crested in 1867 with confederation, the new Canadian nation, though still strongly divided between English and French populations, worked to distinguish a united government and to promote Canadian industry and economic independence. It was a dream made increasingly possible by the completion of the Canadian transcontinental railroad, the opening of the prairies, and the burgeoning settlement of the Canadian West in the last two decades of the century. The development of a national literature was part of this movement. Catherine M. McLay compares the eastern Canadian "literary awakening" after confederation with the "Literary Renaissance" in the United States after the War of 1812.[5] The extent to which Sui Sin Far was aware of this movement is not clear. As a native-born English woman living in a French Canadian neighborhood and as a newswoman, she certainly would have encountered, both personally and professionally, the national and ethnic conflicts involved.

In this atmosphere, many journals, magazines, and periodicals were born, including, in Sui Sin Far's Montreal, the *Dominion Illustrated*. The magazine's credo was stated on the masthead of its first issue, 7 July 1888: "We are for building up a homogeneous, united, patriotic nation, and for ignoring all prejudice of race and sect; marching onward, shoulder to shoulder, to the goal of prosperity that looms ahead." The magazine's literary editor was John Lesperance, a Missourian who had immigrated to Canada after the fall of the Confederacy to become, in the words of James Doyle, "a loyal, conservative, pro-British-Canadian" and "an eminent Montreal man of letters." Because Lesperance was known for "taking on protégés," Doyle conjectures Edith Eaton was one of his writing discoveries; indeed, Doyle sees Lesperance as "a most important literary connection" for both Sui Sin Far and her future brother-in-law Walter Blackburn Harte.[6] The subject of much of the fiction Lesperance printed, following the trend of contemporary magazine fiction in Canada and the United States, was "romantic love," filled with local characters and framed in local settings. In response to the popularity of women writers in such magazine fiction, the Canadian critic Hector Charlesworth coined a counterpart to Hawthorne's "scribbling women": "The fair scribblers pour forth an endless stream of prose and poetry for the edification of their sisters, while to the men it is a mass that is 'erotic, neurotic, and tommyrotic.' "[7]

Sui Sin Far's first *Dominion Illustrated* piece is journalistic in style, and the next five are fiction; all present Canadian characters, settings, and subject matter and focus on gender or family relations. The Montreal audience for these stories would have had to be English, the only language in which Sui Sin Far wrote. All are signed Edith Eaton and are concerned with "romance" in one way or other, with tones ranging from comic to tragic. With the exception of "The Origin of a Broken Nose," all are presented by a third-person-omniscient narrator. In the mode of the late nineteenth century and Victorian melodrama, the style is often "flowery," laced with sensation and plots frequently turning on accidents. A closer look, however, reveals the ironic complexities already at work that mark Sui Sin Far's future writings.

The first of these, "A Trip in a Horse Car," begins with the narrator's announcement that she is taking her readers for a ride in a horsecar. She establishes the setting precisely: from Mile End to Cote St. Antoine in Montreal, at three in the afternoon. As one character after the next boards the car, the sketch becomes a sampler in human interest. There are two French Canadian seamstresses taking coats "to some shop in the city." There is a man who drops his parcels, one of which has "a little stream of sugar . . . oozing out" and has to be tied with "a large red handkerchief." There is "a poor beggar girl" for whom "life holds nothing bright," and "sitting as far as possible from her" are two "rich ladies, good church members," who are "collecting contributions for some mission" yet regard the beggar girl "with faces of disgust." There is "a masher," of whom the young girl he escorts is "very proud," but the narrator manages to introduce a dual vision by observing that although this man "thinks he has mashed a couple of typical old maids," they whisper that they think him "a senseless fellow" (235). On one level the purpose of this piece is simply to take us on a ride through Montreal streets; on another, the writer observes and synthesizes, testing social values and themes against the environments within which they emerge. Sui Sin Far knew what it was like to be termed an "old maid," and she had also been a "beggar girl." Altogether, she uses the horsecar much as Katherine Anne Porter used a ship, as a microcosmic gathering of human beings.[8]

In context, the character on the horsecar who deserves most attention is "the masher," for he introduces a type who will be played off in Sui Fin Far's various other *Dominion Illustrated* stories. "Misunderstood: The Story of a Young Man" presents "a very amiable young man" who is satirized for believing the myths underlying the masher role. The young man concentrates "night and day" on his highest desire—to make all women happy—until an "apparition" appears and tells him that "a woman's happiness is comprised in . . . LOVE," conferring on him the power "of casting a spell over the heart of every girl." He finds himself with six hundred "devotees," each of whom he sees once a week. When the one woman he really loves pines and dies, the others all seek "REVENGE," mobbing the young man and hanging him "by the neck," with no feeling of "pity." "This was the reward of years spent on the happiness of others," the narrator ironically observes in conclusion (314). In its satirization of the idea that love is the key to "a woman's happiness," the story becomes a parable of ironic reversal; romantic expectations topple into absurdity and violent death. The recitation of Alfred Lord Tennyson's refrain from "In Memoriam" ("'Tis better to have loved and lost / Than never to have loved at all") suggests the part "all the great writers" play in perpetuating such fancies.

"Albemarle's Secret" introduces another version of the masher: "a poet—a genius," though "the world did not acknowledge him," who "mashes" women through his poetry. With "dreamy" eyes, a "pale" cheek, "dark" locks, a "noble brow," and "a fascinating melancholy," Albemarle imitates the portrait of a Byronic hero, an image furthered when his life is said to turn on "some strange mysterious sorrow." Though "conscious of the fact that many a fair one viewed him with admiring eyes," Albemarle seeks only a woman "whose mind is elevated enough to converse with mine" and "accompany my spirit in all its ethereal flights." He finds her in "a sylvan bower" and "haunted" her steadily for three weeks—reading verse, singing songs and dropping "many a dark hint of the mysterious sorrow which is eating his heart away." One day she recites a poem to him:

> My other friends have left me,
> The false ones and the true;
> Won't you follow their example,
> Won't you please to say adieu?

Albemarle responds by comparing himself to Byron and by reciting:

> Here's a sigh for those that love me
> Here's a smile for those that hate,
> And whatever sky's above me,
> Here's a heart for any fate.

The woman parodies in reply:

> Here's a whine for those that love me,
> Here's a scowl for those that hate,

> For whatever food I swallow,
> Indigestion is my fate.

In response, "our poet" vanishes and is "never heard of more." The narrator discloses why: "She had discovered what the strange, mysterious sorrow . . . was, and the discovery had broken the charm. . . . Albemarle suffered from dyspepsia." Once again, in the guise of embracing sentimentality, Sui Sin Far shows her scorn for it. The story's feigned seriousness masks its comic revelation that such a homely condition as "indigestion" has been mistaken as "potent charm" by those foolish enough to accept "outward signs" and buy into Albemarle's romantic pose (254).[9]

"The Origin of a Broken Nose" is also a satire on the naiveté of believing romantic rhetoric. Presenting a male first-person narrator who recounts the tale of how he gained "the privilege of calling the dearest little woman in the world my wife," the story is structured around the narrator's opening question, "So you want to know how I got my nose broken?" Textual action moves from the present to the past, when the narrator was "a young man" sitting in his room "ruminating" about a girl who "had ungratefully and heartlessly thrown me over for another fellow." Reading a newspaper article that urges "gallant youths" to prove their chivalry by stationing themselves at icy street corners and being "on the lookout to help any unfortunate maiden who may chance to come to grief," the narrator is inspired to find a "nice slippery corner," where he helps "old ladies" and "a drunken man" but finds "all the girls light and sure of foot." When a girl finally "tottered along" who seems a likely victim, the narrator "sprang towards her," only to slip and break his nose, while she gets "past the perilous place in safety." When a policeman tries to arrest the narrator for "molesting peaceable citizens," the "girl" runs back with the words: "What! take him to the police station? No, you never shall. He is a hero . . . ," and "some months later" the couple is married (302). Maintaining a perfectly deadpan point of view, this story is full of the elements of slapstick; it is also enormously funny and clever. In the gap between a narrator who is naive enough to believe the stereotypes that he reads and an author who knows that images of "chivalrous knights" and "unfortunate maidens" are hogwash, the reader cannot miss the dramatic irony. Who indeed is the "hero" in a situation where the woman that society sends a man out to rescue reverses the course of expectations and rescues him?

Each of these stories reveals the absurdity of literary treatments of "romantic love" so popular in Sui Sin Far's era. Each presents a male protagonist who literally believes the sentimental rhetoric in which his pursuit of a woman or women is framed, rhetoric that the narrative vision proves ridiculous. We can imagine that these characters were modeled on the men Sui Sin Far and her sisters were currently meeting and perhaps being pressed—through the guiles of this very same rhetoric—to consider as husbands. Deconstructing her texts proves that, as a writer, Sui Sin Far approached such rhetoric with ironic detachment and parodied the nonsense in romantic conventions through binary opposites—principle versus practice, rhetoric versus actuality, expectation versus outcome—with a light comic tone.

In "A Fatal Tug of War," her narrative stance moves toward a more somber evaluation of the pitfalls of romantic love as a basis for marriage. The characters' fates illustrate the tragic consequences that can result when romantic formulas bring ill-matched men and women together. The main characters are newlyweds, whose love, the narrator tells us, has "triumphed over every obstacle" and who have "given up everything for its sweet sake." The realities of the marriage, however, collide almost instantly with the expectations of the romance. Both the woman and man have tempers that are "obstinate, proud and unyielding," resulting in "a day when even the Power of Love failed to steer them over the precipice down which they rushed." The reason for the quarrel that incites their downfall is described as "some trifling thing"; of more thematic importance is the quarrel's aftermath. Moving between the minds of both of her characters, the narrator shows how both want to make up but pretend they do not; each prepares for their prearranged date to a concert but disdains to let the other know that she or he cares. The conflict's controlling image comes to rest on a bouquet of "red and white carnations, her favourite," which the man buys but does not give her—leading the woman to reason "that he was still angry with her, and if he had a right to be angry . . . surely she had too." Complication builds on their interlacing anger until after the concert, when she rushes ahead of him out of the theater and he chases her across the street—to be run down by a speeding carriage. Viewing his "manly form lying crushed and limp," the wife suffers "grief bordering on madness," settling "into a gloomy, weak-minded creature whose every hope seemed blighted, whose life light was quenched." "The quarrel was so trivial," the narrator repeats in a Desdemona's handkerchief kind of refrain (362–63). All of the currently popular elements of melodrama are there, yet it is a melodrama to which any married couple can relate.

"If I could have left them happy after the auspicious day which made them one, my story would have been finished, but, alas, I did not," the narrator prophecies at the beginning of "A Fatal Tug of War" (362). This could be a microcosm for Sui Sin Far's vision in the *Dominion Illustrated* stories, a vision undoubtedly based on the experiences of her own family: marriages may begin with the "Power of Love," but the traditional happy ending is inevitably canceled, possible only for a brief moment at love's beginning.

The story "Robin" extends this theme to show another motif Sui Sin Far knows well: it is the children of romantic unions who often most suffer. Robin, "a bright, interesting child," and his little sister Alice are born of "poor, hardworking" parents in Montreal, "a beautiful Canadian city on the River St. Lawrence." One day the father "died suddenly of heart disease, leaving his wife and children destitute." Imitating Sui Sin Far's early career, the mother goes to work "as a type-setter in a printing office" but is "obliged to leave [her children] alone all day while at her work." One day Robin "caught fire" from the wood stove, an accident so traumatizing to the child that "reason was fled." When the mother dies shortly thereafter, the children are turned into street beggars by their "bad and dissolute" uncle, and when Alice drowns, Robin lingers on until he is twelve (394).

In the narrator's juxtapositions between riches and poverty, the motif of class is continually present in "Robin." This is obvious in details, such as when the widow turns to the father's "late employers" for help, and they refuse her with "stony faces and stonier hearts." It is highlighted most centrally in "the storming of the Ice Palace," a symbol of Montreal's pride and affluence in which "every block of crystal ice was cut from the bosom of that noble river and fashioned by Canadian art into a stately edifice. . . ." At the edge of the celebrants surrounding the Ice Palace is Robin. Like one of Zola's children looking from the street into windows at a French banquet, Robin gazes at the "glittering, cold, fairy-like habitation," with the fancy "that in one of those blocks of ice which were hewn out of the river in which his sister was drowned she lives." The imaginative flight of the boy unifies the story's conclusion. Reality is juxtaposed between the eyes of the crowd that witnesses the "pitiful sight" of "a little lad lying dead on the sandy beach of St. Helen's Island" and the "outstretched arms [that] caught his spirit as it escaped from its earthly habitation" (394). In this story, narrative distance largely descends into pathos, yet (the narrator seems to say) so do the lives of children trapped in urban poverty—Robin's environment reflects the conditions in which Sui Sin Far and her siblings were raised.

The conclusion of "Robin" highlights another opposition that recurs in Sui Sin Far's life and early fiction: the duality between the world of duty and imagination, a tug the author recalled most explicitly in the "withdrawn life of thought and musing" she entered at age eleven (Globe). "I love poetry, particularly heroic pieces," she wrote in "Leaves." "I also love fairy tales. Stories of real life do not appeal to me."[10] Sui Sin Far's last two pieces in the Dominion Illustrated, both nonfiction essays, illustrate this "withdrawn life." Amy Ling interprets the first of these, "Spring Impressions: A Medley of Poetry and Prose," as "a key to Sui Sin Far's later work," for here "spring fragrance," the title of her 1912 book, is first introduced.[11]

Sui Sin Far's eight early pieces in the Dominion Illustrated, all signed "Edith Eaton" and with English and French Canadian subjects and settings, should not be dismissed as mere trivia she did early in her apprenticeship, random and disconnected from the remainder of her oeuvre. I see them instead as an important indicator of the early voice of a writer who later self-consciously chose to shift her name and her art from the English to the Chinese side of her heritage. Edith Eaton began writing in an English Canadian voice for her English Canadian audience. Yet these stories reveal the author's ironic stance toward her subjects and her skill at turning the ambiguities offered by life into aesthetic strategies. Though the fiction does not yet acknowledge racial issues, the bridges from early to late work are clear and provocative. The title "Misunderstood," for example, is later reused for a story in the Tales of Chinese Children section of *Mrs. Spring Fragrance*.[12] The Tennyson quote, "'Tis better to have loved and lost / Than never to have loved at all," recurs as a refrain in the short story, "Mrs. Spring Fragrance," published in 1910.[13] The first line of "A Fatal Tug of War" ("They were two people with heads hot enough and hearts true enough to think the world well lost for love." [362]) is also the first line of "Children of Peace"—with the addition of four words: "and they were Chinese."[14] Most significant to this study are the author's attempts to control a dual narrative vision and illuminate sociopolitical incongruities through the tools of irony.

The Growth of Chinese Montreal Populations

Sui Sin Far's ambition to write a book about the "half-Chinese" would have been impeded for many years by various obstacles. Her family apparently maintained a public image as English Canadian, and she grew up in a locale where her acquaintance with individuals of Chinese descent was primarily limited to her mother and siblings. This isolation from her mother's people started to change with the growth of a Montreal Chinese population in the late 1880s. That this growth was taking place at the same time Sui Sin Far was emerging as a writer and newswoman must have had a tremendous impact on her. How did these two circumstances interconnect? Why, as she describes in "Leaves," did local papers begin to give a free-lance journalist calling herself "Miss Edith Eaton" their "local Chinese reporting?" What led her to the choice she would make within the decade: to begin assuming, in her publications, a Chinese-identified voice?

That the catalyst for Sui Sin Far's first steps over the threshold from English to Chinese Canadian communities should have been a clergyman was not entirely accidental. The missionary movement that played a central role in the meeting and marriage of Sui Sin Far's parents in China was reaching a fever pitch in Europe and North America in the 1880s and 1890s, when Canada, England, and the United States were allied in a common march to "save the heathen" and colonize the non-Christian world.[15] With the title metaphor in his sermon "Civilization without the Gospel Is Profitless," the Reverend

J. Chalmers highlighted the missionary-merchant connection: "The Gospel must precede commerce. . . . The rampart can only be stormed by those who carry the cross."[16]

The religious interchange taking place in this era between Western countries and China, and catching fire in the popular imagination largely through missionary literature, can be seen in countless letters in Montreal papers, a correspondence in which women and children played a major part. A "Chinese Letter to an American Sunday School," republished in the *Montreal Daily Star* on 10 January 1891, was sent by Chinese children of the Ngan Chia Miao mission to thank Pennsylvania Sunday school children for the $12.50 they sent—they said it paid for "the chapel entire." A 23 October 1889 report in the *Montreal Daily Star* by the Woman's Missionary Board in Montreal praised the efforts of sisters in Victoria for bringing over Chinese girls who "would yet go back and tell their people of Jesus." Moreover, by this date—approximately thirty years after the Tsetsin Treaties had permitted Western missionaries to move full scale into China—a reverse dynamic was occurring. A whole generation of Chinese converts (younger brothers and sisters to Lotus Blossom) had been trained by Western missionaries and were being sent from China into Europe and North America to appeal for help in "saving" their own people—from China's own traditional religions.

A case in point for Sui Sin Far's Montreal is a woman known only as Mrs. Ahok. Reported in 1890 to have been nine years ago "a heathen, burning incense to her idol" and never venturing more than three miles from home, Mrs. Ahok now had "left her home, her husband, her little boy, her mother, her friends, and all dear to her" and was touring England, the United States, and Canada with the news: "The Chinese are like lost sheep." Claiming through an interpreter that "a million a month are dying without God, and without hope," she pleaded for more missionaries to come to China and "save them." Ironically, when Mrs. Ahok and her maid tried to descend from the train in Montreal, they were told they could not "land on free Canadian soil" without payment of the fifty-dollar head tax per person that the Dominion Parliament had imposed on all Chinese attempting to enter Canada. Furthermore, the two Chinese women were not allowed to sightsee in Montreal without the escort of a customs official, and when they left for Vancouver by the Canadian Pacific Railway to book return passage to China, they were sent through "in bond." The editor of the *Montreal Daily Witness*, a Protestant newspaper that radically criticized Canada's policy regarding Chinese immigration, noted the obvious contradiction: "[Mrs. Ahok] has had the example of one of the great civilized countries . . . and will doubtless wonder at the 'progress' that while opening China to Canada and others, closing [sic] Canada to the Chinese."[17]

As a reporter, Sui Sin Far could have met Mrs. Ahok. Whether or not she did, there is little doubt that as someone with both a political consciousness and a desire to learn about China, Sui Sin Far was aware of the incident and its ironies. Another likely point of meeting for Sui Sin Far with Chinese in Montreal would have been the Protestant church, where "home" mission societies were now in full swing, sponsoring ministries on home soil, channeling new immigrants into mission schools, and trying to obliterate Chinese language, religion, dress, and customs with methods analogous to those used by both Canada and the United States on North American Indians.[18] Alexander Saxton observes a common pattern in whites' treatment of darker-skinned people in the United States, noting that their responses to Chinese Americans in California were influenced by previous responses to Indians, immigrants, and Negro slaves in the Midwest and East.[19] Immigrants from China presented missionaries with a special challenge, partly because of their stereotyped images about the "quaint" and "exotic" nature of Chinese peoples—images created and mythologized largely by the missionaries themselves. Because Chinese immigrants to North America were considered, in the words of the Reverend F. M. Dewey, "birds of passage"—on the continent only temporarily before returning to China—by converting them, the missionaries anticipated "making progress in Christian knowledge that will bear fruit in China."[20]

That Montreal missionaries took their task seriously is evidenced by Chinese Sunday schools, the first of which opened in November 1884 and by August 1896 had grown into a "chain of Chinese Sunday Schools which encircle[d] the city." Established in twelve of Montreal's Presbyterian churches, all were maintained under the supervision of the Reverend J. C. Thompson, "a missionary of the true type," who was said to reach "about 200 Chinamen every Sunday."[21] Teachers were mainly English Canadian women, one assigned to each Chinese pupil, as in this typical scene described by the Reverend F. M. Dewey: "The spacious lecture hall is fitted up with approximately 100 small tables and twice as many chairs. At each table is seated a Chinaman in native dress, at his side is a Chinese worker...."[22] The aim of these schools, as expressed by more than one missionary, was to inculcate new immigrants with the "language, religion and customs of their adopted country."[23] By appealing to the new immigrants' inclination "to learn English and become acquainted with European methods," according to Dewey, missionaries could lure them to an education meant not to supplement but to replace native cultures.[24]

Because of the Eaton family's past connections with the missionary movement and the Protestant church, it seems likely that Sui Sin Far, along with her mother and siblings, would have been part of the Montreal Christian missionary network. We know that Lotus Blossom was "brought up in a Presbyterian college" (Leaves, 126), had been trained as a missionary, and sent her children to Sunday school. That participation in church affairs was a regular part of the Eatons' life is implied in the clergyman's visit, in public and family records, and by Sui Sin Far when she recollects crocheting "a set of mats" for her mother in response to "the church's" request for a donation (*Globe*). Some years later, in the *Boston Globe* article, Sui Sin Far would reflect on having taught "in a Chinese mission school" in Seattle, as well as in Boston. The physical arrangements, aims, and overall strategies of Chinese mission schools in Montreal were typical of what Sui Sin Far would encounter later in the United States in cities with larger Chinese North American populations.

This implies that the writer would have been in close touch—at a level exceeding her own experiences as an individual of Chinese-English parentage from England—with the media-induced stereotypes and racist assumptions that Chinese immigrants in Canada had to face. The historian Anthony B. Chan writes that "racism in Canada did not spring up overnight with the arrival of Chinese immigrants, but was woven into Canada's evolution."[25] The experiences Chinese immigrants had likely been through by the time they reached Montreal paralleled those of Chinese immigrants in the United States, with certain historical distinctions. Chinese migrations to the United States are generally dated by the California Gold Rush of 1849 and to Canada by the Fraser River Gold Rush of 1858. The Chinese came to both countries to make money and because of conditions of war, political chaos, and general hardship in China, conditions partly induced, as noted earlier, by intrusions from the West. North America was seen by Chinese immigrants, as by the rest of the world, as a place to get rich. For the United States and Canada, both involved in the business of "empire building" (expressed in the United States as "manifest destiny" and in Canada—after 1867—as 'Dominion-building") and constructing transcontinental railways, the scarcity of labor was a major problem, and importing Chinese labor came to be one solution.

That politicians viewed Chinese immigrant workers as temporary commodities, welcome in Canada only as a labor resource, is illustrated in a speech delivered by Canada's first prime minister, John A. Macdonald, in response to protests by white Canadians against Chinese Canadian labor in 1882: "I share very much the feeling of the people . . . against the Mongolian or Chinese population in our country as permanent settlers. I believe they would not be a wholesome element for this country. I believe that it is an alien race in every sense, that would not and could not be expected to assimilate with our Aryan populations. . . . [But] it is a simple question of alternatives—either you must have this labor or you cannot have the railway."[26] With this statement, Canada's highest ranking executive legitimized racism in Canada. The discrimination against Chinese by white Canadian workers who saw Chinese as threatening competition was supported and reinforced.[27] When the railroads were completed, the white Canadian majority immediately moved to get Chinese Canadians out of the country. In 1884, the year before official completion of the railroads, thousands of Chinese Canadian laborers under contract were laid off without notice and left to make their way from points throughout Canada back to the West Coast. Head taxes, payable to customs by each incoming Chinese immigrant, began in 1886, "not coincidentally," Chan notes, "just after the completion of the CPR."[28] Originally set at $10, head taxes increased to $50 in 1896, to $100 in 1900, and to $500 plus the immigrant's possession of $200 in cash in 1904.

From the mid-1880s, Chinese individuals—persecuted in the West or stranded somewhere on the prairies—steadily made their way to eastern Canada, seeking community and a livelihood. An "overland internal" migration pattern traced by Rebecca Aiken for Montreal's Chinese Canadian population in the late nineteenth century shows 76 percent arriving from western Canada and the remaining 24 percent from the eastern United States.[29] By the 1890s, the decade when Sui Sin Far opened her stenographer's office, Quebec province claimed the fourth largest Chinese population in Canada, with the majority in Montreal.[30] This does not necessarily imply significant numbers, and accurate demographics are complicated by the phenomena we have observed with the Eatons: persecuted minorities are often invisible on public records, and even numbers that have been documented are inconsistent.

A monograph by Denise Helly indicates that the entire Montreal Chinese community was composed of only 34 men and 2 women in 1891 but grew to 1,030 over the next ten years.[31] An 1895 article in the *Montreal Daily Star* cites 400 to 500 "Chinamen" listed in the city directory for that year and an additional "floating population" of approximately 100, along with 160 Montreal Chinese laundries and stores.[32] A year later, Dewey's article in the *Montreal Daily Witness* reported the 500 total but cited 300 permanent and 200 transient Chinese Canadians living in Montreal. According to Dewey, the Canadian Pacific Railway brought a load of a hundred Chinese through Montreal every three weeks. They were held in the city until "necessary papers" came through and then were moved to South America, the West Indies, or Europe. These transients stayed from a few days at Windsor Station to several months at officially designated Chinese Montreal hotels and boardinghouses. The best-known boardinghouse was owned by Sang Kee, whose name was often surrounded in Montreal newspapers with hints of smuggling. He had a contract with the Canadian Pacific Railway to "board men."[33]

Whether we refer to Dewey's "birds of passage" or the *Star* reporter's "floating population," one fact becomes quickly apparent: many Chinese about whom Montreal reporters wrote at the turn of the century were not "immigrants" but indentured laborers, sold into bondage for the sake of an income during a period of dire conditions in China. Viewing news photographs of Chinese lined up at Windsor Station and looking stoically into the camera as they are held under guard by Canadian Pacific Railway officials is like looking at prisoners—which is, in effect, what they were. The *Star* portrays one group of Chinese who traveled through Montreal during this period: "Last night a party of 80 Chinamen arrived at the Windsor station from the West. They were all in bond and on their way to Cuba via New York, to work on plantations. Accompanying the party were wives of the two Chinese gentlemen in charge of the party. They were dressed in rich flowing silks. The party proceeded to New York this morning."[34] One reason they were so closely guarded was to prevent escapes across the border into Vermont or New York, where the Chinese Exclusion Act had been in effect since 1882. This act, prohibiting all Chinese except scholars, diplomats, merchants, and their wives from entering the United States, partly accounted for the entrepôt role Montreal played in the laborers' transfer.

As the *Star* article also shows, not all of Montreal's "floating" Chinese were indentured laborers: the "two Chinese gentlemen in charge of the party" and their wives "dressed in rich, flowing silks" were presumably merchants. Brochures distributed by the Canadian Pacific Railway in Hong Kong encouraged potential travelers like Mrs. Ahok to come by steamship to Vancouver, then go overland to the East, and then board a second ship at St. Lawrence Port for Havana. Newspaper articles also reveal a pattern of travel by Chinese American merchants from New York and Boston, who went back for visits to China through Canada and returned to homes in the United States the same way. "Yesterday five Chinamen reached the city over the Canadian Pacific Railway from Vancouver, and Mr. Ibbotson was seeing them safely on their way to New York and Boston," the *Montreal Daily Witness* reported on 8 May 1891. "They had been home, and had a good time; and now were coming back to add to their already large fortunes. For these were wealthy merchants who had been 'taking in' China as the successful Colonial Englishman takes in the Old Country."

Such articles make it clear that the route across the continent by Canadian rail was regularly enjoyed by both Canadian and American Chinese with the means to travel for pleasure, proving that the individuals of Chinese descent whom Sui Sin Far encountered in Montreal were more diversified than the categories of either "immigrant merchants" or "indentured laborers" would suggest. Mr. Ibbotson's presence indicates that all travelers of Chinese descent—impoverished or wealthy, indentured or merchants—had in common, if they crossed ports of entry, the legal necessity of traveling in bond. In Montreal such travelers came in at Windsor Station, a few blocks from the heart of the business district and "Miss Edith's" office. In the 1880s and 1890s there were few days passersby could not find them there, waiting for "necessary papers," and they attracted frequent attention from local reporters. As we have seen, Sui Sin Far would have been one of these. "The local papers patronize me and give me a number of assignments, including most of the local Chinese reporting," she recalled about this time in her life. "I meet many Chinese persons, and when they get into trouble am often called upon to fight their battles in the papers" (*Leaves,* 128). It is important to establish what some of those "battles" might have been.

The peak of Sui Sin Far's professional life in Montreal, 1888–97, was also the decade of the "much vexed Chinese question," a phrase that appeared as a recurring refrain in news articles, editorials, and letters to editors during this period. Aiken suggests that because the Chinese were only one of many immigrant groups in Montreal and a small percentage of the city's total population, the "racist climate" was less severe in Montreal than in the West.[35] Local news coverage, however, illustrates increasing racist hostility toward the Chinese Montrealers on the part of both the English and the French. In 1894 the major paper for Montreal's French populations, *Le Presse,* printed "The Chinese Invasion: A Cry of Alarm and Warning," predicting "serious labor troubles if the current trend toward Chinese migration continues" and urging the Canadian government to act "in the interests of Canadian white men." Letters to the editor picked up the "cry" by noting the "alarming increase" of Chinese people in Montreal and the dangers they were said to introduce with their "innate passion for gambling" and for opium, the "curse of the Chinese race everywhere."[36] In April 1896 the city council passed both laundry and water taxes, tactics of legislative discrimination also used in cities in the United States (e.g., San Francisco) to drive Chinese Americans, who frequently went into laundry work as one of few occupations in which they were allowed, out of business. Such captions as "Abusing the Chinee," "How Some White Christians Treat Them," "Rotten Eggs and Stones" recall the Eaton children's "pitched battles" of earlier years.

Accompanying the sinophobic trends of the era were newspaper scare stories of the vices that Chinese immigrants imported, vices used by the media to rationalize the maltreatment of Chinese Canadians. "The Chinese Gambling Case" reported that Fong Mong King, Quin Yick, and Yam Yick were "committed to the Court of Queen's Bench for selling lottery tickets" and that another eighteen Chinese were charged with "frequenting a gambling room."[37] "Three Chinamen Captured" took *Montreal Daily Witness* readers to the nearby U.S. border, where the "Chinamen" in question had been found in Vermont "just this side of the Canadian line . . . trying to *steal* their way to New York City."[38] A dispatch from the *London Standard* described a rebellion on the borders of Kiang Su and Shantung in which "French missions have been destroyed and converts scattered," a "German missionary . . . killed," and "an American or British missionary woman . . . abducted."[39]

Such stories created an international image of the fiendish nature of Chinese behavior, a message brought closer to home with news from Vancouver that a Chinese houseboy had revolted and murdered the white family with whom he lived.[40] On the other hand, some non-Chinese Montrealers were sympathetic with their new neighbors, and missionaries in particular wrote in defense of their Chinese Canadian congregations. A petition asking the city council to repeal the water tax was signed by forty-two members of the European Montreal community.[41] Highlighting the hypocrisy of damning gambling when Chinese Canadians did it was a letter describing Montreal poker tables occupied by gamblers who were white.[42] In response to the "opium danger," a Montreal Chinese merchant reminded newspaper readers that "the English are responsible for it and that it was they who in their greed for gain first introduced it into China."[43]

China and Chinese Canadians were obviously part of Montreal's daily news in Sui Sin Far's era. The views represented, consistent in their prejudice against the Chinese and in the collisions between her mother's and father's people, suggest what she would be ingesting with her tea and papers each morning. They filled the streets she walked, the air she breathed, the words that formed her assumptions. The growth of a Chinese Canadian community in Montreal through the 1880s and 1890s would provide rich source materials for any reporter inclined to do battle, and for a woman of Chinese descent, these materials would offer a depth far beyond professional interest. How did Sui Sin Far define her position and that of her family relative to immigrants from her mother's homeland? How did she define her stance as a journalist writing about them? Her early journalism offers some clues.

The Montreal Journalism

Repeating a pattern from childhood, Sui Sin Far continued to fight the battles of Chinese North American immigrants as an adult, but she moved the site of her struggle from the streets to the papers. Her Montreal journalism is important on more than one level. Practically, it provided the beginning writer with a profession and a partial means of support. It also offered her a comparatively neutral excuse for entering the Chinese community: as a reporter, she was collecting materials for stories. Journalism provided an entrée for Sui Sin Far, allowing her to initiate acquaintance with the culture of the mother's side of her ancestry, which she was eager to know. In terms of her career, it opened doors to a Chinese subject matter that was growing in popularity with publishers and their readers as the century reached its conclusion and North America's interest in "brown people" increased, step-by-step with the annexation of Hawaii and the Philippine and Spanish-American wars. By doing "Chinese reporting," Sui Sin Far stepped into a new context, one in which she would locate her fiction's primary subject matter and begin to establish her literary voice.

Trying to identify exactly which journalistic pieces are hers, however, again reminds one of the spaces stretching between the known facts of Sui Sin Far's life. The roots of the writer's career as a journalist can be set at 1883, when she went to work at the *Montreal Daily Star* as a typesetter. For a "gentlewoman" of this era, the move into journalism at any level would have been daring and of questionable social propriety. In her study of nineteenth-century Canadian newswomen, Susan Crean writes, "Journalism wasn't at all a suitable occupation for a gently reared young lady, working in a smoky office full of shirt-sleeved men, spittoons, and smutty jokes. It was quite as improper as going on the stage."[44] Sui Sin Far was not, of course, gently reared in any conventional sense, and in eastern Canada the "new media" (Crean's term) provided the writer with precedents. There were Sara Jeanette Duncan, Gaetane de Montreuil, E. Cora Hind, and Kathleen Blake Coleman, all born in the decade of confederation and described by Crean as "rebels and adventurers: independent, curious and fired with ambition to act on a wider stage than the one home and custom had allotted them."[45] Beginning with the woman's page of the *Toronto Mail* in the 1880s, Coleman—an Irish immigrant nicknamed "Kit"—would become a correspondent to Cuba during the Spanish-American War. Duncan—popularly known as "Redney"—violated "taboos no woman had yet defied" in 1884 by going to the New Orleans World Fair as a correspondent for the *Toronto Globe*. Crean notes that the Canadian Pacific Railway refused newswomen courtesy passes given as a matter of course to newsmen. That Duncan was "barred from participating in many important events," partly "because she was unmarried," is another disadvantage she shared with Sui Sin Far.[46] The two journalists might have been acquainted, since in 1888 Duncan began writing a column for the *Montreal Daily Star.*

Locating Sui Sin Far's journalism in Montreal papers is particularly difficult because most reporters, especially if they were unknown, were not given a byline. Nineteenth-century editors' standard practice of refusing writers credit for stories is documented in a letter by one of Sui Sin Far's contemporaries, who wrote that she sent four articles to a Canadian "literary weekly," all which the weekly printed without naming or paying the author. The editor's retort was that publication alone was "a compliment to the writer."[47] Because of Sui Sin Far's particular style and empathy with Chinese Canadians, however, it is possible to build a case for her authorship of particular articles. In doing this, my first criterion is that the subject matter be Chinese populations in eastern Canada and that the piece fight their battles in some fashion. My second criterion is the presence of "literary elements" in the article: figurative language, scenic presentation, character development, and irony. A third criterion is a noticeably sympathetic attitude toward Chinese Canadians, one that often reverses the racist assumptions usual among reporters who were Sui Sin Far's contemporaries.

Going by these criteria, I suspect Sui Sin Far was the author of an article appearing in the *Montreal Daily Witness* on 15 March 1890 entitled "In the Land of the Free." The piece is brief and epigrammatic, with the abstract ideal of "free" played off ironically against the reality of the situation in Canada:

> "Goon" was a Chinaman from New York, desirous of taking up his residence in Montreal. He was sent through in bond like a box of traps, and the moment he touched the free soil of Canada he was pounced upon by Customs officer, A. Pare, who demanded in the name of the Queen of this marvelously free country, $50 or his immediate departure from the country. "Goon" gave the officer to understand that if he took him to Hop Sing, 1316 Notre Dame Street, that generous compatriot would put up the amount and, sure enough, Hop Sing did, and "Goon" is now "washee-washee" as happy as a King.

Sympathy for Goon emerges through the narrative voice, which juxtaposes traveling "in bond" against the "free soil of Canada," the rhetoric "of this marvelously free country" against the reality discovered by one Chinese immigrant. The piece's figurative language—the simile "like a box of traps," connoting Goon's reduction to thingness, and the verb "pounced," implying that A. Pare is a predator—carries ironic commentary on Montreal's treatment of Chinese immigrants. The contrast between Goon's encounter with the customs officer and his interaction with Hop Sing, his countryman, reinforces the irony. The comparison of Goon to a "King" in the last line counterpoints with the "Queen," in whose name A. Pare extracted the fifty dollars. The narrator seems to be asking if anyone limited to "washee-washee"—popular slang for doing whites' laundry, labor to which Chinese immigrants were often confined—can really be this happy. Beneath the level of informational news, this article resounds with mockery for the incongruity between Canada's professed freedom and its practice. Both style and message are startlingly similar to Sui Sin Far's short story "In the Land of the Free," which would be published almost two decades later in the *Independent*. [48]

A similar piece, "The Ching Song Episode: The Crazy Chinaman Regains His Senses and Stays in Canada," appeared on 17 April 1890 in the *Montreal Daily Witness:*

> Ching Song is free once more. He had a narrow escape. He was just on the eve of being declared insane. But he suddenly ceased to talk about desiring to go to "China or heaven," and expressed his intention of becoming a good Canadian citizen and engaging prosaically in "washee-washee." So, after being a few days in gaol for safety, Ching Song was liberated, and at once went to pay his respect to the C.P.R. officials, who had suffered greatly on his account last week, not knowing what to do with him. "Tom Lee" came along and handed Ching Sing's $153 to Mr. McNicoll, out of which the Custom's people will have to get $50

before they allow the foreign gentleman to wash as much as a ten cent handkerchief in the Queen's Dominions.

The motifs, similar to those in the former piece, again suggest Sui Sin Far's authorship. Such phrases as "free once more," "narrow escape," and "liberated" are juxtaposed against "just on the eve of being declared insane" and the oxymoronic "a few days in gaol for safety," creating a vision of freedom as a "good Canadian citizen" that is overshadowed by the threat of extortion and imprisonment Ching Song faces. The recurring play on the "washee-washee" stereotype, the refusal by "the Queen's Dominion" to allow Ching Song "to wash as much as a ten cent handkerchief" unless he pays fifty dollars, and Ching Song's concern for C.P.R. officials "who had suffered greatly on his account" when it is these very officials who had caused him to suffer suggest a second level of meaning. The controlling irony in this piece, however, is in its oppositions of "craziness" and "sanity," the former equated with a desire "to go to 'China or heaven,'" the latter with "becoming a good Canadian citizen." Unlike the usual media treatment, this reporter's account suggests that this should be reversed.

Each of these pieces is brief, barely constituting a long newspaper paragraph, but in the midst of factual journalistic pieces, each reads like a miniature short story, in which are compressed the components of fiction. Relatively bold in their satiric challenge to racial stereotypes, these pieces present the Chinese as human, with perhaps more sense than the whites. Goon and Ching Song are betrayed by the rhetoric of "freedom," just as the couple in Sui Sin Far's "Fatal Tug of War" are betrayed by the rhetoric of happy endings in marriage. The styles in which the writer of each piece reveals these betrayals are noticeably similar.

Another unsigned newspaper article to come out during the years when Sui Sin Far was free-lancing from her Montreal office more directly addresses a subject we know was central to her life and sense of identity: the children of Chinese-English parentage whom society labeled "Eurasians." Entitled "Half-Chinese Children: Those of American Mothers and Chinese Fathers," the article appeared in the *Montreal Daily Star* on 20 April 1895 and, according to the reporter, was based on an interview with "an American lady, the wife of a Chinese merchant, now of this City, but formerly residing in the United States of America." Both content and style suggest Sui Sin Far was the reporter. The piece begins by describing numerous Chinese-English unions in Boston and New York that resulted in children "who for the most part live in the Chinatown of the Cities," where "the white people with whom they come in contact that is, the lower classes, jibe and jeer at the poor little things continually, and their pure and unadulterated Chinese cousins look down on them as being neither Chinese nor white." The mothers of these children were described sometimes as "respectable women" but more often as "women whose characters would not stand much investigation." The fathers were described "as a rule, very kind and good to their offspring" but often having "left behind them wives in their own country," which raises questions of the American children's "legitimacy." Consequently, "the conditions under which the American-Chinese child is 'dragged up'" are, according to the reporter, "not favorable."

The language and attitudes recall the ambiguous racial traits that in "Leaves" Sui Sin Far claimed strangers saw in the faces of her siblings and her: "There is occasionally to be seen a half Chinese child with bright complexion and fair hair, and these combined with a straight nose, small mouth and wide eyes might easily deceive a stranger, but a person who has been informed of the child's parentage, notices at once a peculiar cast about the face. . . . It is indescribable but it is there" (3). The last lines voice racial constructs of an era strongly influenced by Darwinian notions that blood would always "tell" and would raise the ever-present threat to those ethnic minorities that, like Sui Sin Far and her siblings, are "invisible" and attempt to "pass": discovery is always imminent. In the news story, Eurasian children's "peculiar cast" calls forth the "mocking cries of 'Chinese' 'Chinese'" and gives rise to street fights paralleling those Sui Sin Far describes in "Leaves." One little boy, for example, was first mobbed by "his tormentors" and then "comforted with a thrashing" by his father when he got home.

More echoes of Sui Sin Far's remembered experience are found in the news story's depiction of children who "appear to be more fortunate"—usually "sons and daughters of wealthy and perhaps Christian Chinamen who live in more respectable parts of the city than Chinatown." According to the reporter, "a certain class of people" patronized these "interesting" children. The children's feelings about these relationships are illustrated in a dialogue between a Eurasian child "who is not susceptible to such petting" and her mother:

"Mamma, I'm not going to see Mrs. G—— today."

"Why not?" said the mother, "she is always so kind to you and gives you more toys than you know what to do with."

"Yes," said the child, "but I don't care for the toys. It is just because I'm Chinese that she likes to have me there. When I'm in her parlor she whispers to some people about me, and then they try to make me talk and pick up all that I say, and I hear them whisper 'her father's a Chinese' 'Did you know' 'Isn't it curious' and they examine me from head to toe as if I was a wild animal—and just because father is a Chinese. I'd rather be dead than a 'show.'"

This passage bears likeness to several in "Leaves";[49] it also appears, with only minor changes, as a scene in "Sweet Sin," a short story Sui Sin Far would publish in 1898.[50] In "Sweet Sin," the title character, "the child of a Chinese merchant and his American wife," has had a street fight in response to the children's calling her "Chinese! Chinese!" (223). Her mother laments after the fight that Sweet Sin is "not fit to be seen" at "Mrs. Goodwin's party tonight":

> "I'm glad," answered Sweet Sin. "I don't want to go."
>
> "Why not?" queried the mother. "I'm surprised, she is so kind to you."
>
> "I do not think so," replied Sweet Sin, "and I don't want her toys and candies. It's just because I'm half Chinese and a sort of curiosity that she likes to have me there. When I'm in her parlor, she examines me from head to toe as if I were a wild animal—I'd rather be killed than be a show." (224)

A clue to the origin of both these pieces may be found in "Leaves," where Sui Sin Far recalls a visit to her office by "a Chinese scholar," the graduate of "an American College," who has "an American wife and several children": "I am very much interested in these children, and when I meet them my heart throbs in sympathetic tune with the tales they relate of their experiences as Eurasians. 'Why did papa and mamma born us?' asks one. 'Why?' " (128). Only the quotation marks offer guidance to where the voice of these children leaves off and Sui Sin Far's voice begins—albeit reversing the roles of "American" mother and "Chinese" father and setting the anecdote not in Montreal but in New York. For children of Chinese-white parentage, the reporter implies, which side of the U.S.-Canadian border one lives on makes little difference.

Finally, the news piece in which Sui Sin Far speaks most explicitly as a champion for the Chinese in Canada appears in a letter to the editor of the *Montreal Daily Star* on 21 September 1896. Captioned "A Plea for the Chinaman: A Correspondent's Argument in His Favor," the letter is signed simply "E.E." The closest that the writer comes to identifying herself as Chinese in this piece is with words that disguise as much as they reveal: "It needs a Chinaman to stand up for a Chinaman." The letter begins by asserting, "Every just person . . . must feel his or her sense of justice outraged by the attacks which are being made by public men upon the Chinese who come to this country." The "attacks" against which she defends the Chinese in Canada and—as the letter proceeds—throughout North America are clarified by an article in the *Montreal Daily Witness* on 30 July of that same year: "A monster petition to the Federal Government for the further restriction of Chinese immigrants to Canada is being circulated. The petition will contain 10,000 names when it is sent to Ottawa. The petition recites that Chinese labor is driving out the white working-man, that the U.S. realizing this, has excluded the Mongolian coolies, and that Canada should also adapt measures to keep them out. It urges that a tax of $500 be levied upon each Chinaman entering the Dominion."

The target of E.E.'s letter to the *Star* is a Mr. Maxwell, the representative of a commission from British Columbia that the writer charges with "persecuting" the "defenceless": "It makes one's cheeks burn to read about men of high office standing up and abusing a lot of poor foreigners. . . ." By citing personal experiences with the Chinese, the writer authenticates her authority to speak as she does and then cuts through stereotypes with a catalogue of diversity: "I speak from experience, because I know the Chinaman in all characters, merchants, laundrymen, laborers, servants, smugglers and smuggled, also as Sunday School scholars and gamblers. They have faults, but they also have virtues."

After defining the major issue—"It is proposed to impose a tax of five hundred dollars upon every Chinaman coming into the Dominion of Canada"— E.E. lays out the charges the commission makes against the Chinese, and one by one she refutes them. To the charge that the Chinese "work cheap," she reminds her readers of the contributions that the Chinese have made to Canada: "helping to build our railways, mine our ores and in various branches of agriculture and manufacturing. . . . act[ing] as an incentive to [other workers] to be industrious and honest." To the charge that the Chinese are "immoral"—in Maxwell's words, "the accumulated filth of Chinese gaols and dens of vice and crime"—she responds in the voice of a hometown aunt defending her nephews: "They are mostly steady, healthy country boys from the Canton district. . . . They have come furnished with a modest sum of money and the hope of adding therein through honest labor." She adds that she cannot recall one ever "being accused of saying or doing that which was immoral. . . ." Illustrating her point from personal experience, she describes a visit to New York's Chinatown "in the spring of this year," contrasting the warnings she received "that Chinatown was a dangerously wicked place," where "if I went in . . . alone I would never come out alive or sound in mind or body," with her reception "by the Chinese there with the greatest kindness and courtesy." Finally, she points up the difference in manners that cause people like Maxwell to misinterpret the Chinese's "quiet dignity" to mean that they are "docile and easily managed." In place of physical violence, Chinese have been trained, she explains, to "treat the rude with silent contempt."

The writer of this letter thus turns the tables on those who accuse Chinese immigrants of being "immoral," demonstrating the immorality of the accusers. In the same strokes with which E.E. argues against the commission's singling out Chinese immigrants for a head tax, she notes the ethnocentric hypocrisy by which Western nations blame the Chinese and ignore their own role in the dynamics of history. To the "sojourner" charge that "[the Chinaman] comes here to make money and with the intention of returning sooner or later," she replies, "In that he follows the example met him by the westerners . . . the ports of China are full of foreign, private adventurers. After they have made their piles, they will return to their homes—which are not in China." Against the pejorative "heathens," she sets the practices of Christian missions: "the Chinaman may be willing to attend Sunday School and learn all that you can teach him, but . . . it never enters his head to convert you to his way of thinking." The letter reverses the notion that westerners have a monopoly on civilization with the assertion, "There are signs that in the future we in this country may attain to the high degree of civilization which the Chinese have reached, but for the present we are far away behind them in that respect." In conclusion, the writer posits racism as the heart of Mr. Maxwell's petition: "I believe that the real reason for the prejudice against the Chinese . . . is that they are not considered good-looking by white men; that is . . . according to a Canadian or American standard of looks . . . that the Chinese do not please our artistic taste is really at the root of all the evil . . . and from it spring the other objections to the Chinese." By observing that "this is not a woman's reason, it's a man's," she relates racism to gender. The letter caps its argument with the humanistic vision that will be repeated throughout Sui Sin Far's short fiction: "What does it matter whether a man be a Chinaman, an Irishman, an Englishman or an American. Individualism is more than nationality. . . ."

The Early Chinese Fiction

To my knowledge, Sui Sin Far's first creative writing about the Chinese consists of six short stories and one essay, all written in Montreal and published in little magazines in the United States between 1896 and 1898. That Sui Sin Far's journalistic work was recognized in the Chinese North American community beyond Montreal is suggested by a reference in "Leaves," which could be a response to the 1896 letter just discussed: "My heart leaps for joy when I read one day an article signed by a New York Chinese in which he declares 'The Chinese in America owe a debt of everlasting gratitude to Sui Sin Far for the bold stand she has taken in their defense' " (129). On the other hand, the writer's listing in *Lovell's* continued to be Miss Edith Eaton until 1897, and we may assume that she continued to protect her "British Canadian" family against their Chinese identity's becoming public. In the eight years since her first *Dominion Illustrated* story was published, however, certain changes took place in Sui Sin Far's family life that must have been significant for her vocation as a writer. Primary was a reduction in household size, a change that presumably allowed Sui Sin Far's role as "second mother" to evolve to "maiden aunt" and freed time and space for her to write.

In 1896, the year that Sui Sin Far visited New York's Chinatown, she published five pieces of Chinese fiction: "The Gamblers," "Ku Yum," "The Story of Iso," "A Love Story of the Orient," and "A Chinese Feud." The first appeared in February in the *Fly Leaf,* a little magazine founded and published in New York by Sui Sin Far's brother-in-law Walter Blackburn Harte. Advertising itself as "A Pamphlet Periodical of the New—the New Man, New Woman, New Ideas, Whimsies and Things," the *Fly Leaf* prided itself on enlisting "the interests and sympathies of our own generation—say those born sometime in the sixties and since" and in stressing democracy over "snobocracy" as seen to be practiced by Mrs. Humphrey Ward (27). Sui Sin Far's third and fourth stories appeared in August and October in the *Lotus,* published out of Kansas City but edited in New York, also by Harte. Her second and fifth stories appeared in June and November in *Land of Sunshine,* a magazine edited by Charles Lummis from southern California. The essay "The Chinese Woman in America" and the short story "Sweet Sin" were also published in *Land of Sunshine,* in January 1897 and April 1898, respectively.[51]

To get a sense of the kind of networks by which the manuscripts of an unknown writer from eastern Canada might travel to southern California, we can look at an ad for *Land of Sunshine: A Magazine of California and the Southwest* that appeared in the same issue of the *Fly Leaf* in which Sui Sin Far's first story, "The Gamblers," was published. That the Eaton sisters were accustomed to reading ads from the United States in Montreal papers is supported by Sui Sin Far's recollection that her sister May found a job in a San Francisco photography studio through a Montreal paper (*Globe*). The novel *Marion* portrays the Eaton sisters as skillful at checking daily ads for job and publishing possibilities. James Doyle has conjectured that Sui Sin Far's first contact with *Land of Sunshine* came through her initial exposure in Harte's journals, the *Fly Leaf* and *Lotus*. If she queried *Land of Sunshine* after reading the ad, this would certainly be plausible.

The ad itself tells something about the magazine in which Sui Sin Far would get her most reliable start and about its editor Charles Lummis, who would publish ten of her stories and become her lifetime correspondent: "Lavishly Illustrated. Monthly, $1.00 a year. No Mars, no Africa, no Napoleon. Just the best Western literature."[52] Almost as ambiguous a figure as Sui Sin Far herself, Lummis migrated from the East Coast to the West Coast in the 1880s and in January 1894 was offered the editorship of *Land of Sunshine,* a magazine founded by the Los Angeles Chamber of Commerce to promote southern California real estate. More interested in literature than in advertising and not wanting the image of a "boom periodical," Lummis obtained editorial license and set out, in the words of Edwin R. Bingham, "to represent the West from a literary and cultural standpoint," without losing the magazine's "promotional objective."[53] Lummis's statement of purpose was both regional and nationalistic: the journal would be "exclusively Western in text, unswervingly American in spirit. . . ."[54] His literary goal of "a short story in each issue" posed problems because *Land of Sunshine* paid low rates and had trouble attracting writers of qualilty—on the other hand, Lummis insisted on "standards." Surmounting this difficulty at first by taking various pseudonyms and doing most of the writing himself, Lummis soon formed the Land of Sunshine League, made up of such names as Charlotte Perkins Gilman, Charles Warren Stoddard, and Joaquin Miller, who agreed to contribute stories in return for stocks in the company. Persuaded by Lummis that only by uniting could "the West . . . match the East in the excellence of its literary product," these known writers formed one part of *Land of Sunshine*'s contributors.[55] Unknown "writers of promise," whom Lummis took pride in encouraging, made up the other part. He was the first, for example, to print Mary Austin, who appeared in the magazine the same years Sui Sin Far did.

That the *Land of Sunshine* ad appeared in the *Fly Leaf,* an eastern journal, indicates Lummis, in his search for "the best Western literature," did not require his writers to live in the West. Bingham perceives *Land of Sunshine*'s "common denominator" to be that "all [stories] dealt with western themes" and were set in California or the Southwest.[56] This may explain why, even though there is no evidence that Sui Sin Far herself had ever been West before 1898, her early *Land of Sunshine* pieces are set in California. Lummis's attraction to her was undoubtedly also connected with his interest in "exotic ethnics," and Bingham argues that it was Sui Sin Far's concern with the "Oriental in the West" that qualified her as a *Land of Sunshine* contributor.[57] Although Indian and Mexican American populations of the Southwest were the "ethnics" Lummis was mainly interested in (an irony when one considers that most of the land exploited by the firm that he worked for came from land "grabbed" from these two groups), as Los Angeles's Chinatown grew along with Chinese immigrant issues, Lummis began to tap local writers for articles on Chinese immigrant themes.

In 1894 *Land of Sunshine* published "The Chinese in Los Angeles," an article by Ng Poon Chew, a San Francisco Christian newspaper editor, citing "between three and four thousand of these strange, little brown men residing in this city and vicinity." In 1895 a photo of a young child captioned "A Chinese Maiden" occupied a full page of the magazine under the heading "Southwestern Types." In 1896, the same year that Sui Sin Far's stories began in *Land of Sunshine,* "Only John" presented Los Angeles's Chinatown as "a Mecca of tourists," and "Some Little Heathens" journalistically toured the "unsightly huts, homes of an alien people" in the "China fish-town" of Monterey. Two of these pieces focused on gambling and opium, and all highlighted white missionary activity among Chinese Americans in California.[58]

Though popularly seen as a crusader against imperialism and a champion of racial tolerance, Lummis did not carry this stand to the point of promoting social or political equality for Chinese Americans in the United States. In 1901 he warned of "the danger that the Exclusion Act, now about to expire, may not be renewed," and he supported popular racist stereotypes about the Chinese as "non-assimilable," an opinion most dramatically illustrated when he compared the United States to a cider mill and Chinese immigrants to potatoes, adding, "But we in the U. S. are looking for something that can be made into cider." Lummis expressed his own belief in assimilation quite overtly when he claimed that the United States "cannot afford a class of non-assimilable aliens. . . ."[59]

Another way in which Sui Sin Far's writing would have fit the needs of Lummis's journal was the *Land of Sunshine*'s emphasis on local color. First popularized in California by Bret Harte in the 1850s and carried on by such writers as Mark Twain and Frank Norris, local color was also popular at the turn of the century among women writers, including Mary Austin, Mary Wilkins Freeman, and Sarah Orne Jewett in the United States and Susanna Moodie in Canada. With its emphasis on local settings and dialects and characters often modeled on immigrant populations, local color was part of the effort to define national literatures on both sides of the border. According to David Arnason, the form emerged in Canada in response to the "new nationalism" after confederation, and it sacrificed considerations of plot in favor of examining "some facet of the Canadian character, such as "French" or "Métis."[60] In creating Chinese and Chinese North American characters, Sui Sin Far was using a more recent ethnic population as material for an already established mode of fiction. Her ability to translate "local color" into marketable forms has been demonstrated in the *Dominion Illustrated* stories. Not surprisingly, Lummis praised her stories for their "excellent coloring."[61]

It is important to note, however, that Sui Sin Far was not simply playing the markets; the earliest stories show what would later become her hallmarks: sensitivity to character, skill with irony, and commitment to political themes. It might have been such touches that Walter Blackburn Harte had in mind when he perceived this major difference between Bret Harte's work and hers: Harte's "sketches" were "too colored by caricature to hold the touch of psychological reality," while "it is in this particular matter of insight that Sui Seen Far excels. . . ."[62] With "The Story of Iso," "A Love Story of the Orient," "Ku Yum," "A Chinese Feud," and "Sweet Sin," Sui Sin Far began to probe issues of identity, gender relations, and filial piety, which would be continuing motifs in her fiction. All deal with young Chinese or Chinese American female characters who face choices between following the mandates of tradition or pursuing their individual destinies. The relationship between females and males (as in the *Dominion Illustrated* stories) is the microcosm within which character conflicts are examined. Another motif these stories introduce—significant to Chinese immigrants in general and to Sui Sin Far's life in the 1890s in particular—is the division of families. Plots imitate the political scene of the times, with families divided by geography, legislation, or ideology, and structures that often move with the rhythms of immigration: from China to California, from California to China, and back again.

The leading female characters in these stories demonstrate the impossibility, in their circumstances as in Sui Sin Far's own, of separating issues of identity from those of gender or filial piety. "The Story of Iso," its beginning set in China and narrated by the old man Tei Wang, illustrates the consequences that can befall a woman who defies cultural convention. In open disdain of the man her family chooses for her, Iso follows her own wishes instead. Going "across the sea" with "some 'red-headed people,' "[63] she is "everlastingly disgraced," with "no more proposals of marriage," and dies "in a strange land, far away from China—the country which heaven loves." Iso is allegorized as "the woman who talks too much," and her own will takes precedence over social laws governing her sex and obedience to her family, making her an outcast even after death (119).

By contrast, the title character of "Ku Yum" obeys the rules laid out for her, crossing the Pacific Ocean from China with her maid A-Toy to marry Tie Sung, "who was living in San Francisco and had become wealthy" (29). The night before leaving, however, Ku Yum sits in her room and weeps because she overhears a conversation between her parents, who reveal that Tie Sung actually believes she looks like the photo her family sent of A-Toy, described as "beautiful," while Ku Yum is "plain." Because she feels humiliated, Ku Yum asks her maid on the ship going over, "How would you like to take my place, dress in my clothes and be Tie Sung's bride?" (30). A-Toy agrees and marries Tie Sung, while Ku Yum masquerades as A-Toy's maid—causing roles to reverse as A-Toy becomes Ku Yum's mistress. When A-Toy begins to abuse her and Ku Yum realizes that the disguise has replaced reality and cannot be reversed, she makes the choice to jump off a balcony to her death. Her body is sent back to China as that of A-Toy, the maid. The mother recognizes her daughter by her "Golden Lily feet,"[64] but the father will not allow her to claim the body, saying "I will not be disgraced." Hence, "Ku Yum was buried among the slaves," and, in a mythical prose that unites Ku Yum's mother with mother figures from classical literature—La Llorona, Rachael, Hecuba—her mother "stood afar off and wept" (31).

Iso and Ku Yum represent two kinds of women: she who defies and she who obeys. Neither achieves happy endings, but the narrator implies that Iso has more fun. Ku Yum tries to follow the rules for her sex, maintain filial piety, and subordinate her personal inclinations; the result is loss of identity, youthful death, and an ironic silencing of her real name for eternity. It is important to remember that in the Chinese language "Ku Yum" is not a name at all but a description, approximating a miserable person or someone in need of help—which in traditional China was virtually synonymous with a daughter: "She's Ku Yum, she's a girl, she's supposed to be miserable."[65] That Sui Sin Far uses this description as a proper noun—it is the most common name for Chinese women and girls in her fiction—may indicate her feelings about what the plight of Chinese women has traditionally been. "A lady reporter" had written in a news article about Chinese immigrant women in Montreal several years earlier, "I looked around the four walls within which her life is spent and I wondered how it was she could laugh and be merry. Is it custom or nature that makes her contented with a life that to the daughters of Europe and America seems worse than death? Obedience, never-failing obedience, is the characteristic of the Chinese woman."[66] The reporter, as I later discuss, was probably Sui Sin Far.

"A Love Story of the Orient" and "A Chinese Feud" depict love stories that basically adapt familiar romantic plots from Western literature to the customs of Chinese marriages. In a Romeo and Juliet tale that turns on surprises, deceit, and misinformation, "A Love Story of the Orient" presents two young people who meet and fall in love independent of family arrangements and without parental knowledge. When the parents of each arrange a betrothal, which turns out to be with each other, the man is told the identity of his intended, but the woman—who again bears the name of Ku Yum—is not. When she protests to her lover that she is being forced to marry another, he, planning to surprise her, tells her to obey her parents. Believing that he no longer loves her, the woman commits suicide, and the man enters a monastery. Formulaic as this tale is, the fact that Ku Yum alone is denied information to which all others in the story have access affirms her invisible—or "miserable"—status. Look at the results of too much "obedience," the story's narrator seems to say. This Ku Yum's death reinforces the silencing of her questions in life.

Fantze and Wong On, the star-crossed lovers of "A Chinese Feud," are the first explicitly identifiable Chinese Americans in Sui Sin Far's stories. She is "American born," and he has "been brought to the States when but nine years of age." They become "engaged just like ordinary Americans who pledge themselves to marry the one (they believe at the time) they love best" (236). This time the obstacle is not marriage customs but a tribal feud between the Sam Yups (Fantze's family) and the See Yups (Wong On's) so severe that it threatens death if they are seen together. One night as Wong On walks to his beloved's home, dreaming of "a boy baby with a round shaven head and Fantze's eyes," there comes "a swish," and "long, skinny arms threw the bleeding body [of Wong On] against the door, on the other side of which sat Fantze dreaming of someone" (237). In the world of imagination—designated here as the "To-Come"[67]—Fantze and Wong On are together. In the external world, society gets in the way. By cutting off the union of a young Chinese American couple and showing that the only children they will ever have are in dreams, Sui Sin Far implies the high cost of perpetuating history's violent and destructive conventions.

"Sweet Sin" is the most unfinished in form of this period's short stories; it skips between time and space without clear transitions and confuses the voices of the narrator and the main character. With "Sweet Sin" comes Sui Sin Far's first fictional treatment of race and her first Eurasian protagonist. As the "child of a Chinese merchant and his American wife" (223), Sweet Sin has something in common with the figures in "Half-Chinese Children," but her home is farther west, in the "California sunshine and the balmy freshness of Pacific breezes" (225). At seventeen, Sweet Sin breaks an engagement with a man named Dick Farrell, offering rationale similar to what Sui Sin Far offers for the Eurasian woman who broke her engagement with a white man in "Leaves":

> "I must leave you now, as I have something to do for father. Dick, do you remember once asking me if my father was a Chinaman; and when I replied yes, you said, 'Doesn't your flesh creep all over when you go near him?' You were about twelve then and I ten."
>
> "I cannot recall things I said so long ago," replied the young fellow, flushing up.
>
> "No! Well, you see this is the day when I remember—the day when you forget." (225)

Subsequently, Sweet Sin's mother dies, and her father prepares to return to China, partially to find "amongst his cousins in China" a husband for his daughter, who was "of a full marriageable age" (225). The night before they are scheduled to sail, Sweet Sin commits suicide and leaves her father a letter, the last paragraph of which evokes the dilemma I perceive to be at the core of Sui Sin Far's own rejection of marriage: "Father, I cannot marry a Chinaman, as you wish, because my heart belongs to an American—an American who loves me and wishes to make me his wife. But, Father, though I cannot marry a Chinaman, who would despise me for being an American, I will not marry an American, for the Americans have made me feel so that I will save the children of the man I love from being called 'Chinese! Chinese!' " (226).[68]

Bingham suggests that Sui Sin Far's stories in *Land of Sunshine* were "translations into print of the writer's suffering and frustration."[69] I suggest instead that they were translations of hope, in the sense that the suicides in all stories open a door labeled "Exit" for women who are otherwise trapped. Consistent with their author's "bird on the wing" philosophy, by choosing death over the options society gives them, these characters find choices over which society has no control; furthermore, they command an attention that was absent in their lives. In this context Dale Bauer's translation of Mikhail Bakhtin's dialogic into feminist criticism is significant: "Through Bakhtin's principle of the dialogization of the novel, we can interpret the silenced or suicidal voice of female characters compelling a dialogue with those others who would prefer to think they do not exist."[70]

These stories illustrate Sui Sin Far's early experiments with the marriage theme in Chinese and Chinese American culture. The message that emerges is parallel to that in the *Dominion Illustrated* stories for English and French Canadian romances: relations between the sexes, arranged or self-determined, Chinese or white, are doomed to disaster. These stories suggest three other factors that contribute to splits in Chinese immigrant families: geography, legislation, and ideology. The first is built into the act of immigration itself. When Iso and Ku Yum sail to North America, they leave families in China; when Wong On's father returns to China, he leaves a son in the United States. The second is caused by the passage of laws. The Chinese Exclusion Act prevented all women except the wives of merchants from entering the United States; the Canadian head tax of five hundred dollars made entry of entire families possible for only the wealthy. Because such issues are addressed in these stories only indirectly, reader awareness of their influence largely depends on external knowledge.

The third factor is even more subtle and focuses on acculturation, or "division" from the Chinese culture, by adopting the manners and ideas of Anglo-dominated North America—what scholars of the late twentieth century frequently term *assimilation* and what Sui Sin Far called *Americanization.* The most frequent catalyst for assimilation in Sui Sin Far's fiction is the female missionary (just as missionaries had been responsible, in Eaton family legend, for taking Sui Sin Far's mother from China). In "A Chinese Feud," the missionary makes her debut, visible in only one clause that connects her to Fantze's adoption of Western culture: "She was in many respects an American girl: for her mother had died when she was in swaddling clothes and her father had allowed the ladies of the Mission to have much to do with the bringing up of his little daughter" (236). In "Sweet Sin" the missionary enters into the plot more explicitly, when Sweet Sin is led home from her street fight "by a couple of much scandalized Sunday-school teachers," who "explained the case [to Sweet Sin's mother] and departed." Sweet Sin "had been brought up in the Methodist Church and her mother sent her to Sunday-School regularly," an omniscient narrator informs us. "Sometimes she felt a missionary spirit" (223–24). In raising the question of whether her "Christian friends" will allow her a "Christian burial" because of her suicide, Sweet Sin's farewell letter sets the teachings of her maternal and paternal religious heritages in opposition: "The Chinese teachers say that the conscience tells us and they teach the practice of virtue for virtue's sake. The Christians point to the Bible as a guide, saying that if we live according to its lessons, we will be rewarded in an afterlife. I have puzzled much over these things, seeking as it were for a lost mind" (226). Was Sui Sin Far, like Sweet Sin, also seeking "a lost mind" in her struggle to understand the implications of assimilation for her own identity—as a writer whose upbringing had largely removed her from her

Chinese heritage yet who had made the breakthrough, by the time she wrote these stories, of signing her name "Sui Seen Far"?

That these stories feature landscapes of the imagination is clear; no evidence indicates that Sui Sin Far had ever been to either China or San Francisco at the time they were published. She presumably knew China from her mother's stories, her own reading, and her interviews with Montreal Chinese immigrants. She could have gained familiarity with San Francisco through Christian missionary networks, correspondence with Lummis, and her sister May's letters. Her personal experience with North American Chinatowns, however, was probably limited to Montreal and New York, which she had visited in the spring of 1896. Her 21 September 1896 letter to the editor of the *Montreal Daily Star,* discussed earlier, shows that she concentrated on Chinatown when she was in New York and that she made the most of the experience: "For two weeks I dwelt amongst them [the New York Chinese Americans], trotted up and down Mott, Pell and Doyer streets, saw the Chinese theatres and Joss Houses, visited all the little Chinese women, talked pigeon English to them, examined their babies, dined with a Chinese actress, darted hither and thither through the tenements of Chinatown, and during that time not the slightest disrespect or unkindness was shown to me."

This passage points to another essential aspect of Sui Sin Far's early stories. With the exception of the all-male "Gamblers," each focuses on women's lives and emphasizes a woman's perspective. Such emphasis on the woman's point of view calls to mind Virginia Woolf's scene in 1929 in *A Room of One's Own,* when Woolf fancied two women, English in heritage, holding a conversation together alone in a room, the likes of which Woolf believed had rarely been portrayed in English literature. Sui Sin Far's stories indicate that four decades before Woolf she was asking similar questions about women of Chinese descent in conversation with one another. In contrast to their multiple silencings in life by Chinese and North American traditions, Sweet Sin, Fantze, Iso, A-Toy, and all the Ku Yums are given the power of speech on Sui Sin Far's printed page—from where we, as readers, hear them speak for themselves for the first time in North American literature.

How well did Sui Sin Far know such women personally? Although she had met Chinese American women during newspaper interviews, mission work, and her brief visit to New York, her personal relationships with Chinese Americans appear to have been limited to her mother and sisters before 1898, and her sisters had largely assimilated the English Canadian culture. As discussed earlier, Sui Sin Far's visit with her mother to the Chinese immigrant bride was pivotal and lead her to recall: "From that time I began to go among my mother's people" (*Globe*). On 4 May 1894 an article appeared in the *Montreal Daily Witness* entitled "Girl Slave in Montreal: Our Chinese Colony Cleverly Described. Only Two Women from the Flowery Land in

Town," written by "a lady reporter," who was likely Sui Sin Far herself. The piece reports an interview with two Chinese Montreal women: Mrs. Ho Sang Kee, who came from China "about two years ago" to marry Sang Kee of the Lagauchetiere boardinghouse, and "Mrs. Wing Sing, who lives in a nice store kept by her husband at the side of St. Lawrence." The women are described as "very exclusive," going out or receiving callers only with their husbands' permission. Neither had bound feet or anything "whatever to do with the Christian faith." Mrs. Wing Sing speaks a few words of English: "good, good," "thank you," "nice boy," "nice girl," "come again," "how do you do," "yes," "no." Since the reporter spoke no Chinese, the interview would have been linguistically limited. With the women is a ten-year-old Chinese girl, who is Mrs. Ho Sang Kee's slave. The reporter describes them as "the only three [Chinese] females in Montreal."

We know something, however, that the reporter either does not know or is not revealing. We know about Lotus Blossom and her nine daughters. In addition, because statistics for persecuted immigrants, especially women, cannot be relied on, we really have no idea how many Chinese women were in Montreal at the dates Sui Sin Far was writing.[71] Whatever the extent of her personal acquaintance with Chinese immigrant women during this period, she was able to identify with them in her writing because she shared their experience. If she could not speak as an immigrant woman from China, she could speak as the daughter of such a woman and as a woman of Chinese descent who had migrated from England. Certainly, she could speak with authority about racist abuse, sexual oppression, and the pressure to marry against one's personal will—all topics her stories address. Sui Sin Far had her finger on women's lot in a global sense.

This empathy with women's condition in general, and with the Chinese immigrant woman's in particular, emerges in "The Chinese Woman in America," Sui Sin Far's only located essay during this period and her last publication signed from Montreal. In the sense that its materials must have been compiled in the East, while its text was published for a *Land of Sunshine* audience with the implication that it was about California women, the piece is a tour de force. The author creates this illusion in several ways. First is the lack of definite setting. The women migrate from China to "America"; their destination never becomes more specific. In addition, the surface treatment is generalized and romantic: "She is a bit of olden Oriental coloring amidst our modern Western lights and shades; and though her years be few, she is yet a relic of antiquity" (59). No individualized female character (a Ku Yum or a Fantze) is ever developed. The "Chinese woman in America" is a composite, a type: "She was born in China, probably in Canton . . . [and] her years slipped away happily until it was time for her to become an American bride" (60). Sui Sin Far's style, which uses the generic "she is," "she resembles," and "she lives," reinforces this impression. The generations over which Chinese women have been migrating are indirectly addressed with the information that the majority are brides, but "some were born here; others are merely secondary wives . . . and there are a few elderly women who were married long before leaving home" (64).

The author's stance is reportorial, that of an outsider offering, after the manner of popular fiction or missionary literature, a peephole into a strange and exotic environment: "The Chinese woman in America differs from all others who come to live their lives here, in that she seeks not our companionship, makes no attempt to know us, adopts not our ways and heeds not our customs. She lives among us, but is as isolated as if she and the few Chinese relations who may happen to live near were the only human beings in the world" (59). Enjoying the rare privilege of paying this woman a visit, the narrator invites the reader to join her, an invitation personalized by speaking in the second-person: "So if you wish to become acquainted with her . . . you must seek her out. She will be pleased with your advances and welcome you with demure politeness, but you might wait for all eternity and she would not come to you" (59). At the same time, the narrative stance is humane and seeks to counteract stereotypes of Chinese immigrants with firsthand experience: "Having broken the ice, you will find that her former reserve was due to her training, and that she is not nearly so shy as report makes her . . . despite the popular idea that the Chinese are phlegmatic people, that she is brimful of feelings and impressions and has sensibilities as acute as a child's" (59–60). While on one level the diminutives ("acute as a child's") may sound condescending, on another they allow a non-Chinese audience to relate to the Chinese immigrant woman on a personal, human basis.

Further details suggest that Sui Sin Far identifies her subject's dream voyage with her own dream of returning to a maternal homeland: "She lives in the hope of returning someday to China" and "would not be a daughter of the Flowery Land were she content to die among strangers" (64).[72] In the meantime, in the quarters above her husband's store, the woman creates icons of her home culture: "Chinese ornaments decorate the tables and walls," there are hangings of "long bamboo panels covered with paper or silk on which are painted Chinese good-luck characters,"[73] and "in a curtained alcove of an inner room can be discerned an incense vase, an ancestral tablet, a kneeling stool, a pair of candlesticks—my lady-from-China's private chapel" (62). Such settings serve as fictional microcosms of attempts to keep Chinese culture alive in North America. Their furnishings will be reassembled for Sui Sin Far's later fictional brides.

Moreover, concepts that are as yet unseen thematically may be subtly suggested in what Henry James has called the artist's hint of experience.[74] In "The Chinese Woman in America," the narrator's line of vision stretches toward the "curtained alcove of an inner room" (62)—a glance that hints at inaccessible and unexplored possibilities in the Chinese woman's apartment. The image recalls a technique Willa Cather used in *The Professor's House*. Based on paintings of Dutch or Italian masters in which a window or door opens, as Stephen Tennant phrases it, "either to sky or sea or mountains, or to the Room Beyond," the hint of some physical area beyond immediate reach allows the artist to suggest experience beyond that which the canvas can literally represent.[75] Similarly, Sui Sin Far's "curtained alcove" suggests experience undisclosed in the text: a consciousness of the other "Chinese woman" in the room, the writer who signs her essay with the name Sui Seen Far.

Other details suggest similar autobiographical parallels. The narrator identifies certain artifacts hidden in the alcove with her own maternal ancestry. In particular, among the Chinese immigrant woman's "memories of home" is her perception of "an image of a goddess called 'Mother,' to whom she used to kneel till her little knees ached" (60). A tone of familial affection (in which we again glimpse the reflexive mirror) informs us that Sui Sin Far's interest in the "exotica" of Chinese women differed in essence from that of writers for whom such women were only features of local color. The narrative voice does not miss this distinction: "Do not imagine for an instant that she is dull of comprehension and unable to distinguish friendly visitors from those who merely call to amuse themselves at her expense" (64).

The question of voice operates in "The Chinese Woman in America" on multiple levels. The women are described as wives of well-to-do Chinatown merchants. This means that traditionally they were not allowed to go out or have visitors without their husbands' permission. Did they speak English, or did Sui Sin Far speak "pidgin," or was the language barrier crossed through an interpreter? Were they aware of their interviewer's common racial heritage? Were they, perhaps, the same women who were interviewed for the article in the *Montreal Daily Witness*? Whatever the answers, in contrast to the women from China, Sui Sin Far had a voice, and she was not afraid to use it. Bingham argues that there is a conflict between "essentially eastern" themes and "spirit" and Western settings and dialogues in Sui Sin Far's *Land of Sunshine* stories, a conflict that parallels the writer's personal ambivalence about heritage and environment and becomes "disruptive of unity."[76] For writers like Sui Sin Far, however, the descendant of an interracial couple whose races are at war with each other, we might say that life in North America was "disruptive of unity" and that—put inversely—these writers' drive to find unity was disruptive of the stereotypes commonly practiced in their cultural environments.

Altogether, the significance of such political and artistic issues to Sui Sin Far as a woman of dual racial parentage and to her voice as a writer can best be measured by the borders we see her crossing on several levels in this decade between publication of her first story signed "Edith Eaton" and her last story signed "Sui Seen Far." On an obvious level, the names become outward manifestations of the ambivalence with which the author inwardly lived. Her experimental spelling shifts (Sui Sin Fah, Sui Sin Far) of the next few years exemplify the wavery lines of the particular "border" that she sought to make the land of her writing.[77] Though it is tempting to think of the name change as marking some glorious identity transformation from English to Chinese, we must remember that the writer's growth at this stage was toward her mother's culture but not necessarily away from her father's. She is "much more on the inside of her theme than are most who pretend to depict the expatriated John," Lummis wrote of Sui Sin Far in 1896.[78] "There are many layers of 'outside,' " Amy Ling wrote some ninety years later.[79]

Notes

1. [Winifred Eaton Babcock,] *Marion: The Story of an Artist's Model* (New York: W. J. Watt, 1916), 99. Hereafter referred to in the text as *Marion*.

2. Edith Eaton, "A Trip in a Horse Car," *Dominion Illustrated* 1 (13 October 1888): 235; "Misunderstood: The Story of a Young Man," *Dominion Illustrated* 1 (17 November 1888): 314; "A Fatal Tug of War," *Dominion Illustrated* 1 (8 December 1888): 362–63; "The Origin of a Broken Nose," *Dominion Illustrated* 2 (11 May 1889): 302; "Robin," *Dominion Illustrated* 2 (22 June 1889): 394; "Albermarle's Secret," *Dominion Illustrated* 3 (19 October 1889): 254; "Spring Impressions: A Medley of Poetry and Prose," *Dominion Illustrated* 4 (7 June 1890): 358–59; "In Fairyland," *Dominion Illustrated* 5 (18 October 1890): 270.

3. Virginia Woolf, *A Room of One's Own* (New York: Harcourt Brace Jovanovich, 1957 [1929]).

4. Sui Sin Far, "Sui Sin Far, the Half Chinese Writer, Tells of Her Career," *Boston Globe,* 5 May 1912. Hereafter referred to as *Globe.*

5. Catherine M. McLay, ed., *Canadian Literature: The Beginnings to the Twentieth Century* (Toronto: McClelland and Stewart, 1974), 75. A classic speech launching literary nationalism in Canada is "The Mental Outfit of the New Dominion," presented by Thomas D'arcy McGee "Before the Montreal Literary Club, November 4, 1867," reprinted in McLay, *Canadian Literature,* 182–85.

6. For information on Lesperance I am indebted to James Doyle. Doyle's unpublished research shows that Sui Sin Far and Harte were both writing for Montreal newspapers at the same time.

7. Hector Charlesworth, "Miss Emily Pauline Johnson's Poems," a review of *White Wampum, Canadian Magazine* 5 (September 1895): 480.

8. Katherine Anne Porter, *Ship of Fools* (Boston: Little, Brown, 1962).

9. Interestingly, one of Ada's suitors in *Marion* is named Albemarle.

10. Sui Sin Far, "Leaves from the Mental Portfolio of an Eurasian," *Independent* 66 (21 January 1909): 128. Hereafter referred to as "Leaves."

11. Amy Ling, "Edith Eaton: Pioneer Chinamerican Writer and Feminist," *American Literary Realism* 16 (Autumn 1983): 292. The second essay is "In Fairyland."

12. Sui Sin Far, "Misunderstood," in *Mrs. Spring Fragrance* (Chicago: A. C. McClurg, 1912), 314–20.

13. Sui Sin Far, "Mrs. Spring Fragrance," *Hampton's* 24 (January 1910): 137–41.

14. Sui Fin Far, "Children of Peace," in *Mrs. Spring Fragrance,* 249.

15. Kenneth Scott Latourette, *A History of Christian Missions in China* (New York: Macmillan, 1929), examines the Christian mission movement in depth. W. Peter Ward, "The Oriental Immigrant and Canada's Protestant Clergy, 1858–1925," *BC Studies* 22 (Summer 1974): 40–55, discusses the paradox that "church leaders were of two minds on the Asian in their midst. On one hand he appealed to their charitable and evangelical instincts. . . . On the other, the Oriental challenged the cultural identity of many Protestant Canadians" (40).

16. Quoted in *Montreal Daily Star,* 4 December 1889.

17. *Montreal Daily Witness,* 4 October 1890.

18. Emily Pauline Johnson, a poet of Mohawk-Anglo descent from Ontario who was a contemporary of Sui Sin Far, speaks to assimilation strategies as they were practiced in Canada on Indians in "Her Sister's Son," a poem in which Johnson, to quote a review in the 4 June 1895 *Montreal Daily Star,* "endeavors to show the bad effects which are likely to be produced by the custom prevailing among the mission schools of the North-West of preventing the Indian children, after leaving their tribe in order to gain a mission school education, from again associating with their own people. They are not even allowed to see their parents again." An ad accompanying the review states that "Her Sister's Son" occupied "the principal place upon [Johnson's] program" when she read it in Montreal's Windsor Hall. Sui Sin Far exposes similar practices perpetrated on Chinese American children in the United States in her later short stories. Whether the two writers met is unknown. What is certain is that they shared common experiences as women of mixed racial parentage in colonized societies and that each dealt with these in her art.

19. Alexander Saxton, *The Indispensable Enemy* (Berkeley: University of California Press, 1971), 47. More specifically, he observes that the discrimination against Chinese in the mining camps and anti-Chinese legislation in California was "replaying the script of an older drama" (15).

20. F. M. Dewey, "No Chinatown Here," *Montreal Daily Witness,* 22 August 1896.

21. *Presbyterian Record* 21 (1896): 11.

22. Dewey, "No Chinatown Here."

23. *Montreal Daily Star,* 15 June 1895.

24. Dewey, "No Chinatown Here." The link between learning to speak English and embracing Christianity is well grounded in North American history.

25. Anthony B. Chan, *Gold Mountain: The Chinese in the Northwest* (Vancouver: New Star Books, 1983), 11.

26. Sir John A. Macdonald speaking to the House of Commons, 1882, file on Chinese Canadians, Canadian Pacific Railway Archives, Montreal.

27. Patricia Roy, *A White Man's Province* (Vancouver: University of British Columbia Press, 1989), sees the competition between white and Chinese workers as the major cause of white Canadians' hostility toward Chinese Canadians. Audrey Kobayashi and Peter Jackson, "Japanese Canadians and the Racialization of Labour in the British Columbia Sawmill Industry, 1900–1930" (Paper presented at the Sixth British Columbia Studies Conference, University of British Columbia, Vancouver, 2–3 November 1990), 2, argue, however, that the racialization of labor is the root problem and that labor competition is mainly "a means of justifyng a negative and hostile reaction."

28. Chan, *Gold Mountain*, 11.

29. Rebecca Aiken, *Montreal Chinese Property Ownership and Occupational Changes, 1881–1981* (New York: AMS, 1989), 52. This was the decade of the Chinese Exclusion Act in the United States.

30. See David Cheunyan Lai, *Chinatowns: Towns within Cities in Canada* (Vancouver: University of British Columbia Press, 1988), 100.

31. Denise Helly, *Les Chinois à Montréal, 1877–1951* (Montreal: Québecois de recherche sur la culture, 1987), 128.

32. "The Chinese Colony: A Visit to Sang Kee's Big Boarding House," *Montreal Daily Star*, 15 June 1895.

33. Dewey, "No Chinatown Here."

34. *Montreal Daily Star*, 20 March 1895.

35. Aiken, *Montreal Chinese*, 51.

36. "The Chinese Invasion: A Cry of Alarm and Warning," reprinted in *Montreal Daily Witness*, 27 February 1894; letters are from the same source.

37. "The Chinese Gambling Case," *Montreal Daily Star*, 11 April 1896.

38. "Three Chinamen Captured," *Montreal Daily Witness*, 8 April 1896 (emphasis added).

39. Reprinted in *Montreal Daily Witness*, 4 July 1896.

40. Ibid., 8 April 1896.

41. Ibid.

42. *Montreal Daily Star*, 15 June 1895.

43. Ibid.

44. Susan Crean, *Newsworthy: The Lives of Media Women* (Toronto: Stoddart Publishing, 1985), 17.

45. Ibid., 16.

46. Ibid., 17.

47. "Our National Literature," *Montreal Daily Witness*, 26 January 1889.

48. Sui Sin Far, "In the Land of the Free," *Independent* 67 (2 September 1909): 504–8.

49. See "Leaves": the "white-haired old man" who "adjusts his eyeglasses and surveys me [Sui Sin Far] critically" (126); "older persons pause and gaze

upon us, very much in the same way that I have seen people gaze upon strange animals in a menagerie" (127).

50. Sui Seen Far, "Sweet Sin," *Land of Sunshine* 8 (April 1898): 223–26.

51. Sui Seen Far, "The Gamblers," *Fly Leaf* 1 (February 1896): 14–18; "Ku Yum," *Land of Sunshine* 5 (June 1896): 29–31; "The Story of Iso," *Lotus* 2 (August 1896): 117–19; "A Love Story of the Orient," *Lotus* 2 (October 1896): 203–7; "A Chinese Feud," *Land of Sunshine* 5 (November 1896): 236–37; "The Chinese Woman in America," *Land of Sunshine* 6 (January 1897): 60–65.

52. *Fly Leaf* 1 (February 1896): n.p.

53. Edwin R. Bingham, *Charles F. Lummis, Editor of the Southwest* (San Marino, Calif.: Huntington Library, 1955), 49. The information on Lummis's editorship of *The Land of Sunshine* comes largely from this source.

54. Quoted in ibid., 57.

55. Ibid., 72.

56. Ibid., 164.

57. Ibid.

58. Documentation for these pieces is, respectively, Ng Poon Chew, "The Chinese in Los Angeles," *Land of Sunshine* 1 (October 1894): 102–3; *Land of Sunshine* 3 (October 1895): 219; J. Torrey Connor, "Only John," *Land of Sunshine* 4 (February 1896): 111–13; and Ella S. Hartnell, "Some Little Heathens," *Land of Sunshine* 5 (September 1896): 153–57.

59. Charles F. Lummis, "In the Lion's Den," *Land of Sunshine* 15 (November 1901): 368–69.

60. David Arnason, ed., Introduction to *Nineteenth Century Canadian Stories* (Toronto: Macmillan, 1976), ix.

61. Charles F. Lummis, "That Which Is Written," *Land of Sunshine* 6 (December 1896): 32.

62. W. B. Harte, "Bubble and Squeak," *Lotus* 2 (October 1896): 216–17.

63. The expression "red-headed people" or a "red-headed stranger" is a stock descriptive phrase used by writers of fiction at the turn of the century for Chinese characters describing Americans.

64. "Golden Lily feet" is the expression North American writers of the period used for the traditional bound feet of Chinese women. It introduces a class issue, in that only women from middle or upper classes have their feet bound. As Ku Yum's mother says, "Ku Yum is pretty enough for me, and she has the Golden Lily feet, which A-Toy has not" (29). The irony is that slaves, maids, and lower-class women have the freedom of using their feet, which upper-class women do not. The further irony in Sui Sin Far's story is that although women suffer footbinding to enhance sexual desirability, the maid is more desirable than the mistress to Tie Sung.

65. Jinqi Ling, Interview, Pullman, Wash., 15 October 1990.

66. "Girl Slave in Montreal: Our Chinese Colony Cleverly Described. Only Two Women from the Flowery Land in Town," *Montreal Daily Witness*, 4 May 1894.

67. The "To Come" occurs in other stories. It always refers to a character's fanciful flight toward some dream, a flight that is immediately cut through with reality.

68. We recall that Sui Sin Far uses *American* to refer to white Americans.

69. Bingham, *Charles F. Lummis,* 172.

70. Dale M. Bauer, *Feminist Dialogics: A Theory of Failed Community* (New York: State University of New York Press, 1988), 14.

71. Before locating these articles, I was repeatedly told that there were no Chinese women in Montreal in the nineteenth century.

72. Compare Sui Sin Far's comment in "Leaves," 132: "As my life began in my father's country it may end in my mother's."

73. Compare lines from "Girl Slave in Montreal": "the walls were hung from top to bottom with long bamboo panels covered with paper, on which were printed Chinese characters, signifying good luck."

74. Henry James, *The Art of Fiction* (New York: Charles Scribner's Sons, 1962 [1907]).

75. Willa Cather, "On the Professor's House," in *Willa Cather on Writing,* with a foreword by Stephen Tennant (Lincoln: University of Nebraska Press, 1988), 30–32 and v.

76. Bingham, *Charles F. Lummis,* 172.

77. James Doyle suggests that the last two syllables of the name's initial spelling may form a pun, read in English as Sui "seen far."

78. Lummis, "That Which Is Written," 32.

79. Amy Ling, "I'm Here: An Asian American Woman's Response," *New Literary History* 19 (1987–89): 152.

3

Pacific Coast Chinatown Stories

Enabled on the one hand to write, to create new worlds and to recreate what should have been home, many writers find the other hand shackled by the expectations and rules of the world of words they have chosen to inhabit. For some, however, the ambiguity and paradoxes inherent in finding a place to write are at least partly resolved by finding a home in writing itself.

—Mary Lynn Broe and Angela Ingram, *Women's Writings in Exile*

Sui Sin Far's migration from Montreal to the U.S. West Coast, with a year's interlude in Jamaica, marks a juncture in her evolution from an English Canadian with a largely closeted Chinese identity to a Eurasian who begins to acknowledge publicly her Chinese heritage, a move earlier witnessed in her "coming out" to non-Chinese colleagues at a luncheon table in the town in the "Middle West." In terms of daily survival, however, this picture is simplistic. As her letters show, Sui Sin Far moved back and forth across the border from Canada to the United States many times, during an era when the Geary Act of 1892 (which extended the Chinese Exclusion Act of 1882 for ten years) made it illegal for her, as a person of Chinese descent, to enter the United States. In 1902 the same imperialistic climate that supported the annexation of Hawaii and a war with the Philippines saw the Exclusion Act extended indefinitely, barring almost all Chinese from entering "any of the insular territory of the U.S." These acts were very specific in "prohibiting and regulating the coming of Chinese persons and persons of Chinese descent into the United States."[1] That Sui Sin Far was able to manage border crossings without, as far as we know, any difficulty suggests her English name and appearance conferred an invisible Chinese status, one that she was forced to exploit whenever she crossed national borders.

The "invisibly" black narrator, Irene, in Nella Larsen's *Passing* offers an example of the trepidation we can imagine that—with each crossing—Sui Sin

Far must have felt. Irene is sitting at a table in the posh Hotel Drayton enjoying iced tea when she gets the feeling that she is being watched: "And gradually there rose in Irene a small inner disturbance, odious and hatefully familiar. . . . Did that woman, could that woman, somehow know that here before her very eyes on the roof of the Drayton sat a Negro? It wasn't that she was ashamed of being a Negro or even of having it declared. It was the idea of being ejected from any place, even in the polite and tactful way in which the Drayton would probably do it, that disturbed her."[2] Irene's full racial status was not discovered, nor, inasmuch as we know, was Sui Sin Far's. Yet Irene's experience presents the inside view of a woman persecuted because of her race, cast by society into the chameleon stance, and forced to play roles to survive as she lives with the perpetual tension of threatened exposure. Being caught in this dilemma presumably reinforced Sui Sin Far's empathy with "the brown people of this earth" in Jamaica and helped her identify with immigrants from China on the U.S. West Coast. Crossing national borders undoubtedly developed her awareness of the conditions of exile and betrayal, disguise and deceit, that she would address through strategy and themes in her short stories.

The feeling of being an exile in a strange land was as central for Sui Sin Far as it was for the Chinese immigrants to North America she would meet in West Coast Chinatowns during the last decade of the nineteenth century and the first decade of the twentieth. The editors of *Aiiieeeee!* speak to the ambivalent position Asian Americans have held in North America: "rejection by both Asia and white America proved we were neither one nor the other."[3] Amy Ling names the condition "between worlds."[4] Born with a parent in each culture, Sui Sin Far described this sense of double exile: "I do not confide in my mother and father. They do not understand. How could they? He is English, she is Chinese. I am different to both of them—a stranger, tho their own child."[5] Sui Sin Far might have felt herself an exile from her family on several other fronts: as a "semi-invalid," as the only daughter who chose not to marry, and as the only sibling who directly sought out her Chinese heritage. In Canada she was an exile from England, and in the United States she was an exile from Canada. The place she could call home was indeed a dilemma.

As Mary Lynn Broe and Angela Ingram have demonstrated for other writers in exile, the drive to "recreate what should have been home" may be the most essential factor in Sui Sin Far's writing from this period onward.[6] Fiction, under such circumstances, can be conceived as the place to probe, to explore, and to conceive an identity that the world apart from the printed page recurrently denies. In this context, "The Sing-Song Woman" of 1898,[7] Sui Sin Far's first located story after her move to San Francisco and her last to be signed "Sui *Seen* Far," may be read as a fantasy solution to her own sense of exile. The story exemplifies how her fiction from this period deals with such issues.

"The Sing-Song Woman" is the tale of two Chinese American women with opposing views about their national and racial preferences: Mag-gee, a "half-white girl" who wants to marry an Irish American and stay in the United States but whose father arranges for her to marry "a Chinaman" who will take her to China; and Lae Choo, "a despised actress in an American Chinatown" who feels stuck in the United States and dreams of returning to her life as a fisherman's daughter on the Chinese Sea (225). As "the fair head and dark head drew near together" plotting "a play" (226), the doubling of the two characters is visually symbolized. The motif of disguise is as central to the plot as it was to the author's life every time she crossed borders. However, whereas Sui Sin Far as a Eurasian must masquerade as white, the Eurasian Mag-gee is forced by her father to masquerade as Chinese. To this end, Mag-gee is portrayed in the stereotypical costume of "red paint, white powder and carmine lip salve" "besmeared over a naturally pretty face" (225), down which—because of Mag-gee's tears—the paint runs "in little red rivers" (226). Lae Choo joins the masquerade by disguising herself as the bride and going through the wedding ceremony as a stand-in for Mag-gee, who escapes with her Irish lover. The overall disguise is enacted, though, when "the play" replaces what was previously believed to be reality. " 'It is but a play like the play I shall act here tomorrow,' " Lae Choo tells Ke Leang, the groom—who, when the veil is lifted, discovers he has wed the wrong woman. Because Ke Leang is able to see Lae Choo's "kind heart" beneath the trick she has played on him, he accepts her as his wife, assuring the actress, " 'Hush! . . . you shall act no more.' " When Mag-gee stays in the United States eating "potatoes and beef" with the "white man" she loves, while Lae Choo returns with Ke Leang to China, the two female characters in "The Sing-Song Woman" reconcile Sui Sin Far's own internal division and create her dreamed of cultural wholeness. " 'It takes a heart to make a heart, and you have put one today in the bosom of a Sing-Song woman,' " Lae Choo says to Ke Leang (228).

"The Sing-Song Woman" also typifies Sui Sin Far's fiction that concerns itself with the subject of exile during this period. Being threatened with expulsion from the homes they prefer is basic to the situations of both Lae Choo and Mag-gee—as it was to Sui Sin Far's familial connection to Montreal and her psychic relation to China. In Sui Sin Far's fiction, the sense of exile is often complicated by the temptation of betrayal by forgetting or abandoning familial or cultural obligations. The ambiguity of potential betrayal inherent in border crossing is at the core of the dilemmas of her fictional characters, as it must have been for their author. How does a person of mixed racial heritage deal with a society that constructs artificial lines between races and then acts on these as reality? Can the borders be negotiated by means other than disguise and deceit? If life lacks logic and justice, should not art turn it over?

Chinatowns of the U.S. Pacific West

I can wash handkerchiefs wet with sad tears;
I can wash shirts soiled in sinful crimes.
The grease of greed, the dirt of desire . . .
And all the filthy things at your house,
Give them to me to wash, give them to me.

—Wen-l To, "The Laundry Song"

To comprehend the significance of the theme of exile in Sui Sin Far's stories, some understanding of the Chinese American context in which Sui Sin Far was moving at the time they were written is vital. Of particular import is the very real feeling of exile experienced daily by Chinatown populations she would meet in the U.S. Pacific West, many of whom were caught in the political dynamics we have already witnessed between their home country of China and Europe or European-dominated North America. In the words of one San Francisco oldtimer interviewed by Victor G. Nee and Brett De Bary Nee, "At this time, you see, we Chinese seemed to be without a country."[8] Sui Sin Far shared these immigrants' sense of exile.

The San Francisco Chinatown Sui Sin Far would encounter when she arrived in 1898 was the oldest and largest in North America. Chinese had been immigrating to Montreal in noticeable numbers for barely a decade, but they had been going to San Francisco for half a century and had founded a community that combined the vitality of new immigrants with the stability of native-born, second-generation Chinese Americans. Though this dynamic cultural climate existed on a smaller scale in Seattle and Los Angeles[9]—the other two cities of Sui Sin Far's West Coast residence—the "city of the Golden Gate" was the main port of entry for immigrants from China and actually the only legal one until 1907, when Port Townsend, Washington, opened.[10] In addition to the arrival of new immigrants, a steady pattern of migration between cities kept the demographics of West Coast Chinatowns continually variable.[11]

Though nineteenth-century Chinese immigrants are generally typed as laborers on the railroads or in the mines, occupations in which the majority were indeed employed, Jack Chen illustrates that early Chinese Americans were just as diverse as immigrants from other countries were. "Chinese adapted their traditional skills to the service of the new land and integrated themselves into the society of pioneering California," Chen writes.[12] Seeing more profit in serving the miners than in mining, over half of Chinese immigrants to San Francisco in the 1850s found work in the city; others dispersed to various locations. They established fisheries up and down the

West Coast, were hired out by Alaskan canneries, started produce farms, and opened restaurants—serving fresh food at low prices and relieving the drab, unhealthy frontier diet. They started herbal shops and offered medical treatment in a land of few or no doctors. They began home deliveries of flowers, fruits, and vegetables and sold imported cloth door-to-door—all very welcome since such goods were at a premium. They cut and delivered firewood, the fuel of the city. They worked in industry, especially in the manufacture of cigars, woolens, shoes, and boots. When employment in construction opened after the Gold Rush, Chinese Americans built houses and streets. In an era when the phrase "bachelor society" applied to all races (Chen notes that 70 percent of San Francisco's total population was male until 1869),[13] the Chinese were in high demand among Nob Hill's elite as servants and cooks, and male and female teams sometimes worked together. They started laundries and delivered clean clothes in baskets carried on shoulder poles.[14] They also participated in entertainment, including opening a Chinese theater that featured juggling, acrobats, plays, puppets, and opera in 1852. In this frontier climate, Chen points out, everyone gambled; favorite games for the Chinese were lotteries and fantan.[15]

By the time Sui Sin Far arrived, near the turn of the century, survival needs of the frontier had been largely met, and services supplied by Chinese Americans were less appreciated than they had been fifty years earlier. The Chinese Exclusion Act was a sixteen-year-old reality. Anti-Chinese hysteria—already manifested in the Scott Act of 1888, which prevented Chinese who left the United States from reentering the country, and in a renewal of the Exclusion Act in 1892—was driving Congress to enact legislation that excluded Chinese permanently in 1902.[16] Simultaneously, Jim Crow restrictions were enacted. Chinese Americans were forbidden to compete with white labor, excluded from many industries, and curtailed by both laws and social attitudes from earning a living. The historian Roger Daniels describes the 1893 resolution passed by the San Francisco Board of Education that authorized "separate schools for children of Chinese Mongolian descent."[17]

The Chinatown where Sui Sin Far would canvas newspaper subscriptions in the late 1890s housed between ten and thirty thousand Chinese Americans (depending on the season) in the eight-square-block neighborhood of the original pioneer settlement around Portsmouth Square, where, in the words of Will Irwin, "an unwritten city ordinance, strictly observed by successive Boards of Supervisors, confined them."[18] Enacting punitive laws against Chinatown residents for the ghetto conditions that the city itself had forced them into, San Francisco passed the Cubic Air Ordinance in 1870, outlawing the rental of rooms with under five hundred cubic feet of air space per person. The Queue Act of 1893 required that "Chinese prisoners" (which any immigrant could become very easily) have their hair cut—"a disgrace to Chinese nationals in those days," as noted by the editors of *Island*.[19] In 1880 the California state legislature extended previous laws prohibiting marriage between "whites" and "Negros or mulattos" to include "Mongolians" and in 1905 declared such marriages illegal and void.

Turn-of-the-century immigrants interviewed by the Nees disprove popular assumptions that Chinese Americans in San Francisco willingly isolated themselves from the rest of the city, and they provide important background about the kind of environment from which Sui Sin Far's fictional characters were drawn. "In those days the boundaries were from Kearny to Powell, and from California to Broadway," recalled Wei Bat Liu. "If you ever passed them and went out there, the white kids would throw stones at you."[20] "The area around Union Square was a dangerous place for us, you see . . . but once we were inside Chinatown the thugs didn't bother us," remembered another.[21] White retaliation against Chinese who fought back duplicated the terrorism of lynchings used to control African Americans in the South. In the American West, Daniels contends, no other group except the American Indians suffered so much violence.[22] One outstanding example occurred in Los Angeles in 1871, when twenty-one Chinese were shot, hanged, or burned to death by non-Chinese males, a travesty that oldtimers surely passed down to new immigrants. Such historical context informs us that Sui Sin Far's stories about immigrants who yearn for their homeland of China are more than simply romantic. Many clung to what Sau-ling C. Wong refers to as the "wish-fulfilling 'myth of the return'" held by many West Coast Chinese Americans.[23]

Before 1985 many scholars argued that Chinatowns on the West Coast originally developed after the completion of the transcontinental railroad and that their growth was spurred in the 1870s by anti-Chinese witch-hunts, which created the need for Chinese Americans to band together for protection.[24] While there is little doubt that Chinatowns served a protective function, recent studies suggest more complex causes. By segregating people of Chinese descent to restricted corners of cities, civic legislators did their share in forcing the growth of separate cultural communities. Doug Chin and Art Chin observe that "restrictive covenants" in real estate relegated Chinese Americans in Seattle to limited parts of the city;[25] Doug Chin and Peter Bacho describe one such area on Seattle's Washington Street, where twenty-seven houses were jammed into about half a block in 1877.[26] In the U.S. West, Sui Sin Far was seeing ghetto areas that were the long-term results of the anti-Chinese discrimination eastern Canada had more recently started to practice.

The solidarity that helped Chinese Americans endure in spite of persecutions was demonstrated by the thousands of San Francisco Chinese, twelve hundred of them members of the Tom family, who came out to view the remains of the body of Tom Kin Yung—a military attaché of a Chinese legation to the United States who suffocated himself with gas because he "had been humiliated and assaulted" by a policeman who "seized [him] at his door when they were coming home from a banquet, then knocked him down and arrested him"—lying in state at the Chinese consulate, to give him a traditional Chinese funeral, and to suspend all Chinatown business by order of the Chinese Six Companies.[27] Such solidarity was a product of both Chinese and North American thinking, evidencing a threshold of Chinese American culture that Sui Sin Far would discern and trace in her fiction. As the Nees put it, the San Francisco Chinatown system was modeled on the combination of "traditional social patterns carried over from the Kwangtung and . . . the specific demands of the American situation."[28]

The tight community structure that Sui Sin Far would have encountered in San Francisco is described by the Nees as involving "three tiers": the Clan Association, the District Association, and the Six Companies. Occupying the bottom tier, the clan system was based on the kinship tradition of China wherein "whole villages were made up of families whose male members claimed direct descent from a common ancestor thirty or more generations back . . . in America . . . broadened to include all those who shared the same last name and, therefore, a mythological common ancestor."[29] In practical terms this meant that Chinese American immigrants—in San Francisco or Seattle, Los Angeles or New York—who shared the same family name would also share rooms and living expenses, help each other find jobs, write letters to families, mail remittance, and, after death, send bones home to rest with their ancestors'. On the second or middle tier, district associations were organized according to the region of Kwangtung from which immigrants came.[30] Larger and more powerful than the clans, the district associations worked to establish liaisons within Chinatowns, between Chinatown communities and the outside society, and between Chinese in China and North America. To keep contact with U.S. government agencies at a minimum, the districts organized independent Chinatown institutions, such as employment agencies, welfare systems, and banks.

Internal disputes occasionally arose between district groups, inherited in part from China but modified in North America. For example, the Sam Yups were generally merchants and craftsmen from the wealthy area of Kwangtung who felt superior to the Sze Yups, illiterate and impoverished rural peasants from southwest of the provincial capital, Canton.[31] In a sense, the feud between these two groups was rooted in class, yet in the cramped quarters of San Francisco it became territorial. To reconcile such internal disagreements, the Chinese Consolidated Benevolent Association of America, popularly known as the Chinese Six Companies, was organized in the first decade of the San Francisco Chinatown's existence. Made up largely of merchants who possessed the most education and wealth, the Six Companies dominated the tier structure and by the turn of the century were, in the words of the Nees, "empowered with supreme jurisdiction within the community."[32] The power of the merchants is illustrated by the control they exercised over which Chinese Americans could return to China and the exit tax they exacted. Pitted against them were the notorious Tongs, described by the Nee study as largely social discontents who reacted against the Six Companies' domination and formed a "parallel network" to maintain justice by their own definition. In Sui Sin Far's era, the Tongs and the Six Companies fought frequent wars for control of Chinatown rackets—generally defined as gambling, opium, smuggling, and prostitution. Both collaborated with San Francisco city officials, many of whom accepted their bribes and closed their eyes to such things as the enslavement of indentured laborers and prostitutes. The Tongs would provide constant fuel for the sensationalist stereotypes of "yellow peril" writers of this period.

In contrast to earlier interpretations that North American Chinatown culture, especially the rackets, derived solely from China, contemporary historians reveal a culture being mutually shaped by China and the United States. Nowhere is this more sharply illustrated than in the situation of the Chinese woman prostitute. Exiles in the starkest sense, a few of these women migrated under individual initiative and plied their trades independently; the rest existed in a captivity that parallels the enslavement of Africans who were kidnapped by Europeans to supply a labor force for the U.S. South. Lucie Cheng Hirata maintains the period she calls "free competition," when San Francisco brothel-keepers like A-Toy and Lai Chow had men standing in line for hours just to look at their faces, lasted from 1849 to 1854, only five years.[33] From then into the 1920s, capitalism took over, as merchants on both sides of the waters cooperated in an intricately organized slave trade across the Pacific.

Sometimes the Chinese women—or, in most cases, girls—who served as raw material for this business were taken by coercion, like thirteen-year-old Lalu Nathoy, a fictionalized hero who, until a bandit threatened her father, threw two bags of soybean seeds at his feet, and pulled Lalu behind him onto a horse, had been her father's "treasure," his "thousand pieces of gold."[34] Sometimes they were taken with sweet talk, as when a "young immigrant man" bought Wong Ah So for $450, promised her impoverished mother that "in America she could support her family by entertaining at Chinese banquets," and then sold Wong Ah So into prostitution.[35] Hirata relates how a woman might be invited for a tour of a steamer anchored at a dock in Shanghai or Hong Kong, only to find herself sailing to America at the bottom of a bucket of coal.[36] Many were barely adolescents—as in the case of Lai Chow, who started her career as one among two dozen twelve-year-olds, all packed in crates labeled "dishware" and shipped from China.[37] An old woman servant in California told of how she had been resold four times, the first at age seven.[38] The "contract" method sounds a little more honest, but because most indentured women could neither read nor write and only signed with a thumbprint where they were told, the degree to which they understood what they were getting into is dubious. As noted by Judy Yung, many women—auctioned off in the barracoons of San Francisco and locked into small cages called "cribs," where they were forced to sexually serve men of all races—died within four or five years, before their contracts were ever "worked off."[39] Yung suggests that women sent to the logging, mining, or railroad camps throughout the Northwest might have had even shorter lives.

Traditional generalizations about Chinese immigrant women as prostitutes must be viewed with caution, however, along with historical stereotypes of Chinese America as a "bachelor society." Chinese American women were part of Chinese American life from its beginning, and their roles were as diverse as those of any immigrants to North America. Part of the problem has been in looking at numbers of women in relation to numbers of men, instead of considering women in their own right. The 1900 Los Angeles census listed 120 Chinese women and 3,089 Chinese men,[40] clearly indicating Chinese American women were part of the Los Angeles population. When Sui Sin Far was canvassing for subscriptions in San Francisco, it was the women of Chinatown who discovered that she had "Chinese hair, color of eyes and complexion, also that [she loved] rice and tea," and it was these same women who "influenced their husbands" ("Leaves," 131). Yung has shown that Chinese women came to North America as early as Chinese men did. Marie Seise, the first known of these, arrived in 1848 as the servant of a family of traders, the Gillespies of New York.[41] Others migrated independently. One "China Mary" ran away from her home in China when she was nine, migrated to Canada by age thirteen, outlived three husbands, and then moved to Sitka, Alaska, where she survived as a fisherwoman, hunter, prospector, restaurant keeper, nurse, laundress, and official matron of the Sitka Federal Jail.[42] Proof that women (probably the wives of exempt merchants) were still migrating from China to San Francisco after the Exclusion Act is given in an 1897 article in the *San Francisco Call,* which reported complaints by Chinatown merchants charging that immigration officials of Angel Island were mistreating Chinese immigrant women by "making them strip for inspection and watching them while they bathed, ostensibly for the purpose of ascertaining whether they take the bath."[43]

Refuting the notion that most Chinese American women were wives of merchants, Hirata notes that the life-style of a merchant's wife "applied only to less than 1 per cent of Chinese married women" and that "at least before 1880 a considerable number of workers also lived with their wives." Women married to laborers had to keep their own houses and also help earn an income; like working-class women of every ethnicity, they did piecework at home and took in boarders. The occupations of these women ranged from entertainer to miner, from seamstress to laborer, the latter of whom worked alongside men building the railroad.[44] From interviews with Chinese immigrant women, Ginger Chih discovered that "women whose husbands were not fortunate enough to own stores found employment sewing in garment factories, canning fruits, or cleaning shrimp."[45] Class distinctions made a difference in the freedom women were allowed. While wives of merchants usually lived in seclusion above their husband's businesses, had servants to do their shopping, and were only permitted in public on special holidays, their working class sisters came and went pretty much as they pleased.

Women from all these walks of life would have been on the West Coast during Sui Sin Far's residence. As in Montreal, one probable place of meeting would have been the Christian "home mission," which was becoming prominent on the edges of Chinatowns during this period. The most renowned of these in San Francisco was Cameron House, which belonged to Sui Sin Far's own Presbyterian church. Staging active campaigns against prostitution-slavery, the mission women, recurring types in Sui Sin Far's fiction, did not wait for Chinese American women to come to them but engaged in regular raids to "rescue" enslaved women and girls, bringing them back to the mission, teaching them Christianity, and "helping" them, to quote Peggy Pascoe, exchange "prostitution for marriage."[46] Ironically, the mission woman's "rescue and training," as Sui Sin Far's fiction would recognize, often interfered with Chinese American family life and separated Chinese American children from their ancestral cultures. Because such attempts included separation from traditional religions, the condition of exile even involved a threat to the spiritual experience of Chinese American immigrants.

Overall, the Chinatowns that Sui Sin Far would have known on the West Coast were in a state of suspension between cultures. "Perhaps never was Chinatown's isolation from [other segments of] American society so great as during the two decades at the end of the nineteenth century and the beginning of the twentieth," the Nee study notes.[47] This was caused by events back in China, as well as by political, social, and religious discrimination in North America. Not all immigrants left their homeland because they were starving or saw the Western world as a place to get rich; many were political exiles in the same sense that immigrants who had fled to the U.S. Northeast from Europe in the seventeenth century were. As John Jeong, an interviewee of the Nees, put it, "We were just the servants of the Manchus . . . if we didn't obey, they cut off our heads."[48] According to the historian Edgar Wickberg, the revolutionaries, led by Sun Yat Sen who was attempting to overthrow the Qing dynasty, and the reformers, who were trying to keep the extant structure but change it from within, were both "seeking bases overseas from which to launch their efforts for change in China."[49] From the 1890s until the Chinese Revolution of 1911, Chinese North American communities would become increasingly political, as revolutionaries and reformers competed with each other and with the Qing dynasty for backing from Chinese Americans and from the governments of the United States and Canada. After the empress dowager backed the Boxers in their uprising against Western missionaries in 1900, support for rebel groups increased among leaders in the Western world.

At a more personal level, the Nee study directly links the eagerness of Chinese Americans to help their home country with "the depth of isolation and frustration which existed in their own lives here in America. It was as if, excluded, rejected, and even physically beaten by the white society around them, they transported the sense of oppression which permeated their everyday lives into the context of Chinese society of which they could still claim to be a part."[50] As a journalist and someone with a deep personal commitment to the Chinatown community, Sui Sin Far was clearly aware of the dynamics of this political climate and North Americans' heightened awareness of Asian peoples at the turn of the century. Where Sui Sin Far stood personally is suggested in random, if ambiguous, clues.

In a 16 September 1900 letter to Charles Lummis, she wrote euphemistically, "Everything Chinese seems to be taking now," asking a couple of sentences later, "Aren't the Boers terrible people? But I forget. You are cheering them on."[51] The latter sounds so steadfastly British that one is tempted to wonder whether Sui Sin Far really missed the parallels between British imperialism in Africa and U.S. imperialism in Hawaii and the Philippines. In the same letter, her observation about the empress dowager sounds more tongue in cheek: "Europeans and Americans are forever talking about the way the Chinese women are kept down. Isn't it strange that the greatest person in China—the one who has the most influence—should be a woman. And the white people howl over the fact and don't like it at all. What do they want?"[52]

That Sui Sin Far herself was pro-reform is indicated in an article she wrote three years later about Leung Ki Chu, who visited Los Angeles in October of 1903 when she worked for the *Los Angeles Express.* In this piece, she referred to Los Angeles as "a stronghold for the reform party," an identification reinforced with the news that Leung's arrival brought out the city's entire Chinese American community, its mayor and civic dignitaries, and the press. Because Leung could not speak English, his secretary spoke for him to the reporters. We may imagine Sui Sin Far interviewing Leung through this translator, writing that he dared not "enter his native land" and that his wife and children were hidden out in Japan. Generally, she perceived that "the Chinamen who by their bearing and intelligence reflect the most credit on their race are those who believe in Leung Ki Chu and uphold his standard. They are men of education, but though entertaining advanced ideas, they are not Americanized Chinese." The world vision we first saw in the 1896 letter to the *Star* editor recurs here: "They are Chinese Chinamen of the sort that a citizen of the world can be proud to know."[53]

Literary Representations

By the beginning of the century, Los Angeles's Chinatown and other Chinatown communities along the West Coast had become popular stops for tourists. In San Francisco Sui Sin Far would have witnessed the phenomenon where, as John Bart Foster points out, "guides called 'lobby-gows' led crowds of gaping tourists" on "slumming expeditions" to see "opium dens and gambling saloons and joss houses."[54] Such sensationalistic display of Chinatown life for popular consumption ironically took place alongside campaigns to stamp out Chinatown areas. We may see Foster's tours as a metaphor for the "Chinatown literature" of the period, wherein popular writers offered their own "expeditions," taking readers on vicarious tours. As Foster puts it, "The Chinatown of the popular imagination, drawing sustenance from the pulp magazines and newspaper supplements, if it ever existed at all existed in the last decade of the 19th century between the passing of the Exclusion Act and the fire of 1906. . . ."[55]

To understand Sui Sin Far's writings, we must see them in relation to this trend, which William F. Wu termed "yellow peril" and described as "the overwhelmingly dominant theme in American fiction about Chinese Americans during this period."[56] The papers for which Sui Sin Far wrote during 1899 offer representative captions: "Confession of Slave Dealer," "Crusade against Foot-Binding," "Gambling Question of Chinatown," "White Baby Sold to Chinese."[57] The same issues of the *Los Angeles Express* that featured Sui Sin Far's series of sympathetic depictions of Los Angeles's Chinatown in 1903 were also concentrating on a ring of smugglers, whose anticipated "invasion" supplied persuasive grounds for tightening the Exclusion Act. "Chinese Are Coming" and "Hordes on Mexican Border Ready to Be Aided across the Line by Smugglers" headlined stories about federal officers lined up against a "flood" of Chinese laborers ready to inundate southern California.[58]

William Purviance Fenn observes that "the sensationalism played up by reporters provided much of the material for the melodrama of the day."[59] Indeed, one would be hard put to distinguish between these headlines and the titles of currently popular fiction. As examples, Fenn cites Joseph Jarrow's *Queen of Chinatown,* published in 1899, and C. W. Doyle's *Shadow of Quong Long,* published in 1900. Centering on a mission worker abducted by the Chinese (in real life, this was usually reversed) and rescued by her white lover, *Queen of Chinatown* includes, in Fenn's words, "opium fiends and highbinders in sufficient quantity to thrill the most insatiable."[60] *The Shadow of Quong Long* portrays "babies drunk with Chinese gin and absolutely depraved adults."[61] Two short stories, Frank Norris's "Third Circle" and Olive Dibert's "Chinese Lily," illustrate typical attitudes of the era, ideas and content that Sui Sin Far's work sought to overturn.

Written in the late 1890s for the San Francisco periodical *Wave,* Norris's "Third Circle" is presented through a white narrator who divides Chinatown into three parts:[62] "the part the guides show you, the part the guides don't show you, and the part no one ever hears of" (1). The story's leading characters, young Hillegas and Miss Ten Eyck, are introduced in the "Seventy Moons" restaurant, described by Miss Ten Eyck as "a dear, quaint, curious, old place." Hillegas tells us that it belongs to the "second part": "This is the way one ought to see places . . . just nose around by yourself and discover things. Now, the guides never brought us here" (2). Calling a Chinese fortune-teller to their table, Hillegas leaves him to tattoo a butterfly on Miss Ten Eyck's little finger, then goes to find out where their food is, and returns to find that Miss Ten Eyck is gone. No "white man" ever saw her again, the narrator tells us—until he does twenty years later, when he is taken by "a Plaza bum" (6) to see a woman named Sadie, who sits rolling "the cleanings of the opium pipes . . . into pills" with two other "white women" in a slave joint under Ah Yee's tan room (7). Now Norris leads his readers into "the third circle," where we may see with our own eyes the "strange, dreadful life that . . . wallows and grovels there in the mud and the dark" (1). Along with him, we witness "a butterfly tattooed on the little finger" that Sadie holds out (10).

Olive Dibert's "Chinese Lily" features Constance Black,[63] a new teacher at a Chinatown mission house and wife to Clifford Black, a news reporter who warns her to stay out of "this filthy Chinatown neighborhood" (184). The plot revolves around Chee Kee, a former "slave girl" who lives at the mission and whom the missionaries are trying "to get possession of" through the courts. Conflicts heighten with the entrance of an "innocent-eyed, smooth-faced Chinese man," who undergoes a "diabolical change" before the eyes of the mission folk, causing them to "shrink back" and Clifford to decide, " 'He's a hatchet-man, sure!' " (185). The "Chinese man" is also desirous of "possessing" Chee Kee and springs the "trap" ("set for a mouse," Clifford says later) with two Chinese lilies that he presents to Constance and Chee Kee. " 'Set um in window' " (186), the man says of the lilies and then uses them to locate Chee Kee's bedroom. Constance's moral—"A symbol of purity has dragged her back to perdition" (188)—points up the main oppositions. The mission teacher's (naive) response to her husband's early warnings, " 'You believe all those dreadful things we've been reading in the papers' " (185), is juxtaposed against Clifford's words to her in the conclusion: " 'With your information about the lily I'll have a two-column story to carry down to the office' " (188). Following the formula of the "Chinatown tour," the tale provides Constance—and the reader—with "evidence" that the horror stories reporters tell about

Chinatowns are not fiction but fact. In the words of the mission matron, " 'Nothing is too bare-faced or too under-handed for a Chinaman' " (187).

Norris's and Dibert's stories play off against each other in the following manner. In "The Chinese Lily," on the night Chee Kee is stolen, Constance sits in her own room alone reading "The Third Circle" and thinking—as "the realism stirred her imagination"—that "Miss Ten Eyck was only the fancy of an over-wrought imagination; but [Chee Kee] was real flesh and blood, perhaps soon to be drawn into the monstrous maw of Chinese depravity" (187). In this intertexual allusion, the "imagined" and "real" turn a flip-flop before the eyes of the reader. But the "monstrous maw" is implicitly "real" in both stories; it is both narrators' common antagonist. No matter how many apparently benign "China boys" appear to take orders ("Third Circle," 3), to "figure up accounts by means of little balls that slide to and fro upon rods" ("Third Circle," 5), or to "never make any noise when they walk" ("Chinese Lily," 185), none is important except in the sense that the "grimy stairs" and "soiled sash curtains" ("Chinese Lily," 184) in the hallway leading to the mission door are important—as signifiers of the ultimate depravity of Chinatown itself. The fates of both Miss Ten Eyck and Chee Kee relay the key message: there is no fantasized evil that the Chinese cannot fulfill.

No Chinese character in either of these stories connects with humanity on a level with which white characters (the bearers of civilization) can identify, and each duplicates all the others. In sum, they recall Fenn's comment about Bret Harte's characters: "Every Chinaman looked like any other Chinaman, wore the ordinary blue cotton blouse and white drawers of the Sampan coolie. . . ."[64] Norris and Dibert both represent Chinatowns as "noisome swamps" ("Third Circle," 1) that "breed crime like a swamp breeds infection" ("Chinese Lily," 186). All discourse in these stories separates "them" from "us" and pits the immoral (Chinese) against the moral (white) in San Francisco. Constance, assuming "woman" and "white" are synonymous, asks, " 'What woman the least impressionable could long endure the sights and smells and subtle evil influences of this bit of heathen Asia, draggling its mire along the edge of the fairest heights of the city' " ("Chinese Lily," 188). In both stories, civilization's only torch shines from the Christian mission: " 'Cut for the Mission House on Sacramento Street—they'll be good to you there,' " Norris's narrator advises Sadie (9); and Constance, though believing herself in danger, "made up her mind to remain at the school and add her mite of Anglo-Saxon leaven." With an irony the story's narrator does not seem to notice, Constance muses rhetorically, " 'What would Chinatown turn into if white people never went there?' " (188).

The rationalization behind the racist assumptions in both pieces is overtly expressed in Constance's musings: it is the burden of "white people" to "civilize" a world that, without them, would degenerate into a "swamp." It is the same rationalization behind the colonist's ethic, which can be illuminated by Glenn Altschuler's theory of "white cultural chauvinism legitimized by 19th century science," within which most populations of southern European descent accepted the superiority of the Anglo-Saxon races as fact and believed that "mixing" races would produce "degenerate offspring" and destroy American civilization.[65] That "degeneration" also could be produced by the Chinatown environment is demonstrated in the difference between Miss Ten Eyck's original "fresh, vigorous, healthful prettiness only seen in certain types of unmixed American stock" (3) and her transformation in the hands of the Chinese into "Sadie," a "dreadful-looking beast of a woman, wrinkled like a shrivelled apple . . . her hands bony and prehensile like a hawk's claws—but a white woman beyond all doubt" (8). The vision becomes apocalyptic when Miss Ten Eyck is described by Constance as " 'suddenly lost in blackest hell as a star is covered by some swift cloud!' " In this ethnocentric perspective, home missionaries see Chinese women like Chee Kee in the same way that foreign missionaries saw children in China, as victims of their own culture: "The thought of the dismal social maelstrom into which these Chinese children are often thrown filled Constance with melancholy foreboding" (187).[66] An implicit belief in the "white man's burden" shapes and is supported by "The Third Circle" and "The Chinese Lily" as clearly as it provided a rationale for imperialism in the Philippine-American war. Both are told from the perspectives of white narrators, whose vantage points are what Mikhail Bakhtin termed monologic, refusing as they do to acknowledge alternate voices and diverse constructions of social reality. Their narrators present white characters as innocents abroad, stumbling into—as Miss Ten Eyck puts it—this " 'little bit of China dug out and transplanted here' " (2). The narrators, the white characters, and implicitly most contemporary readers of these tales believed themselves to be "insiders," holders of the hegemony that privileged white Americans and labeled Chinese Americans "outsiders" in their own community— just as the British labeled Chinese "outsiders" in Shanghai.

Sui Sin Far's Fiction and Journalism, 1898–1905

These stories exemplify the portrayals of West Coast Chinatown communities that appeared regularly in the bookstalls Sui Sin Far would have been frequenting at the turn of the century. Her journalism and fiction of this era present a relatively lonely alternative voice against the solid background chorus of literary imperialism in "yellow peril" literature, a literature that dramatized and effectively reinforced the cultural doctrine England and the United States were currently acting out on a global scale. Such writings as Norris's and Dibert's perpetuated all of the stereotypes that characterized Asians as alien, nonhuman others, who could be treated by nonhuman methods and should not have a place in American society.

By contrast, Sui Sin Far's fiction clearly runs against the grain of contemporary literary treatments of her mother's people in North America. In a 4 December 1903 letter to R. U. Johnson, associate editor of the *Century,* she wrote, "I know I am not a fluent or artistic writer, but I try to depict as well as I can what I know and see of the life of the Chinese people in America. I have read many clever and interesting Chinese stories written by American writers, but they all (the writers) seem to me to stand far off from the Chinaman—in most cases treating him as a 'joke.' "[67] We have seen how such mainstream writers as Dibert and Norris not only treat Chinese and Chinese American characters as "jokes" but also use literature to legitimate racism, segregation, exclusion, and imperialism. Sui Sin Far's earliest editors recognized that she was doing something different. In 1896 W. B. Harte, comparing her fiction with Bret Harte's, noted that the latter "wrote of John as if he did not exactly belong to humankind,[68] but was an isolated puzzle that appealed to one's sense of the ludicrous and mysterious. But Sui Seen Far has struck into the field with a new view of quiet character drawing and humor . . . compressed into a small compass with the natural tact of a born story-teller. . . ."[69] In 1900 Charles Lummis similarly observed, "To others the alien Celestial is at best mere 'literary material'; in [Sui Sin Far's] stories he (or she) is a human being."[70]

As seen in the previous chapter, Sui Sin Far's writings do pick up character types familiar from mainstream discourse and sometimes—as in "A Chinese Feud"—appear to perpetuate the stereotypes of what Fenn calls "Chinatown literature." Readings that stop at this level, however, miss the complexities of aesthetic and political references in the interrelating layers of Sui Sin Far's work. Her writings from 1898 through 1905 obviously used the conventions, character types, and formulas of her literary marketplace, yet S. E. Solberg points out that these sometimes serve as a kind of writer's "shorthand,"[71] creating bridges of common reference between the text and the editor-reader. I further suggest that these were mainly camouflage, beyond which the writer could slip in her message. A significant distinction in Sui Sin Far's fiction is that the stories are told primarily from the vantage points of Chinese or Chinese American characters, and it is these characters' lives that focus her fictional vision. This is a radical change from the usual white American at the center; it not only reverses the traditional protagonist-antagonist relationship but also alters the conventional hegemonic order. As Chinese and Chinese American characters become the focus of the narrative vision, white Americans shift to positions of "outsiders" or "Other"—and function as antagonists to Chinese American characters and the Chinatown community/culture. Furthermore, in Sui Sin Far's stories this angle of vision is carried predominantly by female characters, a strategy that breaks through the silences both Chinese and white North Americans are accustomed to assigning to women. Finally, in contrast to the work of such writers as Harte, Norris, and Dibert, Sui Sin Far's writing about her mother's people in this era is never condescending. In the journalism, her stance is that of sympathetic outsider, with certain insider privileges. In the fiction, her stance is more complex, ironic, and dependent on an audience understanding of cultural context.

Sui Sin Far's sympathetic treatment of Chinatowns might have limited her acceptances for publication. Clearly she wanted to make a living by writing, as illustrated by her cryptic remark in the *Boston Globe:* "One cannot live on air and water alone, even if one is half-Chinese."[72] The marketplace she wrote for, however, was aimed at an audience that expected to have their preconceived stereotypes about "little brown people" not overturned but confirmed in the stories they read. The functions of such stories was, as Elaine Kim observes, "to provide literary rituals through which myths of racial supremacy are continually reaffirmed, to the everlasting detriment of the Asian."[73] To his *Out West* readers in November 1900, Lummis marketed his "half Chinese" author with obvious appeals to such myths: "She is a wee, spiritual body, too frail to retain much strength for literature after the day's bread-winning; with the breeding that is a step beyond our strenuous Saxon blood, and a native perception as characteristic."[74]

In this passage, Lummis might have inadvertently put his finger on the pulse of Sui Sin Far's struggle: to write and try to sell stories could not have been easy for this single, semi-invalid woman who, as Lummis knew, not only had to work for wages but also had to send earnings home. From her 2 December 1898 letter to Lummis, we recall that she had "quarreled" with the *San Francisco Call* editor, had discovered that the *Chronicle* editor "doesn't take fiction," and had "six stories touring around" that she expected to be rejected.[75] In the next few years she placed several fiction manuscripts with eastern editors, but her main fictional outlet remained magazines that Lummis edited: *Land of Sunshine, Overland Monthly,* and *Out West.* Judging by the January 1897 letter Sui Sin Far sent to Lummis from Jamaica thanking him for the check for four dollars, sales here hardly could have provided a living.[76] Her connection with Samuel Clover—who printed one of her stories, wrote letters for her to *McClure's* and the *Century,* and employed her to write a newspaper series in the *Los Angeles Express*—appears to have brought equally limited results. The national network she tried to break into paid off in a scant three publications during this period: "The Coat of Many Colors" in *Youth's Companion* (April 1902), "A Chinese Boy-Girl" in the *Century* (April 1904), and "Aluteh" in the *Chautauquan* (December 1905). Since Frank Mott, an historian of American magazines, ranks the *Century* along with *Harper's* as "[a leader] in the field of national illustrated monthlies devoted to the publication of literary miscellany,"[77] and since Sui Sin Far's story was placed in the same volume with serializations of Edith Wharton's *Roman Villas* and Jack London's *Sea-Wolf,* this was indeed a milestone. Her repeated efforts at further *Century* publications, accompanied by Associate Editor Johnson's repeated rejections, turned this achievement into an anticlimax, however.

Altogether, in the first seven years after she migrated from Canada to the United States, Sui Sin Far's located writings total only thirteen short stories and some miscellaneous journalism, in spite of the fact that, according to her extant correspondence, she was writing and steadily trying to market what she wrote. The struggle cannot have been eased by her knowledge that "Onoto Watanna" was putting out novels from major publishing houses at the rate of almost one a year, the most successful of which, *The Japanese Nightingale,* became a bestseller and was made into a play that ran simultaneously with *Madame Butterfly* on the Broadway stage.[78] The discouragement and growing frustration Sui Sin Far must have felt during this period is understated in the letter she wrote to Johnson on 1 April 1904—a letter in which she expresses her fatigue as a stenographer, her determination to "push" her stories, and her vow, if she does not succeed within the year, to "retire from the field and take up again with the honest old typewriter."[79]

Breaking Stereotypes

In her study *Asian American Literature,* Elaine Kim asserts that the key images of Asian Americans have been the "unassimilable alien" and the "inhuman Asian."[80] The rationale behind these images is essentially the same as the rationale behind the enslavement of black Africans by white Europeans. As suggested previously, *race* used in this manner becomes a social construct, leading to stereotypes that justify maltreatment of the Chinese by stressing, in the words of Kim, "permanent and irreconcilable differences between the Chinese and the Anglo, differences that define the Anglo as superior physically, spiritually, and morally."[81] One way to counteract such stereotypes is to stress a human essence that prevails across racial constructs. Sui Sin Far does this by individualizing her characters and their relationships with the world so readers of any racial descent can relate to them.

The depiction of Chinatowns as "bachelor societies," or communities of men without women except for slaves or prostitutes, was also conventional in the dominant culture's representations of this era and continues in many modern histories of North American Chinatowns.[82] Studies by Hirata, Yung, and other scholars, however, have demonstrated a small but significant migration of lone Chinese women to North America, some in response to the needs of males, others on their own.[83] In Sui Sin Far's fiction, women become vital members of Chinatown communities, participating and performing leadership roles in ways that belie their small numbers. *Linking Our Lives* points out that anti-Chinese hostility in the United States combined with traditional subordination of women in China to obscure the visibility of Chinese immigrant women: "Living in an alien and inhospitable society led these women to cling even more to traditional ideas and reinforced traditional attitudes."[84] Class distinctions also wielded some influence. True to the mores of both societies, working-class women had some freedom to roam, while—as we have seen with the wives of Wing Sing and Sam Kee in Montreal—merchant-class women lived in self-contained urban circles and were confined to household quarters, where their main company was one another. Most, whatever their background, would not have come into social contact with the large numbers of lone, laboring men against whom they are demographically measured. Historians have further diminished women's significance by discussing their presence or absence in frontier communities, including Chinatowns, largely in terms of their roles as traditional holders of the lamp in the window, responsible for any moral lapses by men or society. As the historian Jack Chen succinctly put it, "The lack of women and normal family life fostered gambling, prostitution, and opium smoking."[85]

In Sui Sin Far's short story "Lin John," Lin John's sister makes short work of this rationale when she steals the four hundred dollars her brother has saved to buy her out of prostitution. The sister knew that her brother planned to "send her to their parents in China, to live like an honest woman," but she would rather have "good dinners and pretty things."[86] The portrait of Lin John's sister challenges the assumption that women exist only to serve men or to conform to the moral categories men have assigned them. It challenges Virginia Woolf's metaphor of women "as looking-glasses possessing the magic and delicious power of reflecting the figure of man at twice its natural size" by presenting a woman who breaks the glass.[87] Characters like Lin John's sister act out the dilemma that Carolyn Heilbrun notes: "The choices and pain of the women who did not make a man the center of their lives seemed unique, because there were no models of the lives they wanted to live, no exemplars, no stories."[88]

The categories assigned to Chinese American women often had little to do with women's actual lives as individuals in Chinatown communities. Demographics for women are customarily cited in ratios, and many studies identify women mainly through the perspective of families. William F. Wu, for instance, writes, "In 1860, the male-female ratio for Chinese immigrants to the U.S. was 1,858 to 1; by 1890, it was 2,678 to 9. With statistics like these, one easily understands that few families were formed."[89] By numbering females in relation to males and failing to recognize female populations in their own right, studies have diminished the very real roles women from China have played in North American history. Gerda Lerner argues that authentic historical inquiry requires seeing women not in the context of men or family life but in the autonomous roles women themselves play in history. Lerner cautions that this requires knowing the right questions to ask and looking at data through a lens different from the one historians have traditionally used.[90] In her *Los Angeles Express* articles of 1903, Sui Sin Far used this alternate lens to write about women. Her report that "there are about 4,000 Chinese in Los Angeles, including about 75 women and from 50–60 children" shifts the spotlight to seventy-five individual women who were actively present, each with a journey behind her and a story to tell.[91] In Sui Sin Far's writings, women and children are visible in their own right; indeed, in her writings, they are the main characters. Women carry the points of view and hold the centers of action in eight of her ten stories published in this period, and in the other two they play major supporting roles. By opening women's worlds to her audience and portraying women's perspectives, Sui Sin Far not only breaks stereotypes about Chinatowns as bachelor societies of "alien others" but also depicts communities vibrant with women, children, and family life.

Sui Sin Far's *Express* pieces take us to the heart of Los Angeles's Chinatown, where we see not a swamp of depravity glimpsed from the window of a second floor tea room, as in Norris, or down a "long flight of grimy stairs," as in Dibert, but the daily affairs of a functioning, human neighborhood. In "Los Angeles' Chinatown," we visit a kindergarten where "the cutest of cute things, in their coats of many colors, purple trouserettes and wooden shoes with turned up toes" rush in and out. We are taken inside the schoolrooms to see "Chinese lanterns being swung overhead and tables spread with all kinds of good things and beautifully decorated with plants and flowers" during New Year and Christmas celebrations. The flute that Dibert's narrator heard "wail" from a mysterious distance is carried here by "the flutist" into the party, where he is accompanied by "the banjo man [and] his banjo."[92] In "Chinatown Needs a School," we meet Mrs. Sing, who has ten children ranging in age "from 4 to 20 years," all "native sons and daughters of the Golden West [who] speak both Chinese and English fluently"; we see her home—"furnished tastefully in a semi-eastern, semi-western style"—and view the portraits on her sitting room wall.[93] In "Chinatown Boys and Girls," we watch boys and girls on the street who "play as other children," with "bells, rattles, toys, and knick-knacks of all sorts," but who at the same time wear culturally distinct clothing: "A bright-hued silk Chinese cap decorated in front with a little gold god and a sprig of evergreen" tops the head of a baby boy.[94] In "Chinese in Business Here," we meet "medicine vendors, who comprise with their business fortune telling; undertakers, barbers, cobblers, tinkers, vegetable venders, and . . . the laundry man," many of whom "work at their trade or profession in the streets of Chinatown and sit with their tools, materials or compounds around them." The influence of women and children on this California community extends across the Pacific from China: many of the "curios" displayed in the shops "have been made by Chinese boys and girls living in small, isolated farmhouses and cottages of the Middle Kingdom," and "much of the beautiful embroidery work that we see is done by Chinese women in their own homes, and has provided many a poor family with rice and tea."[95] Moreover, in "Chinatown Needs a School," Sui Sin Far explicitly recognizes the "large number of families with children who ought not to be playing on the streets the greater part of the day."

Altogether, Sui Sin Far's journalistic portraits of Los Angeles's Chinatown reveal a diversity among the inhabitants that makes stereotyping while we read them impossible. The relationship between writer and subject assists this. In contrast to the tone of alienation and antagonism most writers maintain with Chinatown subjects, Sui Sin Far's voice is closely allied with the communities about which she writes, a position that reveals itself intermittently: "I have passed many a pleasant half hour or longer in the Chinese stores, taking a cup of tea here and there and a pinch of instruction in between whiles. . . ." In a passage such as the following, she identifies with her subjects more intimately: "Several times have I heard sounds of laughter issuing from the big laundry of Quong Chung & Co., on East Third Street, and paused to wonder why these homeless, childless, wifeless sons of labor, far from country and kindred, could carry with them into their exile the spirit of content."[96]

This tone of one immigrant alone in a strange land observing another calls to mind W. B. Harte's sense of Sui Sin Far's ability "to touch a pity that lies close to the surface in response to all human feeling."[97] For example, in opposition to the "no tickee, no washee" stereotype of the Chinese laundryman,[98] a figure who never attains intelligence at a human level in most literature of the period, Sui Sin Far introduces us to an individual. We observe his "ingenious method of checking the clothes left . . . to be washed," his choice of a theme such as "the heavenly bodies" for each passing week, and his creation of an original drawing (sun, moon, sky, or stars) that bears out this theme on a laundry check, which, when torn in half, matches laundry with customer.[99] A role that Kim perceives to be "clearly accepted [in America] as menial work for a despised people" is treated by Sui Sin Far with regard and respect.[100] The laundryman viewed by the reader of this piece is not an "alien Asian" but an efficient and imaginative businessman.

Another familiar Chinatown stereotype, the fortune teller, whom we have seen portrayed by Norris as a diabolical figure fronting for white slavers and by Dibert as an accomplice in the kidnapping of a young Chinese woman, is characterized in Sui Sin Far's "Horoscope" as a professional whom people in the Chinatown neighborhood consult as regularly and with the same trust as white Americans consult a doctor or priest: "Sometimes it was the question of the buying of a house, or in regard to some action of the Six Companies, or whether a brother Chinaman could be safely smuggled into the country, or if a sick cousin would recover . . . or a certain betrothal be lucky, and if so, whether the result would be many children."[101] In her *Express* article "Betrothals in Chinatown," Sui Sin Far explained the fortune teller's importance in the business of marriage and the process by which, after initial proposals were made, the parents of the couple must visit the fortune teller, have their children's horoscopes told, and thus discover whether the match appeared favorable.[102]

Fong Toy, the fortune teller in "The Horoscope," is characterized as human and fallible, by no means omnipotent in spite of his culturally granted authority. He informs the powerful Chinatown merchant Him Wing, " 'From the eight diagrams I learn that ill fortune will follow the betrothal of your daughter to the son of Hom Lock,' " a union on which both parents had "set their minds and hearts" so that "the house of Him and the house of Hom should be united." This prediction "by a contrary fortune teller galled them bitterly." Because of Fong Toy's authority, neither father "dreamed of ignoring his horoscope," yet both withdraw their business and use "their influence to draw from him the favor of other patrons" (522).

When the subject of the horoscope, Him Wing's daughter Mai Gwi Far, approaches Fong Toy with hints of her own romantic interest in him, the fortune teller faces an intense human conflict, between personal and professional interests: "Love called to him on one side, while professional pride held him on the other" (523). This dilemma is reinforced by complicated emotions: " 'There are stirrings within me of pleasure, sorrow, joy and anger—all caused through gazing at you.' " The conflicting feelings of Mai Gwi Far reveal themselves in return: " 'If it is not love, what is it? . . . Why was I glad when it was decreed that another was not to have me? Why did I grieve over your own misfortunes? Why am I here?' " (524). Signifying development beyond Sui Sin Far's previous fictional women, Mai Gwi Far does not commit suicide to avoid a betrothal but rather chooses her own husband instead of accepting one arranged by her parents. As the couple's situation emerges through the eyes of Chinese, not white Americans, we view the fortune teller as an ordinary professional undergoing a conflict about love, a subject familiar to every race. Fong Toy's situation demystifies the fortune teller's role, a point Mai Gwi Far makes through hyperbole: " 'Ah! . . . How grave, how dignified is our elegant and accomplished fortune-teller! So awe-inspiring his deportment. One can scarcely believe that he has feelings such as we common mortals' " (524).

White readers at that time obviously held preconceived notions about Chinese as "heathen," a term that in the Christian tradition is equated with "non-Christian," "irreligious," and "uncivilized."[103] Sui Sin Far portrays Chinese and Chinese Americans as generally serious about religion, sometimes following traditional Confucian faiths, sometimes practicing Christianity, and sometimes—reflecting the author's pluralistic attitudes—combining both with no sense of conflict. In "Chinatown Needs a School," Sui Sin Far notes, "In China to have a large family is a religious as well as a natural and political duty." The article "In Los Angeles' Chinatown" recognizes the diversity of Chinese American religion by observing that nine missions of varying Protestant denominations exist in the same neighborhood with three joss houses, from which "the smoke of the burning incense daily ascends to the nostrils of the wrathful or benevolent deities who preside." In describing the missions— "Four native Chinese preachers, backed by American church people, gather in the flock and a Christian Chinese sermon preached to a heathen Chinese congregation can be heard every Sunday"—Sui Sin Far suggests the eclecticism of Chinese Americans and blurs boundaries between organized religions. The narrator of "The Sing-Song Woman" may express the author's own religious views: "One does not need to be a Christian to be religious, and Lae Choo's parents had carefully instructed their daughter according to their light..." (225). The importance of keeping home religions alive in a new culture is highlighted in "Chinatown Boys and Girls" when the parents "called upon [their children] to perform their part" in such religious feasts and ceremonies as " 'The Completion of the Moon,' 'Passing Through the Door,' and 'The Worship of Ancestors.' "

In Sui Sin Far's fiction, religious life—usually defined as life of the spirit—is respected in whatever cultural form it appears. In "The Coat of Many Colors," after the Chinese husband Ke Leang is induced by a " 'red-headed' youth" to cross the sea from China to California, his wife (another Ku Yum) "lighted the sticks of incense before an image of Kuang Ing Huk, the Chinese goddess of mercy, and prayed to the spirit which she believed was in the image to help her husband to make his fortune quickly."[104] Ku Yum's religion is not Christianity, yet this character shares the Christian belief in a spiritual power to which she turns for assistance. Similarly, when Leih Tseih of "A Chinese Ishmael" is shipwrecked while running away from his debt, his "acknowledg[ment] with sorrow to the Parent of All that I have indeed wandered far from the path of virtue, and [vow], if my life were spared, to follow my conscience" taps what is, in Sui Sin Far's fiction, an instinctual human need to contact the spiritual in times of great fear.[105] Yet Sui Sin Far's fictional "spirits" also participate in her characters' daily lives and are evoked to serve a function. In "A Chinese Ishmael," it is a spirit who whispers in (another) Ku Yum's ear as Leih Tseih passes under her balcony: " 'Let fall a Chinese lily' " (43). This Ku Yum's faith in an afterlife transcends the divisions of class that separate her from Leih Tseih, a point made when she forms a pact with her lover to "leap into the Pacific": "Ah! that will be happiness—to enter the spirit-land, hand in hand. When my cousins in China hear of it, they will say, 'How fine! Our cousin,

Ku Yum, who was a slave-girl on earth, walks the Halls of Death with the son of a high mandarin' " (48).

In spite of Sui Sin Far's strong missionary background (maybe partly because of it), and in spite of the Christian faith that she apparently continued to practice, her writings offer no illusions about Christianity's being the only "true religion" or guide to morality—quite the contrary. As we have seen in her *Dominion Illustrated* fiction and in her 1896 letter to the *Montreal Daily Star* editor, some of her most biting ironies are built around the discrepancies between Christian teachings and practice. In "A Chinese Boy-Girl," the ambiguous nature of "spirits," or religious practices constructed by society to exert power over human lives, is illustrated when the Chinese American father Ten Suie explains why he has disguised his fifth son as "Ku Yum": " 'Every year for three year evil spirit come, look at my boy, and take him. Well, one, two, three, four, five, six years go by, I see but one boy, he four year old. I say to me, Ten Suie, evil spirit be jealous. I be 'flaid he want my one boy. So I take my one boy, I dless him like one girl. Evil spirit think him one girl, and go away; no want girl.' "[106] Miss Mason, a white teacher at the Los Angeles Chinatown school who has tried to take this child away from her father in the name of "morality," comes to recognize that by seeking " 'to keep an evil spirit away . . . he brought another, and one which nearly took you [the fifth son] from him [Ten Suie], too.' " By juxtaposing a "heathen" father who goes to drastic lengths to keep the last remnant of his family together and a "Christian" teacher who tries to break that family up, Sui Sin Far illustrates the ambiguity in words like *morality* and how socially contrived categories jump boundaries. Overall, she suggests it is not that the Chinese lack religion but that whites lack understanding of Chinese religion.

In these stories, Sui Sin Far clearly challenged the images of Chinatowns as the moral "swamps" depicted by such authors as Norris and Dibert. She originally spoke out against the "dreadful tales" told about New York's Chinatown as "a dangerously wicked place" from which she "would never come out alive or sound in mind or body" in her 21 September 1896 letter to the *Montreal Daily Star.* Her 1903 *Express* articles continued to reject such representations, replacing them with portraits of individuals going about their lives in their own cultural communities. Even in a melodramatic story like "A Chinese Ishmael," which features a knife-wielding villain in San Francisco's Chinatown, Sui Sin Far portrays a council session of Chinatown's governing body, the Six Companies, contrasting the lawlessness of one individual with a respect for law in the community as a whole.

The scene opens inside the council hall, where the presidents of the Six Companies are gathered and the chief of the Sam Yups is "urging the advisability of expending a sum of money for the relief of some sick laborers." A secretary enters and whispers to "the aged chief of the Hop Wos," after which

Lum Choy, "a repulsive-looking fellow whose forehead bore a huge scar," is admitted. Lum Choy petitions the council to prosecute Leih Tseih for assaulting him and for " 'abducting a slave girl named Ku Yum.' " In response to the Sam Yup chief's announcement that Leih Tseih has paid off " 'the whole of his indebtedness' " and that the council therefore has " 'no legal claim' " against him, Lum Choy protests: " 'What? . . . the powerful Six Companies have no jurisdiction over the men they have brought to this country?' " The ensuing dialogue demonstrates the council's awareness of the tight line they walk between two systems of government. " 'In some cases we have,' " replied the Hop Wo chief suavely, " 'but this case lies with the American courts.' " When Lum Choy protests that " 'I have paid a large sum for [the slave girl, Ku Yum] which Lee Chu will not refund,' " the chief of the Ning Yeongs answers that " 'the purchase of slave girls, which is just and right in our own country, is not lawful in America' " (46–47). In this scene, Sui Sin Far suggests that the Six Companies, Chinatown's governing body, maintain self-conscious boundaries between their laws and those of the broader society while respecting the precedence of the latter. For comparison, we may recall the lack of respect demonstrated for Chinese American culture in "A Chinese Boy-Girl" when "the Superior Court of the State" "decree[d] that Ku Yum, the child of Ten Suie, should be removed from the custody of her father" (829).

Sui Sin Far often made such cultural contrasts more explicitly. In her 21 September 1896 letter to the *Montreal Daily Star,* she asserted, "There are signs that in the future we in this country may attain to the high degree of civilization which the Chinese have reached, but for the present we are far away behind them in that respect." In the midst of "Chinese in Business Here," an otherwise "objective" article for the *Los Angeles Express* in 1903, she offered this comment: "The Chinese did their bookkeeping by the abacus system when the forefathers of the present 'Anglo-Saxon' Americans were living as savages in the British Isles or thereabouts." She wrote in the same article, "There is also this to be said in favor of Chinese ornaments. They are made of good and lasting material and are meant to please the eye for more than a day, which cannot be said of American manufactured knickknacks." By using such words as *savages* and *knickknacks,* she mirrors the condescending tone most of Sui Sin Far's contemporaries assumed toward the civilization of China.

Taking this a step further, Sui Sin Far contrasts the "civilization" of life inside Chinatowns with the pure savagery that her Chinese American characters encounter when they step outside Chinatown borders. In this way her fiction creates a direct inversion of popular stereotypes about Chinatown violence. This contrast is sometimes submerged so casually into the action that we must look twice to see it.[107] In "Ku Yum's Little Sister," for instance, our reader's eye may be so lulled by the simple plot line of a child walking off to try to find herself "a little sister" that we fail to notice it is when the child wanders "outside the precincts of Chinatown" that she feels "something sharp strike her cheek. It was a pebble." Pursued by a boy "joined by others of his kind," Ku Yum "ran pantingly up a hill and sank down exhausted, outside a fenced garden, where she lay sobbing and quivering in the cold and the dark."[108] Because the diction is in the mode of children's fiction and Ku Yum is soon rescued and taken home, the tale resolves itself "happily." As readers, we can dismiss the piece easily without ever realizing that this is the scene of a stoning—the kind remembered by the oldtimers in the Nee study as they walked to San Francisco's Chinatown from the wharf, the kind that could kill a small girl or even an adult if a policeman had not "put a stop to the chase."

White racist attacks against Chinese North Americans in Sui Sin Far's fiction are not in the forefront of the action, but they are consistent: background to the Chinese American living environment, as ever-present as the weather. In "O Yam—A Sketch," we are told, "Like all Chinamen living in America, Wo Kee was subjected to considerable annoyance from thoughtless boys." It is not until the next sentence that the author designates the form this "annoyance" takes: "One day a number of [boys], passing [Wo Kee's] garden and seeing him there, began to pitch earth and pebbles on his back, at the same time making remarks on his dress and features."[109] In this story's "killdeer technique," the reader's (and presumably the editor's) attention is diverted from the exposure of racist abuse to the safer domestic plot of a young girl trying to get to the bedside of her dying father. Brutal attacks against the Chinese American father by what we assume are white American children proceed almost incidentally in the margins of action—perhaps because the author considered these too subversive to be accepted directly. Illustrating Joan Radner and Susan Lanser's strategy of "distraction,"[110] the story line in "O Yam—A Sketch," as in "Ku Yum's Little Sister," is a superficial melodrama, but a closer reading reveals that the story's depths conceal something else.

By such methods Sui Sin Far guides her readers' perceptions to a different stance from what we are used to seeing in literature.[111] Her work invites readers to see life in North America from the vantage points of characters who are of Chinese, not European, descent. In her 21 September 1896 letter to the *Montreal Daily Star,* Sui Sin Far challenged Maxwell for saying the Chinese were "docile and easily managed," arguing that he mistook the "quiet dignity" of many Chinese American immigrants, who had been taught to avoid violence and to "treat the rude with silent contempt." In "O Yam—A Sketch," Sui Sin Far's portrait of Wo Kee, who "paid no attention whatever to his tormentors" (342), captures this quiet dignity. It could represent both Sui Sin Far's sense of the Chinese American stance in a hostile North America and her own stance as artist. Chinese American enclaves in Sui Sin Far's fiction, whether composed of Wo Kee in his solitary garden or thousands of individuals gathered in a community, function for Chinese Americans much as

Plymouth Plantation functioned for William Bradford's English immigrants: a bulwark of civilization against the perceived wilderness of a strange continent. For Sui Sin Far, a child of both sides, perhaps the only garden in which to take refuge was her art.

Assimilation, Americanization, and Cultural Pluralism

In explaining "cultural hegemony," T. J. Jackson Lear argues that relationships in society are not fixed and static but in the process of continual creation; cultural realities fluctuate in an ongoing dialogue between, in Lear's terms, the "ruler" and the "ruled."[112] Sui Sin Far's writings illustrate this process. They deal with the dialogue between Chinese and European immigrants in North America, tracing the dynamics through which a new culture, "Chinese American," is being born."[113] Her description of Los Angeles's plaza in "A Chinese Boy-Girl" in 1903 catches the region's pluralism in action: "The persons of mixed nationalities lounging on the benches. . . . The Italians who ran the peanut-and-fruit stands . . . The Chinese merchants' stores in front of the plaza. . . . A little Chinese girl with bright eyes and round cheeks . . . a woman tourist who was making a sketch of the old Spanish church" (828). But such pluralism in the United States at the turn of the century was at best only tolerated as a marginal phenomenon; in practice, efforts were made to assimilate each new immigrant group into the European-based culture as quickly as possible. In "A Chinese Ishmael," Ku Yum indicates her scorn for assimilative practices as she describes the villain Lum Choy to her benefactress, A-Cheun: " 'He is a man who, wishing to curry favor with the white people, wears American clothes, and when it suits his convenience passes for a Japanese' " (44). A-Cheun's response—" 'Shame on him!' "—signifies Sui Sin Far's attitude toward such pretense, especially when it involves a denial of heritage.

In Sui Sin Far's writings, "Americanization" can be a choice, but often it is a process whereby white Americans force Chinese Americans to relinquish their native traditions and adapt the language, religions, and manners of mainstream America, as modeled on England.[114] The institution that most aggressively functions to assimilate immigrants in Sui Sin Far's view is the Christian mission movement, whose vehicle, the mission school, lures Chinese American immigrants with the promise of teaching them the English language and then strives to convert them culturally. Other institutions exert similar pressure. In her *Los Angeles Express* article "Chinatown Needs a School," Sui Sin Far pinpoints the schools: "[Chinese] children will be admitted into the American schools if they were [sic] dressed in American fashion, but not otherwise, and this is a great hardship and inconvenience to Chinese mothers who in many cases are unable to make the child's clothes in American style and occasionally are too poor to afford the change." Through such passages, Sui Sin Far's writings point to the dangers in "Americanization."

In Sui Sin Far's writings, however, the dynamics by which Chinese become Chinese American are rarely simply a one-sided dialogue between the powerful and powerless but instead express themselves at every level, from descriptive details to theme and plot. The process can begin mentally the instant a Chinese national considers migrating westward. In "The Coat of Many Colors," Ke Leang "was well content and every day gave thanks to having been born in China," until a "red-headed stranger" planted the seed in his mind that he was foolish to work in the rice fields like his father and should "think for himself," because " 'that is what we believe in the West.' " After this encounter, the narrator tells us, Ke Leang "was no longer contented. Like Oliver Twist, he wanted more." The North American culture becomes more deeply ingrained in some characters than in others, especially those of the second generation. When Fong Toy of "The Horoscope" tries to block Mai Gwi Far from leaving his office by standing against the door, the narrator comments, "It was a bold thing for a Chinaman to do, and a strange thing for a Chinese girl to suffer, but it must be remembered that Fong Toy and Mai Gwi Far were living in America, and Chinese people living in America adopt many of the foreign devil ways, despite what has been said to the contrary (523). The narrative voice in Sui Sin Far's stories often reminds the reader that second-generation Chinese Americans hold equal status as native-born Americans. In "O Yam—A Sketch," the title character is described as "a native daughter of the Golden State, even though she did wear a long braid interwoven with many colored silks hanging down her back and reaching almost to the heels of her tiny embroidered shoes" (341).

The relationship between Chinese immigrants and other members of their new society starts becoming coercive when white Americans start dropping hints to Chinese Americans that they should become more like whites. Passing by Wo Kee's garden each day, the white ladies in "O Yam—A Sketch" who are his "patrons" stop for "a few words" with his daughter. "One lady was so interested," the narrator points out, "that she made a request to Wo Kee that O Yam should be sent to her house every day for the purpose of learning all that a little American girl should know. . . ." Though Wo Kee assents, the child fends the ladies off: "O Yam would not be weaned from her father's side for even one hour." Commenting on the closeness of father and daughter, the narrator takes an insider perspective to dash a stereotype about Chinese fathers' not loving their daughters: "And Wo Kee's love for the child and his care of her were such that those whose knowledge of the Chinese was limited to books could not help but express surprise" (341). O Yam in turn defends her father from stone-throwing boys and later stops an express train to journey to his side when he takes sick while away on a trip. Her persistent loyalty to her father's culture is particularly underlined when she forces the train to stop: "Between the rails stood O Yam holding aloft a broom. Tied to the upper end of the broom was a magenta silk garment—O Yam's best blouse.... The train thundered down. Its breath was on the child.... The train stopped, *almost* too late" (342–43). However melodramatic this scene may appear by today's standards, it offers an effective emblem of heroic cultural resistance against the power of white society. In life, that train was not so easily halted.

Four years later "A Chinese Boy-Girl" explores a similar theme, with greater subtlety and deeper complexities. Long before the narrator informs us that the white schoolteacher Miss Mason has obtained a court order to have Ku Yum taken from "her" father and "put into a home for Chinese girls," we know this is a story about the forcible assimilation of the offspring of immigrants—which, at its worst, involves stealing children. Such phrases as "the other pupils were demure little maidens who, after once being gathered into the fold, were very willing to remain" depict the Chinatown school's effort to produce uniformity, and Miss Mason, well-intentioned as she seems ("if ever the teacher broke her heart over anyone it was over Ku Yum"), is the agent for assimilation. Worried about Ku Yum because the child does not "obey orders," is seen "running wild with the boys," and learns rules "only for the purpose of finding a means to break them," Miss Mason convinces herself that "she had a duty to perform toward the motherless little girl," and hence the teacher becomes "determined to act." For a conventional writer of Chinatown fiction, the court order would be considered a triumph and mark the end of the story. For Sui Sin Far, it marks the beginning of Miss Mason's inner conflict ("What had previously seemed her distinct duty no longer appeared so"), and the story turns into an identity farce (829).

After the court order is granted, Ku Yum disappears, "and those who were deputed to bring her to the sheltering home were unable to find her" (829). The teacher's act damages her standing with former Chinese friends, who meet her with "averted faces and downcast eyes, and her school had within a week dwindled from twenty-four scholars to four" (830). The Chinese in this community resist Miss Mason's "well-intentioned" act of cultural arrogance and prove the misguided nature of her perceptions. When Miss Mason meets Ten Suie, the child's father, he reveals that Ku Yum is not as she assumed, a "motherless little girl," but a boy in disguise. Under the Victorian assumptions at work when "A Chinese Boy-Girl" was written, this revelation shifts everything. It adds a gender issue to what has previously focused mainly on race. Because it is more acceptable for a boy to "run wild" on the streets than for a girl, Miss Mason is shocked into second thoughts. When Ten Suie (in his quiet, dignified way) forces this mission schoolteacher to acknowledge her faulty perceptions of her Chinese American students and the abuse of power in her court order, Miss Mason's vision of life is mocked and proved false. Instead of her bringing "light" to this Chinatown community, its people enlighten her. Cultural hegemony is caught changing positions between the "ruler" and "ruled."

As the daughter of Lotus Blossom and the sister of Winifred, Sui Sin Far obviously recognized the fallacies in simplistic views of assimilation. As a person of biracial heritage, she knew that one's race marked the limits of acceptance by the European-dominated North American culture. Wo Kee is performing the culturally neutral act of working in his garden when the boys attack him from over his fence. Ku Yum is only taking a walk when the silk ribbon is pulled from her braid and the boys chase her. In these stories, abuse is based not on how "Americanized" one is but on racial appearance. We know that Sui Sin Far was born in England, reared in an Anglicized environment, and could pass for white, yet she suffered from racist abuse all her life. Mag-gee's dialogue with Lae Choo in "The Sing-Song Woman" could be Sui Sin Far's dialogue with her younger sisters about whether to be "Chinese" or to be "white." When Mag-gee marries an Irishman and stays in the United States, does she completely cross borders, culturally and psychologically? When Sui Sin Far's sisters all married white husbands, did they? How did those choices alter their relationship with the sister who was determined to claim her Chinese heritage?

A tentative pluralistic ideal for a society that respects difference while remaining human across racial lines is implied by Sui Sin Far when the Chinese American title character of "Ku Yum's Little Sister" finally finds "a little sister" in an older "white" woman "who could also speak Ku Yum's language," who "took Ku Yum in her arms and comforted and petted her as Ku Yum had not been petted and comforted since her [Chinese] mother died two years before," and who—instead of "rescuing" the child by keeping her outside of Chinatown—"took Ku Yum home," where "her father talked with her new friend" (4). This ideal is also implicit in "The Coat of Many Colors," symbolized in the garment Ke Leang makes for his son: "It was veritably a coat of many colors and many designs, and had been made by Ke Leang himself, who had delighted in seeing his son roll around in it."[115] Unlike its biblical antecedent, Ke Leang's coat serves as a catalyst for a reunion with his family in China, causes his memory to be restored, and inspires the man to write to his wife that "he had overcome a great evil, an evil which had threatened to separate them forever." Symbolically, that evil was forgetting China.

Giving Voice

Whether in response to the largely silent voice of her Chinese mother, to her siblings' concealment of their Chinese ancestry, to the lack of public recognition for Chinese American women, or to her own lifelong fight for a voice, Sui Sin Far's key concern is with women who emerge from the shadows and demand visibility. We meet them as Ku Yum in a "San Francisco Chinatown tenement" and as O Yam in a rural southern California village. Their relationships with males are many and varied, but it is in bonding with one another that they find special strength and design solutions to their multiple conflicts. In Sui Sin Far's journalism, female children are prominent in scenes of Chinatown streets and are drawn with individualizing details. In "Chinatown Needs a School," we meet such women as Mrs. Sing, "surrounded by a family of ten bright children" in a "pretty house on East Commercial Street." Their intercultural status is recognized with passages like "All these children are native sons and daughters of the Golden West and speak both Chinese and English fluently." The fact that six are daughters signifies an increase in the Chinese American female population.

Sui Sin Far's female characters, even literally, defy neat historical categories. The title character of "The Story of Tin-A," for example, "was born on the island of Formosa, so . . . [is] not a Cantonese like most of the Chinese who come to this country."[116] The unnamed sister who plays the lead in "Lin John" prefers her work as a (successful) prostitute to the only other option held out as available—marriage. The title character in "The Smuggling of Tie Co" is believed by everyone to be a man until customs officers bring her body out of the St. Lawrence River.[117] These characters' relationships with men are as varied as their diverse life-styles permit. Tin-A gives Hum Ling, the chief of a troupe of actors, her jewelry to pay her way to the United States. Lin John's sister steals the bag of gold her brother has saved to buy her out of prostitution. Tie Co jumps into the river to save the life of the white Canadian smuggler Jack Fabian. Even though the mothers of many are (inexplicably) dead, Sui Sin Far's women characters, like the fictional characters of women writers from many cultures, experience their most intense relationships with other women, for it is a woman's world they mostly occupy.[118]

Sometimes they hurt one another—as in "A Chinese Ishmael," when Mrs. Lee Chu, Ku Yum's mistress, beats her—but more often they help. Women who are virtual strangers step forward to offer support in times of need. In "A Chinese Ishmael," "when Ku Yum's screams rent the air in response to her mistress' beating, [the neighbor woman A-Cheun's] heart swelled big with pity" (43), leading her to let Ku Yum and her lover meet in her apartment and to help them escape. Women also regularly serve each other as confidantes, revealing angles of perception to which men have no access. Explaining to her friend E-Sang why she stole the bag of gold from her brother, Lin John's sister observes, " 'Lin John meant well, but he knows little' " (77). Often women will drop everything to help each other in trouble, as in "The Sing-Song Woman," when Lae Choo stands in for Mag-gee as the bride. Women's loyalty to their sisterhood is perhaps best illustrated in Tin-A's reason for migrating: she is escaping the marriage her father has arranged for her as the second wife of her best friend's husband. A letter from that friend, A-Ho, to Tin-A and Tin-A's response demonstrate Sui Sin Far's awareness of the potential complexities in women's friendship:

> A-Ho pleaded with me not to become wife to her husband. She said, "Tin-A, I love him, and cannot bear to see another in my place. My affection for you has never changed, and my eyes long to behold you, but not, oh, not as a sharer in him. . . ."
> My heart burned within me, and the tears that did not fall were behind my eyes. I recalled the hour when A-Ho and I had parted. Between her sobs she had murmured, "Love me always and never grieve me," and clinging to her I had promised that the grave should receive me before act of mine should pain her or my heart prove false. (102)

With Tin-A's choice to defy her father, loyalty to her friend resounds as the woman's priority.

These characterizations that portray women who risk everything to take a voice in their destinies break the stereotype of Chinese and Chinese American women as victims, allowing them to transcend the oppressiveness of their circumstances. As we have seen with the slave girl Ku Yum in "A Chinese Ishmael," this can involve fighting off advances from men they do not want; conversely, it can mean making advances to men they do want. Ku Yum shows that even a slave can assert herself: "Underneath the balcony there passed a young man, and as he went by, some spirit whispered in Ku Yum's ear, 'Let fall a Chinese lily.' Ku Yum obeyed the spirit, and the young man, whose name was Leih Tseih, raised his eyes, and seeing Ku Yum, loved her" (43).[119] Such assertiveness is treated with a comic touch in "The Horoscope." When the fortune teller Fong Toy (who, reflecting the social mores, believes that "every girl desires a husband") first sees "the maiden whose marriage to a promising young man he had been instrumental in preventing," he fears that she has come to his office "to visit her wrath upon his head." Instead, Mai Gwi Far gives him "sweet thanks" and reveals that she is attracted to him. "It was not proper, of course," the narrator tells us, "but even a Chinese girl, under certain circumstances, can be unconventional" (522–23). Within the context of a society that expected women to be reticent, Sui Sin Far's women in these stories are "unconventional"; they even talk, in their author's understated language, about their own sexuality. When Ku Yum says to A-Chuen in "A Chinese Ishmael," "'I am only a slave, but still a Chinese maiden,'" she declares her virginity to this older woman who wants to help her (45).

The female protagonists of both "A Chinese Ishmael" and "The Smuggling of Tie Co" choose death but with motives that are different from those of the earlier suicides—both move to claim love, not to escape it. Most characters of this period opt for life, resolving their conflicts strategically. Mag-gee of "The Sing-Song Woman," Lin John's sister, and Tin-A all escape from unwanted marriages cunningly, by their own wiles. The title character of "Aluteh" is a warrior figure, subtly manipulating the intricacies of the political system of her province in China to save her father, Yenfoh, from ruin. When "she whispers words of consolation" to her father, offering to speak for him to the viceroy, Yenfoh admonishes her, " 'Daughter, be not so frivolous. . . . I am pondering a weighty matter. . . . Ah, that you had been a man child.' "[120] Ironically, this "woman child" ends up rescuing both her father and her future husband, a falsely accused magistrate. Like Abigail, the woman who rescues a man on a Montreal street corner in Sui Sin Far's "Origin of A Broken Nose,"[121] Aluteh reverses gender expectations about who rescues whom.

"The Story of Tin-A" merits further analysis, for its protagonist's conflict is the most complicated and her resolution the bravest. In response to A-Ho's letter, Tin-A reflects on when the two girls, who "were of the same age," played together (perhaps not unlike Sui Sin Far and her sisters), "picking flowers on the hillsides or seaweed from the rocks on the seashore." She recalls her loneliness after A-Ho married and moved away and her feelings upon learning that her father was arranging for her to become the second wife of A-Ho's husband: "both glad and sad—glad because I should again be with my friend, and sad because I was to leave home for the first time in my life." Tin-A reveals that the real truth did not dawn until she received A-Ho's letter: " 'My sin is that I have borne my husband no son, and to you would be given the first wife's place. So Tin-A, so dear, have compassion on your poor A-Ho, and be not the instrument through which she is made a discarded wife.' " With this recognition, Tin-A never considers accepting the situation but strives to find a way out. Going to her father, she "besought him to deliver me from the marriage contract." When he laughs, she goes to her stepmothers, but they "feared my father too greatly to interfere." Finally, she appeals to the chief of a "company of actors" who have arrived in the village to perform—can she travel with them, " 'to be a man and an actor' " (102)?

Assuming the voice of society, Hum Ling, the chief actor, "laughed and said that that was impossible"—because Tin-A "was a woman." Hum Ling does, however, permit Tin-A to immigrate with them to the United States as his wife's "companion," and when he tries to marry her off to "some San Francisco Chinaman," Tin-A refuses, maintaining her own independence. The character's closing lines reveal the pain she lives with as a consequence of her decision to break with tradition: " 'Am I happy? . . . How can that be when the greatest sin of all is to sin against one's parents? . . . Heaven will surely punish me for unfilial conduct' " (103). Such awareness does not, however, stop Tin-A, as it did not stop Sui Sin Far, from the pursuit of her own sense of

right and of her own destiny. Like Sui Sin Far, Tin-A calls out from exile at
the end of the story; she is an immigrant still in search of a geographical and
spiritual center.

Conclusion: The Play's the Thing

The stories examined in this chapter reveal a "trickster" stance in Sui Sin Far's
writing that will become more complex in later stories. We can see the
trickster antics of characters and the author's manipulation of audience
expectations. "The Story of Tin-A" especially plays with allusions to fiction
and fiction-making. At the height of Tin-A's conflict, she witnesses a play
performed by the troupe of actors: "The female characters were taken by boys,
and an old man was represented by a youth wearing a false beard; another
youth with a shrill voice played the part of an old woman." Nothing is as it
appears; the actors construe even social categories of age and gender as
manipulatable constructions. The plot of this play centers on "the joys and
woes of a beautiful princess who flees from her home for love of some humble
young man whom her parents are opposed to" (102). It is while watching it
that Tin-A (like Hamlet) is inspired to act—transferring the message of the
play to her life: " 'Well, this play so excited my imagination that then and there
watching it, I resolved that I too would leave home.' " Yet while the play
clearly offers a mirror image of the story itself, Tin-A's motives ironically
contrast with those of the play's princess. She flees " 'not, however, for love of
any man, more because I feared one' " (102–3). Sui Sin Far's story, in which
female friendship receives the highest priority, contrasts with the play, which
has standard romantic themes.

Survival for Tin-A, as for most women in Sui Sin Far's worlds, often
depends on metamorphosis, or the transformation of socially formulated
realities. This message is continually reinforced by Sui Sin Far's disguises, one
of which I suggest for this story. "The Story of Tin-A" was published in 1899,
the same year Sui Sin Far visited southern California, and the narrator who
reports Tin-A's tale is described as a southern California traveler: "I had been
riding many miles; and feeling tired and hungry, I dismounted and knocked at
the cottage door." A Chinese man invites the traveler into a room, where
her/his eyes "strayed over the garden" and spot Tin-A "bending over a large
bush of scented-geranium." With the questions, "Who was she? Why was she
living there?" the traveler invites Tin-A to share breakfast, draws "her out to
talk of herself, and here gives her story as she related it" (101). Because of the
reader's conditioned responses to gender roles and fictional formulas, it is easy
to suppose that this traveler is male. There are no distinguishing pronouns or
evidence to support this assumption, however. Both Sui Sin Far's biography

and the tone of curiosity lead me to believe that the model for the traveler narrator was Sui Sin Far.

Such play with her audience's expectations marks Sui Sin Far's style in many stories of this period. It is seen in "Lin John," where we are told that someone approaches the title character with "stealthy step" to slip the bag of gold from his sleeve; we do not learn until later that the thief is Lin John's own sister. It is seen in "A Chinese Boy-Girl," where the naive reader is trapped along with Miss Mason into misperceiving reality because of the gender- and culture-bound expectations for a Chinese American "girl." It is seen in "The Smuggling of Tie Co," with the confusion of the Chinese Canadian men in a Montreal laundry who cannot understand how a body "found with Tie Co's face and dressed in Tie Co's clothes" could belong to "a girl—a woman" (104). Sui Sin Far teases her readers by presenting us with situations and characters that appear to fit stereotypes but in fact disprove them.

Sui Sin Far's evolving trickster stance is not confined to fictional representations; it also occurs in her factual pieces. Between 3 February and 9 March 1904, a time when Sui Sin Far claimed that she was writing a "series of articles" from Montreal for the *Los Angeles Express,*[122] a series appeared in the *Express* entitled "Wing Sing of Los Angeles on His Travels."[123] "Wing Sing" is identified as "the pen name of a well-known Americanized merchant . . . [who] recently left Los Angeles to . . . visit his old home in China, going by way of Montreal." He takes the reader on this indirect route (the same Sui Sin Far likely used), going by steamship and rail to San Francisco and Vancouver, then by the "one big train name Canadian Pacific . . . to railway station, Montreal." Upon Wing Sing's arrival in Montreal, he observes, "The Chinese lily, the Chinaman call the Sui Sin Far, it bloom in the house of the Chinese at this time and its fragrance greet me like a friend." Furthermore, as a Chinese American tourist, Wing Sing goes to pay "respects to the Gambling Cash Tiger"—a god repeatedly referred to in Sui Sin Far's fiction, though I have not found it elsewhere.

Radner and Lanser suggest that "in the creations and performances of women—and indeed of other oppressed groups. . . . Coding occurs . . . in situations where some of the audience may be competent to decode the message, but others . . . are not."[124] These critics cite Susan Glaspell's "A Jury of Her Peers" as exemplary: after a woman is arrested for murder, two other women are able to "decode" the message in the quilt blocks in her basket, while the men present, including the sheriff and district attorney, overlook such evidence as insignificant. To the writer who relies on coding, "facts" are important only as they pertain to her purpose. In the conclusion to her 1903 article "Chinatown Boys and Girls," Sui Sin Far prefaced a poem entitled "The Lost Fairy" with the note, "A Chinese mother says the following verses are her daughter's." While it is not stated explicitly, it is implied that this "daughter" belonged to a Chinatown family in Los Angeles in 1903. Only the reader familiar with Sui Sin Far throughout her career would recognize that thirteen years earlier Edith Eaton had published a version of this same poem in "In Fairyland."[125] The following appears in both texts:

> Hast thou forgotten fairyland,
> The maze of golden light
> The flower-gemmed bowers,
> The crystal founts,
> The skies forever bright—
> Save when the evening shadows crept
> Athward the roseal blue,
> And the pale moon whispered to the sun,
> "Say to the earth, Adieu!"[126]

Given that we know Edith Eaton published this poem earlier, we can infer that Sui Sin Far is the "daughter" the *Express* article alludes to and that the "Chinese mother" is Lotus Blossom.

Of primary importance is that Sui Sin Far, who shared the condition of exile with the "Chinese in America" about whom she wrote, was coding herself as one of their community in her writings of the early 1900s. In her *Express* article "Leung Ki Chu and His Wife," Sui Sin Far featured another woman in exile, the wife of the Chinese reformer who, for safety's sake, had been sent to live in Japan. Envisioning this woman's plight, Sui Sin Far imagines her voice: "Those who believe in ideals and hero-worship may picture her—when her children are in bed and her husband over the sea— stretching her arms Chinaward and crying: 'Oh, China! Unhappy country! What would I not sacrifice to see thee uphold thyself among nations?' " In this apostrophe summoned from over the ocean, Sui Sin Far creates a double, another woman with whom she may share the dream of restoration for a lost homeland. By assigning herself an identity as a Chinese American "daughter" who wrote poetry in English, the writer might have been pointing to the most stability that she had yet found as a woman of Chinese-English heritage in colonized North America: "a home in writing itself."

Notes

1. "An Act to Extend the Exclusion Act of 1882 Indefinitely," *United States Statutes at Large,* vol. 32, part 1 (1901–3), 176. The 1882 act forbade any Chinese or person of Chinese descent to enter the United States by either land or sea vessel. The act did not define "Chinese descent."

2. Nella Larsen, *Quicksand and Passing,* ed. Deborah McDowell (Camden, N.J.: Rutgers University Press, 1986 [1929]), 150.

3. Frank Chin et al., eds., *Aiiieeeee! An Anthology of Asian American Literature* (Garden City, N.Y.: Anchor, 1991 [1974]), x.

4. Amy Ling, *Between Worlds: Women Writers of Chinese Ancestry* (New York: Pergamon, 1990).

5. Sui Sin Far, "Leaves from the Mental Portfolio of an Eurasian," *Independent* 66 (21 January 1909): 128.

6. Mary Lynn Broe and Angela Ingram, eds., *Women's Writings in Exile* (Chapel Hill: University of North Carolina Press, 1989), 5.

7. Sui Seen Far, "The Sing-Song Woman," *Land of Sunshine* 9 (October 1898): 225–28.

8. Victor G. Nee and Brett De Bary Nee, *Longtime Californ': A Documentary Study of an American Chinatown* (New York: Pantheon Books, 1972), 61.

9. See Sucheng Chan, *This Bittersweet Soil: The Chinese in California Agriculture, 1860–1910* (Berkeley: University of California Press, 1986), for a study of the Chinese American agricultural community in southern California.

10. Karen C. Wong, *Chinese History in the Pacific Northwest* (Seattle: n.p., 1972), 36, indicates the Chinese Seattle population was 438 in 1900 and 924 in 1910.

11. Jack Chen, *The Chinese in America* (New York: Harper and Row, 1980), 122, contends there were 300,000 Chinese in the United States in 1882.

12. Ibid., 61.

13. Ibid., 58.

14. Though laundry work has been generally seen in the United States as a stereotypically "Chinese" occupation, Elaine Kim, *Asian American Literature: An Introduction to the Writings and Their Social Context* (Philadelphia: Temple University Press, 1982), 99, asserts that laundry work "has been a strictly American phenomena . . . permitted because whites did not want to do laundry work themselves. . . ."

15. Chen, *The Chinese in America*, 60–61.

16. The Chinese Exclusion Act was not lifted until 1943, a move by the U.S. government related to Chinese resistance to Japan during World War II. Roger Daniels, *Asian America* (Seattle: University of Washington Press, 1988), 191–98, examines the repeal of the Chinese Exclusion Act in depth.

17. Ibid., 111.

18. Arnold Genthe, *Old Chinatown: A Book of Pictures,* text by Will Irwin (New York: Mitchell Kennerley, 1913), 43–44. Originally printed by Plimpton Press, Norwood, Mass., 1908.

19. Him Mark Lai, Genny Lim, and Judy Yung, *Island: Poetry and History of Chinese Immigrants on Angel Island, 1910 to 1940* (San Francisco: HOC DOI, 1980), 10. All the laws mentioned are discussed in this text.

20. Nee and Nee, *Longtime Californ',* 60.

21. Ibid., 72.

22. Daniels, *Asian America,* 58–59.

23. Sau-ling C. Wong, "What's in a Name? Defining Chinese American Literature of the Immigrant Generation," in *Frontiers of Asian American Studies,*

ed. Gail M. Nomura et al. (Pullman: Washington State University Press, 1989), 159.

24. Among historians to advance this theory are John Burt Foster, "China and the Chinese in American Literature, 1850–1950" (Ph.D. diss., University of Illinois, 1952); William F. Wu, *The Yellow Peril: Chinese Americans in American Fiction, 1850–1940* (Hamden, Conn.: Archon Books, 1982); and Doug Chin and Art Chin, *Uphill: The Settlement and Diffusion of the Chinese in Seattle* (Seattle: Shorey, 1974).

25. Chin and Chin, *Uphill,* 39.

26. Doug Chin and Peter Bacho, *The International District: History of an Urban, Ethnic Neighborhood in Seattle* (Seattle: International Examiner, n.d.).

27. *Los Angeles Express,* 6 October 1903.

28. Nee and Nee, *Longtime Californ',* 63.

29. Ibid.

30. Most Chinese who migrated to North America were Cantonese from the Pearl River Delta in Kwangtung (alternately spelled Guangdong) Province on the south coast of China. The relationship between these people's diaspora and European/North American interference with China's internal sovereignty is referred to in Harry Con et al., *From China to Canada: A History of the Chinese Community in Canada,* ed. Edgar Wickberg (Toronto: McClelland and Stewart, 1988), 6–7.

31. Nee and Nee, *Longtime Californ',* 66.

32. Ibid.

33. Lucie Cheng Hirata, "Free, Indentured, Enslaved: Chinese Prostitutes in Nineteenth-Century America," *Signs* 5 (1979): 3–29.

34. Ruthanne Lum McCunn, *A Thousand Pieces of Gold* (New York: Dell, 1981).

35. Peggy Pascoe, *Relations of Rescue: The Search for Female Moral Authority in the American West, 1874–1939* (New York: Oxford University Press, 1990), 163.

36. Hirata, "Free, Indentured, Enslaved," 12.

37. Dorothy Gray, *Women of the West* (Millbrae, Calif.: Les Femmes, 1976), 69.

38. Hirata, "Free, Indentured, Enslaved," 17.

39. Judy Yung, *Chinese Women in America: A Pictorial History* (Seattle: University of Washington Press, 1986), 14.

40. As cited in Chinese Historical Society of California, UCLA, *Linking Our Lives: Chinese American Women of Los Angeles* (Los Angeles: Chinese Historical Society of California, UCLA, 1984), 2.

41. Yung, *Chinese Women in America,* 14.

42. Ibid. Yung explains that "China Mary" is a generic name white Americans used for Chinese women, just as they used "John Chinaman" for Chinese men.

43. *San Francisco Call,* 25 June 1897, 10.

44. Lucie Cheng Hirata, "Chinese Immigrant Women in Nineteenth-Century

California," in *Women of America: A History,* ed. Carol Ruth Berkin and Mary Beth Norton (Boston: Houghton Mifflin, 1979), 238.

45. Ginger Chih, *The History of Chinese Immigrant Women, 1850–1940* (North Bergen, N.J.: G. Chih, 1977), 28.

46. Pascoe, *Relations of Rescue,* 11.

47. Nee and Nee, *Longtime Californ',* 60.

48. Ibid., 74.

49. Con et al., *From China to Canada,* 75.

50. Nee and Nee, *Longtime Californ',* 72.

51. Edith Eaton to Charles Lummis, 16 September 1900, Charles Fletcher Lummis Collection, Southwest Museum, Los Angeles, Calif. (hereafter cited as SWM).

52. Sui Sin Far's acquaintance with Chinese political figures is further suggested in an undated news article given to me by Charles Laferrière. Printed in the *Montreal Gazette* and captioned "Sun Yat Sen Paid Visit to Montreal," its description of Sun Yat Sen's secret visit to Montreal in the early part of the century includes the following: "Amongst the few who were in the secret of the Doctor being here was the late Miss Edith Eaton, a clever literary lady, who was Chinese from her mother's side, the latter a full blooded Chinese lady. . . . She had the entry to Sun Yat Sen's suite of rooms for herself and a few selected friends. . . ."

53. Sui Sin Far, "Leung Ki Chu and His Wife," *Los Angeles Express,* 22 October 1903.

54. Foster, "China and the Chinese in American Literature," 145.

55. Ibid., 144.

56. Wu, *The Yellow Peril,* 1.

57. *San Francisco Call,* 2 April, 17 May, 19 May, and 16 August 1899.

58. *Los Angeles Express,* 2 and 4 December 1903.

59. William Purviance Fenn, "Ah Sin and His Brethren in American Literature" (Ph.D. diss., State University of Iowa, 1932), 111.

60. Ibid., 113.

61. Ibid., 116.

62. Frank Norris, "The Third Circle," in *Collected Works of Frank Norris,* vol. 4 (New York: Kennikat Press, 1967 [1928]), 1–10.

63. Olive Dibert, "The Chinese Lily," *Overland Monthly* 42 (August 1903): 184–88.

64. Fenn, "Ah Sin and His Brethren in American Literature," 66.

65. Glenn Altschuler, *Race, Ethnicity and Class in American Social Thought, 1865–1919* (Arlington Heights, Ill.: Harlan Davidson, 1982), 120.

66. Kim, *Asian American Literature,* observes that missionaries showed only the most negative aspects of Chinese culture to reinforce the role of the missionaries as "saviors." She maintains that in many stories the missionaries become the "key to [the Chinese woman's] liberation from her own culture" (17).

67. Edith Eaton to R. U. Johnson, 4 December 1903, Century Company

Records, Rare Books and Manuscripts Division, New York Public Library (hereafter cited as NYPL).

68. *John* was a term applied to Chinese males generically in current popular usage.

69. W. B. Harte, "Bubble and Squeak," *Lotus* 2 (October 1896): 216–17.

70. Charles F. Lummis, "In Western Letters," *Out West* 13 (November 1900): 336.

71. S. E. Solberg, Interview, Pullman, Wash., March 1988.

72. Sui Sin Far, "Sui Sin Far, the Half Chinese Writer, Tells of Her Career," *Boston Globe,* 5 May 1912.

73. Kim, *Asian American Literature,* 20.

74. Lummis, "In Western Letters," 336.

75. Edith Eaton to Charles Lummis, 2 December 1898, SWM.

76. Edith Eaton to Charles Lummis, 30 January 1897, SWM.

77. Frank Luther Mott, *A History of American Magazines, 1741–1930,* 5 vols. (Cambridge, Mass.: Harvard University Press, 1930–68), 4: 113.

78. See Earl Miner, "The Japanese Influence in English and American Literature, 1850–1950" (Ph.D. diss., University of Minnesota, 1955), 354: "Shortly after *Madame Butterfly* became a hit, the Theatrical Trust purchased this novel [*A Japanese Nightingale*] for a play which would compete with Belasco's. It was presented with great display and a boast that its settings were genuinely Japanese in comparison with what one might find in other theaters about town. The play was popular enough, but it did little more than add lustre to Belasco's production, since everybody compared it unfavorably with *Madame Butterfly.*" As cited in S. E. Solberg, "The Eaton Sisters" (Paper presented at the Pacific Northwest Asian American Writer's Conference, Seattle, Wash., 16 April 1976), 12.

79. Edith Eaton to R. U. Johnson, 1 April 1904, NYPL.

80. Kim, *Asian American Literature,* 8–9.

81. Ibid., 4–5.

82. Nee and Nee, *Longtime Californ',* 62, for example, assert that "at the turn of the century, a small number of native-born women, wives of merchants and imported prostitutes composed the tiny female element in Chinatown's overwhelmingly male population," and Chen, *The Chinese in America,* 69, presupposes that the only way women could migrate was with men: "Chinese men, like American men in those days, did not usually bring their wives to the Wild West and it was unthinkable that any proper girl would go off on her own as an immigrant."

83. Yung, *Chinese Women in America;* Hirata, "Chinese Immigrant Women in Nineteenth-Century California."

84. Chinese Historical Society of California, UCLA, *Linking Our Lives,* 9.

85. Chen, *The Chinese in America,* 123.

86. Sui Sin Fah, "Lin John," *Land of Sunshine* 10 (January 1899): 77.

87. Virginia Woolf, *A Room of One's Own* (New York: Harcourt Brace Jovanovich, 1957 [1929]), 35.

88. Carolyn G. Heilbrun, *Writing a Woman's Life* (New York: Ballantine Books, 1988), 31.

89. Wu, *The Yellow Peril,* 72.

90. Gerda Lerner, *The Majority Finds Its Past: Placing Women in History* (New York: Pantheon Books, 1978).

91. Sui Sin Far, "In Los Angeles' Chinatown," *Los Angeles Express,* 2 October 1903.

92. Ibid.

93. Sui Sin Far, "Chinatown Needs a School," *Los Angeles Express,* 14 October 1903.

94. Sui Sin Far, "Chinatown Boys and Girls," *Los Angeles Express,* 15 October 1903.

95. Sui Sin Far, "Chinese in Business Here," *Los Angeles Express,* 23 October 1903.

96. Sui Sin Far, "Chinese Laundry Checking," *Los Angeles Express,* 3 November 1903.

97. Harte, "Bubble and Squeak," 216.

98. Kim, *Asian American Literature,* 12.

99. Sui Sin Far, "Chinese Laundry Checking."

100. Kim, *Asian American Literature,* 99.

101. Sui Sin Far, "The Horoscope," *Out West* 19 (November 1903): 521.

102. Sui Sin Far, "Betrothals in Chinatown," *Los Angeles Express,* 2 October 1903. This piece appeared in the *Express* the month before the short story "The Horoscope" appeared in *Out West.*

103. *Webster's Desk Dictionary of the English Language* (1990) manifests such assumptions by defining *heathen* as "(1) an irreligious or uncivilized person; (2) an unconverted individual of a people that do not acknowledge the God of the Christians, Jews, or Muslims."

104. Edith Eaton (Sui Sin Far), "The Coat of Many Colors," *Youth Companion* 76 (April 1902): n.p. Jingi Ling, Interview, October 1990, offers this information: Kwang Ing Huk is an important and powerful goddess in both the folklore and literature of China. She is a symbol of mercy, and when people are in trouble they call on her and she appears in the sky. She stands on a lotus blossom and holds a vase in her hand, into which she sucks monsters to tame them. She lives in the South Sea. The monk and his disciples call upon her in the Chinese classic, *Pilgrimage to the West.*

105. Sui Sin Fah, "A Chinese Ishmael," *Overland Monthly* 34 (July 1899): 44.

106. Sui Sin Far, "A Chinese Boy-Girl," *Century* 67 (April 1904): 831. This passage illustrates the English language Sui Sin Far typically puts in the mouths of Chinese American characters speaking to white American characters. When Chinese American characters speak to one another, however, their dialogue becomes standard English. I suggest that these "insider-outsider" shifts in language use are further strategies by which Sui Sin Far shows Chinese Americans to use trickster guiles when communicating with whites.

107. Joan N. Radner and Susan S. Lanser, "The Feminist Voice: Strategies of Coding in Folklore and Literature," *Journal of American Folklore* 100 (October–December 1987): 412–25, discuss submersion as a coding strategy in women's writing.

108. Sui Sin Far, "Ku Yum's Little Sister," *Chicago Evening Post,* 13 October 1900.

109. Sui Sin Fah, "O Yam—A Sketch," *Land of Sunshine* 13 (November 1900): 342.

110. Radner and Lanser, "The Feminist Voice," 417, define *distraction* as the "drowning out or drawing away from the subversive power of a feminist message."

111. Lerner, *The Majority Finds Its Past,* ix, uses "alternate stance" as a technique for locating women in history. It can be applied to any people whom traditional scholarship has rendered invisible because of scholars' failure to see from diverse points of view.

112. T. J. Jackson Lears, "The Concept of Cultural Hegemony: Problems and Possibilities," *American Historical Review* 90 (June 1985): 567–93.

113. Compare S. E. Solberg: "She saw the Chinese community becoming by generation an American community." Quoted in Doug Chin, "Edith Maud Eaton: The First Chinese American Writer," *International Examiner* (Seattle), January 1977.

114. Compare Lorraine Dong and Marlon K. Hom, "Defiance or Perpetuation: An Analysis of Characters in *Mrs. Spring Fragrance,*" in *Chinese America: History and Perspectives,* ed. Him Mark Lai, Ruthanne Lum McCunn, and Judy Yung (San Francisco: Chinese Historical Society of America, 1987), 142: " 'Americanization' in Sui Sin Far's stories means the adoption of some basic Anglo values, such as acquiring the ability to speak English and interacting with Caucasians, and nothing more."

115. In the Biblical story, Genesis 37, Joseph's father also "made him a coat of many colors," but when Joseph's jealous brothers sold him into slavery in Egypt, they took his coat and dipped it in the blood of a kid goat and then told their father that Joseph had been "devoured" by "an evil beast." In Sui Sin Far's version, the "evil beast" is assimilation, implied by the fact that in crossing the Pacific to America, Ke Leang suffers a fever that gives him amnesia and thus comes close to losing China forever—of being swallowed into the culture of the red-headed stranger. Seeing the coat he has made for his son revives Ke Leang's memory and makes the garment a symbol of reunion rather than—as in Joseph's story—of severance. The fact that it is the "red-headed stranger" who both tempts Ke Leang to leave China and later brings him the coat that recovers his memory suggests the kind of ambivalence that Sui Sin Far must have felt being both a mission schoolteacher and the daughter of a Chinese mother.

116. Sui Sin Fah, "The Story of Tin-A," *Land of Sunshine* 12 (December 1899): 101–3.

117. Sui Sin Fah, "The Smuggling of Tie Co," *Land of Sunshine* 13 (July 1900): 100–104.

118. Carroll Smith-Rosenberg, *Disorderly Conduct: Visions of Gender in Victorian America* (New York: Alfred A. Knopf, 1985), 60, attributes women's intimacy with one another largely to the "rigid gender-role differentiation within the family and within society as a whole," leading to the segregation of women and men and the creation of "supportive networks . . . that accompanied virtually every important event in a woman's life, from birth to death," and creating a world in which "devotion to and love of other women became a plausible and socially accepted form of human interaction."

119. Notable in this passage are the biblical/mythical rhythms ("and the young man, whose name was Leih Tseih, raised his eyes, and seeing Ku Yum, loved her") typical of Sui Sin Far's prose.

120. Sui Sin Far (Edith Eaton), "Aluteh," *Chautauquan* 42 (December 1905): 341.

121. Edith Eaton, "The Origin of a Broken Nose," *Dominion Illustrated* 2 (11 May 1889): 302.

122. Edith Eaton to R. U. Johnson, 19 March 1904, 1257 Dorchester Street, Montreal, NYPL: "I am going to New York early in April and shall stay for a couple of weeks. When I return I shall go West by way of Chicago—making my way as a Chinaman. I am writing a series of articles for the Express as per enclosed."

123. Dates for this series are 4, 5, 6, 10, and 24 February and 9 March 1904. All are signed "Wing Sing."

124. Radner and Lanser, "The Feminist Voice," 414.

125. Edith Eaton, "In Fairyland," *Dominion Illustrated* 5 (18 October 1890): 270.

126. The first printing features eight stanzas, while the second has six, five of which are identical to the first version.

4

Boston:
The Mature Voice and Its Art

Denied a place in the history of men, the women of Shangjiangxu wrote
their own history, recorded their own knowledge, made themselves central in a literary tradition passed on from mother to daughter for centuries.
. . . Women everywhere, like the writers of *nushu,* connect with sisters
and sames in our own common codes.
—Cathy Silber, "A 1,000-Year-Old Secret"

In the writings of the last period of her literary career, 1909–13, Sui Sin Far
arrived at her mature voice. Her skill with the ironic strategies she had been
practicing since adolescence was sure, and her themes, the "slanted truths" that
mirror her divided racial identity—find harmony in a pluralistic aesthetic.
The "play" we have seen her characters stage in response to undesirable
realities can be treated in the mature fiction in terms of Mikhail Bakhtin's
dialogic—diverse voices challenge the monolithic mainstream of the culture
of imperialistic North America, a mainstream that pretends to speak for all of
its people but in reality speaks for only those of a European-based culture. By
creating trickster characters and playing the role of author as trickster, Sui Sin
Far dramatized strategies for dealing with the contradictions of life faced by
her Chinese American characters, even as she exposed social injustice and
racism for audiences with sufficient insight to see them.

This chapter focuses on writings that most illuminate this overall pattern.
The first section reviews Sui Sin Far's writing career in this period, beginning
in 1909 when, after an apparent four-year hiatus, her publishing voice reappeared
in major markets, highlighting major themes and artistic strategies. The
second section discusses her major nonfiction publications of 1909, "Leaves
from the Mental Portfolio of an Eurasian" and the *Westerner* series, with
particular attention to the public persona Sui Sin Far projects as an Anglo-

Chinese writer on the margins of the Chinese immigrant communities with whom she identifies. The third section examines her separately published fiction of this period under three broad subject categories: (1) *marriage:* "Mrs. Spring Fragrance" (January 1910), "The Inferior Woman" (May 1910), "An Autumn Fan" (August 1910), "The Bird of Love" (September 1910), and "A Love Story from the Rice Fields of China" (December 1911); (2) *intermarriage:* "A White Woman Who Married a Chinaman" (March 1910), "Her Chinese Husband" (August 1910), and "Chan Hen Yen, Chinese Student" (June 1912); and 3) *child theft:* "The Sugar Cane Baby" (May 1910) and "In the Land of the Free" (September 1909). Power relationships among the characters in these stories, which often involve courtship and family matters, tend to become analogues for hegemonic issues in early twentieth-century American society, especially those involving interracial and intergenerational tensions. The chapter concludes with a discussion of "Who's Game?," Sui Sin Far's last located fiction, published in 1912.

Writing Career, 1909 – 12

The hiatus I perceive in Sui Sin Far's publications between 1905 and 1909 may result from our not finding her stories rather than her not writing them. That she might have been publishing during this period is suggested on the acknowledgment page to *Mrs. Spring Fragrance* (1912), where she thanks editors for permission to reprint various unspecified stories, which have not yet been uncovered.[1] Given our current knowledge, however, during these four years Sui Sin Far appears to have fallen silent, as foreshadowed by Robert U. Johnson's repeated rejections of her submissions to the *Century* in 1903 and 1904, a silence unbroken until the publication of "Leaves from the Mental Portfolio of an Eurasian" in January 1909.[2]

Early in 1909, when Sui Sin Far was almost forty-four, her writing career took a turn for the better, first signaled by the publication of "Leaves," then by a letter to Lummis enclosing an announcement for a series of articles she was writing for the *Westerner,* a Seattle monthly published in Earlington, Washington. Entitled "The Chinese in America," the series was scheduled to begin in "March or April and run through the year,"[3] although its last installment actually appeared in August. Regularly published from this time forward in major eastern periodicals, Sui Sin Far had moved to Boston by 1910, judging by the *Boston Globe* article of 1912: "Two years ago I came East."[4] Her first ease from money worries came in this period, for in the *Globe* she mentioned receiving financial assistance from "two of my lawyer friends in Montreal," which freed enough time from earning a living for her to write her first book. A letter of introduction from a Chinese merchant in Montreal to his brother in Boston evidently facilitated her entrance to the Chinese Boston community.[5] The Austins and Mrs. Henderson, sister of "my western friends," also provided her with contacts in the white Boston community (*Globe*). Presumably she continued her periodic trips home to Montreal. The death of her beloved older brother, Edward Charles, which she writes "has affected me more than I can say" (*Globe*), must have taken her there in 1911. Her letters to Lummis, however, document a stable residence during 1911 and 1912, at a single address: 146 Concord Street West in Boston.[6]

During the years from 1909 to 1913, Sui Sin Far clearly established herself in the literary marketplace of the East. She was having her stories accepted by major journals, she was apparently writing and publishing many stories for children as well as for adults, and she found a publisher for a collection of thirty-seven of her short stories in the spring of 1912. Obviously, she was enjoying the largest and most far-reaching audience of her writing career. Before examining the kinds of writing she did in this period, it is useful to look briefly at the journals where she was placing her work—with an eye toward defining the publications' editorial goals and philosophies. In roughly the order in which her writings appeared, these journals were the *Westerner,* the *Independent, Hampton's, Delineator, Good Housekeeping,* and *New England Magazine.*

Subtitled "The Truth about the West," the *Westerner,* like Lummis's *Land of Sunshine,* regarded selling real estate as its first priority. The historian of American periodical publishing Frank Luther Mott describes it as a Seattle monthly, "dedicated to promoting the Northwest while furnishing some literary fare to [its] readers."[7] The same year "The Chinese in America" series by "Sui Sin Far (Edith Eaton)" ran in the *Westerner,* the Alaska-Yukon-Pacific Exposition was held in Seattle, and the *Westerner's* editor, Edgar Hampton, called on "every man or woman of the West who had red blood in his or her veins" to join with the journal in "doing everything in [their] power to make the Exposition a success." Believing that "success" depended on attracting eastern tourists, Hampton urged his twenty-five thousand subscribers to purchase "for some friend of yours back East" a year's subscription to the *Westerner* for twenty-five cents. Moreover, Hampton wrote, "We are carrying on a regular Western Exposition each month in our columns, telling the world as many things as we are able to tell them about Western advantages, offering all the pleasant inducements we know how to offer."[8] Might one inducement have been the depiction of the Northwest's "exotic ethnics" by Sui Sin Far, an English-born and Canadian-bred Chinese-English author?

In contrast to the *Westerner,* essentially a fledgling western journal looking for good regional copy to entice potential tourists and buyers of land, the *Independent* of New York City was a more important new market for Sui Sin Far, one with a national audience. According to Mott, the journal was originally established in 1848 by merchants with "church affiliations," as an organ for the New England Congregationalists to help offset Presbyterian influence on their members moving West. The *Independent* expressed its editorial philosophy in its title and in its statement of purpose: " 'We wish to be, in the highest sense, an independent journal.' "[9] Opposed to the Fugitive Slave Law and supportive of woman suffrage in its early years, the *Independent* would claim Harry Beecher Ward as an early editor and Harriet Beecher Stowe as a leading contributor. Under the ownership of Clarence Bowen, the journal grew increasingly literary and published poets from Elizabeth Barrett Browning and Alfred Lord Tennyson to William Jennings Bryant, Henry Wadsworth Longfellow, and Sidney Lanier. Mott remarks that "the roll of *Independent* contributors reads like a list of the chief poets of the time, which it is."[10] After William Hayes Ward became editor in 1896, the contents grew even more secular, and the journal took pride in its progressive coverage of current social issues and its attention to quality fiction. The fact that Ward had been a Presbyterian clergyman may partially account for Sui Sin Far's contact with the *Independent,* which printed five of her pieces[11] during an era when the periodical was, in Mott's words, "wholly committed to the policy of 'expansion' and 'taking up the white man's burden' " that characterized the "liberal" rationale for American imperialism.[12] Was promoting and publishing a writer from an abused racial group part of that burden?

Hampton's Magazine, another eastern periodical with offices in New York City, had existed only three years when it printed two stories signed "Sui Sin Far (Edith Eaton)" in 1910. Formerly the *Broadway Magazine,* the journal was purchased by Benjamin B. Hampton in 1907 and became, in Mott's words, "a brilliant and aggressive monthly," filled with "greats" in both fiction and nonfiction.[13] It is said to have paid Robert E. Peary ten thousand dollars for the story of his "discovery" of the North Pole, a piece that ran in the same issue containing Sui Sin Far's "Mrs. Spring Fragrance."[14] Tending toward muckraking and an "exposé tone,"[15] *Hampton's* was known for taking on such issues as rights for working women and for attacking monopolies like the Southern Pacific Railroad (in the same issue that ran Sui Sin Far's "Inferior Woman").[16] During the few years of its existence, Hampton boasted that his magazine was "the greatest success on record in the periodical field," as measured by "circulation growth" and "advertising earnings," because, even though "Wall Street hates *Hampton's,* the *people* approve it and buy it."[17] Could one of this radical editor's causes have been to give voice to a "half-Chinese" author, one who represented a viewpoint not usually seen by the U.S. reading public?

As the publishing organ for the Butterick Company, the *Delineator* is described by Mott as having been mainly a fashion monthly until 1894, when Charles Dwyer, the editor, began to expand into literature.[18] From 1907 to 1910, Theodore Dreiser was the general editor, and Mott notes that, though

Dreiser followed Butterick's conservative instructions "never to picture a man smoking a cigarette, never to show a wine glass on a table," he was a crusader and reformist concerning such issues as " 'matrimonial unrest,' divorce, 'race suicide,' women's suffrage. . . . [and] welfare of underprivileged children."[19] Since Dreiser read and approved all stories submitted to the *Delineator,*[20] we may assume that Dreiser approved the two children's stories by Sui Sin Far the *Delineator* published in 1910 and that he found the moralistic lessons these stories convey politically pleasing.[21] It is interesting that Mrs. Spring Fragrance, the central character of both Sui Sin Far stories published in the *Delineator,* is a "safe ethnic," one of her few women to be overtly described as "Americanized."

Good Housekeeping, first published on 2 May 1885 in Holyoke, Massachusetts, was originally subtitled *A Family Journal Conducted in the Interests of the Higher Life of the Household.*[22] Mott describes it as "sub literary" during its first five to ten years, with poems and short stories—usually "decorated"—taking second place to concerns of the home.[23] The magazine's lifelong policy was keeping "close to its readers" by inviting contributions, offering contests, and publishing "reader-written articles." Its circulation in 1908 was over 200,000, and an issue cost fifteen cents.[24] Under James Eaton Tower, the editor in 1909 and 1910, emphasis on fiction, particularly humorous fiction, increased. During these years the magazine published three of Sui Sin Far's stories,[25] two of which, "Ku Yum and the Butterflies" and "The Half Moon Cakes," were specifically aimed at a young audience. The third, "The Sugar Cane Baby," though presenting a child as the central character, was definitely meant to appeal at another level to discerning adults.

Finally, in 1910 Sui Sin Far began placing stories with Boston's *New England Magazine.* Originating in 1884, the *New England Magazine* was published after 1889 by Edwin Doak Mead. Mott describes it as "an important regional magazine," which, although located in New England, "printed much about the South, the West, and Canada." Mott compares it to such major journals as the *Century* and *Scribner's,* on whose pages "social, economic, and literary matters were discussed and a mildly reformatory spirit shown."[26] Between 1910 and 1912 the magazine printed five stories signed "Sui Sin Far" under Frederick M. Burrows's editorship.[27] As will be seen, in terms of craft and maturity of vision, the *New England* stories are among Sui Sin Far's very best work.

Overall, the years from 1909 to 1912 marked the high point of Sui Sin Far's writing career. She had literary patronage and a network of white and Chinese North American friends and professional contacts in the East and the West, in both the United States and Canada. In Boston she was clearly closer to the center of publishing in the United States and had access to national literary markets. In 1912, the same year her sister Grace would pass the Illinois bar, A. C. McClurg of Chicago would bring out Sui Sin Far's first book, the short story collection *Mrs. Spring Fragrance* (printed at Norwood, Massachusetts). Her work in progress included a novel.

Major Themes and Artistic Stance

After 1909 Sui Sin Far's writings were finding, in the words of her *Westerner* editor, "ready space in the best magazines in America";[28] she was publishing one book and had financial support to work on another; and her narrative stance, content, strategy, and ideas were combined with heightened sophistication in her writing. All this indicates that Sui Sin Far's four-year publishing hiatus was not a breach but an expansion, a period of significant growth for the author that culminated in the mature voice we find in her stories of the ensuing four years, the last of her writing life. As in her earlier fiction, Sui Sin Far's subjects and plots continued to focus on marriage, family, and generational conflicts. From her earliest British-Canadian stories in the *Dominion Illustrated* to her mature Chinese American fiction, it is around the core of domesticity that her aesthetic universe builds. This is not surprising. In common with most Victorian women writers, the home was the world Sui Sin Far knew best and the one in which she was typecast by editors.

In *Daniel Deronda*, George Eliot put these words into a female character's mouth ("to protest woman's storylessness," according to Carolyn G. Heilbrun): "To have a pattern cut out . . . a woman's heart must be of such a size and no larger, else it must be pressed small, like Chinese feet; her happiness is to be made as cakes are, by a fixed receipt."[29] If a woman writer of either English or Chinese background wanted to step out of that pattern and talk about broader cultural issues, how, in a society that so confined her, could it be handled? Mary Anne Evans, when she took the masculine pen name of George Eliot, knew that subversive measures were called for. Sui Sin Far knew it also.[30] She would thus choose a metaphor in her fiction that society considered acceptable—marriage and family life—and within its circumference play out the weightiest issues women and Chinese American immigrants of both sexes faced at that time. In particular, the oppositions in her plots between arranged and romantic marriages, between filial piety and rugged individualism, and ultimately between old and new generations and cultures (parents and children) allow her to explore, as she states in the *Westerner,* the dynamics of old and new orders in Chinese American communities, the contrasts between the traditional manners and values of China and those of the European-based majority population in North America, and, in doing so, issues of gender and cultural hegemony.[31] Again we recall that—from the time Lotus Blossom met Edward in Shanghai—such oppositions were integral to Sui Sin Far's heritage.

Issues of hegemony, of the margins of choice that cultures and individuals enjoy or are denied within the established power structure of a society, are the themes of much ethnic and feminist literature. We have seen that Sui Sin Far is not naive about the ways in which societies exercise power or about the effects of hegemonic domination on the daily lives of ordinary people. In her stories, major decisions about power may be made by nations and their institutions, but it is in the lives of individuals, usually in the microcosm of marriage and family relationships, that they are acted out on a daily basis. In the stories she writes during this period, political-moral issues are explored in the plotted narratives of what may appear superficially as formulaic magazine fiction. As a result, her characterizations stress cultural roles or types and the representation of ideas rather than the psychological development of character in any modern sense. Moreover, at the thematic level, her figures often become mouthpieces for particular cultural viewpoints or directly represent the relationships of power between groups.

That most action takes place in gardens, living rooms, or verandas—woman's traditional domain—makes it easy to miss the stories' international settings, which are essential to their concern with the hegemonic and cultural interplay between the Chinese in America and in China and with the effect migration between China and the United States has on these characters' lives. Fictional locales are not limited to one region or even one continent but frequently move back and forth across the Pacific, mirroring the exile-immigrant odyssey we have seen rooted in both history and Sui Sin Far's family experience. Her mature fiction is particularly emphatic in presenting this path across the Pacific as a two-way route, along which people and cultural influences travel in both directions: Americans influence Chinese in Canton; Chinese influence Americans in San Francisco; immigrants become Chinese Americans, and a second or third generation returns to its ancestral homeland. Who is "inside" and who "outside" in her fictional worlds is always changing.

One theme that emerges from this phenomenon concerns the betrayal of the ancestral homeland implicit in the biculturation process. Sui Sin Far's mature fiction examines how families in China felt about their members who went to North America, their hopes, and their fears. Parents want their children to migrate as students or workers, bringing back Western dollars, ideas, and industrial skills—so long as their stays are temporary and they plan to return home. We have seen Ke Leang in "The Coat of Many Colors" (1902) travel to San Francisco and develop amnesia, a metaphor for the "forgotten" obligations to the wife, son, and parents that the coat signifies.[32] Will familial connections be maintained or will they fall away? In her mature fiction, Sui Sin Far addresses this question, one her own lineage might have raised, by exploring how Chinese migrants deal with the temptation to exchange their native country for the new continent on a permanent basis—in one sense, this is the story of immigrant North America.

Sui Sin Far's aesthetic position in this, her career's final phase, is most marked by her reaction to the dominant culture's monolithic voice. As in her earlier writings, the central witnesses to reality are Chinese and Chinese Americans, especially women. The power of her women characters during this period often moves beyond gaining voice within a framework of patriarchy to taking control—of their own lives, at the least, and sometimes of the lives of others. More generally, Sui Sin Far's narrative stance forces her European-based audience to enter into dialogue with those they have customarily conceived as "the Other" and even to see themselves, through alternative eyes, in a position of "Other-ness." Her strategy resembles what Mikhail Bakhtin terms "dialogic," the creation of an environment on the printed page where various cultural voices can speak together and replace a monologic vision of social reality with a climate of pluralism.[33]

The audience Sui Sin Far was writing for by the end of this first decade of the century would have included a few members of the Chinese American communities in which, her writings show, she now had a growing circle of acquaintances. Presumably, most were English-speaking and of the merchant middle-class. To this audience, her stance was that of her mother's loyal daughter, a defender of her "own mother's people," and a provider of empowerment to Chinese Americans by making them visible. Her major audience, however, remained the white, Protestant middle class in which she was socially rooted. It was also the backbone of the mission movement that Sui Sin Far was involved in as a teacher. In her mature writing, her stance toward the mission movement might be described as "a missionary to missionaries"; she held up a mirror reflecting the gap between the principles they professed and their practice.[34] More generally, she continued to write about the Chinese American community for white audiences in ways that disturbed her readers' comfortable stereotypes.

In Bakhtin's terms, Sui Sin Far's mature fiction sets various voices against each other to show her primary audience that these voices—which it does not hear—are speaking continuously, and very close to its ears. Simultaneously, Sui Sin Far has a professional agenda: to write, to sell stories, to have her writer's voice heard.[35] These two impulses—to write against the popular grain and to be accepted in a popular marketplace—seem at odds. The weight that Sui Sin Far gave the first and Onoto Watanna the second may be at the base of why her sister's works sold so easily and Sui Sin Far's sold only after much effort. When S. E. Solberg raises the question of why Sui Sin Far was not more celebrated in Seattle, he suggests, "Perhaps she was too close to Chinatown for comfort"—the comfort, that is, of her white reading audience.[36]

Joan N. Radner and Susan S. Lanser suggest that coding strategies are one way women and ethnic minority writers surmount this dilemma; they develop "a system of signals . . . that protects the creator. . . . in the context of complex audiences, in situations where some of the audience may be competent to decode the message but others ... are not."[37] Sui Sin Far uses such coding—in a voice that takes on various personas and distributes itself in shifting guises. Even in a piece as ostensibly open and direct as her autobiographical "Leaves," Sui Sin Far's masked representations of herself and family members carry levels of meaning that depend on prior knowledge of the writer's life. It is thus relevant to pursue in more detail the concept of tricksterism offered at the conclusion of the previous chapter. Sui Sin Far, like many marginalized writers, implements trickster methods not to mask the truth but to illuminate it.[38] In the words of Zora Neale Hurston, "You hit a straight lick with a crooked stick."[39]

Some attention to historical grounding illuminates these methods. Scholars like William Bright have shown tricksterism to be as old as human history.[40] Bright refers to Paul Radin's depiction of the trickster "as originating in the most psychological primitive strata of the human mind" and Carl Jung's "archetypal psychic structure of extreme antiquity ... a faithful copy of an abstract indifferentiated human consciousness."[41] The trickster is commonly allied with the figure Coyote, who, originating in American Indian legend, has become in Bright's words, "the archetypal trickster known from literature all over the world."[42] Though seeing Coyote as "act[ing] out of impulse, or appetite, or for the pure joy of trickery," Bright also suggests Coyote is "a powerful symbol of a viewpoint that looks beyond abstractions and beyond technology to the ultimate value of survival," one who "may be needed more than ever by modern, urbanized humanity."[43] M. L. Rickett's term "trickster-fixer" sums up one of Coyote's major roles—and defines a key link between Coyote and trickster writers—to "fix up" a world that others have botched.[44] From American Indian mythology, where Coyote preserved speech for the animals, he has been connected with language, the power to create or deceive through the word.

Because Coyote, in Bright's words, is "always male,"[45] an example of tricksterism more precisely related to Sui Sin Far as a woman of Chinese descent may be observed in the inventor of *nushu,* a secret language of women traced legendarily to the Song Dynasty in China (960–1279 A.D.). Though the origins of *nushu* are uncertain, one version has the language originating when a girl who was taken as a concubine to the Imperial Palace devised "a secret code to communicate to her sister back home without the messenger or the Emperor's spies being able to read what she wrote."[46] Remaining alive through the centuries, *nushu* contains about eight hundred words and has been passed down from mother to daughter, orally, in books, or on cloth embroidery. Described by Li Hui as "a system of writing created for and used exclusively by some rural women in a few mountain villages in China," who used *nushu* both to enter a world of story-communication they were denied by formal education and to express emotional ties among women who became "sworn sisters," the practice of *nushu* illustrates how tricksterism can become a survival strategy by which oppressed groups or individuals may attain a certain amount of personal and political autonomy within the restrictions of a dominant system.[47] "*Nushu* was a discourse of resistance: its writers risked the same threats of physical violence that existed for other Chinese women who confronted the inequities of society," Cathy Silber relates.[48]

Similarly, the modern trickster figure can be said to grow out of a political system that oppresses certain cultures and—for purposes here—particularly out of the persecutions of women and ethnic minorities in the immigrant societies of Canada and the United States. The trickster, Mary Dearborn suggests, can "through language, assert the ultimate authority of language against authorities that forbid it."[49] As a writer consigned to marginal status in terms of race, class, and gender, who had to survive in a world of contradictions and find strategies to get published, Sui Sin Far was a natural for trickster methods. Overall, the concept of the trickster offers us one way of looking at this author's writing stance: half playful, half outraged, caught between changing cultures, nations, and family/societal expectations.[50]

A major technique that links a writer's written tricksterism with oral antecedents is ambiguity. In Sui Sin Far's mature fiction, key characters play games of wit with each other, just as the author plays games of wit with her audience. The trickster in these writings appears in two postures: the author as fiction-maker, shape-shifter, and rewriter of cultural scripts; and the characters who perform as mischief-makers, disturbers of the peace, and manipulators of their own and others' destinies. Sometimes this trickster's aim, as we have seen in "The Sing-Song Woman" (1898), is to solve life's dilemmas creatively. At other times, as in "A Chinese Ishmael" (1899), it is to escape personal or social restrictions and to get one's own way, even at the cost of self-destruction. At still others, as we will see in "Who's Game" (1912), the purpose is just to make mischief and turn order into chaos—for purposes similar to Bakhtin's carnivalization, of awakening a world that thinks too restrictively.[51] For Sui Sin Far, tricksterism might have become a tool for survival at age eleven when she separated her psychic world into two compartments, assuming a position of ironic restraint in the devastating situation of having to leave school and assume adult duties. It was the same device, she reported in the *Globe* article, by which she overcame the boredom of legislative reporting in Jamaica by "look[ing] down from the press gallery upon the heads of the honorable members and think[ing] a great many things which I refrained from putting into my report." As we have seen in her 1903 and 1904 pieces for the *Los Angeles Express*, there are points where she plays at "hiding out in the open." She demonstrates Robert L. Welsch's comment that the trickster's genius often lies in disguise, in manipulating the role of "clever deceiver," of appearing to be very stupid (inoffensive), while being in fact exceedingly clever.[52] Finally, to the writer-trickster, truth is approached as in the Emily Dickinson poem, as something "slant" or apart from the usual social perceptions. When ideas become fixed (monologic), the social world freezes—turning an environment pluralistic by nature to one rigid with bigotry, hatred, and the inability to recognize diverse voices.

The Nonfiction: Sui Sin Far's Public Persona

There may be a certain literary prestige in having one's work accepted by the Eastern critics; but my stories and articles in "The Westerner," "Out West" and "Post-Intelligencer"[53] accomplish more the object of my life, which is not so much to put a Chinese name into American literature, as to break down prejudice, and to cause the American heart to soften and the American mind to broaden towards the Chinese people now living in America—the humble, kindly moral, unassuming Chinese people of America.

—Edith Eaton (Sui Sin Far), letter to the editor of the *Westerner,*
November 1909

Two of Sui Sin Far's writings that are factual on the surface, yet hide the soul of the trickster, are "Leaves from the Mental Portfolio of an Eurasian" and the *Westerner* series, "The Chinese in America," both published in 1909. Sui Sin Far's "missionary" voice emits strongly as she observes the oppression that the Chinese in America, including her mother and siblings, have suffered, and simultaneously demonstrates the power of Chinese Americans to survive in a hostile and hypocritical environment. Beneath the public voice of the sober Eurasian woman with a mission, however, lurks the soul of the trickster, recognizable by her shifting roles, her irony, and her playfulness.[54]

Published on 21 January 1909, "Leaves from the Mental Portfolio of an Eurasian" can be seen as a key turning point of Sui Sin Far's career: it was published at the beginning of her most productive period, it signaled the end of her apparent four-year hiatus, and, most important, it represented her first extended public discussion of her mixed racial heritage. She wrote it for the nationwide reading audience of the *Independent,* whose editor, William Hayes Ward, would, as she reported in the *Globe* article, buy four more of her stories and "encourage" her to write her "first book." Arrangements for its publication might have been made for the purpose of promoting an author whom the editor intended to publish in the future. A photo covers half of the first page, the face behind the name "Sui Sin Far" looking intense and somber. The word *leaves* in the title connotes both the leaves we turn reading the essay and the metaphorical leaves the author has turned in a mental portfolio of remembered experiences. All of those she selected to show us involve her mixed racial identity, which she terms "Eurasian." Omitting dates and all but the most general place settings, "Leaves" is structured as a montage of incidents out of memory, arranged in a more or less chronological sequence. Key experiences with both the Chinese and white communities illustrate the marginal status of a child of English-Chinese heritage in the late nineteenth century, a status she and her siblings had known in four countries. Within the microcosm of her family, Sui Sin Far presents various options she had confronted and rejected in her lifelong search for a principled way to live with a sense of integrated identity in a racially divided world. The term *Eurasian* itself suggests a stance on the border where both races meet. The speaker of the autobiography does not exonerate the Chinese community for its attitude toward the children of intermarriage—"My mother's people are as prejudiced as my father's" (130)—but she publicly chooses to stand with and defend her "own mother's people" (129) rather than deny them by concealing her Chinese heritage and passing for white.

Sui Sin Far speaks in a Eurasian voice throughout "Leaves"—an obvious departure from her letter to the *Montreal Daily Star* in 1896,[55] where she spoke as Edith Eaton, an English Canadian defending Chinese Canadians. As denoted by her pronouns and consistent Eurasian identification, the narrative voice in "Leaves" is not that of a sympathetic outsider but rather that of an insider to the experience she relates. The "Sui Sin Far" who does the telling is among the persecuted, the story's central example, as we hear in her question: "Why are we what we are? I and my brothers and sisters. Why did God make us to be hooted and stared at?" (127). At the same time, Sui Sin Far's frequent tone of pride and self-righteousness communicates awareness of her power and her choices: "At eighteen years of age what troubles me is not that I am what I am, but that others are ignorant of my superiority. I am small, but my feelings are big—and great is my vanity" (128). Juxtaposed against anecdotes about the abuse she has endured, this tone makes the speaker sound more like the avenging angel than the patient victim; hers is the voice of controlled outrage asserting itself against persecutors. Her white audience is implicitly accused along with the people with whom Sui Sin Far dines in the "little town" in the "Middle West," who condemn the Chinese in their conversation. The speaker's employer, "Mr. K.," is made to apologize in response to her "I am a Chinese" admission; many of the readers of "Leaves" might join him in saying, " 'I should not have spoken as I did. I know nothing whatsoever about the Chinese. It was pure prejudice. Forgive me!' " (129)

The narrator in "Leaves" does not obviously pose as a "trickster"; she speaks to us with a straightforward sobriety that matches the eyes in the photograph.

Yet even this surface tone ripples with other vibrations, hinting at more figurative levels. Sui Sin Far changes her age, for example, making herself some four years younger when she went to Jamaica than she actually was. "My nationality, if I had only known it at that time, helps to make sales," she recalls of her experiences as "The Little Chinese Lace Girl" on Montreal streets (128). Was it still helping to make sales to such journals as the *Independent?* One catches other sly jokes: Sui Sin Far's landlady in the Middle West dinner scene is reported to have said of the Chinese: " 'I wouldn't have one in my house,' " an ironic contention exposing her inability to recognize a "Chinese"—Sui Sin Far—at her own table. In this same conversation, Sui Sin Far's employer calls her " 'Miss Far,' " a skip between the autobiographical and fictitious, for we know that Edith Eaton was the name the author used in her business life at this time and Sui Sin Far the name she used in "Chinese" fiction. This play on names also occurs earlier, when her nurse says " 'Little Miss Sui is a storyteller' "— earning a slap from her mother, implicitly because she presumed the child lied, even though as readers we know that she was telling the truth. From the byline onward, in fact, Sui Sin Far, the maker of fiction, slips in as the persona of this selective autobiography.

Throughout the piece masked figures appear, many "Eurasians" who have assumed various guises to survive. Most of these, according to Charles Laferrière, Sui Sin Far's grandnephew, are modeled on Sui Sin Far's brother and sisters.[56] The "acquaintance" who "accuses" her of " 'walking with a Chinaman,' " a person whose "notions of righteousness" she "cannot reconcile with my own" (129), was probably Edward Charles Eaton, Sui Sin Far's oldest brother, who camouflaged his Chinese heritage and became assimilated into the British-Canadian community. Another example is the "half Chinese, half white girl," whose "face is plastered with a thick white coat of paint . . . eyelids and eyebrows . . . blackened so that the shape of her eyes and the whole expression of her face has changed." This young woman "pass[ed] as one of Spanish or Mexican origin" and only told her white fiancé the truth "when driven to bay" by an unidentified "American girl, who declares that if the half-breed will not tell the truth she will." As we have seen with Sui Sin Far's sister May, this person "was born in the East, and . . . came West in answer to an advertisement." She had lived "for many years among the working class" and "heard little but abuse of the Chinese" (131). Could "the American girl" who demanded she tell the truth be one of the author's guises? "Leaves" also describes "several half Chinese young men and women [who] thinking to advance themselves socially . . . pass as Japanese"—figures who point to Sui Sin Far's sister Winifred, as do the "funny people" who "tell me that if I wish to succeed in America I should dress in Chinese costume, carry a fan in my hand, wear a pair of scarlet beaded slippers, live in New York, and come of high birth" (132). Through figures of Chinese-English descent who believe they must live in disguise, Sui Sin Far shows her audience what people like her are being forced to do. These figures also serve as a contrast to Sui Sin Far's own strategy of coming out: "There are also Eurasians and Eurasians," she writes. The latter include the Eurasian woman in "Leaves" who breaks her engagement to a white man rather than let it be suggested that she is not Chinese.

Although the form of "Leaves" is autobiographical, its voice addresses, in common with the fiction, dual reading audiences. On one level, Sui Sin Far was announcing to a general American public her Eurasian identity and protesting what people in her position were being put through: "The unfortunate Chinese Eurasians. Are not those who compel them to cringe more to be blamed than they?" (131). On another level, she was announcing to her own family that she would not "cringe," that she rejected the coping strategies of some of her family members—the brother who was a successful businessman in the Montreal British community and did not see his family, the sister who moved to San Francisco and told no one of her Chinese ancestry, the other sister who published bestsellers as a Japanese. Perhaps she was addressing as well the mother who slapped her for being a storyteller. "Though my mother has forgotten it," this voice says, "I have not" (125). This is surely an understatement, for it was in the role of storyteller—of listener, recorder, and transmitter of stories—that Sui Sin Far came into her own during this period.

The role of storyteller is central to Sui Sin Far's *Westerner* sketches "The Chinese in America," where, instead of writing about Chinese Americans as a sympathetic but objective observer as she had in the *Los Angeles Express,* the writer positions herself partially inside the Chinese American community to narrate its stories for a largely white readership.[57] Appropriate to the border position she assumed, the series is bylined with both her names: "Sui Sin Far (Edith Eaton)." From her preface onward, the pieces are not straight journalism but a blend of fiction and fact. The family mythology that both Sui Sin Far and Winifred used in different ways to elaborate a heritage that remains always elusive is voiced in this instance by the *Westerner's* editor, Edgar Hampton, when he describes Sui Sin Far's father as "an English officer" and her mother as "a Chinese lady."[58] By citing a "father who lived in China for many years . . . [and] married a Chinese lady," Sui Sin Far presents her family credentials for speaking about the Chinese in America. Her individual interest she expresses as "perpetual since the day I learned that I was of their race." In the same lines with which she emphasizes her acquaintance with Chinese North Americans, she blurs the boundaries between autobiography and storytelling:

> I have found them wherever I have wandered. In New York are some of my best Chinese friends; nearly every mail brings me news from Chi-

nese Canadians, both east and west. Down in the West Indies I met a Chinese whose intelligence and active heroism in a moment of danger . . . will cause him and his compatriots to be ever remembered with gratitude and a warm feeling of kinship.[59] In Los Angeles, San Francisco and the Puget Sound cities I know Chinese, both men and women, whose lives, if written, would read like romances. . . . ([Author's Preface], 24)

In April 1909, one month before the series started, Hampton announced its subject matter as follows: "the Chinese men and women who live and are part of our life, yet not part of it, here in the West."[60] In his phrasing, the *Westerner* editor characterizes Chinese Americans as marginalized members of Western society, in which "our life" is presumably white and the Chinese men and women are set apart, along with the western flora and fauna that he hoped "red-blooded" easterners would come to see. Sui Sin Far turns the tables on this position at the outset. She redefines her subjects as a definite part of this country—"those Chinese who come to live in this land, to make their homes in America. . . . Chinese-Americans I call them" ("[Author's Preface]," 24)—and uses catchwords from Western mythmakers to place Chinese Americans at the center of Western development: "descendants of the pioneer Chinamen who came to this Coast long before our transcontinental railways were built, and helped the American to mine his ore, build his railways and cause the Pacific Coast to blossom like a rose." To offset her white readers' perceptions of the Chinese as alien, she stresses common human traits: "They think and act just as the white man does, according to the impulses that control them . . . [and] are kind, affectionate, cruel or selfish, as the case may be." She points out that diversity in manners does not change human substance: "[Chinese Americans] hide the passions of their hearts under quiet and peaceful demeanors; but because a man is indisposed to show his feelings is no proof that he has none." In addition, she warns readers of the international political consequences of abusing immigrants from China: "they sustain throughout the period of their residence here, a faithful and constant correspondence with relations and friends in the old country, and what they think and what they write about Americans, will surely influence . . . the conduct of their countrymen towards the people of the United States." She overturns reader expectations about who should learn what from whom in relations between white and Chinese Americans: "If the Chinese can learn much from the Americans, the former can also teach a few lessons to the latter" ("[Author's Preface]," 26).

In the sketches themselves, Sui Sin Far plays out her views in a variety of oppositions: "East" versus "West," China versus America, "old" versus "new." Ambiguity of language allows her to keep a foot on both sides of these issues, a reflection of the plurality of her personal position that maintains the Eurasian middle ground articulated in "Leaves." Such ambiguity is revealed in her "us-them" pronouns: "I have found *them* wherever I have wandered," and the Chinese "came to this coast long before *our* transcontinental railroads were built" ("[Author's Preface]," 24, emphasis added). In "Yip Ke Duck and the Americans," the first paragraph is narrated in the voice of the title figure. " 'I do not like the Americans,' " he begins, and then he claims they are liars and hypocrites and threatens to warn " 'all the Chinese boys that believe in the American Sunday schools and the American Sunday school teachers.' " Sui Sin Far's voice as a "missionary to missionaries" explains that Yip Ke Duck is representative of "some others of his race in this country," who become "bitter and cynical" because of the "wolves in sheep's clothing" among "Christian missionaries and Church women . . . who bring disrepute upon their cause." At the same time, Sui Sin Far qualifies her criticism: "It is such a pity that *they* [the Chinese] do not always see and know the genuine American, the sincere Christian." She assures her reading audience that "the simple yet intelligent Chinese who are with *us* gladly acknowledge that many of the ways of the white man are better than the ways of the Chinese" (24, emphasis added).

The stance of being allied with both the white audience to whom she speaks and the Chinese Americans whose stories she tells continues in "New Year as Kept by the Chinese in America," in which Sui Sin Far writes of "Chinamen [who] take advantage of the holiday season to patronize *our* theatres" and of "*our* black sheep Chinamen" who gamble and smoke opium (25, emphasis added). "Americanizing Not Always Christianizing" juxtaposes "genuine Christian people" against "those to whom religion is but a form" (26), suggesting that the value or harm of religion depends on how it is used. The good missionary is one who abandons monologic assumptions about the absolute truth of Christianity and enters into dialogue with other faiths. In "The Reform Party," similar ideas extend into politics: the Chinese of the Reform Party in America see "a new way of living" and "of thinking," but that includes Christianity only for some: "those of them who have become Christians look forward with bright faith to China's religious reformation" (26).

In all these pieces, we hear the voice of the reporter as missionary, sermonizing not to the Chinese "heathen" but to a white, middle-class reading audience about their prejudices against Chinese Americans and the hypocrisies of their own religious professions. As the editor of the *Westerner* wrote, "Miss Eaton is a woman with a mission."[61] In other sketches, Sui Sin Far exchanges didacticism for whimsy, darting in and out, shifting locations and angles of vision. The narrator of "The Bonze [a Confucian priest]," for example, assumes the persona of a Chinatown tourist, "wandering about the Joss houses . . . and now and then confiscating a piece of sandalwood" for which she "at that time . . . had a rage." She reveals her own ignorance as a relative outsider by asking the priest about the wood: " 'It is sacred, isn't it?' " He answers, with

obvious irony, " 'Not at all. . . . Is it so to you?' " Bringing "forth a letter of
introduction from Chinese friends in my home city," she alleviates some of the
priest's distrust, and he continues to "chat with [her] about Chinese religion."
This conversation draws parallels between Eastern and Western religions: the
priest "declared emphatically that the Chinese worship spirits, not images,"
and "kneel before Mother [Ahmah, the Chinese goddess] as the Catholics
kneel to the Virgin Mary" (38). As a diner at a banquet in "Chinese Food," Sui
Sin Far offers a list of the names of dishes that "passed before me," though she
"could not taste them all" (26). In "Scholar or Cook?" Sui Sin Far plays devil's
advocate, remarking to an immigrant who is making cake in a hotel kitchen,
" 'I thought a scholar in China was not s'posed to know anything about
work.' " His reply demonstrates the flexibility of the Chinese class structure
under the pressures of immigration: " 'When I have enough to live on for the
rest of my life I will return to China and again take up my studies and do
honor to my parents as a scholar' " (26).[62]

In "Like the American," Sui Sin Far is the guest at a wedding feast "on the
top floor of a Chinatown building," where a new proxy bride begins weeping
because she is only a stand-in for the woman her husband expected. The
groom, much like the one in "The Sing-Song Woman" (1898), "comforted
[the bride] . . . bought a marriage license and was married over again by the
Christian missionary." When he asserts that " 'I do as the Americans do. . . . I
marry the woman I love,' " marriage becomes a metaphor for the changes that
some Chinese undergo when they migrate to America. The bride—"an orphan
of adventurous spirit" named Tin-A, who has been "prevailed upon" by a
friend of the same name in China "to undertake the long ocean journey"
(18)— recalls the central figure in "The Story of Tin-A" (1899), who also left
China to help a friend. This figure is only one of several subjects in the
Westerner articles who closely resemble fictional characters and whose stories
resemble fictional plots in Sui Sin Far's previously published work. For
example, "A Chinese Feud" (1896) is mirrored almost exactly in "The Story of
Tai Yuen and Ku Yum," which presents a couple who "fell in love with one
another just as any American boy and girl" (19). Their parents, however,
belong to the feuding clans of the See Yups and the Sam Yups, and the result,
as in the earlier story, is the young man's early death. "A Love Story of the
Orient" (1896) is echoed in "The Bonze." Midway through "The Bonze" the
voice of the writer's "American friend" relates how a priest named Ke Leang
was once in love with a young woman in China, whose parents betrothed her
to another. She wrote to Ke Leang for assurance and received back a message,
which was prompted by "the spirit of mischief" and identical to that in "Love
Story": " 'Marry the one whom your parents have chosen.' " Like her predecessor,
this woman takes her own life in despair, and as a result Ke Leang has become
"a priest in San Francisco's Chinatown" (38). This reuse of characters and story

lines from previously published short stories suggests either that the prior works were based on actual people or that the *Westerner* sketches are fictionalized. Either way, the storyteller as trickster seems to be at work here.

As in the story about the poet-daughter of a Chinese mother in the *Los Angeles Express,* Sui Sin Far again appears in masquerade in her journalism. The story "Wah Lee on Family Life," which reports the title character's experience of growing up in a large family filled with "strife and contention," could be a version of Sui Sin Far's own family life. Though Wah Lee, like Sui Sin Far, asserts that he loves his family and faithfully sends money home, "he did not wish to return to China" anymore than Sui Sin Far wished to live again with her family: " 'Too many tongues in the house interfere with peace.' " Also like the author, Wah Lee had many siblings—fourteen—and "had lived for some years in eastern Canada . . . being smuggled backwards and forwards across the line whenever the fancy pleased him" (19). He laments the " 'poor little' " girls in eastern Canada who, like Sui Sin Far, " 'never have time to play nor to go to school; there are so many babies to be carried,' " and who " 'must go to work for the father has too big a family . . . to support them' " (19, 38). The distance between the Chinese child (that Sui Sin Far perhaps wanted to be) and the Chinese-English Canadian child (that she was) collapses with Wah Lee's conclusion that such families in Canada are " 'just like the big families in China' " (38). Once more, she tells the truth "slant" and manages to slip her family into the series. The Eatons were in many senses, as we know, "Chinese in America."

We also recognize more specific trickster motifs weaving in and out of these sketches: "the spirit of mischief" behind Ke Leang's ambiguous message in "The Bonze" as well as recurring examples of metamorphosis, disguise, and deceit. For instance, in "New Year as Kept by the Chinese in America," the Storm Dragon turns himself into a silkworm and then a butterfly, exchanging storm making for peace; in this same sketch the "fairy fish" "allow[s] itself to be cooked and eaten by [an] old lady," yet it lives on in Sui Sin Far's familiar image of a "little bird" (25). Both these tales are told by Sui Sin Far to illustrate the Chinese fondness for "storytelling, the favorite themes being magic and enchantment"—which, we recall, are also her favorite themes. In "The Story of a Forty-Niner," disguise becomes central to the structure when the scholar Hom Hing switches identities with his laborer brother Hom Long, whom their parents have sold to "agents of certain Chinese Companies . . . to go to America," and goes in his place—reasoning that "in the darkness it would be impossible to distinguish one lad from the other" (18).

Various figures in these sketches use tactics of disguise and reversal that recall Sui Sin Far's own resistance to the premises of the conventional themes of "yellow peril" literature, the writers of which "seem to be so imbued with the same ideas that you scarcely ever read about a Chinese person who is not a wooden peg" ([Author's Preface], 24). Go Ek Ju in "A Chinese Book on Americans" wants to write "a book about the American people" when he goes back to China because " 'we go into the American houses as servants; we enter the American schools and colleges as students; we ask questions and we think about what we hear and see.' " Unlike the Chinese, "the poor Americans ... have no means of obtaining any true knowledge of the Chinese when in China" (26). Go Ek Ju's ambition foreshadows the plot of "The Inferior Woman," a short story Sui Sin Far published in 1910, by implying that it is whites who are in need of being educated by the Chinese. Such a reversal of cultural expectations also figures in "The Bible Teacher" when Liu Went, "a Chinese pupil in [a] Bible class," surprises his teacher by instructing "two American young men" in the Bible, because " 'they cannot read much themselves and wish me to illuminate them' " (26). Sui Sin Far thus upends the monologic assumptions about who "owns" religion at the same time she disturbs the "heathen Chinee" stereotype.

"The New and the Old" features the episodic adventures of the most fully developed trickster in the *Westerner* series. Lu Seek is a Protean figure, who, in a manner that Sui Sin Far recognizes as typical of many who rise to success in the United States, manipulates life against all expectations of logic and still comes out on top. Characterized as the perfect example of one who has been Americanized, Lu Seek comes "to this country at an early age," attends mission schools where he learns both the English language and Western ideas, and then confronts his uncle with the same notion expressed in "The Coat of Many Colors" (1902) by the "red-headed stranger": in America, "a man instead of looking backward and admiring one's parents and uncles, fixes his mind on himself . . . and so acts that his parents and uncles . . . wonder at and admire him" (36). When his uncle refuses to accept this philosophy, Lu Seek takes his inheritance of "fifty silver dollars" and goes off to "seek" his fortune; he finds that he "had a soul above domestic service" (as a cook or laundryman) and was too Western-minded to join his cousin at being a fortuneteller (36): " 'I wanted a business which would call for a telephone and electric lights; not candles, incense, tortoise shells and diagrams' " (37). A solution to this dilemma comes when Lu Seek talks his cousin into setting him up in an employment agency, reasoning that " 'though I could not secure employment myself I might obtain it for others' " (36). When Lu Seek eventually retires to New York and smokes "the pipe of peace" with his uncle, the narrator's irony is clear in the uncle's observation that "the days were over for young men to wonder at and admire their parents and the time had come for the old people to wonder at and admire them" (38).

While pointing out the absurdity in Western thinking, Sui Sin Far's *Westerner* sketches recognize the opposition between "old" and "new" orders in China and Chinese American communities and see the new order—in what she calls "these revolutionary days" ("[Author's Preface]," 24)—as the wave of the future. The sketches were published only one year before Sun Yat Sen's 1911 Revolution, a radical political change that Sui Sin Far undoubtedly anticipated. In "The Story of Wah," Wah, "a leading member of the Chinese Reform Party" in Seattle, declares, " 'We do not think in China as we did in the old days.' " When asked " 'Why did you come to this country?' " he replies, " 'To make money and to learn western ways quicker than I could at home' " (25). But however much Sui Sin Far aligned herself with a "new" and more westernized order for Chinese and Chinese American cultures, she never suggests that the old ways should be rejected or condemned out of hand. Those she admires most manage to occupy a "both/and" position between the old and the new, not an "either/or" stance.

Overall, in "Leaves from the Mental Portfolio of an Eurasian" and the *Westerner* sketches, both published in 1909, Sui Sin Far shapes a public persona for her readers, giving us a glimpse of the storyteller behind the past decade's stories. "Leaves" opens up the biography, revealing the painful past that shaped the stance and voice of the writer who now signs her name "Sui Sin Far." The *Westerner* series also gives us a sense of her evolving role in the Chinese American community—sufficiently "inside" by 1909 to be trusted to hear the stories of the Chinese American culture and pass them along. These pieces show that as a narrator Sui Sin Far was careful to position herself on the borderland, in the "third person" stance she termed "Eurasian," rather than to claim full status as a Chinese American "insider." There was no prescribed place for the Eurasian, born of a union society scorned, at the turn of the century. Yet from this position Sui Sin Far created an artistic identity of her own, through storytelling and writing, that she would pass on to others. The issues she emphasized, and the strategies she evolved to express them, fit her borderline position as a writer faced with a largely white audience to whom she told the stories of Chinese Americans, whose perspectives were almost wholly lacking in literature. Known to that audience largely as "John Chinaman" or "China Mary," Chinese Americans acquire names and speak for themselves as individuals in Sui Sin Far's journalism of this period. In the stories that follow, we see them come to dominate Sui Sin Far's fictional vision.

The Fiction: The Mature Voice

With the exception of two stories, every work of fiction discussed in this section is centered on the issue of marriage: who arranges it, who defies it, and who educates and who becomes educated to "old" and "new" ways of thinking about it. Generational conflicts are at the forefront, as is the issue of whether a woman will acquiesce to a father's marriage arrangement or defy it and choose her own spouse. Marriage and romance were, in the United States as in Canada, the stuff of most popular fiction; they were also important for Sui Sin Far because, in the several cultures that intersect in her life, the family was the basic unit of society. Reared in a Victorian tradition that she defied by remaining single,[63] Sui Sin Far lived in a world where the choices a woman made, or were made for her, concerning marriage both shaped her individual destiny and reflected social assumptions. Moving increasingly in Chinese American circles, she learned that this applied in the Chinese tradition as well. In her Chinese fiction, heroines such as the "Ku Yums" and "Sweet Sins" of her earliest stories would commit suicide rather than "disgrace" the family (society, culture) by open rebellion.[64] In the stories written in the United States from 1898 to 1905, the Tin-As and Mai Gwi Fars find alternate ways to control their own marriage arrangements. After 1909 this pattern continues, while the title character of "Mrs. Spring Fragrance" (1910) will move beyond this to controlling marriage for others. In general, Sui Sin Far's mature fiction relates courtship and marriage to the broader distribution of power in society, as seen in the context of traumatically changing cultural traditions in both East and West during these years just before World War I.

The two stories in this section exempted from these themes each revolve around the "theft" of a child, one a Chinese baby stolen by customs officials enforcing "the law," the other a Hindu baby taken by Catholic sisters representing the church. Though their plots are set in two different countries, the United States and what appears to be British Jamaica, the stories' themes are similar in their exposure of child theft as one way by which white colonizers appropriate culture. Sui Sin Far's texts closely examine this abuse of power by presenting alternate voices with different views of reality. Throughout the stories, trickster figures appear and vanish as catalysts that help disturb the status quo and raise questions that, one suspects, most of Sui Sin Far's readers would prefer to avoid.

Marriage

Printed four months apart in *Hampton's Magazine* (January and May 1910), "Mrs. Spring Fragrance" and "The Inferior Woman" deal with many of Sui Sin Far's central themes and develop her most obvious trickster figure. Mrs. Spring Fragrance is the main character in both stories. "Mrs. Spring Fragrance" presents a comic fantasy world, ruled over by the "quaint, dainty" Mrs. Spring Fragrance, or "Jade," a young immigrant wife who, when she "first arrived in Seattle . . . was unacquainted with even one word of the American language"; "five years later, her husband speaking of her, says: 'There are no more American words for her learning.'" Unlike Chinese Americans in other Sui

Sin Far stories, the Spring Fragrances live not in a Chinatown but in an integrated middle-class Seattle suburb with white neighbors on one side and Chinese on the other. Mr. Spring Fragrance, "a young curio merchant," is what westerners call "Americanized," and "Mrs. Spring Fragrance [is] even more so" (137). Appropriately pluralistic, Mr. Spring Fragrance, when he gets home from his commute, sits in a bamboo settee on the verandah reading the *Chinese World* and feeding pigeons lichis out of his pocket. At the center of their blend of "East" and "West" life-styles is a marriage that combines elements of "arranged" and "romantic": "He had fallen in love with her picture before ever he had seen her, just as she had fallen in love with his! And when the marriage veil was lifted and each saw the other for the first time in the flesh, there had been no disillusion, no lessening of respect and affection, which those who had brought about the marriage had inspired in each young heart" (140).

Desiring this same goal for others, Mrs. Spring Fragrance assumes the role of arranging marriages in both stories. She thus evokes a traditional figure out of Chinese culture, the matchmaker, who traditionally worked for the parents of the bride and groom to arrange marriages in which romantic love played no part. In this instance, however, the matchmaker becomes a catalyst to the Western romantic convention by helping young, second-generation Chinese American lovers outwit their more traditional immigrant parents. In "Mrs. Spring Fragrance," she conspires with the young woman Mai Gwi Far (Laura) to help her marry her "sweetheart" Kai Tzu, a young man whose Western ways are represented by his being "one of the finest [baseball] pitchers on the Coast" and his singing the British classic "Drink to Me Only with Thine Eyes" to Mai Gwi Far/Laura's piano accompaniment (137).[65]

In the midst of Mai Gwi Far and Kai Tzu's romance, Mrs. Spring Fragrance takes on another romance when she travels to San Francisco and introduces Ah Oi—"who had the reputation of being the prettiest Chinese girl in San Francisco and, according to Chinese gossip, the naughtiest"—to the son of a Chinese American schoolteacher and then accompanies the couple on their impromptu elopement (138). Ironically, the San Francisco matchmaking visit puts Mrs. Spring Fragrance's own marriage in jeopardy, because her husband misinterprets her absence and thinks she is having an affair. In a comedy of errors, however, Mr. Spring Fragrance's fears are allayed, and all three matches are happily resolved. When Mai Gwi Far's father, Mr. Chin Yuen, who has been adamantly opposed to his daughter's marriage to Kai Tzu, suddenly accepts her romantic choice with scarcely a hint of dissension, the story's verisimilitude is strongly tested. The metaphor Mai Gwi Far's father voices in consent to the marriage is, however, overtly thematic: "'the old order is passing away and the new order is taking its place, even with us who are Chinese'" (140).

"The Inferior Woman" presents the same title character and matchmaking plot but varies in that this Mrs. Spring Fragrance crosses racial boundaries to arrange a love match between Will Carman, her elitist-thinking, "[white] American neighbor's son," and Alice Winthrop, a woman who "entered a law office at the age of 14" and is now "private secretary to the most influential man in Washington" (729). A letter from Mary Carman, Will's mother, to Mrs. Evebrook (the mother of Ethel, the young woman Mary wants Will to marry) centers the story's major conflict on class: " 'It is incomprehensible to me how a son of mine can find any pleasure whatever in the society of such a girl [as Alice Winthrop]. I have traced her history and find that she is not only uneducated in the ordinary sense, but her environment from childhood up has been the sordid and demoralizing one of extreme poverty and ignorance' " (729).

The contradictions within the women's movement, whose major energies were focused on suffrage when Sui Sin Far wrote this story, are clearly established by the pointed ironies in Mary Carman's own words: " 'Is it not disheartening to our Woman's Cause to be compelled to realize that girls such as this one can win men over to be their friends and lovers...?' " More enlightened is Mrs. Evebrook's daughter Ethel, who explicitly voices the contradictions in Mary Carman's letter and in the white middle-class women's movement that Mary Carman represents. Ethel writes to her mother, " 'Mrs. Carman is your friend and a well-meaning woman sometimes; but a woman suffragist, in the true sense, she certainly is not' " (729). The story's beginning assumptions, that Alice is "the Inferior Woman" and Ethel "the Superior," are upset by Ethel herself when she compares herself with " 'women such as Alice Winthrop who, in spite of every drawback, have raised themselves to the level of those who have had every advantage...' " (729). In the words of Elizabeth Ammons, "Who is Inferior and who is Superior grows murky."[66] The reversal is reinforced when Mrs. Spring Fragrance points out Mary Carman's sexist attitude toward Alice: " 'You are so good as to admire my husband because he is what the Americans call, "a man who has made himself." Why, then, do you not admire the "Inferior Woman" who is a woman who has made herself?' " (731).

The parallels between the lives of Sui Sin Far and Alice, the character with whom she sympathizes, are obvious. On the one hand, both share a continuing struggle to survive independently and pursue a chosen career—what society sometimes calls "liberation"—on the other, neither can identify with the kind of liberation defined by the organized women's movement of the early twentieth century.[67] One may surmise that this is partly because both women see the women's movement as snobbish and middle class, but both also express real feelings of conflict between their feminist precepts and their loyalties to individual men who have helped them. Alice's words as she declines an invitation to speak at a suffrage meeting on the grounds that " 'the men for whom I have worked and among whom I have spent my life . . . have upheld me, inspired me, advised me, taught me' " (730) echo Sui Sin Far's sentiments about the men she sees as her mentors. The women's movement of the era in which Sui Sin Far was writing was clearly another manifestation of the "new" attempting to overtake the "old" order. Sui Sin Far's stories, especially "The Inferior Woman," indicate that she treads a border position on feminist issues as well. Mrs. Spring Fragrance's comment to her husband in the story's last line—" 'I love well the "Superior Woman," but O Great Man, when we have a daughter, may heaven ordain that she walk in the groove of the "Inferior Woman"!' " (731)—may well reflect Sui Sin Far's own ambivalence.

As in "Mrs. Spring Fragrance," the verisimilitude of "The Inferior Woman" also is challenged by a too facile ending. When Mary Carman visits Alice and begs her to " 'return home with me. . . . for the prettiest wedding of the season' " (731), she changes her point of view as readily as Mr. Chin Yuen did in "Mrs. Spring Fragrance." Moreover, the "inferior woman's" superiority is proven by a classic Victorian test—Alice gets the man. As in so many stories about Chinese American women, Sui Sin Far slips her characters' lives into a groove she herself has rejected, that of a fairy-tale marriage. With Mrs. Spring Fragrance as catalyst, the dynamics involved in such marriages are virtually the same for both Chinese and white Americans.

On a deeper level, this storyteller figure plays "tricks" with political as well as romantic messages. For example, an anecdote in Mrs. Spring Fragrance's letter to her husband in "Mrs. Spring Fragrance" subverts the story's surface concern with the arrangement of marriages. This letter highlights Mrs. Samuel Smith, whom Mrs. Spring Fragrance has heard lecture on "America, the Protector of China" and describes " 'as brilliant and [as] great of mind as one of your own superior sex.' " This satirical overstatement spoofs both Mrs. Smith's arrogance and the patriarchal assumptions to which white women in Sui Sin Far's fiction are so frequently handmaidens. The letter satirizes Mrs. Smith's claims about the protection offered to Chinese Americans by " 'the wing of the Eagle, the Emblem of Liberty,' " "protection" that should make Mr. Spring Fragrance " 'forget to remember that the barber charges you one dollar for a shave [and] . . . the American man . . . fifteen cents' " and that " 'your honored elder brother, on a visit to this country, is detained under the rooftree of this great Government' " (138). Clearly Mrs. Samuel Smith, like Ethel Evebrook, exemplifies the "new" woman, who goes beyond breaking silence and steps up to the public lectern in the public arena previously reserved for men, one that Alice Winthrop shuns. While Sui Sin Far herself takes up a public voice as a writer of fiction and journalism, she seems to distinguish between her own role and that of this breed of "new" woman, perhaps because she feels that—unlike the privileged Ethel Evebrook or Mrs.

Smith but like Alice Winthrop—she has earned her voice through long and painful experience.

Mrs. Spring Fragrance's border position—between cultures and individuals, as matchmaker and trickster—mirrors Sui Sin Far's role as author, especially when Mrs. Spring Fragrance turns writer. " 'I listen to what is said, I apprehend, I write it down,' " Mrs. Spring Fragrance says in "The Inferior Woman" (730). Both Sui Sin Far and Mrs. Spring Fragrance arrange marriages, and both do it through fiction. The character's desire to put " 'these mysterious, inscrutable, and incomprehensible Americans . . . into an immortal book' " (728) for "her Chinese women friends" because "many American women wrote books" about the Chinese (727) recalls the author's desire to write about Chinese for Americans and the irony with which she did so. The interplay of author/character identity is deftly revealed in one line in the text, when Mrs. Spring Fragrance imagines Lae-Choo reading her book to Fei and Sie and Mai Gwi Far—all names of characters from various Sui Sin Far stories (727).

Motifs in the two Mrs. Spring Fragrance stories comically present topics we have found in the *Westerner* pieces. Both are concerned with the redistribution of power between races, sexes, classes, and generations, redistributions acted out on the threshold of change from old orders—Victorian England and Imperialist China—as an immigrant people found ways of adapting to new conditions. "Mrs. Spring Fragrance" in particular presents some major problems for interpreting these topics. At several points the story's narrator does not seem aware of the obvious cultural ironies that Mrs. Spring Fragrance's character raises. For instance, the title character is apparently serious in her use of the verse from Alfred Lord Tennyson's "In Memorium" as her refrain throughout—" 'It is better to have loved and lost than never to have loved at all.' " Both Mrs. and Mr. Spring Fragrance call Tennyson "an American poet." Sui Sin Far, reared on British literature when Tennyson was laureate, certainly knew the difference, however, and could be suggesting, satirically, that to her fictional couple—as white Americans say about Chinese in both the United States and China—poets in the United States and England all sound the same.[68] As Ammons observes, "She is forcing us to think about American literature and sentimentality from a place outside white western consciousness."[69] Comments such as Mr. Spring Fragrance's " 'American poetry is detestable, abhorrible!' " (141) certainly recall Sui Sin Far's satiric treatment of romantic fiction in "Albemarle's Secret" (1889). But the reader is given no guide to such irony; the narrator neither corrects nor comments on the Spring Fragrance's erroneous reference to Tennyson as "an American poet."

There are other problems with the Mrs. Spring Fragrance stories. Complex and timely questions that these texts as a whole raise—How does one deal with cultural obedience, filial piety, respect for old customs in this new environment? How does a woman's freedom to do low-paying secretarial labor for a man really speak to problems of class or to the tenets of woman suffrage?—are resolved simplistically. Mr. Chin Yuen readily accepts the "new order," and Mary Carson readily accepts the "inferior woman." Both involve changes in their basic cultural assumptions about marriage and class that take place during a few minutes' chat, which violates the reader's sense of believability. "Mrs. Spring Fragrance" and "The Inferior Woman" solve the problems of living on intercultural borders too easily. They turn comic and cute, and the examination of important issues they open fades back into silence. Is Sui Sin Far caricaturing this "quaint, dainty" woman and the fantasy world she manipulates? Or is she presenting the character she created—one like her authorial self in many ways—as a serious model for negotiating the cultural borders faced by her Chinese American and female characters?

"An Autumn Fan," "The Bird of Love," and "A Love Story from the Rice Fields of China," all published in the *New England Magazine* in 1910 and 1911, more fully reveal Sui Sin Far's skill in using marriage to treat intercultural and intergenerational themes. In "An Autumn Fan," the following exchange occurs early in the text. " 'We are in America and the fault, if fault there be, is not upon thy shoulders,' " Ming Hoan tells Ah Leen's father when he vows not to " 'disgrace his house by giving his daughter to a youth whose parents have betrothed him to another.' " " 'True!' " Ah Leen's mother agrees with Ming Hoan. The father, though, shakes his head: " 'America! . . . Land where a man knows no law save his own' " (700). The voices raised here set into motion a recurrent dichotomy between diverse ideologies common to Sui Sin Far's fiction, in this case one that counterpoints the "rugged individualism" or "lawlessness" of the West against the communal traditions of old China. The conflicting values faced by Chinese immigrant communities in this era are recapitulated in these three stories at the personal level of quarrels between parents and children.

In "An Autumn Fan," Ah Leen's father finds a point of compromise when he allows his daughter and Ming Hoan to marry—but with the "stern decree" that Ming Hoan "must face his parents and clear away the clouds of misunderstanding before he could take Ah Leen." Because this all happens in California and Ming Hoan's parents live in China, the new groom must leave his bride and cross the Pacific, a reversal of the pattern of betrothal and migration that was customary for Chinese American immigrants historically. In a position unconventional for brides of either China or the United States, Ah Leen remains in the world of women in her mother's household in San Francisco, and when she tires of "women's gossip," she sits on the veranda and "gaze[s] upon the moon" in the pose of waiting classic to literary portraits of women. When Ah Leen's father urges her to divorce Ming Hoan and marry " 'a Chinese merchant of wealth and influence,' " he takes the immigrant's option of adapting new cultural mores: "It was not the Chinese way, but was not the old order passing away and the new order taking its place?" Signifying that "new" is open to more than one definition, Ah Leen opposes her father with her own "new" authority: " 'Thou hadst the power to send my love away from me, but thou canst not compel me to hold out my arms to another' " (701). When Ming Hoan does return, Ah Leen and he reunite and thus break through the shifting edicts of society to claim their own power. In the process, hegemonic positions shift; the second generation emerges victorious over the one that proceeded it, and it does so by maintaining faith in both the "new" value of love and the "old" value of marital trust—perhaps Sui Sin Far's vision of an ideal Chinese American family.

When the "American friend" who has urged Ah Leen to get a divorce "steals away"—with the hope that "it is not too late to send a message to someone of recall" (702)—it is hinted that this friend also waits for a lover, has perhaps sent him away, and learns about love from Ah Leen's and Ming Hoan's reunion. As elsewhere in Sui Sin Far's writings of this era, this representative of white culture is in need of more "education" than she is able to give her. But what is the lesson in this case? That if a woman waits long enough, her lover will come? That faith is its own reward? Ah Leen's assertiveness against her father contrasts with her wait for Ming Hoan on the veranda, which complicates the margins between independence and passivity and avoids, through the fairy-tale ending, directly facing the thematic issues involved. "An Autumn Fan," as well as the other two stories, shows the power of love against forces that threaten to dispel it. Yet in the tradition of "Cinderella" or "Sleeping Beauty," in two of these it is the woman who waits.

"The Bird of Love" demonstrates that voices can also lose flexibility when they get locked in traditional perspectives, that characters can become mono-lithic in viewpoint by losing touch with the changing flux of the present.[70] Pau Tsu, a student at the San Francisco Seminary, and Liu Venti, a student at Berkeley, have parents living in China who "had quarrelled in student days, and . . . had ever since cultivated hate for each other . . ." (27). In California, Pau Tsu and Liu Venti meet, fall in love, and decide to marry, violating the Chinese tradition that parents control marriage arrangements. The young couple sends what may be the most dreaded message for Chinese parents with children in the United States to receive: "they were resolved to act upon their belief and to establish a home in the new country." Pau Tsu's father's reply to his daughter—" 'Are you not ashamed to confess that you love a youth who is not yet your husband?' "—rejects her claim of romantic love in the Western mode by evoking Chinese cultural tradition. Liu Venti's reassurance to Pau Tsu sets up the antithesis: " 'Shall I not love thee dearer and more faithfully because you became mine at my own request . . . ?' " (25). The couple marry, and when Pau Tsu gives birth to twin boys whom they are afraid to take to visit their grandparents, a third generation complicates the situation.

To resolve the dilemma, a woman again emerges as the figure who leads in negotiations over a tangled border. One day, watching the babies play, Pau Tsu asserts, " 'Let us go home!' " Even though her "words echoed the wish of [Liu Venti's] own heart," the narrator tells us that "he was not as bold as she" (26). At this impasse, the reader recognizes Pau Tsu as another of Sui Sin Far's trickster figures. We already know that she is a playwright and reminds Liu Venti of a heroine in one of her plays who was "tormented by enemies [who] would make her ashamed of her love." The heroine in question responded with an image that Sui Sin Far herself had used in Montreal twenty years earlier:

> "When Memory see his face and hears his voice
> The Bird of Love within my heart sings sweetly
> So sweetly, and so clear and jubilant.
> That my little Home Bird, Sorrow.
> Hides its head under its wing.
> And appeareth as if dead." (25)[71]

"The light within" helps Pau Tsu realize that the grandparents in China must regret their vow " 'to never forgive us.' " In response, she concocts another "play" aimed at breaking down the grandparents' rigid adherence to a tradition made by them, their own past vows, and their cultural heritage. Against the frozen past of their parents' outdated hate, Sui Sin Far sets hate's antithesis, love, as Pau Tsu and Liu Venti "bade goodbye to their little sons and sent them across the sea, offerings of love to parents of whom both son and daughter remembered nothing but love and kindness, yet from whom that son and daughter were estranged by a poisonous thing called Hate" (26).

Because one child is sent to each set of grandparents, the grandparents are forced to communicate so their grandsons can see one another.[72] The structure of this piece reflects its themes by emphasizing voyages in both directions across the Pacific: Pau Tsu and Kiu Venti originally travel from East to West to study in California; a "ship, sailing from West to East" (25) carries letters from children to parents when the couple write of their marriage; a similar ship carries the babies East to meet their grandparents. On the Chinese shore the twin babies' memories shift this motion into reverse, as "the two little fellows sat down on the sand and began to talk to one another in a queer little old-fashioned way of their own." The reader overhears their conversation and watches them "gaze across the sea with wondering eyes" as they ask, " 'Where is mother and father?' " (26). The role of the grandchildren, the "new" generation that functions as a catalyst for healing a generational conflict, evolves another step when the brothers run away to look for their parents, forcing their feuding grandfathers to unite to find them: "Under the quiet stars they met—the two old men who had quarrelled in student days." The division between the two men thaws as both realize " 'thy grandson is my grandson and mine is thine.' " When the shipborne message, " 'Son and daughter, return to your parents and your children,' " travels from China to Pau Tsu and Liu Venti in San Francisco, the breach is healed (27). Pau Tsu's intervention has opened a discourse between the "old" and "new" orders and among three generations.

By pointing out the absurdity in the grandparents' thinking—"The cause of the quarrel had been long since forgotten; but in the fertile soil of minds irrigated with the belief that the superior man hates long and well, the seed of hate had germinated and flourished" (27)—the narrator shows that tradition rigidly maintained can destroy the present. By implication, the present, when it does not respect the past, is also destructive. A productive future requires opening a dialogue between past and present that makes the future possible without destroying connections. This step back in time's flow suggests the paradox that, for the Chinese immigrant, "filial piety" can best be observed by a challenge to its old precepts. Recalling the probable rift in Sui Sin Far's own family between her parents in Canada and her grandparents in England, Sui Sin Far undoubtedly knew these conflicts well.

In "A Love Story from the Rice Fields of China," themes of "old" versus "new" are explored through a woman's resistance as she waits for her lover. A pluralistic stage is set in San Francisco's Chinatown when Chow Ming, "an Americanized Chinaman," gives a dinner, to which he invites "both his American and Chinese friends, and one friend who was both Chinese and American." After dinner, the male guests begin to tell stories with traditionally moral themes: "the achievements, the despair of lovers, the blessings which fall to the filial and the terrible fate of the undutiful." At the same time, Chow Ming's wife, Ah Sue, slips away with the only other woman present (the narrator of the story) into "her own little room" to tell her "a real true love story—Chinese" (343), which includes the themes of "An Autumn Fan" and "The Bird of Love."

As she begins the story, Ah Sue moves imaginatively from San Francisco to China, where she worked in her father's rice fields and struggled against loving Chow Han, a man who " 'drove the laden buffaloes' " for her father (344). Traveling with her mother to Canton, Ah Sue meets an American woman, who teaches her to speak English, helps her gain the courage to accept Chow Han's advances, and gives her strength to stand up to her father. Ah Sue would do anything for her father except " 'marry the man to whom he had betrothed me' " (343). When Chow Han goes to work in North America, Ah Sue promises to " 'wait,' " and upon getting the news that her lover has been killed in a railway accident, she decides to " 'be brave as the American woman.' " She remains single and starts " 'a small florist shop' "—

against the wishes of her brother-in-law, who wants her to marry and when she will not, refuses to support her (345).

By striking out into independent entrepreneurship, Ah Sue becomes the most liberated of Sui Sin Far's Chinese women. Managing to support herself without men, she is " 'self-made' " in the manner of Alice Winthrop and Sui Sin Far herself. Besides the doctor's sister, Ah Sue's most steady companion becomes a plant, the " 'fragrant leafed geranium' " that Chow Han gave her when he left for America, with the words " 'even if I shall die, my spirit shall fly to this plant, so keep it ever beside you' " (344).[73] Clinging to the geranium as her most valued possession, Ah Sue retorts to the customers who offer to buy it, " 'What! barter the spirit of Chow Han!' " A symbolic substitute for Chow Han as well as an emblem of the independence of spirit that Ah Sue shares with him, the geranium also evokes the spirit of tricksterism, a spirit made flesh in the form of a "stranger" who comes to Ah Sue's shop with face "partly concealed" by a hat, which he sweeps off to reveal himself as Chow Han, returned to take the flower's place in person (345). Like Ah Leen's wait in "An Autumn Fan," Ah Sue's wait has paid off—the spell is broken. Like Sui Sin Far, she has fought for her personal independence, refusing to let her life be stifled by familial and cultural expectations and insisting on her place in life's flow.

Because a woman's friendship empowered Ah Sue to do this, a friendship that portrays a bond between a Chinese and a white woman rarely seen in our literature, this story within a story returns full circle to the two women "snugly ensconced" over its telling in a "little room" in San Francisco, an inner sanctum apart from the world where stories are determined by men. By both its frame and inset tale, this is a story of women bonding as they did in "The Story of Tin-A," of women who create their own realities and share mutual empowerment. More broadly, the scene of Ah Sue and the friend "Sui Sin Far," with whom she shares stories, resonates with the traditions of women, both Victorian and Chinese, within which Sui Sin Far works. It again recalls Virginia Woolf's quest after what two women would say if they were alone in a room together—a query continued by Louise Bernikow as she imagines a fictional "record that includes a woman in a house on a cloudy day talking with her friend."[74] Of more historical profundity, through the intimacy of the fictional women involved, Sui Sin Far connects with the relationship of *laotong* in traditional China, where women became "sames" and remained sworn friends for life, forging links in a woman's network that crossed generations for centuries.[75] Chow Han's trickster role is climaxed when Ah Sue reveals that "my old sweetheart . . . is also my husband Chow Ming," the "Americanized Chinese" who is giving the dinner. Sui Sin Far's trickster stance is revealed in allusions to her own narrative role as transmitter of stories when Ah Sue inserts the narrator's name as the listener to whom she talks: "You forget, Sui Sin Far" (344); "But know this, Sin Far" (345). By inference, this character must also be the "one friend" described in the opening paragraph, "who is both Chinese and American" (343). The most subtle and far-reaching tricksterism in this piece, however, as in many other Sui Sin Far stories discussed, is the secret language of women (a continuation of *nushu?*), about which men haven't a clue.

Without a doubt, all the stories in this marriage group express a "discourse of resistance" in their disturbance of patriarchal authority. All feature daughters who pit their own wills against traditional Chinese and Chinese American fathers and succeed in imposing their own choices on those fathers who oppose them.[76] The old order is typified in attempts to control women through marriage, and the change to a new order is marked by women's rebellion. Yet this rebellion remains restricted because the main options Sui Sin Far holds out to her women remain marrying whom their father wants or marrying whom they want. Like the princesses in old fairy tales, these characters, with the exception of Ah Sue, adhere to the Victorian and Chinese definitions of woman's sphere; they resist their fathers only to go under the roofs of other males. All of these stories show the power of love against forces that attempt to dispel it, yet in the tradition of "Cinderella" or "Sleeping Beauty," it is the woman who waits in "An Autumn Fan" and "A Love Story from the Rice Fields of China." Female characters like Mrs. Spring Fragrance and Pau Tsu exercise their power through fiction-making skills, but they essentially do so within the boundaries of marital relationships. We are left to imagine how power is distributed in the marriages Ah Leen, Ah Sue, and Alice Winthrop choose. Even Ethel Evebrook, the "new woman" in Sui Sin Far's "Inferior Woman," confesses that she is giving the lecture circuit only ten years, partly to "learn about men (not schoolboys), before I choose one" (729). As the lovers embrace, the curtain comes down—portending, as in classic stories (the glass slipper fits her foot, the kiss of the Prince wakes her up), a happily-ever-after-ending.

Carolyn Heilbrun suggests that "what has been forbidden to women is anger, together with the open admission of the desire for power and control over one's life." She cites Eudora Welty's *One Writer's Beginnings* as "the avatar of a simpler world, with simpler values broadly accepted," where women are schooled in the art of camouflage and hence are unable to express the truthful rage of their lives.[77] Sui Sin Far, as a young woman in a British Canadian enclave of the late nineteenth century, also grew up with the assumption that "woman's sphere" was not to be challenged beyond established rules of decorum. Now, in her forties, Sui Sin Far continued to provide her female characters only limited choices: not *whether* they would marry but *whom*—an obvious inconsistency, since the author herself made a third choice. She created in fiction no heroine as independent as her own self-portrait in "Leaves," a fact that raises the question of how much she was guided by what editors in the marketplace would or would not accept.

The Intermarriage Group

In the three stories that follow, marriage or gender relationships are used to represent intercultural and interracial conflicts that Chinese immigrants faced in the United States. The first two are unique, not only in dealing with the taboo subject of miscegenation but also in using a first-person narrator who is a white woman. The third explores a similar motif when a Chinese student falls in love with a young white woman involved in the home mission movement. Without ultimately crossing that threshold, the story speculates on what the results would be if the Chinese-white couple got married. These stories are among the most culturally radical in Sui Sin Far's canon. They dare to speak of the miscegenation taboo that her own parents violated; moreover, they pit white characters against Chinese characters and show the Chinese come out ahead on a human scale. By providing readers with the perspectives of both insiders (the couples involved) and outsiders (society), all these works challenge precepts of logic and justice regarding the laws and attitudes in the United States that forbade intermarriage.

"A White Woman Who Married a Chinaman" and "Her Chinese Husband" were published five months apart in 1910 in the *Independent*.[78] These stories are really one work in two parts; the same female narrator examines the question " 'Why did I marry Liu Kanghi, a Chinaman?' " in the first story and explores her marital relationship with him in the second. Both are told from the point of view of the first-person narrator, who, by setting her personal experience against society's prejudice, exposes society's injustice and lack of logic. Simultaneously, she reasserts the question vital to Sui Sin Far's search for identity: what are the effects of Chinese-white marriages on the children? Oppositional voices carry the stories' development. The voice of the narrator's white husband, James Carsner, opposes that of her second husband, Liu Kanghi; the voice of Liu Kanghi counterpoints that of his white wife concerning their children; and, throughout, the voice of outside society opposes the woman's firsthand experience with a white and a Chinese husband.

The white woman narrator, who remains nameless, "had been a working girl—a stenographer," a job she wants to give up with her marriage. Her husband, James Carsner, however, has other ideas—he wants "to write a book on social reform," so he insists that she continue to work for an income ("A White Woman," 518). When the woman comes home one evening and finds her husband making a pass at Miss Moran, his bookkeeper, she divorces him, taking their baby with her. In their encounters thereafter, James is consistently threatening. Her Chinese husband, Liu Kanghi, is James's antithesis. Finding the woman and her child "homeless and starving," he takes them to friends in Chinatown, who give them a home, and then he provides an outlet for the woman's needlework in his shop ("Her Chinese Husband," 359). The woman credits Liu Kanghi with saving her and her child from "self-destruction"; moreover, her portrait of him rejects popular stereotypes about Chinese American men: " 'I only knew that he was a man,' " and " 'I found comfort in his kind face' " ("A White Woman, 520–21). This view of Chinese Americans extends to the family the woman lives with, who nurse her back to health, care for her baby, and refuse any payment. In contrast to the kindness of this Chinese American family stands the violent prejudice of the baby's white father: " 'So you have sunk!'—his expression was evil. 'The oily little Chink has won you!' " ("A White Woman," 520). The white woman's retort sums up the narrative's contrasting visions of these two men: " 'And what are you that dare sneer at one like him? For all your six feet of grossness, your small soul cannot measure up to his great one' " ("A White Woman," 522).

In this manner, the stories' perspectives bluntly overturn the "yellow peril" portrayals that turn-of-the-century readers expected: the white American with his expression of "evil" and the Chinese American with his "great soul" reverse social stereotypes, showing that what society attributes to one actually exists in the other. Further, as Liu Kanghi and his friends become this woman's defenders, the usual view of Chinatown as alien and violent changes: " 'If you use violence,' [the narrator] declared [to her white husband], 'the lodgers will come to my assistance. They know me' " ("A White Woman," 522). As the white woman joins the Chinese community, her point of view becomes that of an insider looking out on the white world as "Other."

Another radical social revision exists in the harmonious relationship between white and Chinese children. In "A White Woman," the narrator relates, "I watched with complacency my child grow among the little Chinese children." " 'Your child shall be as my own,' " Liu Kanghi assures the narrator when he asks her to marry him (521). The woman's one doubt in accepting this offer enters with the birth of their own baby: "Only when the son of Liu Kanghi lays his little head upon my bosom do I question whether I have done wisely." The border position the woman foresees for this child is analogous to the one Sui Sin Far described in "Leaves" for herself and her siblings: "as he stands between his father and myself, like yet unlike us both, so he will stand in after years, between his father's and his mother's people . . ." (523).[79] Liu Kanghi disagrees in "Her Chinese Husband," voicing Sui Sin Far's frequently extended ideal: " 'What is there to weep about? The child is beautiful . . . he will fear none, and after him, the name of half Chinese will no longer be one of contempt.' " The woman's position—on the borders between the white American society in which she was reared and the Chinese American community into which she marries—keeps her from being convinced: "He could not see, as I, an American woman could, the conflict before our boy." The voices of her former society, assaulting the woman's ears from different directions and disturbing her happiness with her Chinese American husband and his community, maintain the conflict and keep the dialectic in motion: "I had still cause to shrink from the gaze of strangers," and "in a sense I was his, but of the dominant race, which claimed, even while it professed to despise me" (361).

From a social perspective, we can imagine this woman narrator reading such captions in the dailies as "A Distressing Social Condition: Intermarriage of the Mongol Race with the Caucasian," a headline that appeared some years earlier in the paper Sui Sin Far once canvassed for, the *San Francisco Call-Bulletin*. Lamenting that over twenty such marriages existed in San Francisco in 1897 and that "statistics show an increasing tendency," the *Call* reporter argued that one problem the white wives of Chinese men faced was that their husbands might return to China, leaving the women destitute.[80] The character of James Carsner stands between the reporter's implication that white men never leave their wives destitute and the homelessness that Sui Sin Far's narrator faces with her child on the streets. Awareness of current miscegenation laws is implicit in James's threatening question, " 'What will the courts say when I tell them about the Chinaman?' " and in the woman's response, "My little girl pined for her Chinese playmates . . . but I knew that if I wished to keep my child I could no longer remain with my friends" ("A White Woman," 522).

Through the unusual point of view in these stories, in which the white narrator and Chinese Americans look upon white Americans as alien "Others," the reader has access to voices from both worlds and hears the white woman explicitly voice her preference in "Her Chinese Husband": "As my union with James Carsner had meant misery, bitterness and narrowness, so my union with Liu Kanghi meant, on the whole, happiness, health and development" (359). Just as the narrator pits one individual white American against a Chinese American and shows the Chinese American to be superior on a human scale, the reader is left to ponder the white woman's broader judgment of Chinese Americans "as far more moral in their lives than the majority of Americans" (361).[81]

In "Chan Hen Yen, Chinese Student," published in the *New England Magazine* in June 1912, the title character is torn by allegiances to different voices, all roughly dividing into loyalties between old and new orders. In the flirtation between this student from China and the "self-constituted missionary," a sixteen-year-old white woman named Carrie Bray, the story again addresses miscegenation. Carrie and her mother, the widow Carolyn Bray, are not missionaries per se; rather, they support themselves by boarding male Chinese university students and see "missioning" to these young men as part of their duties. As an active volunteer in the Chinese Mission, Carrie takes pride "that through her instrumentality over one hundred Chinese boys have become acquainted with the English language and converted to Christianity." The hypocrisy in the mission movement—indeed, that the mission as the Brays practice it may be used as a sexual hunting ground—is suggested when Carrie invites Han Yen, a new boarder, to " 'come with me to the Chinese Mission sociable' "; scolds that " 'you walk too far away' "; and invites him to sit in the parlor listening to her "playing, singing, and otherwise entertaining her Chinese company." Eventually, Han Yen falls in love with Carrie, and they decide to get married. Nevertheless, Carrie's duplicitous nature is implied by narrative descriptions of her flirting with other Chinese students—"Carrie smiled first at this one, and then at that"—and the disclosure that "she understood [them] much better than they understood her" (463).

In opposition to Carrie, the story's narrator raises voices from Han Yen's Chinese past, voices that enlighten both Han Yen and the reader. We are told that he was chosen to be "the scholar" from his family in Kiangsoo Province and is now being educated at the expense of the Chinese government. In return, Han Yen was expected to "return to the Motherland . . . equipped to render her good service" (462). In addition, Han Yen's cousin, Chan Han Fong, addresses Chinese feelings about marriages between Chinese and whites by raising issues of loyalty to homeland, piety to ancestors, and the effect on future children. Choices polarize when Han Fong reminds Han Yen of his duty: " 'What! . . . you will relinquish your sacred ambition to work for China, dishonor your ancestors, disregard your parents' wishes. . . . all for the sake of a woman of alien blood?' " Han Yen replies in the sentimental language of Western romanticism that we have seen satirized in Sui Sin Far's *Dominion Illustrated* fiction: " 'The feeling which possesses me. . . is divine.' " The political implications—which again reveal Sui Sin Far's awareness of current Chinese politics—are illuminated when Han Fong underlines China's needs by reading something Han Yen reportedly had written six months earlier:

> "Oh, China, misguided country!
> What would I not sacrifice,
> to see thee uphold thyself,
> among the nations. . . ."[82]

A dialogue of divided loyalties is played out between Han Fong's " 'Alas for China!' " and Han Yen's " 'And what is one student to China?' " (464). In a tension that is particularly significant in 1912, two years after the success of Sun Yat Sen's revolution, Han Fong's final argument against his cousin's marriage to a Caucasian proceeds by a metaphor that may demonstrate Sui Sin Far's sentiments about the position of children of diverse racial parentage:

" 'The flowers. . . . of a kind come up together. The sister violet complements her brother. Only through some mistake in the seeding is it otherwise. And the hybrid flower, though beautiful, is the saddest flower of all' " (464–65).

The deceptive nature of these particular "missionaries" is fully revealed when Carrie is unmasked as a sham, whose desire to marry Han Yen is motivated by neither true love nor altruism. When Han Yen informs his fiancée that he will, in Carrie's words to her mother, " 'have to stay in America and live and work here just like a common Chinaman' " after they are married, the vernacular in which Mrs. Bray replies exposes the mother's and daughter's common hypocrisy and suggests that their main interest in Han Yen has been what they perceived to be a step upward in class: " 'Land sakes! . . . Ain't that awful! And I've been telling all around that you was to marry a Chinese gentleman and was to go to China and live in great style.' " When Carrie breaks the engagement with the explanation that Han Yen " 'is not a Christian,' " Han Yen, said to be "wiser than Carrie in that respect," sees through the excuse, realizing that she "has cast him aside, because, oh, *not* because of the reason she has given." With this insight, the Chinese man's enchantment with the Western experience—at least, as represented in "the Lesson of the woman"—is broken (466). Implicitly, Han Yen will go back to China and honor his contract, but he will not return to the "old" order exactly as he has left it, because he will bring back what he has learned of the "new."

These stories illustrate Sui Sin Far's ambivalent feelings about intermarriage. Given an ideal world, racial differences would not be a factor in love relationships; individuals of any race would meet, as had her parents, fall in love, and marry. Up to this point, the premises of her fiction are basically romantic and disregard cultural barriers as casually as her personal declarations do in "Leaves": "I have no nationality and am not anxious to claim any" (131). The practical woman, however—who at age twelve became "advisory head of the household" and who would be represented in 1915 in Winifred's *Me* as the formidable "Ada"—never failed to observe the social consequences of personal intimacy or to remember the punishment recurrently inflicted on both the partners and the children of marriages that crossed racial lines. This kind of double vision is given to the narrator of "A White Woman Who Married a Chinaman." Like that character, Sui Sin Far knows the view from both racial perspectives; through fictional characters and situations, she shows her readers both perspectives as well. The intermarriage stories, in particular, illustrate Sui Sin Far as a realist, who offers neither easy solutions nor happy endings. As in "A Fatal Tug of War," written twenty years earlier, they show that regardless of race "love" does not solve every problem.

Child Theft: Assimilation as Kidnapping

"In the Land of the Free," published in the *Independent* in 1909, and "The Sugar Cane Baby," published in *Good Housekeeping* in 1910, both examine a theme familiar to any colonized culture: child theft, or appropriating a people's culture through their children. In the words of Gail Nomura, "When you steal a people's culture, you steal their past; when you steal their children, you steal their future as well."[83] Because of the scarcity of women and the slow growth of Chinese American communities, children were special treasures for Chinese Americans in the late nineteenth and early twentieth centuries. The news that the title character of "Mrs. Spring Fragrance" finds "more than a dozen babies born to families of her friends" when she visits San Francisco in 1909 is not a casual remark by the story's narrator (138). In a Chinatown community, it is a miracle, promising survival for the evolving Chinese American culture. Missionary efforts, however, undertaken by white American women in positions of influence over children—social workers, schoolteachers, mission workers—were basically designed to squelch that culture by forcing Chinese Americans into the fold of westernization, as interpreted through Christianity.[84]

We have seen the white American culture's attempts to disrupt a Chinese American family in the person of Miss Mason, the schoolteacher who, representing European-based cultural assumptions about correct parenting, tries to take Ku Yum away from "her" father in "A Chinese Boy-Girl" (1904). This story is done with humor, and the Chinese American community comes out ahead. "In the Land of the Free" and "The Sugar Cane Baby" present visions that are considerably darker by dramatizing how the power of the colonizer is brought to bear against colonized peoples through their children, power that may be enacted by individuals but carries the whole weight of the institutional bureaucracy behind them. Though "The Sugar Cane Baby" achieves what could be construed as a happy ending and the child in each story is at least physically returned to his parents, both stories are tragic. Focusing on characters that represent people European and North American societies are colonizing, Sui Sin Far's aesthetic vision in both stories is antithetical to the traditional mainstream.

"In the Land of the Free" features a power struggle between a Chinese American couple and U.S. immigration officials for possession of the couple's child. The story opens with the mother, Lae Choo, returning by ship to San Francisco from China, where she has given birth to The Little One, now held in her arms. The scene is edenic; as they look across the bay at "the hills in the morning sun," mother murmurs to child about how happy they will be in this "home for years to come." Focus shifts to the other side of the water, where "a lone Chinaman" waits on the wharf. It is Hom Hing, a merchant who has been "in business in San Francisco for many years," ready "to board the steamer and welcome his wife and child." A shadow falls with the news that Hom Hing has been "detained . . . by men with the initials U.S.C. on their caps." As the family unites, the ominous forecast moves closer; the father's "proud and joyous eyes" as he lifts his son are juxtaposed against the "customs officer at his elbow" (504). Questioning the parents and "seeing that the boy has no certificate entitling him to admission to this country" (505), two customs officer confiscate The Little One and hold him in a mission nursery for ten months, during which time Hom Hing hands over all of his savings and Lae Choo forfeits her ancestral jewels in their efforts to get their baby back.

The entire plot is structured on contrasts. Lae Choo's initial happiness in viewing the sun with her baby is juxtaposed against her increasing misery, until it becomes "ten months since the sun had ceased to shine for Lae Choo" (505). The honest emotions of the grieving parents counterpoint the manipulations of the white attorney, James Clancy, who declares, " 'You can't get fellows to hurry the Government for you without gold in your pocket' " (508). Hom Hing's naive assurance to Lae Choo that " 'there cannot be any law that would keep a child from its mother!' " clashes against the narrator's ironic comment, "But the great Government at Washington still delayed sending the answer which would return him to his parents" (506). Most important, The Little One who had "looked up into his mother's face in perfect faith" (504) on the boat contrasts with the "little boy dressed in blue cotton overalls and white-soled shoes" who cries " 'Go'way, go'way!' " when his mother is finally allowed to come get him "and tried to hide himself in the folds of the white woman's skirt" (508). In his captivity, the child has indeed been stolen from his mother, forcibly stripped of his parents' language and culture. Juxtaposed against the rhetoric of the U.S. national anthem—"in the land of the free"—is the narrative of this couple's inside experience. Laws in this country do keep a child from his or her mother. This theme is extracted by posing "the law"—an abstraction laid down by white America—against the concrete struggle of this Chinese American family.

Again, it is a woman who leads in that struggle. When Hom Hing feels he must hand his son to the customs officers, we see Lae Choo grab her baby back from his father with words of heroic defiance: " 'No, you not take him; he my son, too!' " (505). When Hom Hing persuades her that this is the law and delivers The Little One to the first officer, her anguished " 'You, too,' " implies that the conflict in this plot is also between the woman and man. Why does Lae Choo finally "yield" the boy? Because, the story's narrator notes, she is "accustomed to obedience"—obedience to her husband, not to the customs officials. That her obedience to Hom Hing's authority as a man is at odds with her love for her child is clear both here and later when Hom Hing tries to console her and she accuses him in these words: " 'You do not know—man. . . .' "[85]

The diversity of voices in this story, with its themes of injustice and child theft, reveals the incomprehensibility of the white bureaucracy from the perspective of a Chinese American couple and the enigma of a male from the perspective of a woman. The hegemonic distribution of power in the story, then, corresponds to that in life and directly opposes images of the era's conventional discourse. Representatives of the white power establishment—customs officers, lawyers, missionaries—are not heroes in these stories but bullies, attacking Chinese Americans who are not mysterious villains but ordinary mothers, fathers, and children trying to survive in an alien land.

By diversifying the subject of "The Sugar Cane Baby" to include a Hindu baby, the author illustrates to an audience that knows her work—the readers of *Good Housekeeping* in which she has already published two sketches about Chinese children[86]—that the assimilative techniques of white colonizers are not limited to Chinese babies or to the United States. Though geography is not specified, descriptive details suggest that the setting is the Caribbean.[87] Once again, the plot is built on oppositions, beginning with the baby, who sits amidst a surrealistically wondrous natural setting of "humming-birds glistening like jewels," "lizards, green, yellow, speckled, black-and-gold," and "green bamboo," near the sugarcane field where his mother is working. The scene is centered by "a green spotted snake. . . . coiling and uncoiling for his delight and pleasure, the most beautiful snake in the world." The perspective is that of the child himself: "At least so thought the sugar-cane baby" (570).

An alternate viewpoint enters when "two serene-faced Sisters of Mercy," who are walking down the road admiring the "miles of green meadows and fruitful plantations undulating toward the sea," spot the snake. With a cry of " 'And, oh, Holy Saints protect it, there's a child!' " they throw a stone at "the coiling shimmering reptile" and kill it. Behind the sisters, and permeating the landscape they enjoy, are centuries of colonization. Behind their terror of this snake stands the biblical expulsion from Eden and, indeed, the whole of Christianity. Their assumptions are no less monolithic than those of the customs officials from "In the Land of the Free," and though their tactics are different, their responses when confronted by customs different from their own are just as intolerant: " 'Oh, these mothers, these mothers! What love have they for their children when they can leave them like this?' " (571).

The reader next sees the baby in "a little white crib in a long white room full of other little white cribs," a scene made even more stark by its contrast—in the baby's memory and ours—with the multicolored nature from which the nuns have extracted him. Replacing it is a pluralistic gathering of babies, presumably the "rescued" offspring of other laboring parents: "Around him . . . were a number of other babies, younger and older than himself. Most of them were pure pickaninnies, but not a few bore the mark of the white man in complexion and feature." The suggestion that many of these babies were the products of unions between the colonizers and the colonized, implying men's sexual exploitation of women, makes the nuns' efforts at cultural homogenization doubly ironic. Through these nuns, women whose only "sexual" union is presumably with a Christian god, the church as an institution participates in the colonial enterprise. The effect of this colonized environment on natural life is evident in the baby's deterioration: "His face did not wear the happy expression it had worn when the bamboo boughs waved above it." At a basic survival level, the child refuses to eat and, in the words of a sister, is " 'wasting away for want of nourishment' " (571).

A third perspective enters with "a young woman" who visits the ward, "a reporter on a local paper, but originally from the United States of America." Questioning the sisters about the baby, the reporter functions as a disturber of their established position, an interpreter between the institution they represent and Hindu culture. Reacting to her observation that " 'I believe the baby is breaking its heart for its mother,' " the sisters initially refuse to listen, declaring, " 'A child of that age! Oh, no!' " Next, the reporter goes to the mother superior, "that wise woman"—a description that turns ironic by the lack of wisdom in her response: " 'it would not be right for us to deliver to [the mother] the child. Is a person who could leave her baby beside a snake on the high road fitted to care for him?' " Because the young journalist opens the dialogue to another perspective—" 'The snake was harmless. . . . it had been trained by the baby's father to guard the little one' "—she educates the mother superior. As a consequence, the child's mother, who was "in the lemon grove—waiting," is sent for. The previously almost lifeless child clings to her, "so tight, so close, that they wondered at his strength" and "suck[s] eagerly" at the sugarcane the mother holds to his lips (572).

As the story ends, the missionary perspective is acknowledged to have limitations. The journalist "looked at the Mother Superior," and "the Mother Superior returned her gaze through a mist of tears," saying, " 'You are right . . .' " (572). The mother superior's conversion recalls that of Miss Mason in "A Chinese Boy-Girl," as Sui Sin Far again suggests, in the manner of Mikhail Bakhtin's heteroglossia, that divergent cultural voices speaking without privilege—in contrast to one voice dominating all others—is the goal toward which the world's peoples must strive. "In the Land of the Free" and "The Sugar Cane Baby" both set various cultural voices into competition, suggesting implicitly that no one has the right to define a single "correct" perspective. Moreover, both show the dire results, cultural and individual, when a particular society decides to set itself up with only one perspective. Who has the right to define a "safe baby" or to make a "law that would keep a child from its mother"? Sui Sin Far's nuns are well-intended, as perhaps the customs officials are. Both sets of characters attempt to uphold what they see as right. Trapped in monolithic assumptions, however, both fail to recognize that there are cultures distinct from their own that regard snakes not as their enemy but as nursemaids for babies. "The Sugar Cane Baby" speaks back to missionaries, in Jamaica or San Francisco, by illustrating that definitions of "abuse" can be culturally based. Simultaneously, the author's "missionary to missionaries" voice speaks with a vengeance, crying out to her readers, "Look at what you are doing."

Conclusion: The "Game" of Sui Sin Far's Mature Fiction

"Who's Game," published in the *New England Magazine* in 1912, encapsulates this chapter's argument that Sui Sin Far's mature fiction depicts marriage as a microcosm within which broader power struggles play themselves out. Sui Sin Far's trickster stance operates in this piece on multiple levels, and the themes reveal the carefully balanced, ironically layered vision that she achieved in many later stories. We recall that Sui Sin Far expressed to *Century* editor Robert U. Johnson the desire to be accepted as a writer on any subject, without being restricted to "Chinese" materials. Apart from the early *Dominion Illustrated* stories and "The Sugar Cane Baby," "Who's Game" is the only known result of this impulse. Unlike Sui Sin Far's other mature fiction, "Who's Game" deals with a white American community and illustrates that Christianity as practiced in the United States does not confine its assimilationist tactics to immigrant cultures or colonized races but marches out against any "stray sheep" that does not join the fold. As Sui Sin Far's last work of fiction to be located, this story offers an anchor for answering the key question of this and the next chapter: "Where did Sui Sin Far arrive with her mature fiction?"

The setting of "Who's Game?" is Zora, a rural village in Washington state, into which moves "the Lonely," a man the church community imagines to be a pioneer-hermit because he "had been living in the vicinity of Zora for at least three months, yet never had his face been seen nor his voice heard, in any church building." The church communities' collective response is to put aside denominational differences under the shared goal of converting a "heathen": "It mattered not whether Baptist, Methodist or Presbyterian. . . ." It is a competitive chase, metaphorically cast as a hunt: "What glory then was in store for whoever could bring him into a fold!" (573). The forerunners in this race dwindle to two, Mrs. William Bennett and Mrs. Thomas Page, who are described as "the best of friends." When the Lonely confides to each woman separately that " 'you will see me in church next Sunday' " (574) Mrs. Bennett suggests it was Mrs. Page who did the converting, and Mrs. Page suggests it was Mrs. Bennett. The Lonely answers both with a riddle: " 'it is someone else's personal magnetism that will draw me into the congregation of the faithful next Sunday'" (575). Comically, each woman, unable in her monolithic thinking to recognize ambiguity, interprets this comment to refer to herself.

The reader learns differently when the Lonely writes in a letter to his absent fiancée, "'Each of the ladies mentioned above is now congratulating herself that she has accomplished my conversion, and I had not the heart to undeceive either'" (575). Words like *undeceive,* in the context of a motif of deception, are sure clues to a trickster presence, as is the "twinkle in the Lonely's hazel eye." An alternate perspective is raised through the eyes of a deer that the man hunts: "Wasn't it great fun to see [the hunter] falling over logs, barking his shins. . ." (574). The man's clumsiness in this hunt mimics the church ladies' clumsiness in their "hunt" to catch him, a parallel reinforced when the Lonely sees himself as "'almost as good sport to them as the deer to me'" (575). The central deception of the tale is uncovered when the Lonely's fiancée, Kate Lesley, arrives in the village and turns out to be the minister's daughter. Kate reveals that the man the villagers believe to be an unredeemed hermit is in truth a professor from "Ohio Wesleyan College," whose "physician had ordered him to rest up in the western woods" (577). The monologic view of reality to which this small town is accustomed thus explodes into a dialogic of ideologies that have nested in their community unrecognized all along.

The Lonely, like the Sing-Song Woman, masks his identity to fool the townspeople, yet it is through their own inabilities to see past their own stereotypes that they have been tricked. The Lonely has disrupted this village's uniformity, not by telling any "untruth," as he reminds Kate when she reprimands him, but by telling the truth "slant"—by letting the church ladies' minds feed on the only conclusions possible within the narrow confines of their thinking. When Mrs. Bennett and Mrs. Page return home from their respective calls to the Lonely, each gloats to her husband that her "'efforts to bring a contrary sheep into the fold are at last rewarded.'" The children of each overhear, and their missionary competition for converts carries on to the next generation when the children subsequently get in a street fight:

> "He did, mama. He said it wasn't you who was getting Mr. Talbot to go to church next Sunday. He said it was *his* mother."
>
> The smile faded from Mrs. Page's countenance. . . .
>
> "Oh, no, daughter, you are mistaken!"
>
> "He did. He said his mother told his father so last night."
>
> "Well, never mind, dear. Come into the house and I will give you a piece of cake." (576)

Sui Sin Far's sense of back-fence gossip is rich and lively with small town realism in the mode of Sarah Orne Jewett: "Mrs. Bennett baked that week, and Mrs. Page made preserves; but there were no sweet exchanges offered or accepted" (577).[88]

Seeing the human cost of the competition between these two women, Kate accuses her fiancé of being " 'at the bottom of the whole mischief,' " underlining for proof the line in his letter: " 'I have not the heart to undeceive either' " (577). When he asks her for a " 'penance,' " the minister's daughter takes her turn at the trickster role, staging a play that " 'seek[s] to explain by actions what cannot be explained in words' ": he must " 'sit beside me in church tomorrow' " (578). Her fiancé agrees to the conditions. Forewarned by the "village gossip" that the " 'fellow to whom Miss Kate engaged herself last winter' " is in town, Mrs. Bennett and Mrs. Page walk to church, albeit separately, and take "their seats in pews across the aisle from one another," from where each sees the Lonely taking "his place beside Bonnie Kate Lesley . . . with an air of lover-like authority" (579).

The truth is revealed. The churchwomen have attempted to trick, but they have been tricked, and in the mutual "gaze [that] turned from the Lonely's back and met across the space between them," both know it. Each initially thinks that she knows what is going on and that her quarry does not. With typical missionary patronization, both report to the minister that the hermit seemed "amiably disposed" and "very intelligent" but held much "ignorance in regard to spiritual" (574). The individual they have tagged an outsider, however, not only is privy to information they do not have but also, by understanding their kind of mindset, teaches the church ladies the folly of judging life by appearance. How fully Mrs. Bennett and Mrs. Page absorb the lesson is another question. Are they aware, as the narrator makes the audience, of the "games" produced by their religious hypocrisies, games each has played on herself? It is ironic that harmony—between them and by implication in the community—is restored over a Methodist hymnal, as they join in singing "Blest Be the Tie That Binds" (579), a pointed reference to precisely the monologic perspective that led to their rift in the first place.

Sui Sin Far's trickster stance in this piece begins with the pun in the title. Does it refer to the slang phrase, "Who's game?" meaning who dares to do it; or is it a rendering of "Whose?" in the possessive case, as in who owns the game? The term *game* has multiple referents in the text itself—the deer as "game" to the hunter/hermit, the hunter/hermit as "game" to the churchwomen, and the churchwomen as "game" to him. Social reality itself is defined here as a set of interlocking games: there is the "game" the women play with the Lonely, reflecting the "game" Christianity plays on the world, under the monolithic assumption that everyone is an outsider unless he or she is converted. There is the game of disguise the Lonely plays on the town and the game of the "play" Kate performs to reveal truth and restore village order. Between the players of all these games is enacted a diverse set of culture-power relations.

The overriding question about these relations is directed at Mrs. Bennett's and Mrs. Page's own hypocrisies, which represent in turn a basic contradiction Sui Sin Far sees in Christianity. In this sense, we can perceive the Northwest town of Zora as Sui Sin Far's microcosm for the mission movement from Shanghai to San Francisco, in which case the figure of the Lonely—an outsider who educates those who think they are inside—occupies the position that Chinese and Chinese American characters take in Sui Sin Far's other writings. The underlying themes of the story—life *is* generally ambiguous, and those who believe in simple answers to its complexities are the real "strays"—might well define the overall vision of Sui Sin Far's art.

In her mature journalism and fiction, we have seen Sui Sin Far define her authorial position—in the Chinese American community, particularly as a storyteller, the role for which she once had been "slapped." Beyond that, these pieces illuminate the sense of the craftswoman, carving and reshaping forms, often repeating fragments of prior content, successfully working with styles and strategies that are able to contain and communicate her ideas.[89] The complexity of her late work imitated the power struggles that she observed and experienced between races, the sexes, and classes and reflected her commitment to bring the diversity of voices involved in these struggles, especially those who had been traditionally silenced, to the printed page. The strategies of her mature fiction involve challenging what Bakhtin has termed monologic visions of social reality with the dialogic of multiple viewpoints, voices that represent those society attempts to make "powerless." These strategies include using trickster figures to expose monologic illusions about society as well as reversing the order of "Other-ness" from usual views in American literature.

The ambivalent stance of her art, one for which Sui Sin Far has been criticized, indirectly reflects her divided life, the division between the colonized and the colonizer in the countries in which she was working, and the vision of ironic wit that she evolved partly as a means of getting published in the marketplace of her era. Bakhtin's condition of "carnival," in which diverse voices and contradictions are released and permitted to speak without privilege, especially applies to Sui Sin Far's mature fictional atmosphere. The nonfictional pieces make her position explicit. She was dealing with the voices of two races as well as that anomalous borderland that society labeled "Eurasian." Her growth as a writer since her earliest *Dominion Illustrated* stories can be measured by the steps she took from being "Edith Eaton" to becoming "Sui Sin Far" and, in 1909, to affirming "Sui Sin Far" publicly by revealing her Eurasian history. Hers was the culture of the trickster, hovering above borders, flitting across them. Always working in a double voice, Sui Sin Far saw reality from two directions at once; she was an ironist who addressed serious issues from both sides of borders. As in Ralph Waldo Emerson's poem "Brahmin," she was both "the doubter and the doubt," both a representative of the culture that in all of its arrogance sent missionaries to convert "heathens" and the "heathen" who rejected being converted. The ambiguity of the writer's life, one might say, provided a center for her art in this period.

Notes

1. Sui Sin Far (Edith Eaton), *Mrs. Spring Fragrance* (Chicago: A. C. McClurg, 1912).

2. Sui Sin Far, "Leaves from the Mental Portfolio of an Eurasian," *Independent* 66 (21 January 1909): 125–32. Hereafter referred to as "Leaves."

3. Edith Eaton to Charles Lummis, 10 February 1909, Charles Fletcher Lummis Collection, Southwest Museum, Los Angeles, Calif.

4. Sui Sin Far, "Sui Sin Far, the Half Chinese Writer Tells of Her Career," *Boston Globe,* 5 May 1912. Hereafter referred to as *Globe.*

5. In 1910 this community is estimated to have numbered nine hundred and to have been concentrated around the Harrison/Beach street area, a railroad construction district that extended to the port of entry at South Station. See Doris C. J. Chu, with the assistance of Glen Braverman, *Chinese in Massachusetts: Their Experiences and Contributions* (Boston: Chinese Culture Institute, 1987), 56, 47. The community was located a mile or two from Sui Sin Far's residence.

6. Edith Eaton to Charles Lummis, 13 July 1911, 23 March 1912, 19 April 1912, Charles Fletcher Lummis Collection, Huntington Library, San Marino, Calif.

7. Frank Luther Mott, *A History of American Magazines, 1741–1930,* 5 vols. (Cambridge, Mass.: Harvard University Press, 1930–68), 4: 108.

8. Edgar L. Hampton, "With the Publishers," *Westerner* 10 (March 1909): 1.

9. Mott, *A History of American Magazines,* 4: 367–79.

10. Ibid., 4: 377.

11. Sui Sin Far, "Leaves"; "In the Land of the Free," *Independent* 67 (2 September 1909): 504–8; "A White Woman Who Married a Chinaman," *Independent* 68 (10 March 1910): 518–23; "Her Chinese Husband," *Independent* 69 (18 August 1910): 358–61; "Chinese Workmen in America," *Independent* 75 (3 July 1913): 56–58.

12. Mott, *A History of American Magazines,* 2: 377.

13. Ibid., 4: 47.

14. Sui Sin Far, "Mrs. Spring Fragrance," *Hampton's* 24 (January 1910): 137–41.

15. Mott, *A History of American Magazines,* 5: 148–49.

16. Sui Sin Far, "The Inferior Woman," *Hampton's* 24 (May 1910): 727–31.

17. Benjamin J. Hampton, "A Statement by Mr. Hampton to the Stockholders and Readers of His Magazine," *Hampton's* 27 (August 1911): 258–59.

18. Mott, *A History of American Magazines,* 3: 483.

19. Ibid., 3: 486–87.

20. Ibid., 3: 486.

21. Sui Sin Far, "The Kitten-Headed Shoes," *Delineator* 75 (February 1910): 165; "The Candy That Is Not Sweet," *Delineator* 76 (July 1910): 76.

22. Mott, *A History of American Magazines,* 5: 126.

23. Ibid., 5: 126–30.

24. Ibid., 5: 132.

25. Sui Sin Far, "Ku Yum and the Butterflies," *Good Housekeeping* 48 (March 1909): 299; "The Half Moon Cakes," *Good Housekeeping* 48 (May 1909): 584–85; "The Sugar Cane Baby," *Good Housekeeping* 50 (May 1910): 570–72.

26. Mott, *A History of American Magazines,* 4: 79–80.

27. Sui Sin Far, "An Autumn Fan," *New England Magazine* 42 (August 1910): 700–702; "The Bird of Love," *New England Magazine* 43 (September 1910): 25–27; "A Love Story from the Rice Fields of China," *New England Magazine* 45 (December 1911): 343–45; "Who's Game?" *New England Magazine* 45 (February 1912): 573–79; "Chan Hen Yen, Chinese Student," *New England Magazine* 45 (June 1912): 462–66.

28. Edgar Hampton, "Miss Eaton's Chinese Sketches," *Westerner* 10 (April 1909): 1.

29. Quoted in Carolyn G. Heilbrun, *Writing a Woman's Life* (New York: Ballantine Books, 1988), 37.

30. Amy Ling, *Between Worlds: Women Writers of Chinese Ancestry* (New York: Pergamon, 1990), distinguishes between the usual use of pseudonyms—as "cloaks in which to hide ones true identity"—and their use by Edith Eaton and Winifred Eaton "to assert and expose their Asian ancestry" (21), as "alternate tactics of survival and negotiation within a hostile environment" (25–26) to which both were born.

31. These are issues Sui Sin Far addresses throughout the *Westerner* articles, particularly in the introduction (May 1909): 24–26.

32. Edith Eaton (Sui Sin Far), "The Coat of Many Colors," *Youth's Companion* 76 (April 1902): n.p.

33. Bakhtin believes that all discourse is "double-voiced," "because it's always shaped by the audience, whose potential reactions must be taken into account from the outset." Quoted in Gary Saul Morson, "Who Speaks for Bakhtin?" in *Bakhtin: Essays and Dialogues on His Work,* ed. Gary Saul Morson (Chicago, University of Chicago Press, 1986), 4.

34. Amy Ling, "Edith Eaton: Pioneer Chinamerican Writer and Feminist," *American Literary Realism* 16 (Autumn 1983): 296, observes that Sui Sin Far hoped readers would "identify" and "condemn the thwarting forces, even if these happen to be their own laws and practices."

35. See S. E. Solberg, "The Eaton Sisters: Sui Sin Far and Onoto Watanna" (Paper presented at the Pacific Northwest Asian American Writer's Conference, Seattle, Wash., 16 April 1976), 23, who declares, "And in the end she wanted desperately to write and to sell what she had written."

36. Cited in Doug Chin, "Edith Maud Eaton: The First Chinese American Writer," *International Examiner* (Seattle), January 1977. Solberg, "The Eaton Sisters," 3, hypothesizes another reason for the difference between the two sisters' publishing records: "Edith Eaton was writing her Chinese stories at a time when the subject no longer constituted a real public issue at the same time her sister Winifred was taking up her Japanese themes as the Japanese question was coming to the front. This may go a good way toward explaining the relative obscurity of Edith against the instant popularity of Winifred."

37. Joan N. Radner and Susan S. Lanser, "The Feminist Voice: Strategies of Coding in Folklore and Literature," *Journal of American Folklore* 100 (October–December 1987): 414.

38. For a book-length study of this subject, see Elizabeth Ammons and Annette White-Parks, eds., *Tricksterism in Turn-of-the-Century American Literature: A Multicultural Perspective* (Hanover, N.H.: University Press of New England, 1994).

39. Zora Neale Hurston, *Dust Tracks in the Road,* 2d ed., ed. Robert E. Hemenway (Urbana: University of Illinois Press, 1984), xxxiv.

40. William Bright, "The Natural History of Old Man Coyote," in *Recovering the Word: Essays on Native American Literature,* ed. Brian Swann and Arnold Krupat (Berkeley: University of California Press, 1987), 339–87.

41. Ibid., 340.

42. Ibid. Examples Bright cites are "Renard the Fox of medieval French legend and Anansi the Spider of West African and modern Afro-Caribbean tradition."

43. Ibid., 349, 346, 379.

44. As cited in ibid., 340.

45. Ibid., 342.

46. Li Hui, "Nushu: A Written Language for Women Only," *Anima: The Journal of Human Experience* 16 (Spring 1990): 109.

47. Ibid., 108, 109.

48. Cathy Silber, "A 1,000-Year-Old Secret," *Ms.* 3 (September/October 1992): 59.

49. Mary Dearborn, *Pocahontas's Daughters: Gender and Ethnicity in American Culture* (New York: Oxford University Press, 1986), 28.

50. See Annette White-Parks, "We Wear the Mask: Sui Sin Far as One Example of Trickster Authorship," in *Tricksterism,* ed. Ammons and White-Parks, 1–19.

51. Compare Bright's observation in "The Natural History," 349, that Coyote "acts out of impulse, or appetite, or for the pure joy of trickery." See also Dale M. Bauer, *Feminist Dialogics: A Theory of Failed Community* (New York: State University of New York Press, 1988), 4, who points out carnivalization is, in part, "to open up another's discourse . . . to make it vulnerable to change, to exposure."

52. Robert L. Welsch, *Omaha Tribal Myths and Trickster Tales* (Athens, Ohio: Sage/Swallow Press, 1981), 17.

53. The "Post-Intelligencer" pieces have not been located.

54. S. E. Solberg, "Sui, the Storyteller: Sui Sin Far (Edith Eaton), 1867–1914," in *Turning Shadows into Light: Art and Culture of the Northwest's Early Asian/Pacific Community*, ed. Mayumi Tsutakasa and Alan Chong Lou (Seattle: Young Pine, 1982), 87, maintains, however, that "Sui Sin Far did reveal as much of herself as she was willing and able" in "Leaves."

55. E.E., "A Plea for the Chinaman: A Correspondent's Argument in His Favor," letter to the editor, *Montreal Daily Star,* 21 September 1896.

56. L. Charles Laferrière, Interview, Montreal, Quebec, Spring 1989.

57. These pieces appear in the *Westerner* in a four-part series entitled "The Chinese in America: Intimate Study of Chinese Life in America, Told in a Series of Short Sketches—An Interpretation of Chinese Life and Character" from May to August 1909. Each issue contained one or more sketches: "[Author's Preface]," "The Story of Wah," "A Chinese Book on Americans," and "Scholar or Cook?" 10 (May 1909): 24–26; "The New and the Old," 10 (June 1909): 36–38; "Like the American," "The Story of the Forty-Niner," "The Story of Tai Yuen and Ku Yum," "Wah Lee on Family Life," and "The Bonze," 11 (July 1909): 18–19; and "Yip Ke Duck and the Americans," "New Year as Kept by the Chinese in America," "Chinese-American Schools," "Chinese Food," "The Bible Teacher," "Americanizing Not Always Christianizing," and "The Reform Party," 11 (August 1909): 24–26.

58. Edgar L. Hampton, "With the Publishers," *Westerner* 10 (April 1909): 1.

59. This allusion to a West Indian Chinese is not referred to elsewhere.

60. Edgar L. Hampton, "With the Publishers," *Westerner* 10 (April 1909): 1.

61. Edgar L. Hampton, "With the Publishers," *Westerner* 11 (November 1909): 1.

62. The man's earlier comment, "My mother was old and needed ginseng and chicken broth, and my father was old and we were poor," duplicates lines from "The Coat of Many Colors," published in 1902.

63. Sui Sin Far, of course, was not alone; many women did remain single in Victorian society. Nevertheless, making this choice meant defying the expectations society laid down for her in the nineteenth century and accepting the consequences of social disapproval.

64. Ling, *Between Worlds,* 4, notes Chinese women's tradition of committing suicide as a means of avoiding societal disapproval: "Chinese wives were encouraged to commit suicide after their husbands' death." For the woman who did so, "the family would erect a stone arch to commemorate her heroism and to inspire other women to follow her example." Ling points out the irony that Helena Kuo, *Peach Path* (London: Methuen, 1940), 136, observes: "Thus, China can boast more monuments to women than any other nation," not for living achievements but for agreeing that "after their husbands died they had no right to live." The suicides of Sui Sin Far's early fictional women occur, by contrast, because they prefer death to marriage. Her later women

prefer the option of life. See Margery Wolf, "Women and Suicide in China," in *Women in Chinese Society,* ed. Margery Wolf and Roxane Witke (Stanford, Calif.: Stanford University Press, 1975), 111–41, for a study of the relationship between suicide and women in traditional China.

65. Lorraine Dong and Marlon K. Hom, "Defiance or Perpetuation: An Analysis of Characters in *Mrs. Spring Fragrance,*" in *Chinese America: History and Perspectives,* ed. Him Mark Lai, Ruthanne Lum McCunn, and Judy Yung (San Francisco: Chinese Historical Society of America, 1987), 142, argue that Mr. Spring Fragrance is "under-developed due to the writer's emphasis on his wife's flamboyant personality." I believe this interpretation misses a major thematic and aesthetic point: within Sui Sin Far's fictional and political vision, a Chinese American woman must maintain the thematic center.

66. Elizabeth Ammons, *Conflicting Stories: American Women Writers at the Turn into the Twentieth Century* (New York: Oxford University Press, 1992), 113.

67. See ibid., 110: "As a liberated, self-sufficient Chinese American woman at the turn of the century, Sui Sin Far obviously resented white feminist's presumption of authority when it came to defining women's issues.... a major theme in the first half of *Mrs. Spring Fragrance* is criticism not only of white racism but specifically of the arrogance and ethnocentricity of white feminism."

68. See ibid., 110: "Distinctions essential to separating British and mainstream white American literary lines are miniscule when looked at globally. Indeed, is white American literature different from British if considered from an Asian American point of view?"

69. Ibid., 111.

70. As noted in chapter 2, "A Fatal Tug of War," *Dominion Illustrated* 1 (8 December 1888): 362–63, features a first paragraph identical to that of "The Bird of Love," except for the last four words: "and they were Chinese."

71. A version of these lines was first printed in Sui Sin Far, "Spring Impressions: A Medley of Poetry and Prose," *Dominion Illustrated* 4 (7 June 1890): 358–59. In that text, it reads: "then that elusive bird called Happiness . . . sings a song so loud and clear that our little home bird, 'Sorrow,' hides its head . . ." (358).

72. At first this is managed through nurses called "Sung-Sungs," a term used by Winifred Babcock Eaton in both *Me* and *Marion* (published in 1915 and 1916, after "The Bird of Love") in reference to an old Chinese servant fictionalized in both works who lived with the Eaton family.

73. Sui Sin Far's personification of this plant recalls the use of symbolic flowers in such works as Nathaniel Hawthorne's "Rappuccini's Daughter" and *The House of Seven Gables.*

74. Virginia Woolf, *A Room of One's Own* (New York: Harcourt Brace Javanovich, 1957 [1929]); Louise Bernikow, *Among Women* (New York: Harper Colophon, 1981), 5. The dialogue of women friends in literature is less of a mystery in the 1990s.

75. Both Li Hui, "Nushu: A Written Language for Women Only," and Silber, "A 1,000-Year-Old Secret," talk about *laotong.*

76. Dong and Hom, "Defiance or Perpetuation," 141, argue that "Sui Sin Far does not offer sympathy for any of these men whose beliefs of filial piety and male authority exemplify the worst Chinese culture can bring to America." I found that Sui Sin Far treats filial piety as a positive value, and while she questions male authority when exercised arbitrarily, she does so in both Anglo and Chinese cultures, as illustrated by the brutal white husband in Sui Sin Far, "A White Woman Who Married a Chinaman."

77. Heilbrun, *Writing a Woman's Life,* 13–14.

78. Referring to these stories, John Burt Foster, "Chinese and Chinese-Americans in American Literature, 1850–1950" (Ph.D diss., University of Illinois, 1952), 205, writes, "So intimately does the author write of mixed marriages that one is tempted to believe that she herself married a Chinese and was enabled in this way to get firsthand information." I find no evidence for this, however. Being born into and raised in the context of a "mixed marriage" certainly supplied her with "firsthand" experience; and we know from her Montreal writings of the 1890s that she had knowledge of, and perhaps personal acquaintance with, other interracial families.

79. Ling, "Edith Eaton," 295, implies this connection when she maintains that this story's final question, " 'What will my boy's fate be?' " is "inspired by a direct, deeply felt experience of the author's own."

80. *San Francisco Call-Bulletin,* 15 August 1897.

81. Here, as elsewhere in Sui Sin Far's work, the term *American* is synonymous with *white,* in keeping with the conventional usage of her era.

82. We as readers recognize this apostrophe as identical to the one that Sui Sin Far attributed to the exiled wife of the Chinese reformer Leung Ki Chu in the *Los Angeles Express* nine years earlier.

83. Gail Nomura, Interview, Pullman, Wash., Spring 1989.

84. See Peggy Pascoe, "Gender Systems in Conflict: The Marriages of Mission-Educated Chinese American Women, 1874–1939," *Journal of Social History* 22 (Summer 1989): 631–52, for a study of the mission-conversion-assimilationist effort, as it affected Chinese American culture on a long-term generational basis. Examining the practices of Protestant mission homes in San Francisco's Chinatown, Pascoe observes that the missionaries, whose explicit purpose was to "rescue" prostituted Chinese American women, did not stop at this but also brought any Chinese American girls the missionaries termed "neglected or abused" into the homes. Through this practice, the missionaries were able to remove the children from their own Chinese American culture and to raise them under white American influence. When the girls reached an age termed as marriageable, the missionaries arranged for them to marry "Christianized" Chinese American men, thus increasing the odds that any children born to the couple would be raised Christian, which further decreased the influence of Chinese American culture and promoted the ideology of white America. Such practices are

acted out consistently, and not all that implicitly, throughout Sui Sin Far's literature.

85. This line could stand as an epigraph to much of Sui Sin Far's writing about practices stemming from the patriarchal assumptions with which her Chinese American women must deal; the men who exercise such authority often "do not know" the viewpoint and experience of women.

86. See note 25.

87. The details may be the product of Sui Sin Far's stay in Jamaica.

88. Judith Fetterley and Marjorie Pryse, *American Women Regionalists, 1850–1910* (New York: W. W. Norton, 1992), 500–501, look at Sui Sin Far as a "local color" writer and regionalist.

89. S. E. Solberg, "Sui Sin Far/Edith Eaton: First Chinese-American Fictionalist," *MELUS* 8 (Spring 1981): 32, alludes to this unique position Sui Sin Far was in as an artist: "As a Chinese-American writer, then, Sui Sin Far had to find a mode that would enable her to deal with her own experience ... but to do that meant to fall outside the boundaries of any of the 'maincurrents' of American writing."

5

Mrs. Spring Fragrance

So I do believe in the timelessness and universality of individual vision.
It [my book] would not just be a family book or a woman's book, but a
world book, and, at the same moment, my book. . . . I hope my writing
has many layers, as human beings have layers.

—Maxine Hong Kingston, "Cultural Misreadings
    by American Reviewers"

Mrs. Spring Fragrance is Sui Sin Far's only book-length collection and—in the
absence of the unlocated novel still in manuscript at the time of her death—the
culmination of her life's work.[1] A deconstruction of the volume's physical
design, marketing strategy, and public reception makes it possible to consider
the publisher's concept of the book and its author. A unifying strategy
informs such essential but distinct details as cover, decorations, layout, and
table of contents, a strategy reflected in how the publishers presented the book
to the public, in its sales, and in reviewer responses. Juxtaposing this against
Mrs. Spring Fragrance's literary contents reveals a balance between the publisher's
appeal to Orientalism and the writer's commitment to introducing an authentic Chinese American voice into American literature. The stories in *Mrs.
Spring Fragrance* that are customarily seen as written for children delineate Sui
Sin Far's voice when it speaks to a young audience and show the common
patterns this voice shares with the work as a whole. Several of the major
stories in the collection, especially those for which no separate printings have
been located, concentrate on the book's major themes and their particular
significance to Sui Sin Far's writing voice during the final phase of her career.

Published in June 1912, two months after Sui Sin Far's forty-seventh
birthday, *Mrs. Spring Fragrance* is the book she "conceived in early childhood
[but] achieved only as I near the close of half a century," as she recounted to a
Boston Globe audience in May of that year,[2] suggesting that the volume
resulted from her lifelong accumulation of experience, ideas, network building,

and purposeful struggle. Publication of the book apparently involved a systematic campaign by eastern publishers to market Sui Sin Far as a writer. For the first time in Sui Sin Far's career she had been freed that past year, thanks to the financial backing of friends, from doing "the work of others," and she was very clear about the priority that her own work now assumed: "Save, however, some visiting among Chinese friends, I do not mingle much in any kind of society. I am not rich and I have my work to do" (*Globe*).

As to what that work was, there are three possibilities. First was the collection and revision of previously published stories for compilation in *Mrs. Spring Fragrance.* With a few exceptions, the stories that have been located in their first printings elsewhere show little evidence of significant rewrite. Second was the composition of new stories, both for periodicals and for original publication in *Mrs. Spring Fragrance.* Because all of the stories discussed in the last chapter carry publication dates of 1910 or later, and because six of these were included in *Mrs. Spring Fragrance,* all were probably being written while she was working on the collection. I have been able to locate separate printings for only eleven out of *Mrs. Spring Fragrance*'s thirty-eight selections, a fact that reinforces my belief that Sui Sin Far wrote some original stories for this volume. Third was her work on "the long novel" that the *Montreal Daily Star* obituary[3] claims was still unpublished at her death in 1914 and that Sui Sin Far mentioned to the *Boston Globe* in 1912: "I have also written another book which will appear next year [that is, in 1913] if Providence is kind." Documentation for the existence of this book manuscript survives in several of her letters to Charles Lummis: the first on 9 August 1911, when she wrote, "I think you will be more interested in my book, when it is written, than in my short stories"; the second on 23 March 1912, when she told him, "The other book, which I submitted to McClurg's, was not rejected by them absolutely. They want it, I think; but they have asked me to cut it down"; and the third on 19 April 1912, when she promised, "Yes, I shall try to please McClurg with my book." The March letter distinguishes between this "other book" and *Mrs. Spring Fragrance* and suggests that Lummis advised Sui Sin Far regarding revisions.[4]

Book Design, Marketing, and Reception

Information about the production of *Mrs. Spring Fragrance* suggests the publisher's interests and explains why the volume is so pretty. The collection was published by A. C. McClurg and Company, a major Chicago publishing house that A. C. McClurg took over in 1886 with the commitment to fight "against cheap bookmaking, which he considered a danger to the trade."[5] In 1911, the year before *Mrs. Spring Fragrance* was published, A. C. McClurg's son, Ogden, assumed control of the company.[6] That McClurg and Company had a modest tradition of giving attention to women and marginalized ethnics is indicated by its publication of George P. Upton's *Women in Music,* their first book in 1886, and W. E. B. Du Bois's *Souls of Black Folk* in 1903. Clarence Mulford's Hopalong Cassidy series and the Tarzan books by Edgar Rice Burroughs, published about the same time as *Mrs. Spring Fragrance,* were among McClurg's bestsellers.[7] The company hired their printing out, in the case of *Mrs. Spring Fragrance* to the Plimpton Press of Norwood, Massachusetts, a printer with a daily output of from twenty-five to thirty thousand bound volumes that described itself as "one of the largest, most modern, and best-equipped plants in the country." Plimpton's considered their bound volumes to be emblematic of their motto "perfect book-making in its entirety" and took pride in "printing as an art."[8] The printer's 1911 yearbook defined "the book beautiful": "It is a composite thing, made up of many parts, and may be made beautiful by . . . its literary content, its material or materials, its writing or printing, its illumination or illustration, its binding or decoration—or each of its parts in subordination to the whole which collectively they constitute. . . ."[9]

This idea of design presumed bookmaking to be what Plimpton's termed a "total concept."[10] To clarify what this concept meant for *Mrs. Spring Fragrance,* I refer back to a letter that Sui Sin Far wrote to Lummis eleven years earlier, in which she observed that "everything Chinese seems to be taking now."[11] She was alluding to the fad of "Chinatown literature" as well as the broader vision of Orientalism, which Edward W. Said has aptly described: "As much as the West itself, the Orient is an idea that has a history and a tradition of thought, imagery, and vocabulary that has given it reality and presence in and for the West."[12] This vision implicitly distinguishes between the Orient as a place on the map and the Orient as imagined in Western fiction. The marketing of Orientalism in Sui Sin Far's era was observed by Edith Noble-Brewer, who claimed that "there is a growing craze in America for the Oriental" in a 1903 article for *New Idea Woman's Magazine,* whose editor Sui Sin Far includes on her acknowledgment page for *Mrs. Spring Fragrance.*[13] The physical appearance of the volume reflects the "imagery" and "vocabulary" of Orientalism, presumably as it was interpreted by the book printer, whether or not in consultation with the author.[14]

Sui Sin Far alluded to one aspect of this imagery when she wrote to Lummis about her book: "It will have a red cover"; the color red, the Chinese color of happiness.[15] In this sense, she sets the stage for the book's subject matter. On the book's front cover, slightly slanted letters in a calligraphic style spell "Mrs. Spring Fragrance" in gold across the top from the left; these are counterpointed by four Chinese characters, also in gold, lined vertically down from the right corner, which approximate the English phrase "signed by Sui Sin Far."[16] A scene of red and green dragonflies superimposed on two white

Chinese lilies, or lotus flowers,[17] emerges from a green water ripple embossed across the cover's center; the Chinese lily motif (a visual translation of Sui Sin Far's name) is repeated in a flower, whose long stem extends down the spine between the gold-lettered title "Mrs. Spring Fragrance" at the top and the publisher's name "A. C. McClurg" at the bottom. The endpapers are "lotus-toned," or off-white, and are etched with the pale gray umbrella of a flowering tree, beneath which float tiny gray fishing boats—the kind that westerners envision set sail from Chinese harbors. The title page and all subsequent pages are from this same paper. Each is decorated with two branches, one of a blossoming fruit tree and one of bamboo, which unite at the margins; on the bamboo perches a pair of evenly spaced, crested birds. The title page also features an etching of four Chinese characters that are repeated in the upper right-hand corner of each subsequent recto leaf. The characters reinforce the motif of the red cover, for they can be approximately translated in English as "happiness, prosperity, and long life."[18] Altogether, according to Jinqi Ling, the paper design suggests a typical scenic drawing of the kind the Chinese paint on mirrors.[19] It is a scene in the mode of Orientalism. Its motif of spring fits the title and, as we shall see, the title character.[20]

The Orientalism so consistently carried out in *Mrs. Spring Fragrance*'s visual design may be illuminated by referring to *Little Folks,* a children's magazine from England that Sui Sin Far lists on *Mrs. Spring Fragrance*'s acknowledgment page as a previous publisher of her stories. With the same avidity that they displayed such acquisitions of Western colonization as the banana palm or the "captive macaw bird," in 1904 *Little Folks* exhibited an African baby, washed and dried by the mother's own tongue, rubbed with lanolin, and hung from a tree in a goatskin, and a little Chinese girl "with feet sturdy as an English child because her family cannot afford to have them bound." In the same issue, the editors marked the distance between humans from colonized countries and the young armchair travelers who made up their readership by reminding the travelers, "You must not think that in these countries which we call uncivilized you will find all the comforts and conveniences of your own happy land."[21] Implicit here was the presumption that people from colonized countries may be quaint and cute but should by no means be considered equal to the people who had colonized them. The assumption of white colonizers, in Europe or North America, was that a nation's people, like its flora and fauna, came with the territory.

Orientalism of varying degrees informed many of the magazines for which Sui Sin Far was writing in the early twentieth century. Evidence that McClurg's drew on stereotyped images of the Chinese as examples of "Other-ness" in its marketing of *Mrs. Spring Fragrance* appears in the ad for the book in the *New York Times Book Review* on 11 July 1912: "Quaint, lovable characters are the Chinese who appear in these unusual and exquisite stories of our Western

Coast—stories that will open an entirely new world to many readers." Sui Sin Far's "Leaves from the Mental Portfolio of an Eurasian," published in the *Independent,* implies that a campaign to market Sui Sin Far as an "exotic" writer had been underway for several years.[22] In this piece, as Sui Sin Far spoke to a national audience for the first time in her own voice as a Eurasian, she related her experiences of what an immigrant woman of Chinese-English parentage had been forced to suffer in England, Canada, Jamaica, and the United States. In spite of taboos against miscegenation, her dual heritage could be exploited. In the Progressive Era, in a liberal journal such as the *Independent,* her story also held out the lure of an exposé, an opening of the reader's mind to what was perhaps a new cause for "reform." Accompanying the story, we recall, was a photo of a face that looked European. Even though the caption described the subject as "Eurasian," her features, set in the standard oval frame of Victorian portraits, would have suggested to a largely white audience that she was a "safe ethnic"—one who looked white.

Moreover, in the minds of the largely middle-class *Independent* readership, the woman who wrote "Leaves," although she had undergone sufferings in the past and her words hardly suggested forgiveness of the racist attitudes she condemned, by now had obviously "made it." Hardship was a motif familiar in American rhetoric, from the trans-Atlantic migrations to the movement West; the important point was that—in the mythic tradition of the Plymouth pilgrims and Horatio Alger heroes—she had overcome difficulties to "pull herself up by the bootstraps," as the American dream said she should. Was not her success proven by the stance from which she faced them, out of the pages of a national magazine?

These clichés in U.S. thinking, implicitly evoked in the pages of "Leaves," were addressed more directly in the *Boston Globe* article on 5 May 1912, a month before the advent of *Mrs. Spring Fragrance* in local bookstalls. Sui Sin Far's introduction of herself as "unusual" and from a life "quite unlike that of any literary worker of whom I have read" hinted at Orientalism and perhaps spoke to the *Globe* article's central purpose, to promote her forthcoming book. Her "exotic" beginnings—the "father who was educated in England and studied art in France," the "mother, a Chinese young girl, who had been educated in England"—and her immigrant status—"When I was 6 years old my father brought us to America"—were established before she moved to her life as a writer. The sequence that followed established a counterpoint between her trials and successes and between her childhood dream—"[I] must have been about 8 years old when I conceived the ambition to write a book about the half Chinese"—and her current achievement: "My collection of Chinese-American stories will be brought out very soon, under the title 'Mrs. Spring Fragrance.'" Though the writer stressed the difficulty of both the creative and marketing process ("I struggled for many months. The Century Magazine took a story from me . . ."), her voice evokes neither a downtrodden woman nor a persecuted minority but a professional who had endured what life sent and now claimed her reward. This attitude is compatible with the Protestant ethic. In line with that ethic, Sui Sin Far did not claim all the credit herself but—like Alice Winthrop of "The Inferior Woman" (1910)—recognized the mentors who had helped in her struggle: Mrs. Darling "who first, aside from my mother, interested me in my mother's people"; Judge Archibald; Charles Lummis; and "the managing editor of the *Independent*," without whose "encouragement" the book "could not have [been] carried to a successful completion." Lastly, Sui Sin Far thanked "two of my lawyer friends in Montreal [who] kindly contributed toward this end." These were her current patrons and individuals Sui Sin Far ostensibly knew would be reading this article.

Overall, both "Leaves" and the *Globe* article suggest that Sui Sin Far's publishers were promoting her as an assimilated or melting-pot immigrant, one who once had faced persecution but had become "Americanized" and now could share her story. Like "Leaves," the *Globe* article includes a photo of a serious-looking woman with a candid face who, in spite of the headline "the Half Chinese Writer" and the caption "Sui Sin Far," looks—as the author described her own mother in "Leaves"—"English bred, with English ways and manner of dress" (127). The marketplace thus managed both to link the writer to Orientalism and to show her as Anglicized and successful. However one reads this marketing of Sui Sin Far, the message seems ironic in retrospect, because both Sui Sin Far and the Chinese American women who populate her stories joined other women of color in the United States in having less access to the "American dream" than anyone else.

Sui Sin Far's personal enthusiasm for her book, and the anticipation that her family would share it, are modestly expressed in the *Globe* article: "My people in Montreal, my mother in particular, my Chinese friends in Boston and also American friends are looking forward to the advent of 'Mrs. Spring Fragrance' with, I believe, some enthusiasm. I am myself quite excited over the prospect. Would not anyone be who had worked as hard as I have—and waited as long as I have—for a book?" The four public reviews of the book that have been located were largely positive. While reflecting the benign Orientalism emphasized by *Mrs. Spring Fragrance*, reviewers recognized that this author was doing something different from simply offering stereotyped portraits of Chinese immigrant life. The first review, which Sui Sin Far wrote to Charles Lummis "was good to read,"[23] appeared on 22 June 1912 in the *Montreal Weekly Witness*. In a response that combined recognition of the volume's Orientalism and "book beautiful" design, the reviewer highlighted the writer's pluralistic identity: "One of the charming gift books of the season comes from the pen of a Canadian Chinese, or half Chinese, woman, whose sympathies range her on the side of the Chinese mother rather than of the English father. 'Mrs. Spring Fragrance,' by Sui Sin Far (Edith Eaton) . . . is a collection of short sketches of Chinese life in the United States and Canada." The words "rather than" emphasize the divisive stance that society has always imposed on Sui Sin Far because of her dual racial parentage. They are prefatory to presenting her as a "Chinese" insider: "Naturally Sui Sin Far can enter into the Chinese thoughts, prejudices, emotions and grievances as no foreigner could do, and yet she understands the friendly attitude of many individuals in the two countries of their adoption towards the Chinese immigrants in contrast with the unfriendly and often heartless treatment meted out to them by the representatives of both governments." The phrase "yet she understands" reinforces the reviewer's point that this Sui Sin Far, understanding of Chinese immigrants though she might be, remains safely in sympathy with the white cultures dominant in both Canada and the United States, if not with the government policies in those countries.[24] It is also apparent that, in contrast to the three U.S. reviewers who claimed Sui Sin Far's sources, inspiration, and identity as part of their nation, the *Montreal Weekly Witness* presented the author of *Mrs. Spring Fragrance* as "a Canadian Chinese, or half Chinese woman."[25]

The second review to appear, on 29 June 1912 in the *Boston Globe,* gave the book three paragraphs. This reviewer also leaned on Orientalist rhetoric in describing the title character Mrs. Spring Fragrance as "that delicious Americanized person" but also recognized that Sui Sin Far's perspective and themes ran counter to literary representations of Chinese or Chinese Americans as alien and threatening: "The tales are told with a sympathy that strikes straight to one's heart; to say they are convincing is weak praise, and they show the Chinese with feelings absolutely indistinguishable from those of white people—only the Chinese seem to have more delicate sensibilities, and more acute methods of handling their problems."[26]

On 7 July 1912 the *New York Times Book Review* devoted one long, substantial paragraph to the book. The reviewer wasted no words on the exotic but rather singled out Sui Sin Far's emphasis on "the lives, thoughts and emotions of the Chinese women who refuse to be anything but intensely Chinese, and . . . the characters of the half-breed children." Despite use of stereotyped language ("half-breed children") and a lack of sensitivity to the complexity of her woman characters (they do not "refuse to be anything but intensely Chinese"), the *Times* review was most astute at observing the unique interracial dialogue opened up by Sui Sin Far's work and its broader significance to literature: "Miss Eaton has struck a new note in American fiction. The thing she has tried to do is to portray for readers of the white race the lives, feelings, sentiments of the Americanized Chinese of the Pacific Coast, of those who have intermarried with them and of the children who have spring from such unions."[27]

The *Independent,* whose editor Sui Sin Far had explicitly acknowledged in both the *Globe* article and a letter to Lummis, did not comment on the book until 15 August 1912, and the comments were only two sentences long:

> Our readers are well acquainted with the dainty stories of Chinese life written by Sui Sin Far (Miss Edith Eaton) and will be glad to know that those published in THE INDEPENDENT as well in other periodicals have been brought together in a volume entitled *Mrs. Spring Fragrance* (McClurg; $1.40). The conflict between occidental and oriental ideals and the hardships of the American immigration laws furnish the theme for most of the tales and the reader is not only interested but has his mind widened by becoming acquainted with novel points of view.[28]

As we might expect from this journal, the remarks clearly recognize the ideological content of the volume, although the reviewer's patronizing assumptions about Chinese immigrants ("novel points of view") and women writers ("dainty stories of Chinese life") are evident.

Even with skillful marketing and positive reviews, it is unlikely that *Mrs. Spring Fragrance* brought in many financial dividends for either the author or her publishers. Sui Sin Far's remarks about the book in a 23 March 1912 letter to Lummis—"I am very tired and hoped to have got some money for it by this time"[29]—suggest her feelings of continuing financial pressure, as does her wish regarding her benefactors expressed in the *Globe* article: "I hope soon to be in a position to repay them." The *Independent's* listed price of $1.40 tells us what *Mrs. Spring Fragrance* sold for, but we do not know the author's royalties. McClurg's initial pressrun consisted of only twenty-five hundred copies,[30] and there is no evidence of further editions. Part of the reason for the apparently poor sales was probably that collections of short stories, then as now, were risky ventures. The deeper reason, I suspect, lay in the nature of *Mrs. Spring Fragrance's* contents, radical far beyond the ability of its Orientalist frosting to camouflage or its reviewers to recognize.

Internal Design

The table of contents in *Mrs. Spring Fragrance* is divided into two sections; the first is entitled Mrs. Spring Fragrance, and the second is Tales of Chinese Children. This table is duplicated below, along with dates of first publication and any changes in titles immediately following each story for which a separate printing has been established.

MRS. SPRING FRAGRANCE

Mrs. Spring Fragrance (January 1910)
The Inferior Woman (May 1910)
The Wisdom of the New
"Its Wavering Image"
The Gift of Little Me
The Story of One White Woman Who Married a Chinese ("A White
    Woman Who Married a Chinaman," 10 March 1910)
Her Chinese Husband (18 August 1910)
The Americanizing of Pau Tsu
In the Land of the Free (2 September 1909)
The Chinese Lily
The Smuggling of Tie Co (July 1900)
The God of Restoration
The Three Souls of Ah So Nan
The Prize China Baby
Lin John (January 1899)
Tian Shan's Kindred Spirit
The Sing Song Woman (October 1898)

TALES OF CHINESE CHILDREN

The Silver Leaves
The Peacock Lantern
Children of Peace ("The Bird of Love," September 1910)
The Banishment of Ming and Mai
The Story of a Little Chinese Seabird
What about the Cat?
The Wild Man and the Gentle Boy
The Garments of the Fairies
The Dreams That Failed
Glad Yen
The Deceptive Mat
The Heart's Desire
The Candy That Is Not Sweet (July 1910)
The Inferior Man
The Merry Blind-man
Misunderstood
The Little Fat One
A Chinese Boy-Girl (April 1904)
Pat and Pan
The Crocodile Pagoda

A review of this table makes a few things apparent. First, a previous printing
for the majority of stories in *Mrs. Spring Fragrance* has never been located, and,

second, most of Sui Sin Far's previously published stories were not included in the volume. The publication's specific principles of inclusion are difficult to discern.[31]

Again, and consistent with Sui Sin Far's work examined thus far, the gap between surface and substance emerges. On the surface, the contents appear to fit the publisher's concept of Orientalism, but a closer look reveals deeper complexities.[32] As in her earlier work, the Chinese and Chinese American characters in these pages speak for themselves; they are not described as "Other" by voices from the dominant culture. Moreover, Chinese Americans, especially women and children, are the leading characters in the stories. Indeed, as the book's reviewers partially recognized, the average white reader of this volume would approach a world in which her or his point of view was not privileged. The effect again recalls Mikhail Bakhtin's "carnival," described in Dale M. Bauer's words: "the realm of desire unmasked, taken out of the law of culture, and involved in an economy of difference. While the authoritative discourse demands conformity, the carnivalized discourse renders invalid any codes, conventions, or laws which govern or reduce the individual to an object of control."[33] If A. C. McClurg and Company had been more aware of *Mrs. Spring Fragrance*'s subversive, anarchic, and carnival character, the publisher might have recognized that marketing Sui Sin Far as a safe ethnic writer was fundamentally incompatible with the character of the book. Carnivalesque is, however, fully consistent with Sui Sin Far's intent to overturn assumed literary concepts of "Other-ness."

If there is any tonal pattern in the sequence of the Mrs. Spring Fragrance section of the volume, it is in an interchange between the comic—"The Gift of Little Me"—and the tragic—"The Wisdom of the New." There is, however, no consistent balancing of dark against light, and most stories reveal the underlying serious strain of Sui Sin Far's dominant themes of this section—the struggle to maintain Chinese American culture in North America and the centrality of women to this struggle. "The Gift of Little Me," for example, is about a white American schoolteacher who is unjustly accused of kidnapping the baby brother of one of her Chinese American students, but the outcome is comic, for it turns out that the student, "Little Me," had taken his brother to his teacher's house and left him in emulation of the Christian myth of the Christ child as a "gift" for Christmas. "The Wisdom of the New," about a Chinese American immigrant bride struggling to "save" her seven-year-old son from the new culture, has no comedy in it but builds toward the bride's tragic solution throughout. Themes of the two stories coalesce around the common question that both characters and readers of each are forced to face: how, in a new continent, do Chinese Americans deal with the continual threat to their native culture?

The most obvious question concerning the book's contents is why they were introduced with "Mrs. Spring Fragrance" and "The Inferior Woman," neither of which is among Sui Sin Far's strongest works. Clearly, any answer must note that these stories bridge the connection between Orientalist motifs in the book's visual design and the complexity of its text. The lotus that blooms on the book jacket, the flowering tree that lines the red cover, and the blossoming branches that decorate the pages all evoke the beauty and fragrance of flowers in the spring. We recall that the protagonist of both stories is the book's title character, and Mrs. Spring Fragrance's own person is likewise surrounded with images that evoke springlike sensations: "Mrs. Spring Fragrance walked through the park, admiring the flowers and listening to the birds singing. It was a beautiful afternoon, with the warmth of the sun cooled by a refreshing breeze." This alliance between the spring season and the title character's personality is developed in the two stories themselves, with such phrases as "she walked, sniffing the rose-heavy air delicately" and "Oh, Mrs. Spring Fragrance, you are *so* refreshing!"[34]

Even more significant thematically is the visual and textual conjunction between "Chinese" and "American" images. The balance between English letters (on the front cover's left top) and Chinese characters (on its right bottom) introduces this motif. The joining of "Mrs."—an English term of address—with "Spring Fragrance"—a common name for women in rural China[35]—in the book's title, title story, and that story's main character positions this cultural oxymoron at the book's center and subtly sets up the expectation that the volume will deal with both Chinese Americans and a pluralistic environment. This expectation is reinforced by the contents. The stories themselves all concern Chinese, Chinese immigrants to North America, or Chinese Americans, and they focus on a dynamic that Sui Sin Far's fiction systematically deals with, that of a culture in various stages of growth.[36]

I have already discussed Mrs. Spring Fragrance as a figure who invokes Sui Sin Far's authorial stance. Reading her stories in the context of the volume as a whole, we recognize that Lae-Choo, the friend to whom Mrs. Spring Fragrance dreams of reading her book about "Americans," shares her name with the protagonist in "The Land of the Free" and "The Sing-Song Woman," stories also collected in the volume from earlier printings. Indeed, Mrs. Spring Fragrance's dream of writing a book about the "mysterious Americans" for Chinese readers is ironically fulfilled, albeit in mirror fashion, by Sui Sin Far's publication of her own book about the "mysterious Chinese" for white readers—as Amy Ling notes, a humorous inversion of "the character/reader relationship" that mocks the concept of Chinese inscrutability.[37]

In the context of the book, the stories achieve dimensions beyond their separate publications. For example, within the text as a whole, the experience of the Jade Spring Fragrance figure partially typifies the stories of many Chinese immigrant women characters who follow her in subsequent pieces.

Though her present environment is Seattle, or the urban United States, her name is rooted in rural China, and though she is currently described as "just like an American woman," five years earlier she was an immigrant bride. She lives on the Chinese American threshold that Chinese immigrant women like the title character in "The Americanizing of Pau Tsu" will resist stepping over. Like Fin Fan of "The Prize China Baby" and Pau Lin of "The Wisdom of the New," she has birthed and lost babies. Like the author, she has friends and neighbors who are both Chinese and white, but unlike Sui Sin Far, she moves across borders between cultures without full consciousness of the complexities. With the exception of Jade Spring Fragrance's satiric letter to her husband in the title story, she does not seem to share the author's keen awareness of and anger about racism or her understanding of the complexity of being marginalized by race and gender. Her glib solutions to complex problems glare like a caricature of the American dream and stand in stark contrast to the struggles of the other women of Chinese descent in Sui Sin Far's fiction, whose problems are not solved so easily. Sui Sin Far shares many traits with Mrs. Spring Fragrance, including, as Ammons observed, the "strong, independent, critical voice that is not going to be controlled either by officious white women or by superior Asian men."[38] But if she is completing the book that her title character started, she does so in ways that ironically qualify her character's sweet-tempered optimism.

Tales of Chinese Children

Mrs. Spring Fragrance, "Mrs. Spring Fragrance," and Mrs. Spring Fragrance—as book title, as short story, as section heading, and as leading character—set the stage for stories whose plots all revolve around women, children, and family life, thus demonstrating—even though men composed the demographic majority in Chinese American communities—the cultural significance of women. They precede and enclose the heading of the second section, Tales of Chinese Children. In many ways, the motif of children binds the entirety of *Mrs. Spring Fragrance.* It begins with the metaphor on the acknowledgment page, where Sui Sin Far thanks twenty-four editors "who were kind enough to care for my children when I sent them out into the world, for permitting the dear ones to return to me to be grouped together within this volume." The metaphor of children as the progeny of creative endeavors has long been a convention. In European-based American literature, it began with Anne Bradstreet's comments on the 1650 publication of her poems:

> Thou ill-formed offspring of my feeble brain,
> Who after birth didst by my side remain,

> Till snatched from thence by friends, less wise than true,
> Who thee abroad, exposed to public view. . . .[39]

Sui Sin Far's usage, however, reveals original dimensions. The stories collected in *Mrs. Spring Fragrance,* the book she has worked on for nearly "half a century," are not only the "children" she never bore biologically; they are the "children" of Chinese American culture for whom she has been "in labor" throughout her life, for whom others (readers, editors) have had temporary "care," but whom now, at age forty-seven, their mother again gathers around her to present to the world. In this sense, the metaphor of "children" operates on dual levels: in the conventional sense, it likens the imagination to a "womb," but in Sui Sin Far's unique case it carries further connotations of the birth of Chinese American literature. Unlike Mrs. Spring Fragrance's two stillborn babies, this is a birth for which the author anticipates ongoing life, an expectation that readers in our own time help fulfill when we pick up *Mrs. Spring Fragrance.*

On a more literal level, children are central to the book's content and themes. The second section, Tales of Chinese Children, devotes the last 102 pages, or almost one-third of the volume, to stories in which children are the main subject matter. The preposition *of* used in this heading is inclusive, for the section includes tales that are *about* children and tales that are *for* children. Even when young readers are the explicit audience, many of these stories involve themes that demand an adult level of insight. Children also receive more than usual attention in the Mrs. Spring Fragrance section. Children are central in four of these stories: little Yen in "The Wisdom of the New," Little Me and his baby brother in "The Gift of Little Me," the Little One in "In the Land of the Free," and the nameless infant in "The Prize China Baby." The criterion for inclusion in the first section does not seem to be simply audience level, however, for the thematic complexity of several stories in Tales of Chinese Children clearly suggests adult reading skills. Consistent with Sui Sin Far's "bird on the wing" style and identity, the categories of the book's two divisions do not remain fixed. Like the boundaries between race or class in the world of her stories, the division seems both ambiguous and arbitrary. What the contents of both sections have in common is the overriding theme of the future of the Chinese in North America,[40] a theme that a concern with children invokes.

Sui Sin Far's stories directed specifically at a child's audience, those in the *Delineator* and *Good Housekeeping* as well as in *Mrs. Spring Fragrance,* illustrate her knowledge of the child's world and her sensitivity to the current marketplace. Isaac Kramnick observes that children's literature was developed in England and the United States in the eighteenth century as "another vehicle for transmitting the values of the new bourgeois society to succeeding generations."

Communicating the needs of a changing class structure, such literature was at its zenith during Sui Sin Far's writing lifetime. The form it took in the United States, Kramnick notes, included a "heavy dose of ethics."[41] The central didactic purpose fit with the mission movement: there was not a Protestant denomination that did not teach its own version of "children's literature" in its Sunday school program as a tool promoting conversion and inculcating "morality." Structured on formulas where rewards and punishments fell with Calvinistic assurance in response to particular behaviors—the former to "good" children and the latter to "bad"—much of this literature aimed not to entertain but to instruct and control.

In its review of *Mrs. Spring Fragrance,* the *Montreal Weekly Witness* recognized the didactic character of children's literature and applied it to tales in the volume: "The child's stories are delightful and have highly moral lessons, as all true fairy tales should have."[42] Sui Sin Far fit the pattern of a writer of children's literature on several counts. First, she understood children, having grown up with thirteen siblings and helping socialize them into the roles they would be expected to take in a society of adults. Her repeated greetings to Charles Lummis's daughter, "little Turbesé," in letters to him suggest that her interest in children did not wane with adulthood or in the absence of bearing babies of her own. Second, her work in mission schools made her well acquainted with Sunday school stories and such moral forms as the allegory and parable. Third, she was a woman, and editors frequently typecast children's writers as women. From the view of the marketplace for children's stories, her gender, if not her race, could be regarded as "safe"; the subject matter alone placed her among the assumed "trite" and nonthreatening in a woman's domain. That this was not necessarily true from the position of a female author is suggested by Joan Radner and Susan Lanser's comments on the strategy of "trivialization": "women have used this strategy by exploiting or hiding behind the very forms that men already consider nonliterary or inferior—the letter, the diary, children's literature, and the 'feminine' novel—to express ideas those same women might never express in an essay or a poem."[43]

Sui Sin Far's stories for children in *Mrs. Spring Fragrance* are marked by both the didactic purposes Kramnick emphasizes and an appearance of "trivialization" that masks more complex meaning. A few follow simple moralistic formulas. "The Peacock Lantern" for example, is about a little boy, Ah Wing, who insists that his father buy him a lantern painted with a peacock, even after the lantern man explains, " 'It is the one lantern of all which delights my own little lad and he is sick and cannot move from his bed' " (247). Ah Wing's father buys him the lantern, but when Ah Wing gets it home, he cannot "laugh and be merry," and he asks his father to take him to see the "little sick boy," to whom he hands the lantern over—not only for the sick boy himself but to share with " 'an honorable hunchback,' " who is the sick boy's best friend (248). The moral: one does not gain happiness by making others unhappy; moreover, those who are well off have an obligation to help those who are not.

In another tale, "The Candy That Is Not Sweet," Yen is home with his old grandfather, who is asleep, while his mother visits a neighbor. The cry of Bo Shuie, the candyman, entices Yen to take three coppers from his mother's string of cash on the wall and buy himself three twists of colored candy. After eating a little, Yen finds he does not like the candy and tries to get rid of it by feeding the rest to his grandfather. The equation between the methods by which the candy was purchased and Yen's lack of enjoyment is explicitly told in the little boy's words after his mother returns: " 'Honorable mother, the string of cash is less than at morn, but the candy, it was not sweet' " (306). Yen's punishment, as Ah Wang's, is meted out not by any external hand but by his own conscience.

A similarly explicit moral informs "The Deceptive Mat," in which two brothers are playing "battledore and shuttlecock" when a stranger interrupts to ask if he may spread his mat on their green. The boys give their permission, but when the mat turns out to fill the whole space, they want to change their minds. Their father appears and tells his sons that because " 'the word of a Tsin must be made good,' " they have to let the stranger stay, causing Tsin Yen, as a man, to always think "for three minutes before allowing any word to escape [his] lips" (299). Another tale, "The Dreams That Failed," uses a jack-in-the-beanstalk motif to illustrate the trouble two little boys find themselves in when they sit "loafing under a tree" and spin dreams of what they will buy with money from pigs they are taking to market (295). Predictably, the pigs climb out of the baskets at their feet and escape. The boys feel the practical effects of forsaking duty for dreams when they are ordered back to the farm to keep raising pigs and, instead of shoes and caps for school, receive a hard caning.

While these tales all portray Chinese or Chinese American children, the lessons their characters learn roughly parallel the basic messages that Kramnick finds in Anglo children's literature: "success comes to the self-reliant, hard-working, independent individual," and, conversely, those who "loaf" receive failure and punishment.[44] Woven throughout are themes of filial piety, or respect for parental authority. In other stories, however, Sui Sin Far reverses such lessons, or, after the models of her previous stories, ironically qualifies them. "Ku Yum and the Butterflies," published in 1909, features a little Ku Yum (miserable creature) who has been told by her mother to stand for one hour with her hands behind her back because she has "spilled her rice over her blue blouse." The child takes her instructions so seriously that even when a butterfly lights on her eyebrow and her "fan lay within her sleeve . . . she raised it not and suffered the butterfly to remain." This extreme of "goodness" startles even the mother, who exclaims when she returns an hour later, " 'Heavens, child!... Why do you not brush that poisonous insect away from your face? Have you no fan?' "[45] Complete obedience to authority is absurd, this tale seems to say—one must always temper it with individual judgment. The treatment here is comic, but the point raised recalls the Chinese Exclusion Act and Hom Hing's obedience to U.S. immigration laws when he hands his son to the customs official in "In the Land of the Free."

"Misunderstood," a more complex children's story in *Mrs. Spring Fragrance,* develops the relationship between morality and obedience by opening the issue to diverse viewpoints. Throughout the narrative, the child's voice speaks side by side with the parents'. A little girl, again a Ku Yum, abducts her baby brother, Ko Ku, from the bed where he has been left in his Ceremony of the Moon finery to await the first shaving of his head that afternoon. The point of view is the sister's; as she watches the sleeping baby, we gain access to her thought processes: "To Ku Yum, he was simply gorgeous, and she longed to get her little arms around him and carry him to some place where she could delight in him all by herself.... Poor baby! that never got any rice to eat, nor nice sweet cakes. Ku Yum's heart swelled with compassion. In her hand was a delicious moon cake.... Surely, the baby would like a taste" (315). As Ku Yum takes the baby out the window, lays him down in the grass, tells him stories about the "worms and ants which she arranged on leaves and stones" (317), and tries to feed him her cake and dip his feet in a mud puddle, the reader knows her motives are kind, not malevolent. This is contrasted with her family's perspective when they come running out. Ku Yum's father says she is " 'possessed by a demon,' " her mother believes she has an " 'evil spirit,' " and her grandmother attributes the act to the " 'demon of jealousy' " (319–20). The bamboo cane that Ku Yum's great-uncle has sent from China to help his grandniece "walk in the straight and narrow path laid out for a proper little Chinese girl living in Santa Barbara" threatens in the background (319), as Ku Yum "wailed low in the grass, for there were none to understand" (320). None, that is, except this story's narrator and the readers. The punishment, in this case, simply shows that those who have power can use it against those who have none and that such power can be used at any level for cruel and unjust ends.

Sui Sin Far's "children's stories," like her other writings, continually defend those who stand at the lower rung of society's ladder. Society may be a family in which the parents abuse their authority over a child; it may be a community that ignores members who are disabled or otherwise different. In "The Story of a Little Chinese Seabird," the central point of view is given to a bird with a broken wing, whom all the other birds have flown off and left. When boys come to the birds' island hunting eggs, their plan—to return that night, catch the seabirds, and eat them—is overheard by the wounded bird. She pulls a red cord from a boy's queue and holds it in her beak that night while she tells her brothers and sisters "a story—a true one" (282). After hearing the story, the other seabirds are ready to fly off without her again until "the eldest sister, she with the satin-white under-wings and spreading tail," urges them to " 'make a strong nest for our broken-winged little sister. . . .' " The conclusion is a fantasy of community acceptance: the birds build the nest, pick it up, and "[soar] together far away up in the sky, the little Chinese seabird with the broken wing happy as she could be in the midst of them." (284).[46]

The importance of mutual kindness within communities that society has segregated on the basis of race or class is perhaps Sui Sin Far's favorite lesson. It is consistent with her imagined ideal of "one family," a kind of ultimate sense of human community that transcends all contrived groupings. "The Banishment of Ming and Mai" involves another animal parable that invokes such concerns by overturning the power hierarchy between humans and animals. A brother and sister, Chan Ming and Chan Mai, are banished to a land that is familiar in fairy tales: "a wild and lonely forest, which . . . could only be reached by traveling up a dark and mysterious river in a small boat" (266). The boatmen voice human stereotypes about nonhuman life; they are "mortally afraid of the forest" because of its "innumerable wild animals, winged and crawling things" (267). Against these stereotypes, the tale's narrator juxtaposes the children's actual experience after the boatmen put them out of the boat and leave them alone. A crocodile guides them to a soft, mossy bed, from where they wake in the morning to find themselves encircled by "a great company" of animals of various species that unite to protect Ming and Mai (269). After "many a moon" (272), when the children's nurse comes to rescue them, her cry of " 'wild beasts' " is answered by the children's " 'They are not wild beasts. They are elegant and accomplished superior beings' " (274).

Sui Sin Far's parable here involves the dissolution of boundaries by opening communication between species; in the context of *Mrs. Spring Fragrance,* the parable suggests the possibility of breaking through fixed ideas, the monologic assumptions and ethnocentric prejudices, that divide human cultures. When the children first confront the "beasts," Ming (the brother) speaks from the assumption of human supremacy: " 'These honorable beings have to be subdued and made to acknowledge that man is master of this forest. I am here to conquer them in fight.' " The remark is ludicrous in this situation. It proceeds from Ming's learned stereotypes about human and male supremacy and causes Mai (the sister) to feel that her brother's "words made him more terrible to her than any of the beasts of the field" (270). What happens next recalls carnivalization, represented in this instance as a breakthrough across borders between humans and animals: "The tiger smiled in return, and advancing to Ming, laid himself down at his feet, the tip of his nose resting on the boy's little red shoes. . . . Thus in turn did every other animal, bird, fish, and insect present" (271).

The history behind the animals' kindness to these particular children reinforces the vision: centuries ago, an ancestor of Mai and Ming was "so kind of heart . . . that he could not pass through a market street without buying up all the live fish, turtles, birds, and animals that he saw, for the purpose of giving them liberty and life" (265); the animals that help the descendants of this man are themselves descendants of the animals that he set free in this forest. The point, that love is stronger than hate and artificially contrived social borders, is explicitly stated when the tiger tells Ming, " 'There is, therefore, no necessity for a trial of your strength or skill with any here. Believe me, Your Highness, we were conquered many years ago—and not in fight' " (271).

"The Banishment of Ming and Mai" can be read as an allegory of, specifically, how whites should treat Chinese immigrants in America or, more broadly, how the people of any nation should ideally treat humans of every culture. In effect, the statement that this story makes is compatible with Sui Sin Far's one-family vision. Her parable of shattering boundaries between human-animal worlds speaks against the imperialistic assumption that any human group can claim the right to assume hegemony over another. In addition, the parable rewrites a biblical verse well known to the author—the virtues of the fathers, as well as their sins, can be visited on later generations. Finally, to highlight the gender issues in this story, it is Ming (the brother) who believes he must go into combat with the forest animals to preserve his assumed—if absurd in this situation—human "supremacy," while Mai (the sister) accepts the animals at face value and is quite as horrified at her brother's response, as was the sister who spoke up for the wounded title character in "The Story of a Little Chinese Seabird" when all her brothers were ready to fly away. Sui Sin Far's "children's stories," like her tales for adult audiences, stress a special sensitivity with which females relate to life, a characteristic furthered through the sisterly bonds girls and women in her fiction repeatedly and almost intuitively forge with each other.

"The Heart's Desire" presents a conventional fairy-tale plot, with a beautiful young girl whose riches cannot make her happy because she lacks a soul mate or companion. Plot development, however, performs a rare twist in what is otherwise formulaic fairy-tale language. "Her name was Li Chung O'Yam, and she lived in a sad, beautiful old palace surrounded by a sad, beautiful old garden, situated on a charming island in the middle of a lake," we are told. Though Li Chung O'Yam "wore priceless silks and radiant jewels," ate from gold plates, and drank from silver goblets, she "was not happy" (300). Her attendants, assuming Li Chung is lonely, bring the girl a father, a mother, and a courtyard full of boy dancers. Rejecting them all, Li Chung declares, " 'I will find my own heart's ease' " (301), and she sends her carrier dove off with a note. The dove returns with the poor and homeless Ku Yum, who is "hugging a cat to keep her warm and sucking her finger to prevent her from being hungry." In spite of her under-class status, Ku Yum is Li Chung's double, a point underlined when the latter exclaims, " 'How beautifully you are robed! In the same colors as I. And behold, your dolls and your cats, are they not much like mine?' " Informing her attendants, " 'Behold, I have found my heart's desire—a little sister' " (302), Li Chung moves Ku Yum into her palace, where we are told that "forever after O'Yam and Ku Yum lived happily together in a glad, beautiful old palace, surrounded by a glad, beautiful old garden, on a charming little island in the middle of a lake" (303). At a glance, the happily "forever after" is a formulaic fairy-tale ending. The radical nature of this particular tale transpires when we realize that it is two girls (instead of a prince) who rescue each other: Ku Yum saves Li Chung from loneliness, and Li Chung saves Ku Yum from the streets. As Amy Ling notes of the revisionist conclusion—where "sad" is changed to "glad" in lines that otherwise echo the opening—the girls' union not only crosses class lines, as in "Cinderella," but also mocks the tradition (recalling Sui Sin Far's "Origin of a Broken Nose") of the male rescuer.[47]

"The Heart's Desire" is obviously a story of female bonding in the tradition of "The Sing-Song Woman" (October 1898), "The Story of Tin-A" (December 1899), and "Ku Yum's Little Sister" (October 1900). In all these stories, voices are set into motion that dissolve the social divisions of age, race, class, and gender by presenting women who flaunt usual categories and come together as doubles. "The Chinese Lily" similarly presents a young girl, Mermei, a human counterpart to the little Chinese seabird. Mermei never goes among the "other little Chinese women" who live in her "Chinatown dwelling-house," because "she was not as they were. She was a cripple" (178). She is unable to move without the help of her brother, Lin John, who (like the title character of "Lin John") accepts the responsibility of brotherly care. Mermei's only diversion, like the title character in "Ku Yum's Little Sister," is pressing her face to the window and watching the street. One day a young girl, whose name, Sin Far, is obviously close to the author's, comes to Mermei's door and extends to her "a blossom from a Chinese lily plant." The friendship that develops between the two women causes Mermei to forget "that she was scarred and crippled" (180). It creates a special world, where women find value that is missing in the world of men. This becomes explicit when Mermei compares her new friend with her brother: " 'Lin John is a dear, but one can't talk to a man, even if he is a brother, as one can to one the same as oneself' " (180–81). Sin Far agrees: " 'Yes, indeed. The woman must be the friend of the woman, and the man the friend of the man. Is it not so in the country that Heaven loves?' " (181).[48] After Mermei's brother falls in love with Sin Far, a fire breaks out in the dwelling-house, forcing him to choose which woman to rescue. When Sin Far makes the decision for him, that he should rescue his sister, the story rewrites the biblical induction: "A greater love hath no man than this, that he lay down his life for his brothers"—if we translate "his" to her and "brother" to sister.[49]

Obviously, no firm line exists between Sui Sin Far's stories for children and her stories for adults in *Mrs. Spring Fragrance*, especially when the text opens up socially conceived notions of power and human relationships and shows they are not absolute. The stories assume that what is considered "right" by those in authority at every social level can often be wrong. In "The Inferior Man," for example, a schoolmaster canes every boy in his class for eating "unfragrant sugar" and then discovers the culprit is his own daughter, who, grasping "two sticky balls of red and white peppermint candy," hides under his desk between his legs (311). In general, Sui Sin Far's stories for children carry through themes and strategies consistent with the rest of her fiction, but often they raise more radical questions than her other work does.

The author's sense that the imagination was freed from adult demands of probability by the conventions of fairy tales, indeed by storytelling in general, is best illustrated in "What about the Cat?" The title is the refrain of a repeated question asked by a princess as she moves from one member of her court to another. Each responds with a different but equally entertaining story: "It is sitting on the sunny side of the garden wall, watching the butterflies"; "She is seated in your honorable father's chair of state" (285); "It is dancing in the ballroom in a dress of elegant cobwebs and a necklace of pearl rice" (286). Finally, the princess lifts her arm and out of her sleeve crawls the cat: "It had been there all the time." When she accuses her court of telling untruths, the courtly chamberlain ventures the moral: " 'Princess . . . would a story be a story if it were true?' " (287).[50]

In the imaginative arena of children's literature—the fairy tale, the animal fable, the biblical parable, all clothed in deceptively simple mythical rhythms— Sui Sin Far allowed the unrestricted fantasy world of the carnival and her often subversive messages to play within formulas that were conceived to indoctrinate monologic moral lessons. The *Montreal Weekly Witness* review of *Mrs. Spring Fragrance* notes that "some fairytales . . . come straight from the flowery kingdom."[51] With few exceptions, however, Sui Sin Far disengages her children's stories from the restrictions of place.[52] By so doing, she shows that traditions from both sides of her heritage, Chinese and Victorian, participate in the creation of structures that elevate a select few and push many down to the bottom. Such gradations may be decided by an individual's class, race, gender, or level of physical ability—by whether one is human or animal, parent or child. Peopled by Chinese or Chinese American characters who act within a world of images, conventions, and ideas derived from both the Victorian and Chinese traditions,[53] these stories are filled with beings who must find their own way within a world of arbitrary expectations, as did Sui Sin Far herself. On one hand, they fill the function that Kramnick observes, of "transmitting the values of the new bourgeois society." On the other, they continue a major theme of Sui Sin Far's other work: until adults teach them those "values," children freely embrace all of life, unrestricted by socially contrived categories that divide living beings.

Key Stories in Context

To recognize how the children's stories connect to other texts in *Mrs. Spring Fragrance,* two aspects of the work must be emphasized, both previously seen in Sui Sin Far's writing. The first is the reversal of conventional literary positions of race, a reversal that places Chinese, not white Americans, at the center of the fictional vision. The second is the reversal of gender priorities, a reversal that places females, women or girls, at the center of portrayals of the Chinese American community. *Mrs. Spring Fragrance*'s overriding theme is the future of Chinese North American culture. It is thus appropriate that the main emphasis is on children (symbolic of the future in any culture), the family (the basic cultural unit), and women (the traditional mainstay of both children and family and the central propagators of culture). Indeed, the women in some of the volume's stories grow beyond seeking the power to choose their own mates to exercising authority in various spheres. In particular, we find Sui Sin Far's married women taking almost fearless stands against everyone, even their husbands, when their traditional cultural values are threatened by the white American culture around them.

The challenge Chinese Americans of either sex in these stories face—the challenge of breaking through white America's refusal to accept them and their culture on an equal basis—is an assumed, if not always explicit, backdrop of their lives. Throughout the volume, the right of cultural survival is continually under siege, not only by laws that excluded Chinese and established a head tax but also by a double standard that whites assume toward Chinese at all personal levels. In the title story "Mrs. Spring Fragrance," a section of dialogue between Mr. Spring Fragrance and his young, white, male neighbor is added to the text that was not in the story's originally published version: " 'Haven't you ever heard that all Americans are princes and princesses, and just as soon as a foreigner puts his foot upon our shores, he also becomes of the nobility—I mean the royal family,' " asks the white neighbor. " 'What about my brother in the Detention Pen?' " retorts Mr. Spring Fragrance. But, the neighbor asserts, " 'we . . . *real* Americans are up against that—even more than you. It is against our principles.' " " 'I offer the *real* Americans my consolations that they should be compelled to do that which is against their principles,' " replies Mr. Spring Fragrance (12–13, emphasis added).

With language such as "foreigner," "real Americans," and "our principles," the insider-outsider situation is clear and provocative; it reflects core and often unconscious differences between these two neighbors, both Americans but one Chinese and one white. The fact that the latter, "a star student at the University of Washington" (4), sees himself as the Spring Fragrances' friend furthers the irony. Whites, even when well intended, fail to recognize Chinese Americans as a "real" part of the nation both occupy. Moreover, in this scene, Mr. Spring Fragrance is the character with superior knowledge and insight into the dramatic irony being employed. Even when these two neighbors appear to converse, they speak from two sets of assumptions, the potentially tragic implications of which will be traced to extreme consequences in "The Wisdom of the New."

Such dual perceptions and their ironic implications are emphasized in the first paragraph of "Tian Shan's Kindred Spirit":

> Had Tian Shan been an American and China to him a forbidden country, his daring exploits and thrilling adventures would have furnished inspiration for many a newspaper and magazine article, novel, and short story. As a hero, he would certainly have far outshone Dewey, Peary, or Cook. Being, however, a Chinese, and the forbidden country America, he was simply recorded by the American press as "a wily Oriental, who, 'by ways that are dark and tricks that are vain,' is eluding the vigilance of our brave customs officers." As to his experiences, the only one who took any particular interest in them was Fin Fan. (224)

Tian Shan, an expert at smuggling himself across the border between Montreal and upstate New York, is placed on center stage in the first line, but by the end of the paragraph the focus has moved to Fin Fan—Tian Shan's "kindred spirit" and the character who will act as protagonist throughout the story's development. Such strategies as use of passive voice ("simply recorded by") and duplication of media rhetoric ("daring exploits," "thrilling adventures," "eluding the vigilance") push the "American press" to the sidelines, looking on with a considerable absence of insight. Representative of white America, the press uses the adjective *brave* to describe customs officials, who, we have observed in "In the Land of the Free," steal babies. Such, ironically, are the standards for heroism in the dominant white culture that Sui Sin Far addresses in this 1912 volume. Such phrases as "a wily Oriental" and "ways that are dark" ironically mock the stereotypes of Chinatown literature that we have seen Sui Sin Far satirize, as a voice for her mother's people, throughout her career.

Comparable in style to "The Land of the Free," which also performs its reversal by placing the perceptions of a Chinese American woman at the fictional center, "Tian Shan's Kindred Spirit" introduces abstractions in its first paragraph, examples of media rhetoric that the story will stretch out and tease against a development of human character that renders those abstractions absurd. We see that Tian Shan really is "wily" because "everytime he crossed the border, he was obliged to devise some new scheme"; at the same time, this character is "heroic," for he "usually succeeded" (226). Fin Fan is "wily" too, disguising herself as a man and slipping over the border behind her lover so that she will be arrested and deported with him back to China. Since her aim is to get out of North America rather than in, such wiliness clearly takes a different twist from that intended by the "American press." Both Tian Shan and Fin Fan, in fact, are wily in the mode of the trickster figure in Sui Sin Far's other fiction. Antithetical construction ("Had Tien Shan been an American"; "Being, however, a Chinese" [224]) clearly acknowledges the duality with which Chinese and whites are perceived in America. Whiteness—or "[reducing] all America to the compulsive, bloodless reality of a guy named Joe," to borrow a phrase from James Baldwin[54]—sets the standard for humanness in a European-based culture. Sui Sin Far's narrators reject this assumption. Characters in the *Mrs. Spring Fragrance* stories are valued not for how closely they adhere to a white standard but for their assertions against those assimilative forces in North America that would deny Chinese immigrants individual and cultural integrity.

The characters who assert themselves most markedly in the *Mrs. Spring Fragrance* stories are female. The conditions they fight against are grounded in history, primarily in the conditions under which men and women migrated. The men of the Chinese American merchant class, to which the male characters in most of these stories belong, chose to migrate mainly for the reasons expressed by Old Li Want, a peddler in China in "The Wisdom of the New": " 'For every cent a man makes here, he can make one hundred over there' " (47). Conversely, many of the women in these stories are shipped from their Chinese homeland to North America in response to men's needs and with little or no choice in the matter. In spite of this, the women we meet in *Mrs. Spring Fragrance* are by no means powerless. Within the limits of the hierarchies that both Chinese and European-based cultures impose, they decide their own actions, influencing, in turn, the lives of others.

For example, Sie in "The God of Restoration" is contracted to marry Koan-lo the First, a man she has never met and "one of the wealthiest merchants in San Francisco" (193). In exchange, Koan-lo the First is buying Sie's father from slavery in China. When the prospective and elderly groom sends his young and penniless cousin, Koan-lo the Second, to meet his bride, the cousin and Sie discover they have loved each other in China and run off together. There is one hitch. Sie believes Koan-lo the Second to be the man to whom she is legally contracted, and the stand-in for the real groom does not tell her otherwise. A pertinent point here is that it is men who have made the explicit decisions, from Sie's father (to sell her), to Koan-lo the First (to buy her), to Koan-lo the Second (to deceive her). Yet once she learns the truth, Sie moves into the position of choosing whether to maintain the deception or to keep the original bargain, and at this point she assumes a position of power over the three males involved. The five years of servitude that Sie proposes to give Koan-lo the First lead to a bondage that paradoxically results from her own decision to be Koan-lo the First's servant. Because her motivation is to free her father, the daughter in one sense maintains "filial piety," not by acquiescing to duty but by assuming responsibility for her own life.[55]

That the men in these stories migrate alone to America and become economically situated before sending for brides means they have experienced the initial difficult years of adjustment before the women arrive. For the characters in *Mrs. Spring Fragrance,* this difference in the immigrant status of men and women produces various traumas. In "The Wisdom of the New," three weeks before he sets sail, Wou Sankwei marries Pau Lin in China in direct compliance with his mother's demand that he find a wife to bear a son to comfort his mother in his absence. By the time Pau Lin is invited to join her husband, their son is six, and "Wou Sankwei's memory of the woman who was his wife was very faint" (51). Though Sankwei has become a successful bookkeeper in San Francisco, during seven years of separation he has never written Pau Lin a letter. "It is the Chinese custom to educate only the boys," so the immigrant bride "can neither read nor write" (53). That the distance between this couple yawns wider than geography is communicated in many scenes, the first when Pau Lin is portrayed on the steamer, clad in a "heavily embroidered purple costume," her son "leaning his little queued head against her shoulder." The wife's "feminine desire to make herself fair to see in the eyes of her husband" is measured against Sankwei's inability—when "he came at last" (54)—to distinguish Pau Lin from other Chinese women awaiting their men, and "only when the ship's officer pointed out and named her, did he know her as his" (55).

Complicating the plot is the presence of Mrs. Dean, Sankwei's wealthy white benefactor, and her niece Adah Charlton, both of whom, the Chinese American husband explains to his wife, "were there to bid her welcome; they were kind and good and wished to be her friends as well as his." In spite of this gesture, Sankwei's words to the white women, "'She cannot understand you'" (55), make it clear that the new immigrant cannot speak English; she remains isolated linguistically and culturally. As the couple's life unfolds in San Francisco, Sankwei is described as "always kind and indulgent" in satisfying Pau Lin's material needs (56), and he pays homage to Chinese tradition by "erect[ing] . . . a chapel for the ancestral tablet and gorgeous goddess which she had brought over the seas with her" (57). Yet, the narrator informs us, Sankwei sees his wife as "more of an accessory than a part of his life"; he focuses his real attention on the "Western training" of their son, without consulting Pau Lin; and he is frequently in the company of the white women.[56] And, though Pau Lin "observed faithfully the rule laid down for her by her late mother-in-law: to keep a quiet tongue in the presence of her man" (56), the narrator reveals that she shows "no disposition to become Americanized" (58).

This immigrant woman's lack of enthusiasm about instant changes in culture is shared by the female lead in another story in the collection, "The Americanizing of Pau Tsu," in which the title character is betrothed to Lin Fo before he leaves China, then waits to be sent to her fiancé by his parents in a few years time. While Lin Fo is described as "one of the happiest and proudest of bridegrooms" (147), he is also "quite at home with the Americans" and eager for Pau Tsu "to acquire the ways and language of the land in which he hoped to make a fortune" (149). When he brings his bride to the apartments he has "furnished in American style," however, Pau Tsu shows her independence, bringing out the Chinese furnishings she has carried over the seas and transforming "the American flat into an Oriental bower" (148). When her husband presents her with elegant dresses, saying, " 'I wish you to dress like an American woman when we go out or receive,' " Pau Tsu "bowed upon the floor and wept pitifully" (153). Her lament—"And why, oh! why, should she be constrained to eat her food with clumsy, murderous looking American implements instead of with her own elegant and easily manipulated ivory chopsticks?" (151)—strikes the heart of the agony these wives experience at being pressured to alter the most minute, homely details of their daily lives. Lin Fo's admonition when Pau Tsu protests against taking English lessons— " 'What is best for men is also best for women in this country' " (149)—suggests that while the United States and China uphold different languages, both share common patriarchal traditions.

Using such painful details, Sui Sin Far shows these immigrant women's plights, their estrangement not only from China, their home country, but also from the men who were their sole reasons for leaving it. How do they survive? What are their options? Their most frequent and natural decisions follow the pathways that women throughout history have taken—they bond together, offering mutual consolation and help. After daily housekeeping duties, Pau Lin "spent most of her time in the society of one or the other of the merchants' wives who lived in the flats and apartments around her own" (56). When Pau Tsu has had enough (it happens when she gets sick, and Lin Fo sends her to a male, American doctor, before whom her breast is exposed and the "modesty of generations of maternal ancestors was crucified," 155), she leaves Lin Fo and moves with her maid A-Toy into the home of "a woman learned in herb lore" (160).[57]

Similar acts by Sui Sin Far's other Chinese and Chinese American female characters teach us that these women's external reticence, bred by centuries of tradition, should never be mistaken for passivity. They are determined, ingenious, and independent of spirit. Beneath their acquiescence to duty a cautiously held rebellion finds its own outlets, rising to its most intense when their children are threatened. Rarely does Sui Sin Far portray a married woman who is not cradling a baby, often with a passionate vigilance against forces ever posed to take that treasure from her. For the young immigrant women in *Mrs. Spring Fragrance,* babies become especially important, because their parents often have left all other family behind; theirs is the responsibility for starting new ancestral lines—the first generation of Chinese Americans—and ensuring cultural continuity. As we have seen, antagonists to such continuity in Sui Sin Far's fiction can be members of the white bureaucracy—customs officer, mission workers, or schoolteachers—but they also can be, as in "The Prize China Baby," a child's own father.

In this story, Fin Fan, a slave who was sold to Chung Kee for a wife in San Francisco's Chinatown, has a baby girl, who is her "one gleam of sunshine" (214). Mindful that Chung Kee does not want the baby because it takes too much of her time from winding tobacco leaves in his factory, Fin Fan gets up very early and goes to bed very late, trying to make as much money for Chung Kee as she did before the child's birth. Hearing that Presbyterian mission women are staging a "Chinese baby show," Fin Fan rolls her baby into her shawl and slips out, hoping that if the baby wins a prize Chung Kee will value the child. The irony that the mother believes she must turn outside her own culture for proof that a female child has value is not lost on the author, nor is the parallel irony that the prize is awarded for "beauty." Enraged to find his slave-wife gone, Chung Kee shouts orders to send the baby away but is interrupted by two men bearing Fin Fan and her dead baby home on a stretcher. They have been run down by a butcher's cart. The last words by the story's narrator—"Fin Fan's eyes closed. Her head fell back beside the prize baby's—hers forever" (219)—ironically emphasize the desperate means by which this woman finally found a security with her child unknown to either in life.[58]

The most frequent and insidious forms of child loss, however, are not physical but take the form emphasized in "In the Land of the Free"—the theft of the child's Chinese culture, rending her or him internally white. In the ironically titled "The Wisdom of the New," the threat is clear from the instant that Pau Lin is introduced to Mrs. Dean and Adah. She notices "Adah Charlton's bright face, and the tone in her husband's voice when he spoke to the young girl," and she feels "a suspicion natural to one who had come from a land where friendship between a man and woman is almost unknown" (56). Because Sankwei frequently takes little Yen to visit the white women, Adah takes "a great fancy to him" and sketches the boy "in many different poses for a book on Chinese children which she was illustrating" (57). Pau Lin does not see this as a compliment. As days go by and Sankwei spends his time with these women instead of her, women come to symbolize in the immigrant mother's mind the culture that has taken her husband and threatens to take her son.

On the evening that Pau Lin burns her son's hand for speaking "the language of the white woman," Sankwei retaliates by taking little Yen out to supper and a show with these parting words to Pau Lin, " 'The child will have to learn the white man's language' " (59). The women of the Chinatown neighborhood then gather around the immigrant mother in a circle of comfort, in one of the most poignant scenes of female bonding in Western literature. " 'You did perfectly right. . . . Had I again a son to rear, I should see to it that he followed not after the white people' " (60), old Sien Lau leans over her balcony to say. " 'One needs not to be born here to be made a fool of,' " adds Pau Tsu (61). " 'In this country, she is most happy who has no child,' " Lae Choo offers, "resting her elbow upon the shoulder of Sien Lau" (60).

The next day after another outing with his father, little Yen pulls off his cap and announces, " 'See, mother . . . I am like father now. I wear no queue' " (63). The enormity of Pau Lin's feelings as she lays her son's queue in her trunk has been foreshadowed in other stories in *Mrs. Spring Fragrance* that describe the Ceremony of the Moon, a ritual in which the foundation for a boy baby's queue and his future cultural manhood is laid.[59] We have seen her son's "little queued head" resting on Pau Lin's shoulder and realize that with the severance of that queue, the mother believes her boy's past and future, as well as her own, have been cut away. From the scenes in which Sankwei and Adah Dean meet alone, we as readers know that their relationship is sexually innocent, yet the issue at stake is larger than infidelity. From her initial recoil on the steamer, Pau Lin is aghast at a friendship foreign to her experience, and Sankwei is not reassuring when he defends the "white women" against her. When Pau Lin gives birth to a second son and the "white women" pay her a visit, the story's narrator underlines the immigrant woman's alienation from the communication these women share with her husband: "The American women could not, of course, converse with the Chinese. . . ." Finally, Sankwei's comparison of Adah to a Chinese symbol, " 'a pure water-flower—a lily' " (66)—the image behind Sui Sin Far's name on *Mrs. Spring Fragrance*'s cover—implies the depth to which the Chinese American husband has transferred his allegiance to the white American culture.

All these details, reinforced by the death of her new baby, accumulate toward Pau Lin's terror and her determination to act. When Pau Lin grinds the picture Adah has painted of the baby under her foot, crying, "She would cast a spell! She would cast a spell!" (67), the climax where she poisons her son Yen is foreshadowed. If it seems a monstrous act, we must pause and consider Pau Lin's expressed motive: " 'He is saved,' smiled she, 'from the Wisdom of the

New'" (84). Earlier, we have seen the mother lift the sleeping Yen from his bed and rock him, expressing the vow, "'Sooner would I, O heart of my heart, that the light of thine eyes were also quenched, than that thou shouldst be contaminated with the wisdom of the new'" (68). Like the African American mother in Toni Morrison's *Beloved* who kills her infant daughter to save her from slavery, Pau Lin sacrifices her child's body to save his spirit. In leading her to this desperate act, the story's narrator underlines the importance of the continuation of Chinese cultural heritage in Chinese America, a heritage that Sankwei's enthusiasm for the "new" threatens to kill and that Pau Lin makes her ultimate sacrifice to protect.

It is an event that has been built toward as carefully as the denouement in Greek tragedy, triggered finally by Sankwei's news that Yen must attend an "American school." Appropriately, Sankwei precipitates the act out of hubris. He does not learn until too late that there are limits to both patriarchy and Americanization over which one cannot step without paying the price. From the beginning, the narrator of this story shows the failure of communication between the white and the Chinese immigrant women and places the responsibility on Sankwei, who occupies the role of translator across cultural and racial borders. When Adah urges Sankwei to include Pau Lin in his plans— "'What does your wife think of a Western training for [Yen]?'"—Sankwei answers, "'A woman does not understand such things'" (57). Sankwei lacks respect for Pau Lin's intellect and feelings and for Chinese tradition and the emerging Chinese American culture. By rejecting Pau Lin's voice, he rejects China; in one desperate act, his wife makes him listen.[60]

Within the context, Pau Lin's act is "successful," for Sankwei now returns with her to China, by implication healing the cultural gap and their marriage.[61] The Chinese American husbands in these *Mrs. Spring Fragrance* stories are not villains; like their Chinese American wives, they operate within the assumptions of male-female roles by which they too have been raised, roles complicated by having to deal with the changing values and life-styles of the new capitalist culture.[62] Led by their women to acknowledge that staying in the United States may lead to cultural demise, the two husbands in "The Wisdom of the New" and "The Americanizing of Pau Tsu" reassert ancestral heritage by returning to China. "'I will not care if she never speaks an American word, and I will take her for a trip to China, so that our son may be born in the country that Heaven loves,'" asserts Lin Fo as he reunites with Pau Tsu. This return, unlike the one in "The Wisdom of the New," is clearly temporary and symbolically sets the stage for the birth of a child that will maintain his Chinese heritage.

"The Wisdom of the New" reveals some of the most complex development of theme and character in Sui Sin Far's fiction, for it reflects a Chinese American culture struggling to be born from the mergence between "East" and "West," regions long conceived by society to be marked by irreconcilable differences of race, customs, and religions. Of special note are the roles of Mrs. Dean and her niece Adah Charlton, white women characters whose lives are deeply entangled with those of a Chinese American family and who serve as guides, mentors, patrons, and friends of the family, as well as catalysts of its tragic destiny. Only Adah is sensitive to the cultural complexities; still Adah remains, to quote the story's narrator, "secure in the difference of race" (66). As a white woman, even Adah is powerless to cross the cultural gap.[63] Regardless of the strategic roles they play, however, the perspectives of neither Adah nor Mrs. Dean become central in the text; their viewpoints function to assist the reader's understanding of the positions of Pau Lin and little Yen and Sankwei but remain those of sympathetic outsiders. As in all *Mrs. Spring Fragrance* stories, the visions of white American characters are clearly subsidiary to the narrator's concern with showing the reader the perspective of the Chinese American family and, at its center, the Chinese immigrant woman.

In "Pat and Pan," the central point of view is carried by a little Chinese American girl, Pan, one of Sui Sin Far's most effective trickster figures. Nothing could be more "quaintly oriental" than the portrait with which this story opens. The two title characters—Pat, a five-year-old white boy; and Pan, a three-year-old Chinese girl—are framed in the entry to a Chinatown joss house: "Her tiny face was hidden upon his bosom and his white upturned chin rested upon her black, rosetted head." Depicted in the diction and rhythm of fairy tales, this is a cameo of races in harmony, but the narrator does not let it last long. In the third sentence, it is exactly "that white chin that caused the passing Mission woman to pause and look again at the little pair" (333). Amazed, she questions a lichi vendor—a Chinese girl and white boy intimately positioned together?—and learns, as do we, that Pat was given as a baby by his dying white mother to her Chinese friends, the Lum Yooks, to raise. Playing the role of the Edenic serpent, the mission woman, Anna Harrison, purchases lichis that she offers to the children as a lure. More astute than the mythical Eve, though, Pan does not eat directly but feeds her companion until he is full. "Whereupon," we are told in language that imitates biblical cadences, "the little girl tasted herself of the fruit." Implications of danger intensify as the Chinese mother, Ah Ma, runs out and calls in her children. Described as "a sleek-headed, kindly-faced matron in dark blue pantalettes and tunic," the mother receives affectionate obedience from Pat, the eldest, and when the little boy "jumped up with a merry laugh" and runs toward her, danger is temporarily alleviated (335).

The mission woman will not give up, though. This we know, not only from having read previous stories but also because we have heard her protest to the lichi vendor, " 'But he is white!' " (333); we have seen her shocked response when the children wake and chat (in the private language tricksters are famous for) and she realizes Pat does not speak English; and we have had our eyes guided by hers toward the entrance of the joss house, with its suspected "heathen" rituals waiting unseen inside. Somewhere in the tension between image and idea, form and content, what frightens Mrs. Lum Yook frightens us. Anna Harrison is after her children—all too often, in Sui Sin Far stories, the task of a mission woman. In the case of Pat and Pan, the mission woman's purpose is doubly complicated: not only of winning a child who is Chinese but also of reclaiming one who is white.

Thus, in scene two, when Anna Harrison opens "her school for white and Chinese children in Chinatown," it is with the determination that Pat shall "learn to speak his mother tongue" (336). Mr. Lum Yook, a fair-minded man who respects native traditions, agrees that his adopted son should "learn 'the speech of his ancestors,' " and both children are enrolled in the school. When Pat will not attend school without Pan, Anna Harrison, having no interest in her except as a decoy, seats the girl "in a little red chair" with "a number of baby toys": "Pan was not supposed to learn, only to play" (337). The mission woman's insincerity and lack of authentic interest in Chinese culture is suggested by the narrator's language and reports of Anna Harrison's thoughts. For instance, Anna sees Pat "with a number of Chinese *urchins*" and at "*some kind of* Chinese holiday," and she feels that for the boy "to grow up as a Chinese was *unthinkable*" (336, emphasis added). The story's reversal of the woman's expectations turns on the simple sentence: "But Pan did learn"—to recite verses, sing hymns, and pronounce a wide English vocabulary—while Pat, "poor little fellow, was unable to memorize even a sentence" (338). As precocious a trickster figure as her cleft-hoofed namesake, Pan is also "the originator of most of the mischief which Pat carried out with such spirit" (340).

The ambiguity of the value of the lessons taught at the mission school is clear in the image of Pan singing, " 'Yesu love me' "—words Pat cannot learn—while the little boy mutters, " 'I hate you, Pan' " (340). At this point we recognize that the mission woman (ostensibly, in the name of Christian love) has introduced violence, competition, and hate into the garden. That such as Anna Harrison—recurrently the assimilationist, or destroyer, of Chinese culture in Sui Sin Far's aesthetic vision—has the power to dissolve bonds of human love is revealed through the step-by-step process by which she disconnects Pat from his Chinese American family. As three years pass, Ah Ma's heart moves from happiness to hang "heavy as the blackest of heavens," in response to the " 'many tongues wagging because [Pat] lives under our roof.' " In Sui Sin Far's understated style, the news of the actual arrival of "the comfortably off American and wife who were to have the boy and 'raise him as an American boy should be raised' " is delivered by an omniscient narrator and so subtly tucked within other action that a reader could easily miss it (341). This information is followed, however, by a scenic portrayal of the parting between Pat and the Lum Yooks in which tension climactically rises.

" 'You are a white boy and Pan is Chinese' " (342), Mr. Lum Yook replies to Pat's protest that " 'I will not leave my Pan!' " (341). Posed against the family's earlier intercultural harmony, the response suggests an introduction of racism into the children's awareness, in the same way that racism was introduced to the woman who married Liu Kanghi in "A White Woman Who Married a Chinaman" (1910), or that the two nurses who wheeled Sui Sin Far down "a green English lane" introduced her to racism.[64] " 'I am Chinese too!' " insists Pat. " 'He Chinese! He Chinese!' " the voice of Pan reinforces. "But," the narrator inserts, "Pat was driven away" (342). By whom or for what? The shift to passive voice leaves us to wonder.[65] " 'Yes, him white, but all same, China boy,' " the lichi vendor replies with dual racial perspective to Anna Harrison's original question about Pat's race; the vendor gives the question the attention he feels it deserves when he asks, " 'Lady, you want to buy lichi?' " (334). Of what significance are white chins or black heads in the arena of human love, he seems to be asking. The multiple voices raised by the narrator suggest that the mission woman's racist absolutism is absurd in a multiracial, pluralistic culture, where, as Mrs. Lum Yook observes, if it had not been for her and her husband's care of Pat, "there would have been no white boy for others to 'raise' " (341).

"Pat and Pan" is a superficially simple story, placed in *Mrs. Spring Fragrance* under the heading Tales of Chinese Children. Yet the story confronts some of the taboos society most profoundly professes: miscegenation, incest, and cultural genocide. The mission woman sees the two children "asleep in each others arm's" in what, if we did not know their ages, could be the pose of adults after lovemaking (333); Pat sits stoically through his own caning at school but shakes his fist at the teacher and, when Anna Harrison begins to slap Pan, shouts "in a voice hoarse with passion: 'You hurt my Pan again!' " The narrator explicitly observes of Pat and Pan: "They were not always lovers—those two" (339). As readers, we recognize what Anna Harrison must have: between this girl and boy from races society has put into severance lies the potential for sexual relations, childbearing, and marriage. The story addresses fears in the dominant white culture of loss of their "own" people to those they term "other," fears faced even more directly in "A White Woman Who Married a Chinaman," whose title character learns to prefer the Chinese community to the white American community.[66] Clearly, the author of *Mrs. Spring Fragrance* does not shy away from positing the underlying reasons why the mission woman believes she must "save" Pat from "Chinese" culture—reasons that highlight the racism of the dominant white culture to which most of Sui Sin Far's readers belonged.

The ironic results of Anna's efforts reveal themselves when the children are brought together for two final meetings. In the first, Pat tells Pan that he is learning " 'lots of things that you don't know anything about,' " to which Pan laments: " 'Pat, you have forgot to remember' "—for Pat admits that he has forgotten A-Toy, " 'the big gray meow' " (343). Once again, the acquisition of knowledge in one world—the "new"—is set against its loss in another. Subsequently, such gains and losses move from the material world into the deepest realms of the spirit. At the children's last meeting, Pan exclaims, " 'Ah, Pat! . . . I find you!' " in response to which Pat's new friends taunt, " 'Hear the China kid!' " Counterpointing an earlier scene in which Pat "was driven away," now he drives Pan with the shout, " 'Get away from me!' " The last line, though, is given to the Chinese American girl, as she calls back, " 'Poor Pat! . . . He Chinese no more . . .' " (344). Even though Pan is the one left to shake her head "sorrowfully," it is Pat for whom the reader feels the most pity. Pan knows who her mother is and, even with a broken heart, can still think of Pat as a brother, while Pat has lost a sister, a family, and a culture. The story is elegiac. It mourns the fate that Pau Lin killed her son to avert—the loss of a soul. In conclusion, conventional expectations are overturned, as he who appears to gain loses, and she who is perceived "only to play" carries the author's thematic intentions. Through the eyes of childhood there is no difference in race, as there was none for Sui Sin Far as a toddler in England, until society implants the division.

Earlier, I suggested that Sui Sin Far grants her fictional heroines the limited freedom of exchanging family-arranged marriages for the right to choose their own mates but is seemingly reluctant to expand their choices to her own—that is, the right not to marry. In the *Mrs. Spring Fragrance* stories, this does not change, but something else does: the authority of the female voice within family relationships to speak out for her children and culture, whether against the dominant white society of North America or against her own men. Fin Fan, Pau Lin, Pau Tsu, Sie, and Pan dare to challenge threats to the life of their culture, and the first three figures assume the powerful roles of educators of males who let capitalist glitter (the "new") momentarily lead them astray. In contrast to the stereotype of passivity and silence popular in Orientalist literature, the Chinese American women in many *Mrs. Spring Fragrance* stories stop at nothing to fight being assimilated. They are, to borrow Dale Bauer's imagery, "women 'on the threshold' of a social or cultural crisis [who] become powerful in the marginal realm which constitutes the carnival world."[67]

Conclusion: "Its Wavering Image"

" 'Its Wavering Image,' " the fourth story in the collection, epitomizes Sui Sin Far's sensitivity to the complications of her own border position. With painful directness, this story confronts the conflicts and struggles for resolution that women of Chinese-white descent faced in North America. In brief, the conflict of Pan, a young woman of Chinese and white parents, comes to the fore through her romance with Mark Carson, a white reporter, who is sent by his newspaper into San Francisco's Chinatown for a story and meets Pan in her father's shop. Early in their courtship, Mark Carson makes the heretofore satisfied Pan feel that "until his coming, she had lived her life alone." In return, Pan plays the border guide for Mark Carson, leading him into parts of Chinatown to which he would not otherwise be allowed access but where "for her sake he was received as a brother" (87). Though Mark Carson spends many hours in Pan's "high room open to the stars, with its China bowls full of flowers and its big colored lanterns" (88), we surmise that their time together is sexually innocent. When Mark Carson says, " 'Kiss me, Pan,' " the narrator comments, "It was the first time." It was, however, the kiss of Judas: "Next morning Mark Carson began work on the special-feature article which he had been promising his paper for some weeks" (91).

The central theme of the tale includes not only Pan's betrayal by Mark Carson—who "had carelessly sung her heart away, and with her kiss upon his lips, had smilingly turned and stabbed her" (92)—but also Pan's sense that, by providing Mark Carson with access to the secrets of her father's people, she has betrayed herself. Unfolding more subtly is the related betrayal of Pan's identity, whose dual racial nature was inherent at birth but only begins "wavering" after her meeting with Mark Carson: "All her life had Pan lived in Chinatown, and if she were different in any sense from those around her, she gave little thought to it. It was only after the coming of Mark Carson that the mystery of her nature began to trouble her" (85). The reasons why are illuminated when Mark Carson asks his city editor, "What was she? Chinese or white?" (86), and when he introduces Pan to racial ambivalence: " 'Pan . . . you do not belong here. You are white—white. . . . Your real self is alien to them [Chinese people].' " The white American man tries to force the Chinese American woman to split herself in half and discard one part or the other: " 'Pan, don't you see that you have got to decide what you will be—Chinese or white? You cannot be both' " (90). Pan's reaction, " 'No! No!' " (89), parallels that of the protagonist of the same name in "Pat and Pan" when the child is told she must give up her white brother. Both Pans express shocked resistance when a representative of the external white culture tries to force a division that to both is unnatural. " 'Oh, do not speak in that way any more' "

(89), Pan tells Mark Carson; " 'I do not love you when you talk to me like that' " (90).

Yet the identity conflict has been raised, and in her days with Mark Carson, Pan feels "at times as if her white self must entirely dominate and trample under foot her Chinese" (87)—in language that echoes the very divisions upon which Mark Carson insists.[68] Throughout the story, Sui Sin Far uses juxtapositions and dramatic irony to warn her readers that there is more to the reporter than what, through Pan's naive eyes, we see. Descriptions of Mark Carson as "clever," with manners that "easily won for him the confidence of the unwary" (86), foreshadow his capacity to deceive; his cool-headed awareness of his motives is implied by his "clear eyes" (87). " 'How beautiful above! How unbeautiful below!' " he exclaims, looking both literally and figuratively down on Chinatown's "lantern-lighted, motley-thronged street" from Pan's balcony (89). The words with which he justifies his news article to Pan recall the attitude of Anna Harrison: Chinatown's beliefs are " 'mere superstition' " that must " 'be exposed and done away with' " (94).

Pan and the Chinese American culture have the last word when, after writing his article, Mark Carson disappears for two months and then returns confident that with "a healing balm, a wizard's oil which none knew so well as he how to apply" (93), he can win Pan. The young woman's answer is to appear in "Chinese costume," which causes Mark to shiver, and Pan to affirm, " 'I would not be a white woman for all the world' " (94–95). In " 'Its Wavering Image,' " the heroine's pluralistic identity, internally harmonious until Mark Carson arrives, "wavers" when the reporter tries to force her to segregate her own being. Her final statement, " 'And *what* is a promise to a white man!' " (95), seems to offer a voice for all races of non-European descent in colonized North America.

" 'Its Wavering Image' " is the most self-referential piece of writing in Sui Sin Far's mature fiction. Pan's dual racial parentage is the mirror image of the author's. Pan's preference for "her father's people," with whom "she was natural and at home" (85), parallels Sui Sin Far's preference for her mother's. With the "people" of the other (white) parent, Pan, like Sui Sin Far as a child, "felt strange and constrained, shrinking from the curious scrutiny as she would from the sharp edge of a sword" (85–86). Like Sui Sin Far, who felt no different from other Macclesfield children until alerted by the whispers of neighbors, Pan "gave little thought" to being "different in any sense to those around her" until "after the coming of Mark Carson" (85). Pan, like her author, was "born a Bohemian, exempt from the conventional restrictions imposed on either the white or Chinese woman" (86). Finally, Pan's decision against marriage may well reflect Sui Sin Far's, and for similar reasons.

The story's self-referential characterizations also include the figure of Mark Carson. The white reporter seeking to ferret out Chinatown's secrets is a stock character in "Chinatown literature." We have seen him in Olive Dibert's "The Chinese Lily," scouring Chinatown's back corners and basements to emerge with sensationalist stories that reinforce his reading audience's stereotypes. It is this reference that Pan calls up when, after reading Mark Carson's story, she feels as if things "sacred and secret to those who loved her [have been] . . . cruelly unveiled and ruthlessly spread before the ridiculing and uncomprehending foreigner" (92). In the sense that Mark Carson is an example of an unscrupulous outsider who can bring harm to Chinese American lives, his role as a reporter is an implicit contrast to Sui Sin Far's insider stance.

Sui Sin Far, however, was also a reporter, a writer, and a collector of Chinese American stories, who, as her pieces in the *Westerner* indicate, must have frequently depended on hospitable members of Chinatown as her guides. Unlike Mark Carson, who apparently felt no conflict, but like Pan, Sui Sin Far must have repeatedly faced difficult decisions about how to use the "secrets" that Chinese Americans and her own interracial family entrusted to her care. Did Sui Sin Far, when *Mrs. Spring Fragrance* was published, also compare the stories she divulged to the act of physical stripping, feeling, in the manuscripts she sent out to the public, "that her own naked body and soul had been exposed" (92)? Pan's dilemma, when seen in these terms, may reveal much about Sui Sin Far's identity as a writer as well. Concerning the complexity of Chinese-White relationships, Pan is portrayed as an innocent, but, at the time she compiled *Mrs. Spring Fragrance,* Sui Sin Far was not. She recognized the fragility of her stance on the border, was aware that attempts to serve as a voice both for a Chinese American community and to an Anglo American readership could result in misunderstandings. Consistent with the recurring motif of borders we have seen throughout Sui Sin Far's work, " 'Its Wavering Image' " confronts the entangled choices that a writer of mixed racial heritage must make in a racist society.[69]

In sum, *Mrs. Spring Fragrance* as a volume displays the doubleness familiar by now to this study. The motif of exotic, nonthreatening Orientalism, staged by the marketplace and conveyed in the book's physical design, is juxtaposed against the saga of Chinese North American culture in its struggle for birth. As we have seen in her earlier writings, Sui Sin Far's representations of that culture treat it not as a bachelor society but as a community informed by the vitality of women and children, whose influence on the evolving shape of Chinese America, as viewed in her fiction, far outweighs demographical numbers. Throughout the volume we hear a clash of voices. This stems in part from the tension created between the book's benign physical appearance—which presents the author as a "safe" if exotic woman of Chinese heritage—and the contents of particular stories that challenge a racist culture to consider the suffering it imposes on Chinese Americans. The contents stage Mikhail Bakhtin's carnivalesque, which, as Dale Bauer describes, "reveals the characters as subjects of their own discourse rather than objects of an official line or finalizing word."[70] The reader who may be soothed by the first two Mrs. Spring Fragrance stories in the collection—stories that entertain relatively easy solutions to Americanization and to generational, racial, and class conflicts—must then face the disturbing anguish of "The Wisdom of the New," in which an immigrant bride feels driven to murder her own child to make her voice heard. The range of the book's trickster figures is as diverse as its voices: the happy, only occasionally ironic, immigrant bride, Mrs. Spring Fragrance, who introduces the volume; the actress in "The Sing Song Woman," who works her tricks at its center; and the Chinese American girl, Pan, who controls the next to last story. If we envision each of these pivotal female characters holding a string pulled across the more than three hundred pages between, we can imagine the tension generated between their three voices. The first presents an intercultural dream fantasy of easy solutions; the second works out a solution through disguise and deceit; the third probes the depths of intercultural nightmares where, unless society wakes, no solutions are possible. Like these figures and consistent with her evolving art as we have traced it, in *Mrs. Spring Fragrance* Sui Sin Far necessarily wrote from a stance that straddled boundaries. The collection is undoubtedly a compromise, Sui Sin Far's answer to the particular challenge faced by a writer attempting to satisfy the dual demands of the marketplace and her own personal vision.

Notes

1. Sui Sin Far, *Mrs. Spring Fragrance* (Chicago: A. C. McClurg, 1912). Unless otherwise mentioned, all the stories discussed in this chapter are in *Mrs. Spring Fragrance,* and the in-text page citations refer to this volume.

2. Sui Sin Far, "Sui Sin Far, the Half Chinese Writer, Tells of Her Career," *Boston Globe,* 5 May 1912. Hereafer referred to in the text as *Globe.*

3. "Obituary," *Montreal Daily Star,* 7 April 1914.

4. Edith Eaton to Charles Lummis, 9 August 1911, 23 March 1912, and 19 April 1912, Charles Fletcher Lummis Collection, Huntington Library, San Marino, Calif. (hereafter cited as HL).

5. John Tebbel, *A History of Book Publishing in the United States,* vol. 2 (New York: R. R. Bowker, 1975), 442.

6. "A. C. McClurg & Co., Chicago's Largest Booksellers," *Publisher's Weekly* 93 (29 June 1918): 1297–98. Anonymously written, this article explains that since 1842 the company that would become "A. C. McClurg's" had been a major bookstore; its still extant rare book department, which Eugene Field named the "Saints' and Sinners' Corner," "became a gathering place for literary figures of the Midwest, including Field, James Whitcomb Riley, Bill Nye, Emerson Hough, and Henry B. Fuller" (1298).

7. Peter Dzwonkoski, ed., *Dictionary of Literary Biography,* vol. 49 (Detroit, Mich.: Gale Research, 1986), 1638.

8. *The Plimpton Press Year Book: An Exhibit of Versatility* (Norwood, Mass: Plimpton Press, 1911), 78.

9. Ibid., 6.

10. Ibid., 70.

11. Edith Eaton to Charles Lummis, 8 January 1901, Charles Fletcher Lummis Collection, Southwest Museum, Los Angeles, Calif.

12. Edward W. Said, *Orientalism* (New York: Pantheon Books, 1978), 5. Although Said's "Orientalism" calls up the far more complex layerings of East-West relations in general, the examples cited here illustrate the way in which the idea was exploited by the marketplace.

13. Edith Noble-Brewer, "The Craze for the Oriental," *New Idea Woman's Magazine* 9 (January 1903): 81–82. To my knowledge, Sui Sin Far's work in this magazine has not been located.

14. Elizabeth Ammons, *Conflicting Stories: American Women Writers at the Turn into the Twentieth Century* (New York: Oxford University Press, 1992), 119, questions the part Sui Sin Far played in the material aspects of her book's publication and asks, "Did [Sui Sin Far] resent the infusion of femininity and Orientalism, the two collapsed into one visual statement on every page of her book?" She concludes that "it is not at all clear whether the most obvious and inescapable formal choice of the book—its insistently 'Orientalized,' hyper-feminized pages—came from the author or the publisher."

15. Edith Eaton to Charles Lummis, 23 March 1912, HL.

16. I am grateful to Jingi Ling for this translation.

17. This design duplicates the lotus flower on the cover of the periodical *Lotus,* which Walter Blackburne Harte edited and which published Sui Sin Far's "The Story of Iso," *Lotus* 2 (August 1896): 117–19, and "A Love Story of the Orient," *Lotus* 2 (October 1896): 203–7.

18. Jinqi Ling, Interview, Pullman, Wash., January 1991.

19. Ibid. The typeface of the text complements the images on the paper; it is comfortably unobtrusive, in the direct and well-spaced lettering of twelve-point Scotch.

20. See Amy Ling, *Between Worlds: Women Writers of Chinese Ancestry* (New York: Pergamon, 1990), 41, who points out, "Like Winifred's novels, which had appeared before this, the physical appearance of the book [*Mrs. Spring Fragrance*] attests to the publisher's attempt to promote sales by appealing to a particular notion of things 'oriental' as exotic, delicate, and lovely."

21. *Little Folks* 43 (1892): 24.

22. Sui Sin Far, "Leaves from the Mental Portfolio of an Eurasian," *Independent* 66 (21 January 1909): 125–32. Hereafter referred to as "Leaves."

23. Edith Eaton to Charles Lummis, 22 June 1912, HL.

24. The reviewer's conclusion is questionable and implies that Sui Sin Far is assuming a stance of "mediation" in the sense described by Mary Dearborn in *Pocahantas's Daughters: Gender and Ethnicity in American Culture* (New York:

Oxford University Press, 1986), for many ethnic women writers "stress samenesses rather than differences," "explain" a subordinate to a dominant group, and ultimately "bridge" cultures. Although Dearborn does not directly discuss writers of Chinese descent, her theories lead me to ask, first, was Sui Sin Far a "mediator" in Dearborn's sense, and, second, what does *mediation* mean when we are dealing with racism? What it comes down to is the attitude a writer assumes toward the culture(s) about which she is writing and the audience for whom she is writing. The *Witness* reviewer obviously ignores the extent to which Sui Sin Far shows racism affecting the Chinese North American immigrant in all aspects of life; her criticism is hardly confined to "governments."

25. "Mrs. Spring Fragrance and Her Friends, Chinese and American," *Montreal Weekly Witness,* 22 June 1912. *Montreal Daily Witness*'s change from a daily to a weekly is signified by the corresponding change in its name.

26. "Book Reaches the Heart," *Boston Globe,* 7 July 1912.

27. "A New Note in Fiction," *New York Times Book Review,* 7 July 1912.

28. "Literary Notes," *Independent,* 15 August 1912.

29. Edith Eaton to Charles Lummis, 23 March 1912, HL.

30. "McClurg Publications" (1935), McClurg Archives, Newberry Library, Chicago, Ill.

31. Ling, *Between Worlds,* 42, describes the contents as "unpretentious, gentle, sometimes sentimental" and comments on the "basic human themes—love of men and women, parents and children, brothers and sisters, [through which] she draws forth the reader's empathy." Focusing on the Mrs. Spring Fragrance section, Ammons, *Conflicting Stories,* 109, pinpoints "an implicit two-part structure," wherein the first eight stories concentrate on relationships between Chinese and white Americans, especially women, while the last nine stories concentrate more on issues within the Chinese American community.

32. See S. E. Solberg, "Sui Sin Far/Edith Eaton: First Chinese-American Fictionist," *MELUS* 8 (Spring 1981): 34, who observes, "Taken out of context, what does the title [*Mrs. Spring Fragrance*] suggest? Perhaps the exotic, that could be traded on, at worst, the quaint, but hardly the struggle toward realism that is found in the pages."

33. Dale M. Bauer, *Feminist Dialogics: A Theory of Failed Community* (New York: State University of New York Press, 1988), 13–14.

34. Sui Sin Far, "The Inferior Woman," *Hampton's* 24 (May 1910): 727, 729, 730.

35. Jinqi Ling, Interview, Pullman, Wash., January 1991.

36. With few exceptions, such as "The Sugar Cane Baby," Sui Sin Far includes only characters of Chinese or European descent in her fiction. We know from reading "Leaves" that she was well aware of the racism suffered among individuals descended from Africa and Mexico. The restriction of her fictional representations to Chinese and white characters probably results from her deep personal and artistic commitment to becoming a voice for her mother's (and her own) people in North America. To this end, true to the history, white North Americans were her primary antagonists.

37. Ling, *Between Worlds,* 43.

38. Ammons, *Conflicting Stories,* 112.

39. Anne Bradstreet, "The Author to Her Book," *The Tenth Muse Lately Sprung Up in America* (Boston, 1678; reprinted as *The Works of Anne Bradstreet in Prose and Verse,* ed., John Harvard Ellis [Charlestown: A. E. Cutter, 1867]).

40. See Ling, *Between Worlds,* 48, who maintains that "Sui Sin Far's major theme, of course, was the plight of the Chinese in America"; and Ammons, *Conflicting Stories,* 109, who argues that the two sections share themes, "such as admiration for acts of loyalty and sacrifice or of outrage at racial bigotry," but are "highly separable because of their distinct audiences."

41. Isaac Kramnick, "Children's Literature and Bourgeois Ideology: Observations on Culture and Industrial Capitalism in the Later Eighteenth Century," in *Culture and Politics: From Puritanism to the Enlightenment,* ed. Perez Zagorin (Berkeley: University of California: 1980), 209, 208. I thank Carolyn Karcher for sharing this article with me.

42. "Mrs. Spring Fragrance and Her Friends, Chinese and American."

43. Joan N. Radner and Susan S. Lanser, "The Feminist Voice: Strategies of Coding in Folklore and Literature," *Journal of American Folklore* 100 (October–December 1987): 421.

44. Kramnick, "Children's Literature and Bourgeois Ideology," 209.

45. Sui Sin Far, "Ku Yum and the Butterflies," *Good Housekeeping* 48 (March 1909): 299.

46. Amy Ling, "Edith Eaton: Pioneer Chinamerican Writer and Feminist," *American Literary Realism* 16 (Autumn 1983): 293, reads this story as "a parable of Eaton's own relationship to the Chinese community; the seabird with the broken wing saves the lives of her brothers and sisters by telling them of a plot to destroy them."

47. Ling, *Between Worlds,* 48, conjectures that this story, along with "The Chinese Lily," is "suggestive of a lesbian sensibility, which the author herself would not have approved and would have striven to repress." I suggest that the intimate bonding of Sui Sin Far's women, which occurs in many stories, is not sexual but essentially psychological and spiritual, a bonding envisioned by the author as springing from women's common experience—as mothers, victims of the patriarchal system, preservers of culture—and with roots in both sides of her heritage. In the Chinese tradition, the love relationship by which Li Chung O'Yam and Ku Yum "rescue" each other demonstrates a continuance of the intimate bonding of Chinese women. As previously mentioned, Cathy Silber, "A 1,000-Year-Old Secret," *Ms.* 3 (September 1992): 58–60, discusses it within the context of *nushu,* the secret language that Chinese women created and used to communicate both orally and in writing for more than ten centuries. Relationships as *laotongs,* or "sames," allowed women to become best friends forever, bonding not only with each other but to a network that crossed generations and could include all female family members. "Women everywhere, like the writers of *nushu,* connect with sisters and sames in our own common codes" (60), Silber concludes. Rooted in the European side of her heritage, Sui Sin Far's "Heart's Desire" taps into the

woman's world explored by Carroll Smith-Rosenburg, "The Female World of Love and Ritual: Relations between Women in Nineteenth Century America," in *Disorderly Conduct: Visions of Gender in Victorian America* (New York: Alfred A. Knopf, 1985), 53–76, where women nourish one another in a realm separate from men, perhaps including but not limited to what society terms *lesbianism,* and are committed to helping each other survive.

48. This is a standard phrase and continuing refrain for China used in Sui Sin Far's writing.

49. See Ling, *Between Worlds,* 46–47, who contends, "Here we find not only the woman-bonding theme, but the ideal of self-sacrifice or martyrdom, as the ultimate expression of love."

50. Ling, "Edith Eaton," 292, suggests "a feminist ring to the symbolic reverberations of a princess having the object of her inquiries up her own sleeve."

51. "Mrs. Spring Fragrance and Her Friends, Chinese and American."

52. Two of these are "The Banishment of Ming and Mai," set in China, and "Misunderstood," set in Santa Barbara, California.

53. Xiao-Huang Yin, a Chinese doctoral candidate at Harvard University, observes that many of Sui Sin Far's stories come out of Chinese folklore and seem very authentic. Interview by the author, 15 February 1991, Pullman, Wash.

54. James Baldwin, "Everybody's Protest Novel," in *Notes of a Native Son* (Boston: Beacon, 1955), 17.

55. See Lorraine Dong and Marlon K. Hom, "Defiance or Perpetuation: An Analysis of Characters in *Mrs. Spring Fragrance,*" in *Chinese America: History and Perspectives,* ed. Him Mark Lai, Ruthanne Lum McCunn, and Judy Yung (San Francisco: Chinese Historical Society of America, 1987), 148, for their interpretation of Sie as "the epitome of filial piety" who "sees no conflict between her duty as a daughter and her own desires."

56. Dong and Hom, ibid., 160, categorize the white women in both "The Wisdom of the New" and "The Americanizing of Pau Tsu" as "White Goddesses," who "are put on their pedestal and worshipped or loved by Americanized Chinese men" and in "their racist ignorance" judge these men's quality by how nearly they resemble "a white person in feelings and behavior...." I consider this a simplistic reading in that it observes the stereotype of white women that Sui Sin Far raises but misses the satirization by which she turns their "pedestals" upside down.

57. Dong and Hom, ibid., 153, see this as "an ironic act because in Pau Tsu's stubborn resistance to Americanization she has nonetheless become Americanized by resorting to a Western marital solution, divorce, to define her own way of life," and they suggest "that Sui Sin Far has imposed a Western cultural characteristic on a character who is consistently depicted as extremely Chinese and anti-American as perhaps an artistic flaw." This is to ignore that divorce in this story is only a pseudosolution, which the author explores and rejects—another example of her attitude toward Western stereotypes.

58. See ibid., 149: "Fin Fan's defiance has brought her a kind of peace that she would not have had in life. At the very least, she does accomplish her goal: she will never be separated from her baby."

59. Two stories in *Mrs. Spring Fragrance* concentrate on this ceremony: "The Silver Leaves" (242–45) and "Misunderstood" (314–20).

60. See Ammons, *Conflicting Stories,* 114, who observes, "Denied voice, Pau Lin murders her son, her most wonderful creation; she renders herself barren, without offspring"; and Ling, *Between Worlds,* 45, who sets the blame for the tragedy in "the situation itself, in the clash between cultures and the fragility of the people caught in this clash."

61. Ammons, *Conflicting Stories,* 114, views Sankwei's "overnight reform" as unbelievable and a problem in the story, one example of Sui Sin Far's "idealization of Chinese men."

62. Dong and Hom, "Defiance or Perpetuation," 145, suggest in their critique of Sui Sin Far's treatment of Chinese and Chinese American male characters that "after a tragic lesson involving the death of his son, Sankwei . . . returns to China with his wife in defeat," and they conclude that "the fate of Americanized men in Sui Sin Far's stories perpetuates antimiscegenation." My study does not support this conclusion. Its thesis instead is that as a Eurasian, a writer who saw both sides from the border, Sui Sin Far looked at these stories from a more complex and ambiguous stance and recognized border crossing as a process fraught with perils for Chinese American immigrants of both sexes.

63. Carolyn Karcher, Letter to Annette White-Parks, 6 April 1990, compares the contrast that Sui Sin Far draws between Mrs. Dean and Adah Charlton with "Americanization versus a feminist sisterhood that includes sensitivity to the culture of non-Western women." Karcher also "associate[s] the older woman with an earlier model of feminism that was much more bound up in white middle-class cultural attitudes than the one we are now striving toward."

64. Sui Sin Far, "Leaves," 125.

65. Solberg, "Sui Sin Far/Edith Eaton," 35, considers that "the most impressive aspect of [Sui Sin Far's] writing is the conviction that environment is more important that [sic] heredity, that race is an accident, and, when, as with the Eurasian, there is a question of choice, the individual has the power to make that choice"; Solberg cites "Pat and Pan" as the writer's "most dramatic statement of the theme of choice." While such might hold true for the adults, I question the extent of this power in the case of Pan, a little boy who, as with all Sui Sin Far's children, is portrayed as largely at the mercy of adult decision making.

66. There are interesting parallels here to the "white Indian"—white captives of American Indians, especially women, who came to prefer and to remain with Indian culture—studied by James Axtell, *White Indians of Colonial America* (Fairfield, Wash.: Ye Galleon Press, 1979).

67. Bauer, *Feminist Dialogics,* 13.

68. Compare this passage with a similar one in "Leaves," 126: "the white blood in our veins fights valiantly for the Chinese half of us."

69. Compare Dong and Hom, "Defiance or Perpetuation," 161–62, who have a different interpretation of Sui Sin Far's "two Eurasian women," Pan (in "'Its Wavering Image,'") and Mag-gee (in "The Sing Song Woman"): "Unfortunately they do not reveal much in terms of the turmoil experienced by Eurasian women at the time or the reasons why such a woman would choose one identity over the other.... The two Eurasian characters are fixed in their respective cultural roles without any significant growth. This is perhaps the biggest disappointment among Sui Sin Far's stories, because as an Eurasian, she would have been in the best position to describe the trials and tribulations of an Eurasian woman living in America at the turn of the century." I believe that this reading is the reverse of what Sui Sin Far actually does—it was exactly those "trials and tribulations" that Sui Sin Far recorded in her literary work.

70. Bauer, *Feminist Dialogics,* 14.

Conclusion

What hurts is the discovery of the measure of our silence. How deep it
runs. How many of us are indeed caught, unreconciled between two
languages, two political poles, and suffer the insecurities of that straddling.
—Alma Gómez, Cherríe Moraga, and Mariana Romo-Carmana,
   Cuentos

The final two years of Sui Sin Far's life emerge as the last of the intermittent
silences that punctuated her existence, recurring spaces in both her life and her
art that elude public scrutiny but in their own way speak louder than words
and recall Adrienne Rich's assertion that "all silence has a meaning."[1] The
preceding pages illustrate Sui Sin Far's determination to come to terms with
that meaning and the frustrating isolation of her struggle as a woman
marginalized not only by gender but also by race and class: as a daughter of an
interracial couple living in racist societies; as a child born into the rootedness
of a well-to-do, merchant-class family who experienced the severance of
immigration and an impoverishment so severe that she and her siblings were
taken from school before adolescence to help earn a living; as a semi-invalid;
and as an artist foraging work as a stenographer to survive. It is obvious that
Sui Sin Far was not silent. She wrote constantly but often in fragments, after
"the work of others" was finished. There was never enough left of either time
or energy, not just for the writing but for the working out of a style and the
search to find markets. Opportunities to develop the kind of network enjoyed
by such nineteenth-century writers as Harriet Beecher Stowe or Helen Hunt
Jackson, who, to quote Susan Coultrap McQuin, "sustained and encouraged
each other's efforts,"[2] or by modernist writers, who, Gillian Hanscombe and
Virginia L. Smyers observe, have read each other's work and kept a mutual
dialogue going in their memoirs,[3] were unavailable to a writer in Sui Sin Far's
circumstances. Regarding her acquaintance with other "literary worker[s]," so
vital to all stages of the writing process, she said late in her life, "I have never
met any to know."[4]

Given the numerous obstacles that stood between Sui Sin Far and creative achievement, her literary work is all the more remarkable. Elizabeth Ammons says it wonderfully: "That Sui Sin Far invented herself—created her own voice—out of such deep silencing and systematic racist repression was one of the triumphs of American literature at the turn of the century."[5] We have seen that nothing extinguished her "ambition to write a book" (*Globe*) or distracted her from her goal: "to fight [the] battles" of Chinese North Americans "in the papers."[6] Her fiction presented portraits of turn-of-the-century North American Chinatowns with a sympathy and understanding that had not been seen before and would not resurface for many more years.

From the late nineteenth century, critics have recognized Sui Sin Far as a founder of Asian American literature in the United States, a recognition that this study extends to include Canada. As a Eurasian, she stands as a foremother to North American women writers of Chinese descent, a position illustrated by her life as well as her art. A comparison may be drawn to the vital connection Paul Lauter sees between African American writers of the present and those of the past: "There is a vital dialectic between the recognition of a writer like [Toni] Morrison and the need to understand her predecessors, like Frances E. W. Harper, Nella Larsen, Ann Petry, and Gwendolyn Brooks; but more, between the creative aspirations of such writers and the lived experience of black women in American society."[7] The empowerment and visibility that Maxine Hong Kingston achieved for Chinese American women and children in *A Woman Warrior* in 1976 finds a precedent in the female characterizations of *Mrs. Spring Fragrance* in 1912. Amy Ling's account of the writer Chuang Hua, whose parents' migrations from China to England to the United States endowed Chuang Hua, in Ling's words, with "a rich experience of cultural diversity at the expense of a sense of centeredness,"[8] parallels Sui Sin Far's odyssey and its effects almost exactly.

Because Sui Sin Far was the first to give not only voice but also leading roles to Chinese, Chinese Canadian, and Chinese American women—dramatizing their authority in the domestic sphere, affirming their significance to the growth of Chinese American culture, showing the sisterly bonds they forge with one another, and portraying the friendships and conflicts they experience with North American women of European descent—I see her as also central to women's literature on an intercultural scale. Through epigrams, I have tried to communicate my own excitement at finding motifs throughout Sui Sin Far's work that tap the vast cobweb of women's literature from many cultures. Like Alma Gómez, Cherríe Moraga, and Mariana Romo-Carmana, she dealt with the insecurities of cultural "straddling." Like the women Carolyn Heilbrun describes, she knew the struggle "between the destiny of being unambiguously a woman" and the "desire, or fate, to be something else." And she would certainly have understood the frustration of Alice

Walker's grandmothers, who "died with their real gifts stifled within them." Alice Murong Pu Lin puts it this way: "Womanhood knows no national or ethnic boundaries. Our shared secrets bridge the centuries and continents."[9]

Similarly, Carmen Salazar-Parr discusses a "special female self-awareness,"[10] which she connects to Patricia Spacks's "female perspective," within which women writers share more with female writers of other historical periods than they share with male writers of their own lifetimes.[11] Sui Sin Far's vision is integrally woven into that perspective. When the Eurasian woman in "Leaves" writes in her diary after breaking her engagement, "Joy, oh joy! I'm free once more," (131), she joins thematic hands with Estela Portillo Trambley's Beatriz, who, after killing the tyrant to whom she is married, recalls a girlhood without him: "It was a joyous idea. . . . Free . . . free";[12] and with Kate Chopin's narrator, who, upon hearing the news of her husband's death, whispers almost identical words: "Free! Body and soul free!"[13] In these stories, the voices of three different writers join across nearly a century of time and three races/cultures to offer spontaneous joy in a freedom hard won and not taken for granted, an exclamation with which any woman can identify.

It was in "Leaves" that Sui Sin Far also extended the most ancient and futuristic of all women's visions: "Only when the whole world becomes as one family will human beings be able to see clearly and hear distinctly" (129).[14] This philosophy, markedly global in an ethnocentric environment, fits appropriately with the short forms within which Sui Sin Far chose to work, forms whose very structures counter the dominant modes of "rugged individualism" and allow her, as Ammons notes, "to present many different people's stories, with the cumulative effect in *Mrs. Spring Fragrance* of giving us a glimpse into a community bound together by shared traditions and problems but composed of individual lives, no one more important than another."[15] Such a fusion of forms and content, as a whole urging her readers to replace competition with cooperation for survival, reinforces Sui Sin Far's contemporary significance.

Since I started this research, the past that Sui Sin Far represents has moved to the present in other ways. In the fall of 1992 in eastern Canada, where a hundred years earlier a young woman listed in *Lovell's Montreal Directory* as "Miss Edith Eaton" fought the battles of the Chinese as a journalist, approximately three hundred Chinese Canadians rallied on Ottawa's Parliament Hill for restitution for the head tax that was forced upon Chinese immigrants who sought to enter Canada between 1885 and 1923. Many of the marchers carried in their pockets Sui Sin Far's 1896 letter to the *Montreal Daily Star* protesting that head tax. The letter was translated into Chinese and included Sui Sin Far's picture.[16] Her dream to "fight their battles in the papers" continues eighty years past her death.

Nevertheless, it is also clear that over the century Sui Sin Far has been double-silenced in the sense that Michelle Cliff describes when women's works, difficult to get published originally, go and remain out of print: "Our silences originate in interruption. And our silences lead to interruption."[17] To these silences I can relate personally, not only as a woman and a writer but also through the responses I have experienced trying to get Sui Sin Far and other little-known writers reprinted. Overwhelmingly, these come back to the question offered at this book's beginning—"Is she any good?"—with assumptions of quality depending on terms like *standards* and *literature*. Such critics as Jane Tompkins and Paul Lauter have spoken in depth about such terms, which have been used in the canon we erroneously label "American" to exclude all but select writers, mainly male and white colonist in their perspective.[18] Feminist scholars can inherit this same fallacy if we are not careful. " 'Literature' is not a stable entity," Tompkins reminds us, "but a category whose outlines and contents are variable . . . a function of the political and social circumstances within which anthologists work."[19] Relating what goes down in print to who has power in society, Lauter observes, "One must ask, then, not how to apply a given and persisting set of standards, but where standards come from, whose values they embed, and whose interests they serve."[20]

Concerning Sui Sin Far in particular, let me return to this book's thesis, that the issue of quality in her writings cannot be addressed in the absence of the cultural and literary contexts within which she wrote. Lauter claims that "to some degree, every text inscribes the social ground against which it was created."[21] For Sui Sin Far, context consistently revolves around the ambiguity epitomized by her stance on the border, a position that reflects the marginalization of her life and her ongoing attempt to negotiate a—if not comfortable, at least manageable—balance. Eight years before the publication of *Mrs. Spring Fragrance,* W. E. B. Du Bois, whose first edition of *The Souls of Black Folk* was also published by A. C. McClurg, described a similar stance for African Americans when he wrote of a "double-consciousness" through which "one ever feels his two-ness—an American, a Negro; two souls, two thoughts, two unreconciled strivings; two warring ideals in one dark body. . . ."[22] Sui Sin Far was caught in what Ling calls "the between world condition"[23]—a condition akin to what Gloria Treviño Velásquez terms "cultural ambivalence."[24] Sui Sin Far's condition was a duality (trilogy?) inherent at birth, given the split that society conceived between Europe and Asia ("West" and "East"), the regions of her two parents. She consciously recognized it, she recalls in "Leaves," at age four, "on the day on which I first learned that I was something different and apart from other children" (125).

This ambivalence of identities is further complicated in that the same message she received from society in general was reinforced by the marketplace. Like many turn-of-the-century writers, she discovered that finding a style in which to write and get published required accommodating the monologic, racialized views of white America. For a writer committed to her own people, it also required breaking through them. Such a schizoid transaction could only be handled subversively or by finding strategies to negotiate with a dual audience. I have shown that Sui Sin Far created those strategies. My findings support the hypothesis offered at this book's beginning, that Sui Sin Far was able to use the very bifurcations handed to her by birth to ground an identity and establish a form and style for her art.

Finally, Sui Sin Far's career reveals a pattern that merits broader exploration. Her struggle to write, to find markets, and to get significant pieces published, only to have her work remain out of print for most of the twentieth century, could serve as a paradigm of the careers of other writers marginalized by race, gender, or class at the turn of the century. To resurrect such voices from silence is obviously central to current attempts to redefine the American literary canon. In *Literary Democracy*, a study limited to male writers of the white middle and upper classes, Larzer Ziff sought an aesthetic unique to the United States, one made possible by factors that began on this continent after the arrival of Europeans.[25] In *Women's Fiction*, Nina Baym laid a solid base for examining how women became major participants in the literature that was developing in the United States during the nineteenth century, but the focus was restricted to writers of European descent.[26] Elizabeth Ammon's *Conflicting Stories* presents pioneer work on women writers from diverse cultures, Sui Sin Far among them, who were a prominent part of the publishing scene just when American literature was coming into its own at the turn of the century, writers whose group of works, Ammons suggests, "brings into view a large and important body of work . . . held together at one and the same time by common features, and, even more important, by heterogeneity and difference."[27] I suggest that the particular tension between surface and substance in Sui Sin Far's style, and in the styles of many writers marginalized by race, gender, or class of her era, demonstrates one of these features and is a hallmark of this body. Developing from factors that arose in the Americas after the first invasions from Europe, followed by migrations from all over the world, the innovations these writers created to survive must also be recognized as uniquely "American." Out of their circumstances they developed a writer's stance that may be termed *tricksterism*.[28]

In this book's preface, I stated that when I started my research in 1985, one of my major goals was to locate women writers, especially those who had written and published from the perspectives of racial, ethnic, or class minorities, and to see them, in Jane Tompkins words, "represented in the picture America draws of itself."[29] If my study helps make Sui Sin Far part of that picture, it will do what I intended. I would like to close with a line from a poet I once heard, whose name I cannot recall but whose words express the relationship I have felt closely throughout, "Ancient sister, I reach backward to take your hand."

Notes

1. Adrienne Rich, "Disloyal to Civilization," in *On Lies, Secrets, and Silence* (New York: W. W. Norton, 1979), 308.

2. Susan Coultrap McQuin, *Doing Literary Business: American Women Writers in the Nineteenth Century* (Chapel Hill: University of North Carolina Press, 1990), 6.

3. Gillian Hanscombe and Virginia L. Smyers, *Writing for Their Lives: The Modernist Woman, 1910–1940* (Boston: Northeastern University Press, 1987).

4. Sui Sin Far, "Sui Sin Far, the Half Chinese Writer, Tells of Her Career," *Boston Globe*, 5 May 1912. Hereafter referred to in the text as *Globe*.

5. Elizabeth Ammons, *Conflicting Stories: American Women Writers at the Turn into the Twentieth Century* (New York: Oxford University Press, 1992), 105.

6. Sui Sin Far, "Leaves from the Mental Portfolio of an Eurasian," *Independent* 66 (21 January 1909): 128. Hereafter referred to in the text as "Leaves."

7. Paul Lauter, *Canons and Contexts* (New York: Oxford University Press, 1992), 169.

8. Amy Ling, Foreword to *Crossings*, by Chuang Hua (Boston: Northeastern University Press, [1968], 1986), 3.

9. Alice Murong Pu Lin, *Grandmother Had No Name* (San Francisco: China Books and Periodicals, 1988), v.

10. Carmen Salazar-Parr, "La Chicana in Literature," in *Chicano Studies: A Multi-Disciplinary Approach*, ed. Eugene Ysidro Ortiz and Francisco Lomeli (New York: Columbia University Press, 1984), 120.

11. Patricia Spacks, *The Female Imagination* (New York: Avon Books, 1976), 39.

12. Estela Portillo Trambley, "If It Weren't for the Honeysuckle," in *Rain of Scorpions and Other Writings* (Berkeley, Calif.: Tonatiuh-Quinto Sol International, 1975), 108.

13. Kate Chopin, "The Story of the Hour," in *Kate O'Flaherty Chopin: The Complete Works*, ed. Peter Seyersted (Baton Rouge: Louisiana State University Press, 1969), 353.

14. Compare Michelle Cliff, "Resonance of Interruption," *Chrysalis* 8 (August 1979): 32: "*Female culture* is a record of the survival of a group of human beings who are innately opposed to the destruction of life, and whose artifacts more often than not demonstrate this opposition with an expression of disloyalty to the norms of the dominant culture."

15. Ammons, *Conflicting Stories*, 118. Ammons, ibid., refers to Sandra Zagarell, "Narrative of Community: The Identification of a Genre," *Signs* 13 (Spring 1988): 498–527, as, though not exact, useful here, in that "occupying ['the narrative of community'] center is not, as in standard western long narratives, the all-important individual, but rather the configuration of figures who make up a group." In a different but related comparison, Dale M. Bauer, *Feminist Dialogics: A Theory of Failed Community* (New York: State University of New York Press, 1988), xiii, discusses differences between male

and female writers concerning concepts of community: "By adding a feminist turn to it, the dialogic community Bakhtin theorizes becomes a much more ambivalent territory."

16. I am grateful to L. Charles Laferrière for this information. The translation was by Desmond Wu. The Montreal Chinatown community also honored Sui Sin Far as their foremother in a recent celebration. Plans are currently underway to name the ballroom at the Chinatown Holiday Inn and the Chinatown subway stop in her honor. According to Laferrière, Sui Sin Far is emerging as a hero to a current generation of Chinese Canadians.

17. Cliff, "Resonance of Interruptions," 30.

18. See Lauter, *Canons and Contexts,* 35: "Obviously, critics did not propose as a dictum that only white men could be 'major' writers, but it was preeminently the works of white males like themselves that they selected."

19. Jane Tompkins, *Sensational Designs: The Cultural Work of American Fiction, 1790–1860* (New York: Oxford University Press, 1985), 191.

20. Lauter, *Canons and Contexts,* 104.

21. Ibid., 110.

22. W. E. B. Du Bois, *The Souls of Black Folk* (Millwood, N.Y.: Kraus-Thomson Organization, 1973 [1903]), 3.

23. As Ling, *Between Worlds: Women Writers of Chinese Ancestry* (New York: Pergamon, 1990), 44, uses it, this phrase applies to characters who are, in her words, "Eurasians wavering between the cultures and peoples of the parents; whites adopted by or married to Chinese; or Chinese who have assimilated white ways but still are tied by Old World bonds."

24. Gloria Trevino Velásquez, "Cultural Ambivalence in Early Chicana Literature," in *European Perspectives on U. S. Hispanic Literature,* ed. Genevieve Fabre (Houston: Arte Publico Press, 1986). As Velásquez uses it, *cultural ambivalence* refers to the dual tug Mexican American women writers feel, nationally, emotionally, and psychically, between Mexico and the United States.

25. Larzer Ziff, *Literary Democracy: The Declaration of Cultural Independence in America* (New York: Viking, 1981).

26. Nina Baym, *Women's Fiction: A Guide to Novels by and about Women in America, 1820–1870* (Ithaca, N.Y.: Cornell University Press, 1978).

27. Ammons, *Conflicting Stories,* 4.

28. I realize that "tricksterism" has existed among Native Americans for thousands of years. Here I speak to the concept specifically as it pertains to literature developing in North America after European colonization. See Elizabeth Ammons and Annette White-Parks, eds., *Tricksterism in Turn-of-the-Century American Literature: A Multicultural Perspective* (Hanover, N.H.: University Press of New England, 1994).

29. Tompkins, *Sensational Designs,* 201.

Bibliography

Primary Sources

A Chronological Listing of Sui Sin Far's Writings

"A Trip in a Horse Car." *Dominion Illustrated* 1 (13 October 1888): 235.

"Misunderstood: The Story of a Young Man." *Dominion Illustrated* 1 (17 November 1888): 314.

"A Fatal Tug of War." *Dominion Illustrated* 1 (8 December 1888): 362–63.

"The Origin of a Broken Nose." *Dominion Illustrated* 2 (11 May 1889): 302.

"Robin." *Dominion Illustrated* 2 (22 June 1889): 394.

"Albemarle's Secret." *Dominion Illustrated* 3 (19 October 1889): 254.

"Spring Impressions: A Medley of Poetry and Prose." *Dominion Illustrated* 4 (7 June 1890): 358–59.

"In Fairyland." *Dominion Illustrated* 5 (18 October 1890): 270.

"Girl Slave in Montreal: Our Chinese Colony Cleverly Described. Only Two Women from the Flowery Land in Town." *Montreal Daily Witness,* 4 May 1894.

"The Gamblers." *Fly Leaf* 1 (February 1896): 14–18.

"Ku Yum." *Land of Sunshine* 5 (June 1896): 29–31.

"The Story of Iso." *Lotus* 2 (August 1896): 117–19.

"A Plea for the Chinaman: A Correspondent's Argument in His Favor." Letter to the Editor. *Montreal Daily Star,* 21 September 1896.

"A Love Story of the Orient." *Lotus* 2 (October 1896): 203–7.

"A Chinese Feud." *Land of Sunshine* 5 (November 1896): 236–37.

"The Chinese Woman in America." *Land of Sunshine* 6 (January 1897): 60–65.

"Sweet Sin." *Land of Sunshine* 8 (April 1898): 223–26.

"The Sing-Song Woman." *Land of Sunshine* 9 (October 1898): 225–28.

"Lin John." *Land of Sunshine* 10 (January 1899): 76–77.

"A Chinese Ishmael." *Overland Monthly* 34 (July 1899): 43–49.

"The Story of Tin-A." *Land of Sunshine* 12 (December 1899): 101–3.

"The Smuggling of Tie Co." *Land of Sunshine* 13 (July 1900): 100–104.

"A Chinese Tom-Boy." *Montreal Daily Witness,* 16 October 1900.

"Ku Yum's Little Sister." *Chicago Evening Post,* 13 October 1900.

"O Yam—A Sketch." *Land of Sunshine* 13 (November 1900): 341–43.

"The Coat of Many Colors." *Youth's Companion* 76 (April 1902): n.p.

"In Los Angeles' Chinatown." *Los Angeles Express,* 2 October 1903.

"Betrothals in Chinatown." *Los Angeles Express,* 8 October 1903.

"Chinatown Needs a School." *Los Angeles Express,* 14 October 1903.

"Chinatown Boys and Girls." *Los Angeles Express,* 15 October 1903.

"Leung Ki Chu and His Wife." *Los Angeles Express,* 22 October 1903.

"Chinese in Business Here." *Los Angeles Express,* 23 October 1903.

"Chinese Laundry Checking." *Los Angeles Express,* 3 November 1903.

"The Horoscope." *Out West* 19 (November 1903): 521–24.

"Wing Sing of Los Angeles on His Travels." *Los Angeles Express,* 4, 5, 6, 10, and 24 February 1904; and 9 March 1904. All signed "Wing Sing" (Sui Sin Far authorship attributed).

"A Chinese Boy-Girl." *Century* 67 (April 1904): 828–31.

"Aluteh." *Chautauquan* 42 (December 1905): 338–42.

"Leaves from the Mental Portfolio of an Eurasian." *Independent* 66 (21 January 1909): 125–32.

"Ku Yum and the Butterflies." *Good Housekeeping* 48 (March 1909): 299.

"The Half Moon Cakes." *Good Housekeeping* 48 (May 1909): 584–85.

"The Chinese in America, by Sui Sin Far (Edith Eaton): Intimate Study of Chinese Life in America, Told in a Series of Short Sketches—An Interpretation of Chinese Life and Character." *Westerner* 10–11 (May–August 1909):

["Author's Preface"], "The Story of Wah," "A Chinese Book on Americans," "Scholar or Cook?" 10 (May 1909): 24–26.

"The New and the Old." 10 (June 1909): 36–38.

"Like the American," "The Story of a Forty-Niner," "The Story of Tai Yuen and Ku Yum," "Wah Lee on Family Life," "The Bonze." 11 (July 1909): 18–19, 38.

"Yip Ke Duck and the Americans," "New Year as Kept by the Chinese in America," "Chinese-American Sunday Schools," "Chinese Food," "The Bible Teacher," "Americanizing Not Always Christianizing," "The Reform Party." 11 (August 1909): 24–26.

"In the Land of the Free." *Independent* 67 (2 September 1909): 504–8.

"Mrs. Spring Fragrance." *Hampton's* 24 (January 1910): 137–41.

"The Kitten-Headed Shoes." *Delineator* 75 (February 1910): 165.

"A White Woman Who Married a Chinaman." *Independent* 68 (10 March 1910): 518–23.

"The Inferior Woman." *Hampton's* 24 (May 1910): 727–31.

"The Sugar Cane Baby." *Good Housekeeping* 50 (May 1910): 570–72.

"The Candy That Is Not Sweet." *Delineator* 76 (July 1910): 76.

"An Autumn Fan." *New England Magazine* 42 (August 1910): 700–702.

"Her Chinese Husband." *Independent* 69 (18 August 1910): 358–61.

"The Bird of Love." *New England Magazine* 43 (September 1910): 25–27.

"A Love Story from the Rice Fields of China." *New England Magazine* 45 (December 1911): 343–45.

"Chan Hen Yen, Chinese Student." *New England Magazine* 45 (June 1912): 462–66.
"Who's Game?" *New England Magazine* 45 (February 1912): 573–79.
"Sui Sin Far, the Half Chinese Writer, Tells of Her Career." *Boston Globe*, 5 May 1912.
Mrs. Spring Fragrance (Chicago: A. C. McClurg, 1912).
"Chinese Workmen in America." *Independent* 75 (3 July 1913): 56–58.

Letters

Dartmouth College Library, Special Collections
1 letter, Edith Eaton/Sui Sin Far to Harold Rugg
Huntington Library, Charles Fletcher Lummis Collection, San Marino, Calif.
5 letters, Edith Eaton (Sui Sin Far) to Charles Lummis, Editor
Century Company Records, Rare Books and Manuscripts Division, New York Public Library, Astor, Lenox and Tilden Foundations
7 letters, Edith Eaton to Robert Underwood Johnson
1 letter, Samuel T. Clover to R. U. Johnson, Esq.
Southwest Museum, Charles Fletcher Lummis Collection, Los Angeles, Calif.
11 letters, Edith Eaton to Charles Lummis, Editor

Interviews

Charbonneau, Réjean. Montreal, Quebec, Spring 1989.
Kobayashi, Audrey. Vancouver, British Columbia, 2 November 1990.
Laferrière, L. Charles. Montreal, Quebec, Spring 1989.
Lewis, Eileen. Telephone interview, Pullman, Washington, 20 September 1990.
Ling, Jinqi. Pullman, Washington, October 1990 through January 1991.
Nomura, Gail. Pullman, Washington, 1987–89.
Rooney, Elizabeth. Toronto, Ontario, November 1989.
Rooney, Paul. Toronto, Ontario, November 1989.
Roy, Patricia. Vancouver, British Columbia, 2 November 1990.
Solberg, S. E. Pullman, Washington, March 1988.
Sumida, Stephen. Pullman, Washington, 1987–89.
Wing, James. Montreal, Quebec, Spring 1989.
Xiao-Huang Yin. Pullman, Washington, 15 February 1991.

Newspapers

Boston Globe, 1910–13. Boston Public Library.
Los Angeles Express, 1900–1906. Los Angeles Public Library.
Montreal Daily Star, 1880–1914. McLennan Library, McGill University.
Montreal Daily Witness, 1880–1912. Bibliothèque Centrale, Ville de Montréal.
Montreal Gazette, 1885–1912. McLennan Library, McGill University.
San Francisco Call, 1897–1900. San Francisco Pubic Library.

Public Documents

"Act to Extend the Exclusion Act of 1882 Indefinitely." *United States Statutes at Large,* vol. 32, part 1, 1901–3.

Baptismal Records. Archives Nationales du Québec, Montreal.

Birth Certificate, Edith Maude Eaton, registered 8 April 1865. District of Macclesfield, Subdistrict of Prestbury, County of Chester, England.

Boston, Mass., Ward 12, Sheet 23. Thirteenth Census of the United States, 1910.

Burial Records. Mont Royal Cemetery, Montreal, Quebec.

Census Report, 1881. District no. 91, S. District E., No. 1, 29, Village of Hochelaga, Quebec.

Crocker-Langley San Francisco Directory, 1897–1900. San Francisco Public Library.

Death Certificate, Grace Eaton, Reg. No. 13638, 9 May 1922. Department of Health of the City of New York, Bureau of Records, State of New York.

Death Notice, Edith Eaton. *Montreal Daily Star,* 7 April 1914.

Funeral Notice, Edith Eaton. *Montreal Daily Star,* 11 April 1914.

Lovell's Montreal Directory, 1870–1925. Bibliothèque de Ville de Montréal.

Macclesfield Census Records. County of Cheshire, England, 1851.

Macclesfield Census Records. County of Cheshire, England, 1871.

Marriage Records. Archives Nationales du Québec, Montreal.

Persons of the Community of the Nuns of Charity of the Province. Archives Province, 12055 rue Grenet, Montreal.

President's Correspondence. Canadian Pacific Rail Corporate Archives Collection, Windsor Station, Montreal, Quebec.

Protestant Board of School Commissioner of the City of Montreal. *Report, 1847–1889.* Montreal: Protestant Board of School Commissioner of the City of Montreal, 1889.

Royal Commission on Chinese and Japanese Immigration. Sessional Paper No. 54. Ottowa: King's Printer, 1902. University of British Columbia.

Sepulchre Register. Archives du Québec, Montreal.

Trow's New York City Directory, vol. 81. Compiled by H. Wilson (year ending 1 May 1868). New York City Library.

White's Cheshire Directory, 1860.

Other Primary Sources

[Babcock, Winifred Eaton]. *Marion: The Story of an Artist's Model.* New York: W. J. Watt, 1916.

———. *Me: A Book of Remembrance.* New York: Century, 1915.

Chopin, Kate. "The Story of an Hour." In *Kate O'Flaherty Chopin: The Complete Works,* edited by Peter Seyersted, 352–54. Baton Rouge: Louisiana State University Press, 1969.

"Edith Eaton Dead: Author of Chinese Stories under the Name of Sui Sin Far." *New York Times,* 9 April 1914.

Hampton, Benjamin J. "A Statement by Mr. Hampton to the Stockholders and Readers of His Magazine." *Hampton's* 27 (August 1911): 258–59.

Hampton, Edgar L. "With the Publishers." *Westerner* 10 (March 1909): 1.
——. "With the Publishers." *Westerner* 10 (April 1909): 1.
——. "With the Publishers." *Westerner* 11 (November 1909):1.
Harte, Bret. *The Works of Bret Harte.* New York: Houghton Mifflin, 1882–83.
Harte, W. B. "Bubble and Squeak." *Lotus* 2 (October 1896): 216–17.
"Home Duties First." *Presbyterian Record* (1885): 305.
Hurston, Zora Neale. *Dust Tracks in the Road.* 2d ed. Edited by Robert E. Hemenway. Urbana: University of Illinois Press, 1984.
Jarrow, Joseph. *The Queen of Chinatown: A Four Act Drama.* New York: n.p., 1899.
Larsen, Nella. *Quicksand and Passing.* Edited by Deborah McDowell. Camden N.J.: Rutgers University Press, 1986 [1929].
McCunn, Ruthanne Lum. *A Thousand Pieces of Gold.* New York: Dell, 1981.
Macmillan Dictionary of Canadian Biography. 3d ed. London and Toronto: Macmillan, 1963.
Norris, Frank. "The Third Circle." In *Collected Works of Frank Norris,* vol. 4, 1–10. New York: Kennikat Press, 1967 [1928].
Plimpton Press Year Book: An Exhibit of Versatility. Norwood, Mass.: Plimpton Press, 1911.
Roy, Gabrielle. *The Tin Flute.* Toronto: McClelland and Stewart, 1947.
Trambley, Estela Portillo. "If It Weren't for the Honeysuckle." In *Rain of Scorpions and Other Writings,* 97–109. Berkeley, Calif.: Tonatiuh-Quinto Sol International, 1975.
Watanna, Onoto [Winifred Eaton Babcock]. *The Daughters of Nijo: A Romance of Japan.* New York: Macmillan, 1904.
——. *The Heart of Hyacinth.* New York: Harper and Bros., 1903.
——. *A Japanese Nightingale.* New York: Harper and Bros., 1901.
——. "The Loves of Sakura Jiro and the Three-Headed Maid." *Century* 65 (March 1903): 755–60.
——. *Miss Nume of Japan: A Japanese-American Romance.* Chicago; Rand McNally, 1899.
——. *The Wooing of Wisteria.* New York: Harper and Bros., 1902.
"Well-Known Author of Chinese Stories Who Died Yesterday." *Montreal Daily Star,* 8 April 1914.
Wen-I To. "The Laundry Song." In *Twentieth Century Chinese Poetry: An Anthology,* translated and edited by Kai-Yu Hsu, 33. Ithaca, N.Y.: Cornell University Press, 1962.
Whitaker, Joseph. *Whitaker's Almanac.* London: J. Whitaker, 1874.
Wong, Jade Snow. *Fifth Chinese Daughter.* 2d ed. Seattle: University of Washington Press, 1990.
Woolf, Virginia. *A Room of One's Own.* New York: Harcourt Brace Jovanovich, 1957 [1929].

Secondary Sources

"A. C. McClurg & Co., Chicago's Largest Booksellers." *Publishers Weekly* 93 (29 June 1918): 1297–98.

Adamson, John William. *English Education, 1789–1902*. Cambridge: Cambridge University Press, 1964.

Agosin, Marjorie. *Women of Smoke: Latin American Women in Literature and Life*. Translated by Janice Molloy. Trenton, N.J.: Red Sea Press, 1989.

Aiken, Rebecca. *Montreal Chinese Property Ownership and Occupational Changes, 1881–1981*. New York: AMS, 1989.

Altschuler, Glenn. *Race, Ethnicity and Class in American Social Thought, 1865–1919*. Arlington Heights, Ill.: Harlan Davidson, 1982.

Ammons, Elizabeth. *Conflicting Stories: American Women Writers at the Turn into the Twentieth Century*. New York: Oxford University Press, 1992.

Ammons, Elizabeth, and Annette White-Parks, eds. *Tricksterism in Turn-of-the-Century American Literature: A Multicultural Perspective*. Hanover, N.H.: University Press of New England, 1994.

Anzaldúa, Gloria. *Making Face, Making Soul—Haciendo Caras: Creative and Critical Perspectives by Women of Color*. San Francisco: Aunt Lute Books, 1990.

Arnason, David, ed. *Nineteenth Century Canadian Stories*. Toronto: Macmillan, 1976.

Atherton, William Henry. *Montreal: 1535–1914 under British Rule, 1760–1914*. Montreal: S. J. Clarke, 1914.

———. "Montreal, 1535–1891: An Historical Sketch." *Dominion Illustrated* 7 (1891): 1–17.

Axtell, James. *White Indians of Colonial America*. Fairfield, Wash.: Ye Galleon Press, 1979.

Baldwin, James. "Everybody's Protest Novel." In *Notes of a Native Son*, 13–23. Boston: Beacon, 1955.

Barrett, Eileen, and Mary Cullinan. *American Women Writers: Diverse Voices in Prose since 1845*. New York: St. Martin's Press, 1992.

Bauer, Dale M. *Feminist Dialogics: A Theory of Failed Community*. New York: State University of New York Press, 1988.

Baym, Nina. "Melodramas of Beset Manhood." *American Quarterly* 33 (Summer 1981): 123–39. Reprinted in *The New Feminist Criticism*, edited by Elaine Showalter, 63–80. New York: Pantheon Books, 1985.

———. *Women's Fiction: A Guide to Novels by and about Women in America, 1820–1870*. Ithaca, N.Y.: Cornell University Press, 1978.

Bernikow, Louise. *Among Women*. New York: Harper Colophon, 1981.

Bingham, Edwin R. *Charles F. Lummis, Editor of the Southwest*. San Marino, Calif.: Huntington Library, 1955.

Bright, William. "The Natural History of Old Man Coyote." In *Recovering the Word: Essays on Native American Literature*, edited by Brian Swann and Arnold Krupat, 339–87. Berkeley: University of California Press, 1987.

Broe, Mary Lynn, and Angela Ingram, eds. *Women's Writings in Exile.* Chapel Hill: University of North Carolina Press, 1989.

Brown, Wesley, and Amy Ling. *Imagining America: Stories from the Promised Land.* New York: Persea Books, 1991.

Carby, Hazel V. *Reconstructing Womanhood: The Emergence of the Afro-American Woman Novelist.* New York: Oxford University Press, 1987.

Cather, Willa. "On the Professor's House." In *Willa Cather on Writing,* with a foreword by Stephen Tennant, 30–32. Lincoln: University of Nebraska Press, 1988.

Chan, Anthony B. *Gold Mountain: The Chinese in the Northwest.* Vancouver: New Star Books, 1983.

Chan, Sucheng. *This Bittersweet Soil: The Chinese in California Agriculture, 1860–1910.* Berkeley: University of California Press, 1986.

Charlesworth, Hector. "Miss Emily Pauline Johnson's Poems." Review of *White Wampum. Canadian Magazine* 5 (September 1895): 478–80.

Chen, Jack. *The Chinese in America.* New York: Harper and Row, 1980.

Chih, Ginger. *The History of Chinese Immigrant Women, 1850–1940.* North Bergen, N.J.: G. Chih, 1977.

Chin, Doug. "Edith Maud Eaton: The First Chinese American Writer." *International Examiner* (Seattle), January 1977.

Chin, Doug, and Art Chin. *Uphill: The Settlement and Diffusion of the Chinese in Seattle.* Seattle: Shorey, 1974.

Chin, Doug, and Peter Bacho. *The International District: History of an Urban, Ethnic Neighborhood in Seattle.* Seattle: International Examiner, n.d..

Chin, Frank, Jeffrey Paul Chan, Lawson Fusao Inada, and Shawn Wong, eds. *Aiiieeeee! An Anthology of Asian American Literature.* Garden City N.Y.: Anchor, 1991 [1974].

Chinese Historical Society of California, UCLA. *Linking Our Lives: Chinese American Women of Los Angeles.* Los Angeles: Chinese Historical Society of California, UCLA, 1984.

Chu, Doris C. J., with the assistance of Glen Braverman. *Chinese in Massachusetts: Their Experiences and Contributions.* Boston: Chinese Culture Institute, 1987.

Clark, Michele. Afterword. In *The Revolt of the Mother and Other Stories,* by Mary E. Freeman. New York: Feminist Press, 1974.

Cliff, Michelle. "Resonance of Interruptions." *Chrysalis* 8 (August 1979): 29–37.

Con, Harry, Ronald J. Con, Graham Johnson, Edgar Wickberg, and William E. Willmott. *From China to Canada: A History of the Chinese Community in Canada.* Edited by Edgar Wickberg. Toronto: McClelland and Stewart, 1988.

Connor, J. Torrey. "Only John." *Land of Sunshine* 4 (February 1896): 111–13.

Coward, T. A. *Cheshire.* Cambridge: Cambridge University Press, 1910.

Crean, Susan. *Newsworthy: The Lives of Media Women.* Toronto: Stoddart Publishing, 1985.

Cunningham, Lucia Guerra, ed. *Splintering Darkness: Latin American Women*

Writers in Search of Themselves. Pittsburgh: Latin American Literary Review Press, 1990.

Daniels, Roger. *Asian America.* Seattle: University of Washington Press, 1988.

Danylewycz, Marta. *Taking the Veil: An Alternative to Marriage, Motherhood, and Spinsterhood in Quebec, 1840–1920.* Edited by Paul-André Linteau, Alison Prentice, and William Westfall. Toronto: McClelland and Stewart, 1987.

Davis, Margery W. *Women's Place Is at the Typewriter: Office Work and Office Workers, 1870–1930.* Philadelphia: Temple University Press, 1985.

Dearborn, Mary. *Pocahontas's Daughters: Gender and Ethnicity in American Culture.* New York: Oxford University Press, 1986.

De fil en aiguille: Chronique ouvrière d'une filature de coton à Hochelaga en 1880. Montreal: l'Atelier d'Histoire Hochelaga-Maisonneuve, 1985.

Dewey, F. M. "No Chinatown Here." *Montreal Daily Witness,* 22 August 1896.

DiBiase, Linda Popp. "A Chinese Lily in Seattle." *Seattle Weekly,* 10 September 1986.

Dong, Lorraine, and Marlon K. Hom. "Defiance or Perpetuation: An Analysis of Characters in *Mrs. Spring Fragrance.*" In *Chinese America: History and Perspectives,* edited by Him Mark Lai, Ruthanne Lum McCunn, and Judy Yung, 139–68. San Francisco: Chinese Historical Society of America, 1987.

DuBois, W. E. B. *The Souls of Black Folk.* Millwood, N.Y.: Kraus-Thomson Organization, 1973 [1903].

Fenn, William Purviance. "Ah Sin and His Brethren in American Literature." Ph.D. diss., State University of Iowa, 1932. Published in Peiping [Beijing], China: College of Chinese Studies Cooperating with California College in China, 1933.

Fetterley, Judith, and Marjorie Pryse, eds., *American Women Regionalists, 1850–1910.* New York: W. W. Norton, 1992.

Fishe, Turbesé, and Keith Lummis. *Charles F. Lummis: The Man and His West.* Norman: University of Oklahoma Press, 1975.

Fleming, Robert E. *Charles F. Lummis.* Western Writers Series. Boise, Idaho: Boise State University, 1981.

Foster, John Burt. "China and the Chinese in American Literature, 1850–1950." Ph.D. diss., University of Illinois, 1952.

Freeman, Mary E. *The Revolt of the Mother and Other Stories.* New York: Feminist Press, 1974.

French, Marilyn. "The Gender Principle." In *Shakespeare's Division of Experience,* 21–31. New York: Summit Books, 1981.

Genthe, Arnold. *Old Chinatown: A Book of Pictures.* Text by Will Irwin. Norwood, Mass.: Plimpton Press, 1908; reprint, New York: Mitchell Kennerley, 1913.

Gómez, Alma, Cherríe Moraga, and Mariana Romo-Carmana, eds. "Introduction." In *Cuentos: Stories by Latinas,* vii-xii. New York: Kitchen Table Women of Color Press, 1983.

Gray, Dorothy. *Women of the West.* Millbrae, Calif.: Les Femmes, 1976.

Hair, William Ivy. *Carnival of Fury: Robert Charles and the New Orleans Race Riot of 1900.* Baton Rouge: Louisiana State University Press, 1976.

Hanscombe, Gillian, and Virginia L. Smyers. *Writing for Their Lives: The Modernist Woman, 1910–1940.* Boston: Northeastern University Press, 1987.

Hartnell, Ella S. "Some Little Heathens." *Land of Sunshine* 5 (September 1896): 153–57.

Hassell, Susan Whitcomb. *A Hundred and Sixty Books by Washington Authors: Some Other Writers Who Are Contributors to Periodical Literature.* Seattle: Lowman and Hanford, 1916.

Heilbrun, Carolyn G. *Writing a Woman's Life.* New York: Ballantine Books, 1988.

Helly, Denise. *Les Chinois à Montréal, 1877–1951.* Montreal: Québecois de recherche sur la culture, 1987.

Him Mark Lai, Genny Lim, and Judy Yung. *Island: Poetry and History of Chinese Immigrants on Angel Island, 1910 to 1940.* San Francisco: San Francisco Study Center, 1980.

Hirata, Lucie Cheng. "Chinese Immigrant Women in Nineteenth-Century California." In *Women of America: A History,* edited by Carol Ruth Berkin and Mary Beth Norton, 222–44. Boston: Houghton Mifflin, 1979.

———. "Free, Indentured, Enslaved: Chinese Prostitutes in Nineteenth-Century America." *Signs* 5 (1979): 3–29.

L'Histoire du logement ouvrièr à Hochelaga-Maisonneuve. Montreal: l'Atelier d'Histoire Hochelaga-Maisonneuve, 1980.

Hiura, Arnold Ti, and Steve H. Sumida. *Asian American Literature of Hawaii: An Annotated Bibliography.* Honolulu: Hawaii Ethnic Resources Center, Talk Story, Inc., 1979.

Jackson, P. *Race and Racism.* London: Unwin Hyman, 1987.

James, Henry. *The Art of Fiction.* New York: Charles Scribner's Sons, 1962 [1907].

Jordan, Winthrop D. *White Over Black: American Attitudes toward the Negro.* Chapel Hill: University of North Carolina Press, 1968.

Kim, Elaine. *Asian American Literature: An Introduction to the Writings and Their Social Context.* Philadelphia: Temple University Press, 1982.

Kimball, Nell. *The Life of an American Madam.* New York: Macmillan, 1970.

Kingston, Maxine Hong. "Cultural Misreadings by American Reviewers." In *Asian and Western Whites in Dialogue: New Cultural Identities,* edited by Guy Amirthanayagam, 55–65. New York: Macmillan, 1982.

Klinck, Carl F. *Literary History of Canada: Canadian Literature in English.* Vol. 1, 2d ed. Toronto: University of Toronto Press, 1965.

Kobayashi, Audrey, and Peter Jackson. "Japanese Canadians and the Racialization of Labour in the British Columbia Sawmill Industry, 1900–1930." Paper presented at the Sixth British Columbia Studies Conference, University of British Columbia, Vancouver, 2–3 November 1990.

Koppelman, Susan. *Women's Friendships.* Norman: University of Oklahoma Press, 1991.

Kramnick, Isaac. "Children's Literature and Bourgeois Ideology: Observations on Culture and Industrial Capitalism in the Later Eighteenth Century." In *Culture and Politics: From Puritanism to the Enlightenment,* edited by Perez Zagorin, 202–15. Berkeley: University of California Press, 1980.

Kurian, George Thomas. *The Directory of American Book Publishing: From Founding Fathers to Today's Conglomerates.* New York: Simon and Schuster, 1975.

LaFargue, Thomas. *China's First Hundred: Educational Mission Students in the United States, 1872–1881.* Pullman: Washington State University Press, 1988.

Lai, David Cheunyan. *Chinatowns: Towns within Cities in Canada.* Vancouver: University of British Columbia Press, 1988.

Latourette, Kenneth Scott. *The Chinese: Their History and Culture.* New York: Macmillan, 1959.

———. *A History of Christian Missions in China.* New York: Macmillan, 1929.

Lauter, Paul. *Canons and Contexts.* New York: Oxford University Press, 1992.

Lauter, Paul, Juan Bruce-Novoa, Jackson Bryer, Elaine Hedges, Amy Ling, Daniel Littlefield, Wendy Martin, Charles Moesworth, Carla Mulford, Raymond Paredes, Hortense Spillers, Linda Wahner-Martin, Andrew Wiget, and Richard Yarborough, eds. *The Heath Anthology of American Literature,* vol. 2. New York: D. C. Heath, 1990.

Lears, T. J. Jackson. "The Concept of Cultural Hegemony: Problems and Possibilities." *American Historical Review* 90 (June 1985): 567–93.

Lerner, Gerda. *The Majority Finds Its Past: Placing Women in History.* New York: Pantheon Books, 1978.

Li Hui. "Nushu: A Written Language for Women Only." *Anima: The Journal of Human Experience* 16 (Spring 1990): 107–10.

Ling, Amy. *Between Worlds: Women Writers of Chinese Ancestry.* New York: Pergamon, 1990.

———. "Edith Eaton: Pioneer Chinamerican Writer and Feminist." *American Literary Realism* 16 (Autumn 1983): 287–98.

———. Foreword to *Crossings,* by Chuang Hua. Boston: Northeastern University Press, 1986 [1968].

———. "I'm Here: An Asian American Woman's Response." *New Literary History* 19 (1987–89): 152.

———. "Revelation and Mask: Autobiographies of the Eaton Sisters." *a/b Auto/Biography Studies* 3 (Summer 1987): 46–53.

———. "Writers with a Cause: Sui Sin Far and Han Suyin." *Women's Studies International Forum* 9 (1986): 411–19.

Lummis, Charles F. "In the Lion's Den." *Land of Sunshine* 15 (November 1901): 368–69.

———. "In Western Letters." *Out West* 13 (November 1900): 336.

———. "That Which Is Written." *Land of Sunshine* 6 (December 1896): 32.

McClung, Nellie. *Clearing in the West.* Toronto: Thomas Allen, 1935.

McCunn, Ruthanne Lum. *Chinese American Portraits: Personal Histories, 1828–1988.* San Francisco: Chronicle Books, 1989.

McGee, Thomas D'Arcy. "The Mental Outfit of the New Dominion." In *Canadian Literature: The Beginnings to the Twentieth Century,* edited by Catherine M. McLay, 182–89. Toronto: McClelland and Steward, 1974.

McLay, Catherine M., ed. *Canadian Literature: The Beginnings to the Twentieth Century.* Toronto: McClelland and Steward, 1974.

McQuin, Susan Coultrap. *Doing Literary Business: American Women Writers in the Nineteenth Century.* Chapel Hill: University of North Carolina Press, 1990.

MeiBenburg, Karen. *The Writing on the Wall: Socio-Historical Aspects of Chinese American Literature, 1900–1980.* Frankfurt: Wissenschaft und Forschung, 1986.

Minor, Earl Roy. "The Japanese Influence in English and American Literature, 1850–1950." Ph.D. diss., University of Minnesota, 1955.

Morson, Gary Saul. "Who Speaks for Bakhtin?" In *Bakhtin: Essays and Dialogues on His Work,* edited by Gary Saul Morson, 1–19. Chicago: University of Chicago Press, 1986.

Mott, Frank Luther. *A History of American Magazines, 1741–1930.* 5 vols. Cambridge, Mass.: Harvard University Press, 1930–68.

"Mrs. Spring Fragrance and Her Friends, Chinese and American." *Montreal Daily Witness,* 18 June 1912.

Nash, Roderick. *Wilderness and the American Mind.* New Haven, Conn.: Yale University Press, 1973.

Nee, Victor G., and Brett De Bary Nee. *Longtime Californ': A Documentary Study of an American Chinatown.* New York: Pantheon Books, 1972.

"A New Note in Fiction." *New York Times Book Review.* 7 July 1912.

Ng Poon Chew. "The Chinese in Los Angeles." *Land of Sunshine* 1 (October 1894): 102–3.

Noble-Brewer, Edith. "The Craze for the Oriental." *New Idea Woman's Magazine* 9 (January 1903): 81–82.

Olsen, Tillie. *Silences.* New York: Dell, 1965.

Pascoe, Peggy. "Gender Systems in Conflict: The Marriages of Mission-Educated Chinese American Women, 1874–1939." *Journal of Social History* 22 (Summer 1989): 631–52.

———. *Relations of Rescue: The Search for Female Moral Authority in the American West, 1874–1939.* New York: Oxford University Press, 1990.

"People of the Golden Mountains." *Edmonton Journal* 16 (September 1983): n.p.

Pollard, Lancaster. "A Checklist of Washington Authors." *Pacific Northwest Quarterly* 31 (January 1940): 3–96.

Presbury, Frank. *The History and Development of Advertising.* New York: n.p., 1979.

Pu Lin, Alice Murong. *Grandmother Had No Name.* San Francisco: China Books and Periodicals, 1988.

Radner, Joan N., and Susan S. Lanser. "The Feminist Voice: Strategies of Coding in Folklore and Literature." *Journal of American Folklore* 100 (October–December 1987): 412–25.

Ramsey, Jarold. *Reading the Fire: Essays in the Traditional Indian Literatures of the Far West.* Lincoln: University of Nebraska Press, 1983.

Rich, Adrienne. "Disloyal to Civilization." In *On Lies, Secrets, and Silence,* 39–58. New York: W. W. Norton, 1979.

Roy, Patricia E. "A Choice between Evils: The Chinese and the Construction of the Canadian Pacific Railway in British Columbia." In *The Canadian Pacific Rail West: The Iron Road and the Making of a Nation,* edited by Hugh A. Dempsey, 13–34. Vancouver: Douglas and McIntyre, 1984.

———. *A White Man's Province.* Vancouver: University of British Columbia Press, 1989.

Rudinger de Rodyenko, S. P. "Chinese Characters in American Fiction." *Bookman* 58 (November 1923): 255–59.

Said, Edward W. *Orientalism.* New York: Pantheon Books, 1978.

Salazar-Parr, Carmen. "La Chicana in Literature." In *Chicano Studies: A Multi-Disciplinary Approach,* edited by Eugene Ysidro Ortiz and Francisco Lomeli, 120–34. New York: Columbia University Press, 1984.

Saxton, Alexander. *The Indispensable Enemy.* Berkeley: University of California Press, 1971.

Shepherd, Charles. "Chinese Girl Slavery in America." *Missionary Review* 46 (1923): 893–95.

Silber, Cathy. "A 1,000-Year-Old Secret." *Ms.* 3 (September/October 1992): 58–60.

Smith-Rosenberg, Carroll. "The Female World of Love and Ritual: Relations between Women in Nineteenth-Century America." In *Disorderly Conduct: Visions of Gender in Victorian America,* 53–76. New York: Alfred A. Knopf, 1985.

Solberg, S. E. "Bibliographic Note." 7 April 1976. In author's possession.

———. "The Eaton Sisters: Sui Sin Far and Onoto Watanna." Paper presented at the Pacific Northwest Asian American Writer's Conference, Seattle, Wash., 16 April 1976.

———. "Sui Sin Far/Edith Eaton: First Chinese-American Fictionist." *MELUS* 8 (Spring 1981): 27–39.

———. "Sui, the Storyteller: Sui Sin Far (Edith Eaton), 1867–1914." In *Turning Shadows into Light: Art and Culture of the Northwest's Early Asian/Pacific Community,* edited by Mayumi Tsutakasa and Alan Chong Lou, 85–90. Seattle: Young Pine, 1982.

Spacks, Patricia. *The Female Imagination.* New York: Avon Books, 1976.

Spelman, Elizabeth V., and María C. Lugones. "Have We Got a Theory for You! Feminist Theory, Cultural Imperialism and the Demand for 'The Woman's Voice.' " *Women's Studies International Forum* 6 (1983): 573–81.

Stanley, Timothy. "Defining the Chinese Other: White Supremacy and Leading Opinion in British Columbia, 1885–1925." Paper presented at the

British Columbia Studies Conference, University of British Columbia, Vancouver, 2–3 November 1990.

Steele, William Paul. *The Characteristics of Melodrama: An Examination through Dion Biocicault's "The Poor of New York."* Orono: University of Maine Press, 1968.

Tachibana, Judy M. "Outwitting the Whites: One Image of the Chinese in California Fiction and Poetry, 1849–1924." *Southern California Quarterly* 61 (Winter 1979): 379–89.

Tebbel, John. *A History of Book Publishing in the United States.* 4 vols. New York: R. R. Bowker, 1972–81.

Tompkins, Jane. *Sensational Designs: The Cultural Work of American Fiction, 1790–1860.* New York: Oxford University Press, 1985.

Tsuchida, Nobuya. "Asians and California's Anti-miscegenation Laws." In *Asian and Pacific American Experiences,* 16–31. Minneapolis: Asian/Pacific American Learning Resource Center, University of Minnesota, 1982.

Velásquez, Gloria Treviño. "Cultural Ambivalence in Early Chicana Literature." In *European Perspective on U. S. Hispanic Literature,* edited by Genevieve Fabre, 75–89. Houston: Arte Publico Press, 1986.

Walker, Alice. "In Search of Our Mothers' Gardens." In *In Search of Our Mothers' Gardens,* 361–83. New York: Harcourt Brace Jovanovich, 1974.

Ward, W. Peter. "The Oriental Immigrant and Canada's Protestant Clergy, 1858–1925." *BC Studies* 22 (Summer 1974): 40–55.

———. *White Canada Forever: Popular Attitudes and Public Policy toward Orientals in British Columbia.* Montreal: McGill-Queens University Press, 1978.

Watters, Reginald Eyre. *A Checklist of Canadian Literature and Background Materials, 1628–1960.* 2d ed. Toronto: University of Toronto Press, 1972.

Welsch, Robert L. *Omaha Tribal Myths and Trickster Tales.* Athens, Ohio: Sage/Swallow Press, 1981.

White-Parks, Annette. "Introduction to 'Wisdom of the New,' by Sui Sin Far." *Legacy: A Journal of Nineteenth-Century Women's Literature* 6 (Spring 1989): 34–49.

Winks, Robin W. *Canadian-West Indies Union: A Forty-Year Minuet.* London: Athlone Press, 1968.

Wold, Alan. "Theorizing Cultural Differences: A Critique of the 'Ethnicity School.'" *MELUS* 14 (Summer 1987): 21–33.

Wolf, Margery. "Women and Suicide in China." In *Women in Chinese Society,* edited by Margery Wolf and Roxane Witke, 111–42. Stanford, Calif.: Stanford University Press, 1975.

Wong, Karen. *Chinese History in the Pacific Northwest.* Seattle: n.p., 1972.

Wong, Sau-ling C. "What's in a Name? Defining Chinese American Literature of the Immigrant Generation." In *Frontiers of Asian American Studies,* edited by Gail M. Nomura, Russell Endo, Stephen H. Sumida, and Russell C. Long, 159–67. Pullman: Washington State University Press, 1989.

Wong Chin Foo. "The Chinese in New York." *Cosmopolitan* 5 (June 1888): 25, 298–311.

Woolf, Virginia. "Professions for Women." In *Women and Writing,* 57–63. New York: Harcourt Brace Jovanovich, 1979 [1904].

Wu, William F. *The Yellow Peril: Chinese Americans in American Fiction, 1850–1940.* Hamden, Conn.: Archon Books, 1982.

Xiao-Huang Yin. "Between the East and West: Sui Sin Far—The First Chinese American Woman Writer." *Arizona Quarterly* 7 (Winter 1991): 49–84.

Yung, Judy. *Chinese Women in America: A Pictorial History.* Seattle: University of Washington Press, 1986.

Ziff, Larzer. *Literary Democracy: The Declaration of Cultural Independence in America* New York: Viking, 1981.

Index

A. C. McClurg and Company, 48, 148–49, 196–97, 204, 230*n6*, 240

Ahok, Mrs. (Chinese traveler in Canada), 71, 75

Aiiieeeee! (Chin at al.), 2, 102

Aiken, Rebecca, 74, 76

"Albemarle's Secret" (Sui Sin Far), 66–67, 168

Altschuler, Glenn, 115

"Aluteh" (Sui Sin Far), 117, 133

"The Americanization of Pau Tsu" (Sui Sin Far), 206, 219, 222, 234*nn56–57*

Ammons, Elizabeth: critical consideration of Sui Sin Far, 2–3, 238; on Sui Sin Far's narrative stance, 168, 206, 242*n15;* on Sui Sin Far's view of feminism, 192*n66;* on boundaries of American literature, 192*n68;* on *Mrs. Spring Fragrance,* 231*n14,* 232*n31,* 233*n40,* 235*nn60–61,* 239; on women writers, 241

Angel Island, 109

Antimiscegenation law, 38

Archibald, Judge John Sprott, 26–27, 48, 63, 200

Arnason, David, 87

Assimilation: fallacy of, 15–16

A-Toy (San Francisco brothel owner), 108

Austin, Mary, 86, 87

Austin family, 47–48

"An Autumn Fan" (Sui Sin Far), 169–70, 172, 173

Axtell, James, 235*n66*

Babcock, Bertram Whitcomb, 43

Babcock, Winifred Eaton (Onoto Watanna): use of Japanese pseudonym, 4, 33, 40, 45, 189*n30;* on Eaton family history, 10, 11, 16–18 passim, 21, 24–28 passim, 30–34

passim, 50, 63, 85, 192*n72;* baptism of, 23; responsibilities of, to Eaton family, 26; concealment of Chinese ancestry, 28, 34; in Jamaica, 31, 32–34, 57*n69;* fiction of, 32, 40, 118, 140*n78;* necessity of "passing," 33; as a stenographer, 33; relationship with Sui Sin Far, 33, 50; contrasted with Sui Sin Far, 33–34, 45–46; attitude toward Eaton family, 34; publishing success of, 40, 45, 118, 151, 190*n36,* 231*n20;* marriage of, 43; as writer of Sui Sin Far's obituary, 50; name of, 53*n6;* as possible funder of Sui Sin Far monument, 62*n139;* Sui Sin Far's representation of, 156, 179. *See also* Eaton family

Baboyant, Marie, 9

Bacho, Peter, 106

Bakhtin, Mikhail: on carnival, 5, 153, 187, 204; on dialogism, 115, 144, 151, 183, 187, 189*n33,* 242–43*n15*

Baldwin, James, 217

"The Banishment of Ming and Mai" (Sui Sin Far), 211–12

Bauer, Dale M.: on carnival aesthetic, 5, 190*n51,* 204, 226, 229–30; on women's silence, 90; on dialogic community, 242–43*n15*

Baym, Nina, 241

Bell, G. T., 36

Bernikow, Louise, 173

"Betrothals in Chinatown" (Sui Sin Far), 122

Bingham, Edwin R., 85, 86, 90, 95

"The Bird of Love" (Sui Sin Far), 169, 170–72

Bosse, Karl, 31, 57*n66*

Bosse, Sarah Eaton, 16–17, 27, 31

Boston: living conditions in, 61*n123;* Chinese community in, 145–46, 188*n5*

Boston Globe, 199–200, 201, 202